The Jack Benny Show

The Jack Benny Show

Milt Josefsberg

ARLINGTON HOUSE·PUBLISHERS
NEW ROCHELLE, NEW YORK

Third Printing, May 1977

Library of Congress Cataloging in Publication Data

Josefsberg, Milt, 1911-
   The Jack Benny show.

   Includes index.
   1. Benny, Jack, 1894-1974. 2. Comedians—United States—Biography. I. Title.
PN2287.B4325J6   791.4′0924 [B]   76-56172
ISBN 0-87000-347-X

Manufactured in the United States of America

Contents

To Jack,
the cast, the crew,
and all the people
who made The Jack Benny Show
the wonderful memory
it will always be . . .
and, of course, to Hilda

Acknowledgments

No book that is biographical in nature can be written without the aid of dozens of people who assist in various capacities. The author is deeply indebted to those who helped, knowingly and unknowingly, in hundreds of ways. Some confirmed facts, dates, and anecdotes. Some filled missing chronological gaps and supplied elusive names and incidents. Some corrected my grammar, syntax, and punctuation. Some served as secretaries, transforming my sloppy copy into a neat readable manuscript. Some were sounding boards for ideas. Some spent days doing research in libraries such as that of the Academy of Motion Picture Arts and Sciences. Some spent countless hours digging through the dusty files of the networks, unearthing early photos and information. Some furnished me with treasured personal photographs. (Bob Hope, Lucille Ball, Milton Berle, Dennis Day, Sheldon Leonard, Mel Blanc, Frank Nelson, Dr. George Weine, Harry Wolarsky, Gene Lester, Allen Studley, Frank Worth, Hal Kanter, and Hugh Wedlock, Jr., deserve extra thanks for this.) Some wrote books, magazine articles, or newspaper columns which I used as references. To some, for diverse reasons, I owe posthumous thanks, and these include Fred Allen, George D. Lottman, George B. Evans, Kermit Lyons, Mark Hellinger, Bill Morrow, Bert Scott, Walter Winchell, David O. Alber, John Tackaberry, and, of course, Jack himself.

To those listed below, I offer my thanks. To those I inadvertently omitted, my apologies.

Goodman Ace
Steve Allen
Army Archerd
Lucille Ball
George Balzer
Sheldon Bardach
Baskin-Robbins
Ed Beloin
Jack Berle
Milton Berle
Ruth Berle
Mel Blanc
Jesse Block
Frank Buxton

Sharyn Burg
Dr. Nathaniel Comden
Kellem deForrest
Dennis Day
Jeanette Eymann (Barnes)
Mort Fleischmann
Rudolf Friml, Jr.
Fred S. Fox
Haskell Frankel
The Friars Club
Sid Garfield
Hank Garson
Lloyd Gaynes
Hal Goldman

Al Gordon
Hank Grant
Bernard Green
Beverly Grey
Ben Gross
Joan Gilmore
Rodney Hooks
Bob Hope
Seaman Jacobs
Ken Jensen
Alan Roy Josefsberg
Hilda Josefsberg
Steven Kent Josefsberg
Hal Kanter
Elliot Kozak
Dr. Samuel Kurtzman
Mort Lachman
Sheldon Leonard
Charles Lee
Gene Lester
Ralph Levy
Joan Hurlow Lord
Sam Lutz
Howard MacClay
Maureen McCaffrey
Arthur Marx
Irving Mansfield
Garry K. Marshall
The Masquers
Gary Morton
Frank Nelson
Dorothy Ohman

Bill Owens
Ed Perlstein
Sam Perrin
Al Rylander
Irvine Robbins
Leo Rosten
Al Schwartz
Sherwood Schwartz
Gilbert Seldes
Jules Seltzer
Arthur Shulman
Raymond E. Singer
Charles Smith
Bernard Sobel
Chuck Stewart
Allen Studley
Alice Tapp
David Tebet
Bob Thomas
Jane Tucker
Dr. George Weine
Bernard Weitzman
Earl Wilson
Lawrence Welk
Larry Wilde
Kathleen Williams
Gail Winson
Rabbi Aaron M. Wise
Harry Wolarsky
Frank Worth
Roger Youman
Earl Ziegler

* * * * * *

To various libraries, especially those of the Academy of Motion Picture Arts and Sciences and the University of Wyoming (and the President, William Carlson, and Gene Gresley).

* * * * * *

To the broadcasting networks, ABC, CBS, NBC, and also RCA.

* * * * * *

To the motion picture studios, including Paramount, MGM, Twentieth Century-Fox, and Warner Brothers.

* * * * * *

To my co-workers at Tandem Productions who tolerated me when my mind was on this book in lieu of *All in the Family:* Lou Derman, Bill Davenport, Larry Rhine, Mel Tolkin, Ben Starr, Carroll O'Connor, Jean Stapleton, Rob Reiner, Sally Struthers, Paul Bogart, Don Nicholls, Micky Ross, Bernie West, Lloyd Turner, Gordon Mitchell, Jay Moriarty, Mike Milligan, Brigit Jensen, Gail Liberte, Douglas Arango, Phil Doran, Jack Elinson, Michael Loman, Sandy Clemente, Michael Mount, Jerry Jacobious, Barbara Brogliatti, Deanne Johnson, Jody Jill Greenwood, Nancy Pomeroy, Bea Dallas, Carol Summers, Linda Neece, Jady Joe, George Sunga, and Norman Lear.

* * * * * *

To two long-time friends who gave me assistance and information far beyond the call of friendship: Hugh Wedlock, Jr., and Maurice Zolotow.

* * * * * *

And finally, thanks to a trio of men I never met but who helped immeasurably with their encouragement and editorial advice: Scott Meredith, Dallas Mayr, and my editor and pen pal, Martin Gross.

Foreword

by Lucille Ball

In November 1963, while talking to Milton Berle, I mentioned that I was contemplating hiring a script consultant and head writer for my television series. Berle immediately recommended Milt Josefsberg, a man I had heard of as a veteran member of Jack Benny's and Bob Hope's scripting staffs.

Some time later I ran into Jack and asked him about Josefsberg. I had no hesitancy about doing this because I knew I would get an honest answer, since we were very close friends in and out of business. Like all those who knew Benny well, I not only adored him but trusted his judgment implicitly.

I first met Jack when I was a newcomer to Hollywood and he was an established superstar on radio. At that time I asked him for some advice on a minor career problem and he counseled me wisely and at great length. So, once again, I asked Jack's advice, this time about Josefsberg's ability as a writer.

Knowing Jack quite well, I was aware of his habit of describing everything as the greatest, whether it was a glass of water, Turkish towels, or a hot pastrami sandwich. However I was not prepared for the way he raved about Josefsberg. Jack praised Milt, both as a talent and a person, for nearly an hour. When Jack finished I didn't know whether I wanted to hire Josefsberg or marry him, but I arranged a meeting.

As a result of the interview, Milt went to work for me. He lived up to Benny's and Berle's advance notices and remained a highly valuable member of my staff for eight years, practically an entire career for anyone toiling in TV. During those years I found that Milt more than returned Jack's admiration. Although I was a close friend of Jack's, and lived next door to the Bennys for years, Milt told me many things about him I had never known before—warm interesting insights and hilariously funny anecdotes. As Milt narrated them with affection, you could tell how much he loved and respected Jack.

In the eight years Milt was with my series he wrote at least a full program or a cameo role for a guest appearance for Jack each season. We all looked forward to the weeks Jack worked with us, not only because it was a pleasure and an education to watch him perform, but also because it was amusing and absorbing listening to Jack and Milt reminisce about the old radio and early TV days. And whenever Jack failed to remember a date, routine, punch line, or blackout of a show or event that took place many years ago, he would turn to Josefsberg who would invariably supply the missing information immediately.

During our first months of association I had learned first-hand that Milt was blessed with an extraordinary memory, but in those wonderful Koffee Klatch sessions I realized that he knew as much about Jack as anybody. He was a walking encyclopedia on Benny's background, career, and idiosyncrasies.

If Josefsberg's book contains only half the amusing anecdotes, fascinating incidents, and revealing stories he knows about Jack, then this book is bound to be a treasured memory—a warm, witty, fitting tribute to a man we all loved as a person and revered as a performer.

Foreword

by Bob Hope

To paraphrase an old saying in show-business terms, one might say "No comedian is a superstar to his writers." Producing a top comedy show requires the concerted efforts of individual talents which are coordinated by the comedian, who must decide what to use and what not to use. This often leads to tension and hurt pride unless that comedian is so respected and inspires such loyalty and affection among his writers that they are able to put their egos on "hold" for the good of the show.

Jack Benny was just such a comedian, as this warm remembrance of him by Milt Josefsberg proves so convincingly.

Milt, who also served time in my think-tank, was one of Jack's top writers for many years and remained a close friend of Jack's all his life.

Josefsberg, with his capacity for total recall, is especially well-equipped to bring us this loving, perceptive, and witty portrait of one of the most beloved entertainers of our time. The proof of this is that as time goes on, we miss him more and more.

Jack and I were pals for over forty years. Professionally, we worked very well together. The nicest tribute a confirmed ham like me can pay Jack is that I was actually pleased when he got the big laugh.

Personally, there was a bond between us which grew over the years, nurtured by our respect for each other's talent, and in my case, by his kindness, gentleness, and genuine modesty despite his world renown.

That is why I welcome this candid, unadorned anecdote-filled recollection by Milt Josefsberg. All of us who miss Jack will treasure this book because it's almost as enjoyable and as rewarding as spending an hour or so swapping stories with Jack.

Milt, thanks for the memories....

Prologue

At 11:52 P.M., December 26, 1974, the world lost a little of its sorely needed laughter. I lost a friend, a former boss, and a man I much admired and loved. Jack Benny was gone.

If Jack had lingered for eight minutes more he would have left at the stroke of twelve and presented us with one final silent comment to the long list of gags he had pulled about his less than successful movie, *The Horn Blows at Midnight.* It probably would have given him a smile to leave us at midnight, but for once in his brilliant career his superb timing was faulty.

Like so many others, when I heard that Jack was seriously ill, I kept hoping against hope for a miracle and that the inevitable would be postponed. However, the radio and TV blared forth the sad news, and the following day the papers headlined the event. Its final reality was brought home to me when I received a phone call from Bob Hope's head writer and producer, Mort Lachman. Bob had been selected to be co-eulogist with George Burns, and he thought that I might have some heartwarming facts to incorporate in his funeral oration. With a heavy heart I tried to type up some notes, but it was difficult selecting a few short lines concerning a man who had given me a million memories.

The world's final goodbye to Jack Benny was impressive. It was attended by thousands—the Who's Who of the worlds of entertainment, business, and politics. Rabbi Edgar Magnin conducted traditional, though simple, Jewish services. George Burns, Jack's best friend for over half a century, and still showing the effects of recent serious surgery, tried to deliver a short eulogy, but he broke down— a fact far more impressive than any words he was prepared to say. Bob Hope followed and commented that no obsequies over Benny could be as touching a tribute as George's simple tears. Hope, more serious than humorous for once, was magnificent, and he thanked several people, myself included, who had helped him to prepare his notes.

And so on Sunday, December 29, 1974, Jack Benny was buried the way he lived—with love, respect, and dignity. I sat in the chapel while the thousands of people who crowded the cemetery, some merely curious but most visibly grief-stricken, filed reverently past his closed casket. I couldn't help thinking that it was fitting yet ironic that Jack Benny was interred on a Sunday.

Sunday. This was always "Jack Benny Day." In radio and then

television, Sunday was synonymous with Jack Benny. For nearly half a century Sunday *was* Jack's day. Like many millions of others, though I didn't know him then, I listened to *The Jack Benny Show* in the early 1930s. He was about the only thing we could laugh at during those depression days. Other comics and programs changed their nights and time slots, but not Jack. He was one of the few constants we could rely on in a rapidly changing world. His name became so identified with Sundays that his network, in one of those self-aggrandizing yet meaningless gestures, deeded Sunday to Jack Benny as his permanent time slot on the air.

And on Sunday, December 29, it did indeed become everlasting. For Jack was buried on a Sunday, and the *Mourners' Kaddish,* the ancient Jewish prayer for the dead, was intoned by his friends of the faith while those of other religions bowed their heads in silent invocation. Thus Sunday did become his permanent niche in the week.

Then, on December 31, 1974, I sat at my typewriter and wrote a special eulogy of my own, but not for the general public. It was meant exclusively for The Writers Guild Newsletter, the official, once-monthly trade paper published by and for screen, television, and radio writers and those others who, like myself, earn their bread via words. It was an esoteric essay dealing with Jack Benny's respect and kindness toward writers in an industry where many comedians resent their script staff as a necessary, yet indispensable, evil.

I thought that my article would be of interest exclusively to my peers. It detailed how Jack, in his over forty years of broadcasting, employed a total of less than ten writers. Many comedy shows use more than twice that number in a single season, and several comics have hired and fired hundreds of them. The eulogy told how he, contrary to most other comedians, publicly praised his writers and was generous in giving them both credit and cash.

The Writers Guild Newsletter published my article. After it appeared in print I received many phone calls and letters from friends and strangers who were fellow guild members. All of them complimented me, but more emphatically they asserted how greatly they envied me for my long, loving association with Jack.

As a result of the publication of that eulogy I have been asked to write a book about Jack Benny—not so much a formal, statistical biography, but a personal portrait as I remember him. Thus what follows will be my memories of him at two levels: Jack Benny the *man,* and Jack Benny the *comedian.*

It was a difficult task to undertake. His passing affected everyone who knew him, but to me it was a traumatic shock. It took me a long time to return to some state of normalcy. I can't say I got over it. I don't think I ever will.

A close friend of mine remarked that I seemed to mourn Jack's passing almost as much as my mother's and father's. Perhaps that's true, but there's a reason. You see, ever since I was old enough to understand, I realized that someday my parents would no longer be with me because they were mortal. I always thought that Jack Benny was immortal. I still do.

1
The Journey to Waukegan

Where do you start the story of a man you love? Of a man you mourn, and yet every time you think of him, a smile lights up your heart despite an occasional moistening of your eyes? Of a man who has enriched your memory with so many heartwarming moments that every anecdote you think of reminds you of another before you're half through telling it?

You can't catalogue the over thirty years you've known him in precise chronological order. Something that caused you to laugh with him when you first met him, casually, in 1939, causes you to laugh at a related incident in 1974.

So for the most part this book will not proceed in day-to-day chronology as a formal biography would. It will skip months and years and sometimes blend two anecdotes separated by a quarter of a century. Yet, like the hundreds of pieces of a complex jigsaw puzzle, they will all fit together, eventually giving you, I hope, a complete picture of a warm, humorous human being you will remember. As Bob Hope quoted in his eulogy, "This was a man."

Jack Benny's ancestry, as far as he could trace it, started in Russia and Poland, and his original name, Kubelsky, shows traces of each of these countries. In the 1880s, Jack's grandfather owned a small tavern in a Russian village or *shtetl,* where he sold wine and vodka. Like so many European Jews in that era, and even today in Russia, his ambition was to get out of there. If he couldn't escape the harsh life and constant pogroms of the ghetto, he would at least arrange for his son, Mayer Kubelsky, to migrate to the "Goldeneh" land, America.

Mayer Kubelsky arrived in America at the Castle Garden, the immigrants' promised land, later known as Ellis Island. When he was permitted to enter the country, he went, not to New York as the great majority of "greenhorns" did, but to Chicago. His father had friends, "landsmen," in the Windy City, and according to Biblical teachings, which were adhered to far more closely in those days by members of all religions, a Jew must give help to anyone in need.

In Chicago, Mayer Kubelsky was helped by his father's friends as much as they could, and they got him a twelve-hour-a-day job in a sweatshop. In those days that was a stroke of good fortune. Besides, Mayer Kubelsky was in his very early twenties and hard work meant nothing to him. He wanted to save enough money and emulate his father by opening a tavern, or saloon, in America.

Mayer lived frugally and saved most of his meager earnings to buy a horse and wagon. The wagon he stocked with notions, pots, pans, clothing, and any other merchandise he thought marketable, and he became a peddler. He visited the towns around Lake Michigan, remaining a few days in each.

However, any trip involving overnight stays was a problem to men like Mayer Kubelsky, since Orthodox Jews will not eat certain foods. No meat of the pig is acceptable. Seafood that has neither scales nor fins, and this includes any and all shellfish, is inedible. Certain fowl, and animals with paws, such as rabbits, are proscribed. And even the fowl and meats that are considered kosher have to be slaughtered in a ritual manner or they too are taboo.

If a Jewish peddler in those days found some family in town of the same faith, he usually lodged with them. If not, he went to the least expensive boarding house and lived almost exclusively on hard-boiled eggs, fruits, and vegetables.

Whenever Mayer Kubelsky came to Waukegan, he considered himself lucky because that town had a huge Jewish population— five families. And the most zealous, if not the wealthiest, head of these five families was an Orthodox Jewish tailor named Solomon Schwartz. All followers of Judaism found a haven in his house. Sometimes Mayer Kubelsky shared the small extra room with two or three peddlers of his faith, but they were all happy because they had a roof over their heads and kosher food to eat. Moreover, it was delicious kosher food because Solomon Schwartz's wife was an excellent cook. Finally, the price was right—it was free. Mayer Kubelsky and his fellow peddlers who used the Schwartz home as a temporary inn always left some gift to pay their way, but Solomon Schwartz wanted none of these material things, for he was after bigger game. He wanted to save their souls, and, at the same time, his own and his family's.

Jewish tradition demands that for any prayer meeting, marriage, circumcision, bar mitzvah, or other similar religious rituals to be legal, there must be a *minyon*. This word is literally translated as "a quorum," and to Jews this means a minimum of ten male adults who practice the faith. Such practice does not necessarily have to be zealous, as long as there is exhibited even the faintest vestige of belief in the Almighty.

With the hopes of eventually increasing Waukegan's pre-twentieth-century Jewish population to ten families, Solomon Schwartz convinced Mayer Kubelsky that this booming village was an ideal spot to open his planned tavern. And so Jack Benny's father settled in Waukegan and opened a small saloon which provided him with a comfortable, if not luxurious, living.

Now, to light the fuse for a population explosion, a bachelor is better than nothing, but not as good as a married man. Therefore, Mr. Schwartz convinced Mayer that he should follow the Bible and "go forth and multiply," but get married first. And Mayer, figuring that he was an established old man of twenty-three, agreed to do this. However, at that time there were no suitable maidens in Waukegan, so Solomon took him to Chicago and introduced him to a *schadchen*.

Now a *schadchen* (pronounced shotgun, and, because of this, sometimes a source of humor) is a marriage broker. Contrary to the saying, "Marriages are made in heaven," in the days before the twentieth century most of them were made by marriage brokers.

A *schadchen* arranged a meeting and, in time, a marriage between Mayer Kubelsky and Emma Sachs, a union to bring laughter and love to all America via their first-born—a son named Benjamin Kubelsky.

The Kubelsky marriage did not take place immediately. First Mayer had to tell his future wife and her family what business he was in. Being a saloon keeper ranked quite low on the list of acceptable occupations. Mayer Kubelsky got out of this situation the way his famous son, years later, got in and out of spots. He talked his way out of it. He didn't lie. He merely bent the truth ever so slightly. He said that he was in the restaurant business and he did sell a little liquor. This was no out-and-out falsehood because in those days all saloons furnished free lunch to their patrons.

So they were married, and a year later, on St. Valentine's Day, February 14, 1894, the Waukegan Wit was born—only he wasn't

23

born in Waukegan. Benjamin Kubelsky came into this world in a hospital in Chicago.

Jack told me that he never really knew whether his mother wanted to have him born in a bigger city, with the most modern medical methods, or whether she wanted to be near her family who lived in Chicago. Whatever the reason, the Windy City was his actual birthplace. His mother went through the entire term of her pregnancy in Waukegan, and after his birth she returned there with him. Therefore, outside of his several days spent in that Chicago hospital, Jack was truly a native of Waukegan.

2
The Early Years

All of the Kubelskys' friends were overjoyed at the birth of the baby, but none more so than Solomon Schwartz. Now he had a potential sixth member for the *minyon*. True, baby Benjamin Kubelsky would have to wait till his bar mitzvah, his thirteenth birthday, before being accepted as an adult, a man, old enough to understand, and thus be able to be counted in religious meetings, but Mr. Schwartz was a patient man and he could wait. Fortunately he didn't have to wait long, because a dozen years before little Benny Kubelsky attained the age of thirteen, Waukegan's Jewish population had swelled to ten families, and now there was a full quorum of adult males to make every prayer meeting official. True, they had no temple, or synagogue as they probably called it because they were all Orthodox. This didn't deter them. They met on Sabbath evenings and mornings at alternating homes, and they followed this custom during the High Holy Days of Rosh Hashonah and Yom Kippur and the many holidays in between. In any event, Jewish prayers emanating from Waukegan were now acceptable in heaven.

In 1901 Waukegan got its first synagogue, and on his thirteenth birthday Jack became a full-fledged member of the Congregation Ahm Echod when he celebrated his bar mitzvah there. However the years between his *b'ris* (circumcision) and bar mitzvah were not uneventful.

At the early age of four, Benjamin Kubelsky showed an aptitude for music. His mother had taken piano lessons as a girl, and once, while visiting some friends or relatives of means, she sat at their piano and played some tunes. Little Benjamin then surprised everyone by going over to the piano and almost faultlessly one-fingering the same melodies. It was clear to his parents that God in His greatness had given them the gift of a musical genius. But God didn't give them the whole "schmeer." Little Benny's hands were small, even for a four-year-old, and in addition to this the cost of pianos was prohibitive. Therefore, they decided to give him violin lessons instead.

Even for this they had to wait. While Mayer Kubelsky made a living via his restaurant that happened to sell liquor, money was not easily come by. To buy their boy a tiny violin and see him immediately outgrow it would have placed a financial burden on the family. Thus they postponed the prodigy's lessons for a couple of years.

Jack started his musical career at the age of six. His father bought him a half-size violin for one hundred dollars—a small fortune at the turn of the century. They enrolled him with a teacher who charged fifty cents a lesson, but Jack's ability was so great that the tutor told his parents that they should send him to a better and more expensive teacher named Professor Lindsay. He was the finest musical expert in all of Waukegan, which was evident because he charged the exorbitant fee of a dollar per lesson. Little Benny outgrew him in less than two years.

Mayer Kubelsky then took his budding, not quite nine-year-old, virtuoso back to his birthplace, Chicago, and enrolled him in that city's college of music under the tutelage of Dr. Hugo Kortschalk at the then unheard of fee of fifteen dollars a lesson. Dr. Kortschalk was both an honest man and a music lover. He wouldn't accept students unless they showed definite signs of talent, and the little Kubelsky boy made an indelible impression on him. Although fifteen dollars a week for a lesson, plus the time and cost of trips from Waukegan to Chicago, severely strained the not too robust Kubelsky family budget, which now had a fourth mouth to feed—a second child, Florence—they let their son study under Dr. Kortschalk.

Dr. Kortschalk impressed on the elder Kubelsky that his son had a rare gift, but that even though his technique and knowledge were remarkable in one so young, it was quite evident that little Benjamin wasn't practicing enough—and if he expected to remain one of Kortschalk's students, he must practice at least two hours a day. To Mayer Kubelsky, who worked twelve hours a day in a sweatshop on his arrival in America, two hours a day of practicing the violin was indeed an easy way to fame and fortune. Therefore his son continued to study under the watchful eye of Dr. Kortschalk. Unfortunately, Kortschalk's eyes couldn't see from Chicago to Waukegan or he would have observed Benny playing games instead of practicing the violin.

Soon the son of Mayer Kubelsky began to have problems—school problems. His marks were declining, his work was bad, and his behavior was nothing to brag about either. If all of this had been a direct result of studying music, it might have been forgiven, but this wasn't the case. Benny was now neglecting his violin more and more, rarely practicing even half of the minimum two hours daily.

Many times in his later years when he practiced four and six hours a day, with no parents to goad him into it, and no childish hopes of becoming the world's greatest violin virtuoso, Jack would wonder why he neglected his schoolwork and his music studies as a youngster. He once said, "I don't know. Maybe music came too easy and school came too hard."

In the ninth grade Jack quit school. Thus at the age of thirteen he became a man in the eyes of his forefathers and a school drop-out in the eyes of his principal. Just as in later years he regretted his lack of interest in the violin, so did he have remorse about his lack of formal education. Jack often laughed at the ironic twist of fate that caused the city of Waukegan to name a school after him. "And," Jack added proudly, "a high school—at least a junior high."

In his early teens young Benjamin Kubelsky started to study bookkeeping in hopes of a career in accounting. This was one of his shorter careers. He worked a few hours a day in his father's place, and he managed to earn a couple of dollars via the violin. He was a member of a small band that played at all the social functions in town, but this was no way to earn a living. Let's face it: In the first decade of the twentieth century there was no "dolce vita" in Waukegan.

Jack's ability with the violin led to one advantage all adolescents hope for—popularity with the opposite sex. Girls found his soulful music, beautiful blue eyes, and brown, almost blond, curly hair extremely romantic. If Jack hadn't been so shy he would probably be remembered in his home town as "The Wolf of Waukegan." Jack had no trouble getting the girls, but he said he wasn't quite sure of what to do with them.

At a luncheon I had with him some years ago he was in a mellow mood and he reminisced about those days. What he told me was, in effect, "I liked girls and they liked me, but I was painfully shy. The best times I remember were the warm summer evenings when with one girl or another, I'd go up to the roof of a building to cool off.

Sitting there in the darkness of the roof those warm summer nights, girls weren't too bashful about loosening their voluminous clothing. That's where I was partially initiated into the joys of sex, through our mutual fondling and fumbling. I guess I was the original 'Fiddler on the Roof.'" Jack laughed at his joke, and I didn't know whether he was describing actual experiences or had invented the entire roof business just to get off that punch line. However he gave me the impression that his teenage sexual exploits could be filmed in explicit detail and still go unnoticed in a Walt Disney movie.

At about the age of sixteen Jack got his first regular job in show business. He was hired as the violinist in the orchestra of the Barrison Theatre, a vaudeville house. Jack's parents were disappointed, for they had expected much more. Young Kubelsky defended himself by saying, "But I'm playing in an orchestra. I'm a violinist." Jack's father said, "Benny, to you, you're a violinist. To me, maybe you're a violinist. But to Jascha Heifetz, you're a *bummekeh*"— which was a Yiddish word for bum.

To digress here for a moment, every Jewish child who studied the violin in this century had to contend with the competition of Jascha Heifetz and Mischa Elman, not to mention Fritz Kreisler. When, as a child, my parents thought that I should be given violin lessons, this imposing trio had become a quartet of my competitors with the addition of Yehudi Menuhin who was approximately my age and was already considered the greatest child prodigy in history. Today's kids not only have this quartet, but also Isaac Stern, David Oistrakh, and others.

It seems odd that in any list of the world's ten best violinists the great majority are Jewish. Jack once explained this to me, and I'll pass his thought along, whether it be fact or fiction. The reason why the violin is sometimes considered a Jewish instrument is basically the same reason why most immigrant mothers of that faith wanted their sons to be doctors, lawyers, dentists, accountants, or any other form of professional men. The reason, Jack said, can be found in that one horrible word "pogroms." When the Jews in a small village in Europe heard rumors of an impending pogrom, they'd grab their most valuable possessions, put them in a pushcart or wagon, and run to hide. A piano can't fit into a wagon. A violin can. It is small and light and can be carried and hidden.

Jack was successful as the violinist in the orchestra of the Barrison Theatre. He was so good that Minnie Palmer offered him the job of permanent violinist for her sons' vaudeville act. Her sons were named Herbert, Milton, Julius, Arthur, and Leonard. Later they became Zeppo, Gummo, Groucho, Harpo, and Chico. Minnie told

Jack that if he would travel with the Marx Brothers she would double his current salary. This wasn't difficult to do because it meant he'd go from earning seven and a half dollars a week all the way up to fifteen dollars—the exact figure Mayer Kubelsky had paid Dr. Hugo Kortschalk when he had visions of seeing his son's name in lights over concert halls throughout the country.

Jack's parents made him reject this offer, since they felt that he was too young for the gamey life of touring vaudeville theaters. Then something happened, as it usually did to Benjamin Kubelsky during his eighty years. The Barrison Theatre did an "el foldo" and went out of business. Thus at the age of eighteen, Jack was unemployed with no unemployment office to go to.

In the Barrison Theatre's orchestra there was a matronly pianist around forty-five years old named Cora Salisbury. She thought that she and Jack might form an act and try their luck at vaudeville. Once again Mayer Kubelsky rejected the offer. Jack was now a young adult of eighteen, and he probably could have gone without his parents' consent—but whoever heard of such a wild thing in those pre-World War I days? However, Jack's mother had a talk with Mrs. Salisbury, who was even older than Mrs. Kubelsky, and she decided that that woman, though a Gentile, was a *shayner mensh*. This is Yiddish for "beautiful person," but the "beautiful" doesn't apply to exterior beauty. Rather, it describes what is inside the heart. In this usage it meant that Mrs. Salisbury was a decent human being, morally upright, and trustworthy. Thus the act entered vaudeville as "Salisbury and Kubelsky, From Grand Opera to Ragtime."

Benny briefly considered changing his name to one that sounded more American, but then he figured that Kubelsky had a nice rhythm to it for a violinist, and he was right—too right. After a semi-successful theater tour of several weeks, Jack received a letter from a lawyer representing an established vaudeville violinist named Jan Kubelik, and the lawyer accused violinist Kubelsky of trying to capitalize on violinist Kubelik's reputation. Despite the fact that he insisted his name was truly Kubelsky, he was advised to change it. He argued against this, but in order to avoid a lawsuit he took a different name. Although he had given the matter thought, Jack didn't change his name because he was afraid that it sounded too Jewish. He changed it because he was afraid of lawyers.

He decided to switch his first name into his surname, and the act became known as "Salisbury and Benny." Now he needed a first name, so he called himself Ben Benny. This didn't last long because there was a vaudeville orchestra leader, later to be involved in a mock radio feud with Walter Winchell, named Ben Bernie, "The Old Maestro" of "Yowsah, Yowsah" fame, and so eventually Jack had to change his name from Ben Benny to something else.

In 1914 when Cora Salisbury had to quit the act to take care of her mother who was ill, Jack found a fine young pianist, a few years older than he was, named Lyman Woods. They formed an act, only this time Jack got first billing. And he changed his name again, or at least the way he spelled it. The act was known as "Bennie and Lyman." Jack hadn't heard of Ben Bernie's objections yet, and he called himself Ben Bennie. He thought that spelling the name with "ie" instead of "y" lent it a little class.

"Bennie and Woods" was a top second-rate vaudeville act getting between three and four hundred dollars a week. Also, and more important, they were getting a few laughs. Jack still didn't speak on stage, but he and Woods would do comedy numbers, mugging along with the music. The act began to get better notices and more bookings, and soon, in 1917, they reached the seventh heaven of every vaudeville performer. They played the historic Palace Theatre on Broadway.

And laid the biggest bomb in history.

At the time it hurt young Benny, or Bennie. He was only twenty-three years old, and he thought that he had attained his goal. What he didn't realize until he was more seasoned was that he and his partner were booked at the Palace for the "number two" spot—the second act. They were preceded by an animal act. And although the animals were well behaved, so bad was the reaction to his act that Jack walked off the stage feeling as though he had stepped into something. He was dejected and depressed. During the act there was no applause. There was no laughter. There was no reaction. And there was practically no audience.

Later he learned that in those days the audience really didn't start coming into the Palace until midway through the third act. It was the fashionable thing to do. Therefore, if you were booked at the Palace in the first or second spot, you could be sure that your act would get a livelier reception at a morticians' convention. But at the time Jack was ignorant of this tradition and thought he was a failure.

Something else happened to Jack in 1917. He got one of his longest bookings and went back to his original name of Benjamin Kubelsky. That's the way the United States Navy listed him when he saw service at the Great Lakes Naval Training Station. It was there, in a Navy camp show, that Jack first started speaking, and getting laughs, on a stage.

The man who was instrumental in this was named William O'Brien. Fifteen years later he gained movie fame under the name of Pat O'Brien. Jack appeared in his camp's show as a classical violinist, and at his debut, in front of an audience composed entirely of sailors, Jack played his first number, "The Rosary," completely straight. He didn't try for laughs. He didn't get any—or any applause either. This wasn't the empty Palace Theatre but an auditorium jammed with men in uniform—and he was rewarded for his long-hair musical efforts by a smattering of boos and hisses.

Pat O'Brien was scheduled to appear in a sketch later on in the show. From the wings he noticed Jack's embarrassment and sauntered out on the stage and whispered to Jack, pretending that it was a scheduled scene in the show. He said, "Put down that damn fiddle and talk to them." Then O'Brien stood next to Jack, arms akimbo, grinning the broadest grin he could. Jack thought for a second and said, "Fellows, this morning I was having an argument with O'Brien here. . . . Yes, O'Brien and I were arguing about the Irish Navy." A small but welcome laugh came from the audience. Jack continued: "He got mad at me because I said that the Swiss Navy is bigger than the Irish Navy . . . and the Jewish Navy is bigger than both of them put together." A roar of laughter greeted him. Then Jack went on to tell a joke which in later years he said he couldn't remember whether he ad-libbed or had heard someplace else. He said, "I know that all you sailors complain about the food. Well, you've got no right to complain. The enlisted men here get the same food as the officers get . . . only *theirs* is cooked." The loud scream of laughter and applause that greeted that line changed a violinist into a comedian.

At that time, back East, the Army had put on a successful fund-raising show called *Yip, Yip, Yaphank,* featuring a song, "Oh How I Hate To Get Up in the Morning," written by a young man named Izzy Balin who had changed his name to Irving Berlin. The Navy decided to go into competition with the Army, so they produced their own show, *The Great Lakes Revue,* at the Great Northern Auditorium in Chicago. Jack was the comedy hit of the show playing the role of "Izzy There, The Admiral's Disorderly." They had a couple of big weeks in Chicago and went on tour to Detroit, Cleveland, St. Louis, and several other cities.

At the end of the tour, Jack became a civilian again.

3
Early Success

In 1919 Jack went back to vaudeville. He also went back to using the name Ben Benny. As a gesture to his real name, Kubelsky, he called himself "Ben K. Benny," and it was shortly after this that he got a phone call from Ben Bernie's lawyer. The attorney pointed out that Bernie had a prior claim to the name, and Ben Benny sounded too much like Ben Bernie. To avoid legal complications he suggested that Jack go back to a name sounding more like his original one. Jack said, "Okay, I'll call myself by my real name, Benjamin Kubelsky, if Ben Bernie uses *his* real name, Benny Anselowitz."

So Benjamin Kubelsky, who became Ben Benny, and Ben Bennie, and Ben K. Benny, now became Jack Benny. Later, Jack and Ben Bernie became good friends. During the height of his radio fame, Jack once said to him, "You know, I'm glad you forced me into using the name Jack Benny. I'd feel silly every week opening my broadcast by saying, 'Hello again, this is Benjamin Kubelsky!'"

Jack started his renewed vaudeville career as a single. He worked alone, and he did comedy. He billed himself, before hearing from Ben Bernie's lawyer, as "Ben K. Benny, Fiddle Funology." Jack's jokes were an odd assortment. He couldn't afford a writer, so he borrowed a few gags, stole a few, switched a few, and made up a few, played his violin a little (hit songs, not classical), and sang a few numbers, including two special material songs. One was "I Used to Call Her Baby, But Now She's a Mother to Me." The other was a topical tune about the advent of Prohibition, and its title was, "After This Country Goes Dry, Goodbye, Wild Women, Goodbye." It may have been a good song, but it was a lousy prophecy.

Gradually Jack played the violin less and less, and finally not at all, but he always carried it on stage with him as a prop. It served more or less as a four-stringed security blanket. The less he used the violin, the more he relied on humor. He had now talked to Ben Bernie's lawyer, so he billed himself as "Jack Benny: Aristocrat of Humor." He did a sophisticated casual act, and he always opened his performance by greeting the audience, "Hello, folks." Then he would lean over the orchestra pit and ask the conductor: "How's the show been up to now?" And the leader would say "Fine," and Jack would snap back, "Well, I'll fix that!"

Jack's reviews, especially in the larger cities, were generally good. In the smaller ones the audiences didn't always understand his material or why he carried a violin without ever playing it. Some critics said that the violin was a distraction, and that if Jack wasn't going to use it, he shouldn't carry it onstage.

Jack tried working without it once and found himself flopping and sweating. His next appearance was much better—but he was again carrying his violin. Despite many more suggestions that he leave it offstage, Jack couldn't bring himself to abandon his crutch. Besides he was now, in the early 1920s, making five hundred dollars a week. He was not a star by any means, but doing quite well, and why tamper with success?

Some of Jack's happiest days were spent in vaudeville, and like his friends and fellow comics, George Burns and Bob Hope, Jack loved to reminisce about his adventures in that medium. He told hundreds of tales of those carefree times and one certainly bears repeating.

During that period performers would play the "Gus Sun," "Keith-Albee," "Klaw and Erlanger," and other circuits of theaters scattered from coast to coast. Sometimes they were fortunate enough to appear in several successive cities with the same group, but soon the time would come when they would have to part company and move on to different destinations. And needless to say, in the weeks they appeared together, fast friendships and bitter rivalries would develop.

During one such engagement Jack appeared on the bill with two performers whose names were Violet and Daisy Hilton. Most people don't remember the Hilton Sisters nowadays, but in the 1920s they were very well known—not so much for their talent, which was considerable, but because they had one thing in common that was extremely rare. Violet and Daisy Hilton were Siamese twins. A trick of nature had joined them, I believe, at the hips, and because surgery sixty or seventy years ago was not as perfected as it is today, they were not separated but remained in tandem throughout their lives.

However Violet and Daisy Hilton refused to become side show freak attractions. They were attractive and talented. They played musical instruments and learned to dance a few steps, and were in some demand as a novelty act in vaudeville. Jack once was booked on a tour of theaters with the girls, and he appeared on the same bills with them for several weeks. In his usual manner, he went out of his way to be nice to them and yet treat them as he would other performers, trying to ignore the fact that nature had joined them together for life. Eventually, however, the two acts were scheduled for different theaters and they went their divergent ways.

Jack didn't run into the twins again for several years until he was booked into a theater in a large midwestern town. He was doing his three or four performances a day at this vaudeville emporium, and at this particular moment was resting between shows when there was a knock on his dressing room door. He crossed to open it and was pleasantly surprised to see the famed Siamese twins. Joyfully he embraced them and said, "Violet! Daisy! It's so good to see you again." At which Violet turned to her sister in all seriousness and said, "See, Daisy, I told you he'd remember us." Jack said he had to bite on his lips to keep from getting hysterical, but he didn't dare laugh for fear of hurting the girls' feelings.

Jack relished recounting other anecdotes of his vaudeville career, but it was a dying art form. However, through a combination of luck and his usual perfect timing, Jack ventured into another branch of entertainment—a Broadway show produced by J. J. (Jake) Shubert. At that time Jake was feuding with his brother and partner, Lee, and he decided to produce a show alone while brother Lee was in Europe. He had seen Jack's act and said that he'd hire him for the show, *The Great Temptations*, only he wanted a comedian, not a violinist. Jack therefore decided to work with a cigar in his hand. Shubert then sent Jack a script, marking off the sketches he was to appear in. Jack read them and immediately rejected all of them. He later said that the show was the *Oh, Calcutta* or *Hair* of its day. It was filthy, in Jack's opinion. He finally agreed to do about sixteen minutes of monologue and also appear in a clean sketch with a girl named Dorothy McNulty. She eventually went on to fame as "Blondie" using the name of Penny Singleton. The show was soundly slapped by the critics for its bawdiness, but Jack personally got the kind of reviews that make actors believe in Santa Claus.

Walter Winchell of the *New York Daily Mirror* raved about Jack, Burns Mantle of the *New York Daily News* called him "amusing," Percy Hammond of the *Herald Tribune* (it may have been just called the *Tribune* then) said Benny was "pleasant," and the critic for one of the other papers said several complimentary things about Jack but spelled his name "Denny." Now these reviews may not sound like overenthusiastic praise, but since he was in a show that was being ripped to pieces, the reviewers' reactions to Jack were like pearls in a dung heap. And the best was yet to come.

It came from famed humorist Robert Benchley who was the drama critic on the old *Life* magazine. This was not *Life,* the picture magazine that stopped weekly publication a few years ago, but a humor magazine that expired in the late 1920s. Possibly with the stock market crash and the depression people didn't feel much like laughing, so it suspended publication. But the first *Life* was still going strong in 1926, the year Jake Shubert's show *The Great Temptations* opened, and Benchley's review in that magazine was devoted almost exclusively to Jack. Benchley used a few lines to tell his readers how awful and tasteless *The Great Temptations* was, and then he devoted the rest of his column to raving about Jack Benny.

The Great Temptations became a smash hit because, as Jack readily admits, the public had read how dirty the show was and they came to see a lewd nude performance. Jack didn't think his excellent reviews brought in one percent of the customers.

Jack was now making over one thousand dollars a week for only eight appearances—one performance every night, except on Sundays, and matinees on Saturdays and Wednesdays. He knew that he was in for a steady, sizable salary for a long run of easy work, but he regarded this success with mixed emotions.

The reason? Jack was in love, and his girl was in Los Angeles. Her name was Sadye Marks, which she later changed to Mary Livingstone, but she preferred to be known as Mrs. Jack Benny. Jack first met her through the Marx Brothers, Sadye's very distant relatives. It happened in Vancouver where Jack was appearing at the Orpheum Theatre on the same bill as the Marx Brothers. He was spotted in the "deuce" or number two position, and the Marx Brothers, now stars, had the enviable dream of all performers. They were on last—the closing act, and thus the main attraction.

Zeppo invited Jack to a party the Marx Brothers were going to attend. He told Jack there would be wine, women, and song, and it wasn't a lie. There were wine, women, and song at the party. It was a Passover *seder,* and drinking at least four cups of wine and singing joyous chants describing the Exodus from Egypt are important parts of every *seder.* The women were the wife of their host, Henry Marks, and his two daughters, Ethel, about nineteen, and Sadye, fourteen years old. Also there was a younger son named Hilliard who, as the youngest male, asked the age-old "four questions" of the *seder*, beginning with the words: "Wherefore is this night different from all other nights?"

One of the reasons "this night was different from all other nights" for Jack Benny was because it was the first time that he laid eyes on Sadye Marks. However, not until years later did Jack realize that this night was indeed different.

Sadye, like all girls of fourteen, tried to appear older. She wore her big sister's long dress and high-heeled shoes, but to Jack, who was twenty-eight years old, she was just a kid—cute, all right, but still a kid. And what really turned Jack off was that she was an amateur violinist. She favored the group with a couple of numbers, but Jack hardly listened to her musical offerings. What mature man shows an interest in a child half his age? And after the evening was over, Jack quickly forgot Sadye Marks—for two years.

At that time Henry Marks moved his family from Vancouver to San Francisco. Jack was playing the Pantages Theatre there, and as he hurriedly left the building for an appointment one day, a sixteen-year-old girl greeted him by saying, "Hello, Mr. Benny, I'm..."

Now vaudeville performers in those days were frequently accosted by stage-door Janies who, like the "groupies" of today, regarded it as an honor to get sexually acquainted with stars of any kind, but Jack wanted no part of a sixteen-year-old girl who was good looking, but still jailbait—San Quentin quail. He gave her a polite "Hello" and continued walking. Thus for the second time in two years Jack ignored Sadye Marks.

About two years later, early in 1926, Jack was appearing in Los Angeles on the same theater bill with a pair of violinists, "The Bernovici Brothers." They were friends because they weren't competitors, since Jack still carried, but no longer played, the violin in his act. He was strictly a comedian now.

One night Jack went out to dinner with Al Bernovici and his wife. A blind date had been arranged for Jack with Mrs. Bernovici's younger sister. While Jack thought that Mrs. Bernovici looked vaguely familiar, her sister looked even more familiar. She was Sadye Marks. Now eighteen years old, she was no longer a child but a young lady, and this time Jack didn't ignore her. He fell in love with her at first sight. It was actually third sight but Jack never really looked at Sadye the first two times.

At dinner that night Jack could only stare at her. He couldn't make any conversation. The glib, witty remarks that made his reputation on the stage stuck to his mouth like peanut butter. Perhaps if he had been holding his fiddle he would have found it easier to talk, but all his hands held were a knife and a fork, so instead of talking, he ate. If Sadye had any inkling that Jack was remotely interested in her that night, neither his actions nor hers showed it.

The following day Jack discovered via Sadye's sister that she worked in the hosiery department of The May Company, a fact that was to be mentioned so often on his radio and television shows. Jack went there and pretended to be surprised at seeing Sadye. He also pretended that he wanted to buy a birthday present for his younger sister Florence.

In an old hit song called "I Found a Million Dollar Baby in a Five and Ten Cent Store," the lyrics described how boy meets sales-girl behind the crockery counter in Woolworth's and woos her by buying china until the other customers get wise. Jack did the same thing with Sadye and silk stockings, except that there was no crowd to "get wise," just Sadye, and she knew exactly why Jack was there. She had made overtures to him on two separate occasions and he had paid no attention to her. Now she was enjoying the reversed positions. She asked Jack questions which in those years would have embarrassed any mere male. How sheer did he want the stockings? Were they to be worn rolled above or below the knees, with garters or garter belts? What size? Jack bought several dozen pairs of stockings, and while Sadye was wrapping them he blurted out an invitation to lunch which she accepted.

While he worked in Los Angeles, Jack appeared at The May Company as often as he appeared at the theater, and he kept buying hosiery. During that week, nearly half a century ago, Sadye Marks probably set a record for selling stockings which still stands at The May Company today. At the end of the week Jack continued his tour of West Coast theaters, ignorant of the fact that Sadye, although not engaged, was going steady with another fellow.

Jack would drop Sadye postcards and letters from the various cities in which he appeared. There would also be an occasional long distance phone call, but never once did Jack tell her that he was in love with her, nor did she tell him that there was another man.

Jack found out about his rival late that year while appearing in Chicago with the Jake Shubert show *The Great Temptations.* It was Sadye's older sister Babe, as she was affectionately called, who broke the news to him. He met Babe one day and they conversed over a friendly cup of coffee. Then Babe casually dropped the bomb. "By the way," she said, "my kid sister Sadye may be getting married soon." Jack was shocked, but for once he was vocal without his violin. "She can't do it," he said to Babe. "She's only a kid. She's a baby. She's too young to get married. Call her on the phone. Tell her she's just a child. Tell her anything, but don't let her get married."

Babe called her sister, but she played no "John Alden" to Jack's

"Myles Standish." She told him to speak for himself, and Jack did. He convinced Sadye that she was too young to get married and that she shouldn't take such a serious step before having a long heart-to-heart, in-person talk with her sister. "And," Jack added boldly, "with me."

Sadye came to Chicago. She talked to her sister. She talked to Jack. Then they all drove to Lake Forest where Jack's father was now living. They talked to him. Next they drove to Jack's home town where they had a wild time as he showed her the sights of Waukegan. She met Julius Synakin, a dear but older friend of Jack's. They talked to him. And on January 14, 1927, in Julius Synakin's suite at the Clayton Hotel in Waukegan, at an Orthodox Jewish wedding presided over by a rabbi named Farmer, Sadye Marks became Mrs. Benjamin Kubelsky, better known as Mrs. Jack Benny.

Like all Jewish weddings, it concluded with the groom stamping his heel on and breaking a wine glass. As Jack's foot came down on the goblet, shattering it with a resounding crunch, Sadye fainted dead away.

4
Stage and Screen

Like almost all vaudeville stars, especially those who were in love with their mates, Jack worked his wife into his act. As a concession to her new profession, Sadye changed her black hair to honey blonde, knowing it would look better under the spotlights. And since one rarely sees a name like Sadye on theater marquees, she called herself Mary. She also had her nose bobbed. So, in a very short time, she changed her name, her hair, her nose, her occupation, and her residence. She no longer lived in a house, but in whatever hotel they stayed at in whatever town they were playing.

The newlyweds had a good life and many friends. Most of them were husband and wife vaudeville teams such as George Burns and Gracie Allen, Jessie Block and Eve Sully, Benny Fields and Blossom Seeley, Fred Allen and Portland Hoffa, and George Jessel and whomever he was married to at the moment. They frequently saw Eddie and Ida Cantor, Jane and Goodman Ace, and many others, all of whom had one thing in common—show business.

Jack and Mary didn't limit their friends to co-workers, but because of their close association with these people on the road and the mutual interests they shared, they had far more friends in the business than out of it. Frequently their tours would find them playing various theaters a week before or a week after some of their dearest friends were scheduled to appear. They would find notes from those who preceded them, and they in turn always left notes for those who followed.

The Bennys were happiest when Jack was cast in a Broadway show. If it clicked they could count on at least several months in New York, and they would then rent a small apartment there as a welcome change from hotel living on the road. However, they rarely had anything resembling a permanent home until Hollywood decided that Jack might make a good movie star. And while Jack would have loved to be a really big movie star, he also would have been happy just to make a good movie.

Jack was signed to a five-year contract at around a thousand dollars a week, with semi-annual increases, by none other than the legendary boy genius of MGM, Irving Thalberg. On the strength of this, Jack and Mary rented—not bought, but rented—a large home, with a swimming pool yet, and Jack started his career in films.

Jack's maiden effort in movies was an epic called *Hollywood Review of 1929.* It was one of the first all-talking, all-singing, all-star, all-dancing, all-hodgepodge movies made. In discussing it Jack would smilingly admit that his debut had been anything but auspicious. He said, "I made my first film in 1929, which shows that that year was a lousy one for the movies as well as the stock market." The picture was, as its title indicates, a review. Jack Benny was cast as a suave sophisticated master of ceremonies named Jack Benny. All the stars in this pastiche performed under their actual names—that is, the actual names under which they achieved their stardom.

In nostalgic moments Jack always would tell of an incident that happened in this picture. As the MC it was his duty to introduce each of the other stars who would then sing, or dance, or participate in a sketch. One of these stars was Conrad Nagel. Jack did a couple of jokes and then said, "And now, it's my pleasure to present one of Hollywood's brightest stars, Conrad Nagel, a name to conJURE with." Because the script directed him to do so, Jack purposely mispronounced "conjure." When Nagel came on screen his first line was to thank Jack for the compliments, and then he added, "But I'd like to correct you on one point. You said conJURE. It's not conJURE. It's CONjure."

Then Benny's big bellylaugh was supposed to come when he said, "Oh, I see. Sort of like La Jo-lah, which is pronounced La Hoya."

Although the scene was filmed that way, when the editors cut the film they snipped out Nagel's correction and Jack's punchline, but they still left in the introduction where he misprounced it conJURE.

Jack didn't realize this until he attended the premiere of the picture. Obviously he was embarrassed when he heard himself mis-prounce the word with no joke to explain it, giving the audience the impression that he was either unfunny or ignorant, or both. And to make matters worse, a movie critic, reviewing the picture, wrote: "If Jack Benny wants to pretend that he's a suave master of cere-monies, he'd better learn how to speak English first."

Despite this incident, MGM picked up Jack's option, gave him a raise, and cast him in another film, *Chasing Rainbows.* Then the studio picked his option up again, increased his salary once more, but gave him no other chores to perform. Meanwhile Jack got an offer to star in Earl Carroll's *Vanities* at an attractive salary. He went to Irving Thalberg and asked for his release, but even though they had no parts for Jack to play and they were paying him a sizable salary, MGM wanted him to stay with them.

A few months later he again asked Thalberg for his release but was turned down. The third time he asked, he got his release. How-ever, when he then called Carroll and told him he was ready and available for the show, Carroll was quite cool to him, perhaps be-cause he figured Jack had personally turned him down several weeks earlier. Carroll said in effect, "Don't call us, we'll call you."

Jack applied for work at other studios—studios that had made lavish offers to him when he was under contract to MGM—and found that there was an underwhelming demand for his services. Finally he signed for a secondary role in a "B" picture made by a tiny independent studio. In discussing this period, Jack invariably said, "It was an independent studio, but what they had to be indepen-dent about I never knew." The picture was called *The Medicine Man,* and a few days after Jack signed to appear in it, Earl Carroll called him again. He was ready to produce another version of his *Vanities,* and he again wanted Jack as the star. Fortunately the movie, like all low-budget "B" movies, was filmed and finished quickly. Then Jack and Mary went back to New York, giving up the house with the swimming pool for a Manhattan apartment.

Earl Carroll had been called Flo Ziegfeld's closest competitor when it came to producing lavish musical stage extravaganzas, but his taste was more like Jake Shubert's. When I was a teenager I remember reading all the New York tabloids of the day about a sensationally lewd party Carroll had hosted at which champagne was served from a bathtub that was filled with the beverage. It was also filled with a nude chorus girl named Joyce Hawley. There were various whispered stories about Miss Hawley's conduct in the tub, and how, and with what, she served the champagne to Carroll's guests.

Carroll eventually was sentenced to jail for this escapade—not for doing anything lewd or pornographic, but on the grounds that by serving champagne he had broken the Volstead Act, which was the law that had ushered in "Prohibition." Oddly enough this created sympathy for him, because by this time the 18th Amendment had been broken more times in less than a dozen years than the combined Ten Commandments in nearly forty centuries.

Carroll didn't serve his full sentence, being given time off for good behavior. But while his behavior had perhaps improved, his taste hadn't, as the latest edition of his *Vanities* showed.

A famous incident in this *Vanities* became one of Jack's favorite anecdotes. One of the sketches starring him was based on a "Farmer's Daughter" type joke with Jack playing a traveling salesman city slicker. The show was having its out of town tryout week in Washington, D.C., and Carroll, a stickler for realism, insisted on using real ducks, chickens, pigs, and a cow in the farm scene, much to the dismay of city-bred Benny who hadn't much affinity for animals. In the sketch Jack was supposed to be on the make for the milkmaid who was tending to the cow, but when they started their dialogue the cow began to urinate. As Jack told me, "I don't know what animal owns the endurance record for pissing, but that cow was a logical contender. It kept going, and going, splashing over the scenery, the stage, and the musicians in the pit, and moistening the first five rows of the audience. The girl playing the milkmaid tried to climb to safety on the stool, but she slipped, causing further laughter. The audience was uncontrollable for several minutes, enough time for even me to think of a good ad-lib." (Jack always furthered the false theory that he couldn't ad-lib because it was inherent in his character.) Then he said, "When that cow finally finished pissing, I walked to the only dry spot I could find on the stage and held up my hand for silence. When the people quieted down I said, 'Folks, you'll have to forgive the cow, but this is opening night and she's just as nervous as we are.' " Jack added that his ad-lib not only got a great laugh, but it convinced Earl Carroll to use a papier-mâché cow.

However, while the cow incident was accidental, the rest of the risqué humor was intentional, and, as in his earlier experience with Jake Shubert, Benny rejected every vulgar and obscene scene he was written into. Again he made a famed Broadway producer let him have his way. Jack appeared in the *Vanities* doing some short monologues and appearing in a couple of acceptable sketches.

Once again the drama critics' reviews ripped the show to shreds but praised Jack personally. They were unanimous in condemning *The Vanities of 1930* as the dirtiest show to ever appear in Manhattan, and they warned their readers that they would be better off skipping this revue because they would be offended and shocked at its smut.

With reviews like that, naturally the show was a big hit and had a long run. It was a phenomenon in show business. But another phenomenon had come along in show business—radio. Unknowns like "Sam 'n' Henry" were broadcasting from Chicago and making five thousand dollars a week. They earned far more than that when they changed their names to "Amos 'n' Andy." Many of Jack's friends, like Eddie Cantor, Ed Wynn, and others, were earning fortunes by broadcasting. And not only that, but with a radio contract you stayed put in one city. You didn't travel from town to town each week, packing and repacking, living out of trunks and in hotels. Therefore, Jack decided to try radio—but nobody wanted him.

After the *Vanities* engagement was over, for a year or more Jack had no regular engagements. He played a theater here and there, but vaudeville was gasping its last. He made a few more movies, but he wasn't truly a star of the silver screen. He eventually made many other pictures, and some of them were good—darn good, in fact, particularly *Charley's Aunt* and *George Washington Slept Here.* His best was probably Ernst Lubitsch's *To Be Or Not To Be* in which he co-starred with Carole Lombard.*

Jack didn't click big in movies, but the broadcasting medium was made for him. His mellow voice, his timing, and his delivery were all manna for the microphone. His personality not only came across the airwaves, it caressed you, shook hands with you, and became your best friend for life. Some big stars of the stage and screen flopped on radio, and the alibi was always, "His personality just didn't come across." On the other hand, one famous comic never scored in radio because, as one wit said, "His personality did come across."

But Jack in the very early 1930s could get no broadcasting jobs. In fact, his first radio appearance was a "freebie"—in other words, for no salary.

In 1932 Ed Sullivan was the Broadway columnist for the *New York Daily News.* He also was doing a radio show on a local station, WHN, where he gave his listeners an earful of the latest show business gossip and interviewed any stars willing to take a chance on the new medium. He asked Jack to come on his program, saying that there was no script and they'd just ad-lib.

This was fine with Jack, but he took the precaution of having Al Boasberg, soon to become his first radio writer, prepare a few remarks. Jack's first spoken lines on radio were, "This is Jack Benny talking. There will be a slight pause while you say, 'Who cares?' . . . I'm going back to motion pictures in a few weeks. I'm going to be in a new picture with Greta Garbo. When the picture opens I'm found dead in the bathtub. It's a mystery picture. I'm found dead in the

*See Appendix A for a discussion of Jack's movie career.

bathtub on *Wednesday* night . . . but you'd like Garbo. She and I were great friends in Hollywood. She used to let me drive her car all over town . . . of course she paid me for it."

This was Jack's first appearance on radio. He did a friend a favor, and fate was kind to him and repaid his kindness to Sullivan.

An advertising agency executive named Douglas Coulter heard Jack on Ed Sullivan's show, and he liked what he heard. He thought Jack was a "natural." Furthermore, his agency had a client, Canada Dry, which wanted to sponsor a radio show. Coulter, who was sold on Benny, now sold Benny to Canada Dry to advertise their ginger ale. Jack went on the NBC-Blue network (now split off and competing with NBC and CBS) and he acted as MC on two weekly half-hour shows, Mondays and Fridays. At the end of his first season he was voted "Most Popular Comedian on the Air" by a poll of radio editors throughout the country—and his sponsor dropped him.

In 1934 he was signed by Chevrolet, which dropped him at the end of two years because the president of the company, William Knudsen, said that he didn't think Jack was funny. However, despite the negative reaction of his first two sponsors, the public loved Jack, and he signed with General Foods, makers of Jell-O, his trademark for years. He soon moved to the West Coast, and this time the Bennys had a permanent home that they bought, not rented. They also adopted Joan, a beautiful little baby girl, in 1935.

As Jack's radio shows became more and more popular, his cast kept changing in those early years. He had orchestra leaders like Don Bestor, Johnny Green, Ted Weems, Frank Black, and George Olsen, and singers like James Melton, Michael Barlett, Frank Parker, and Kenny Baker. His announcers included George Hicks, Paul Douglas, and Alois Havrilla.

By the time that I first went to work for Jack in October 1943, he already had the great and rarely changed cast that most people think he always had—Mary Livingstone, Phil Harris, Rochester, Dennis Day, and Don Wilson. My co-writers and I augmented this never-to-be-forgotten group with numerous supporting players who appeared so frequently on the show that they seemed to be regulars.

I didn't know Jack during his early years. There was a two-decade difference in our ages. I first met him in the late 1930s, and became a close associate some time later. The pages that follow are based on that association and on personal and intimate contact with him for over thirty-five years. The events described are all true. I know they are true because I saw or heard them all personally.

"Bennie & Woods"—that's the spelling and billing of Jack's early vaudeville act, 1916. Lyman Woods is at the piano.

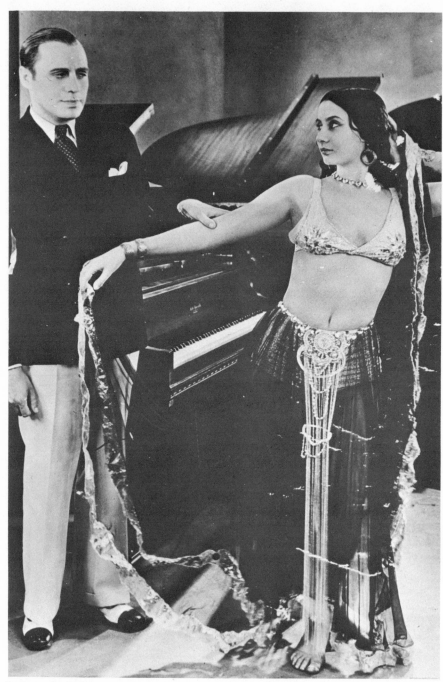

In the early 1920s.

Jack, January 1940.

Jack in front of an NBC mike in the early 1930s.

Alone in his Maxwell, February 1938.

A 1940 radio rehearsal. Jack, Mary, Phil Harris, Dennis Day, Rochester, and Don Wilson.

Jack listening to his own program on board a train, February 1941.

With harmonica virtuouso Larry Adler (right) in Omdurman, Egyptian Sudan, during a break from entertaining the troops in 1943.

Entertaining the troops in 1944, the South Pacific.

Jack, Alice Faye, Phil Harris (front seat), Edgar Bergen, and Harriet and Ozzie Nelson in another Maxwell, October 1948.

May 1964.

5
Kindness and Humility

For those purists who are interested in facts and dates, I will list them briefly. I first met Jack in late 1938 or early in 1939 in a funny but embarrassing way. I was one of the writers on the Bob Hope show which was beginning its successful struggle for the upper ratings. In a sketch on this particular program we did a scene where Hope, playing the part of a gangster who was arrested on charges of burglary, claimed he couldn't have been the burglar because he had a perfect alibi—at the time that the burglary took place, he had witnesses to prove he was committing a couple of murders. Hope said, "That was the night I bumped off Louie the Lug and Mendel the Momzer." The last name was inserted by me because of my ego, a trait you will encounter more than occasionally in these pages. My name is Milton, and the affectionate Jewish version of Milton is "Mendel." Furthermore the word *momzer* in Jewish means "rascal" or "clever little devil." It also has another meaning, but I wasn't aware of it at that time. Thus when Bob wanted to know its meaning before putting it in the script, I explained that "Mendel the Momzer" was an affectionate term my father frequently used in reference to me and that it meant "Milton the Rascal." Hope graciously let me have my little joke which would amuse my family back East, but the network censor objected. He suggested a change, saying the Yiddish word *momzer* was not polite usage, since its actual meaning was "bastard." I received digs from fellow writers because I had mentioned that my father called me *momzer,* and the consensus of opinion was that if anyone should know the facts of my legitimacy, my dad probably had first-hand knowledge. At this point Jack Benny stepped into our rehearsal hall for some now long-forgotten reason. Hope immediately asked Jack, "What does *momzer* mean?" Jack smiled and said, "Don't tell me your sponsor is calling you that already." Jack then explained that *momzer* literally meant "bastard."

Embarrassed as I was prior to this, I became more so in the presence, for my very first time, of the great Jack Benny. With a deep blush, which I hoped he mistook for sunburn, I told Jack that my family frequently but fondly referred to me as "Mendel the Momzer." That was the first of many times that Jack rescued me. He pointed out to Bob and the others that *momzer* was also a term of endearment, usually meaning "rascal." He then put his arm around my shoulder and consoled me by saying that as a child his father would occasionally refer to him as a *momzer* too. At this point Hope broke us all up by pointing to Jack and me and saying, "If we can get rid of these two bastards we can continue rehearsing."

And now I must skip a few years to October 1943, when an almost similar mistake was made by the late John Tackaberry who, like myself, had just joined Jack's writing staff. John was an always happy orbicular Texan who usually spoke in tones some few decibels louder than the air raid sirens that were prevalent during those war years. Even though John was a WASP, he fell in love with the Yiddish word *schmuck.* Now through the years the word *schmuck* began to mean an ineffectual, harmless, good-natured slob. In fact, it was used so commonly that in the late 1930s the staid *Saturday Evening Post* ran a short story by a non-Jewish writer in which he referred to a movie producer's brother-in-law as "a pleasant little *schmuck*." However, the original and true meaning is entirely different. In Yiddish, *schmuck* means the male sex organ.

On this cold autumn afternoon in New York, Jack was supposed to meet his writing staff in Lindy's Restaurant for lunch. We writers arrived a bit early and were seated at a table. Jack came in a few seconds later, but his entrance from the cold outside air to the warmth of the restaurant caused his glasses to fog up, and he looked around the room for us, blinking like a near-sighted owl. Tackaberry spotted him first, and he rose from his seat and bellowed, "We're over here, *schmuck*."

For those unfamiliar with Lindy's Restaurant in 1943, let me point out that from an ethnic standpoint it was not the Vatican. If there were two hundred diners in the room, it was a safe bet that ninety percent were Jewish and the other ten percent were show-business oriented and understood a smattering of Yiddish. Thus when John bellowed at Benny, calling him "*schmuck*," all eyes turned to Jack as he embarrassedly walked to our table. Instead of being mad, he was laughing, and instead of chastising Tackaberry, he enlightened him as to the actual meaning of the word. He concluded his remarks by saying, "It's all right to call me '*schmuck*' in private, but please, never call me that again in Lindy's—or in a synagogue."

In October 1943 I started my twelve-year scripting stint with Jack Benny, and during those first weeks in his employ I discovered that this world-famous star, who was ranked first in all the popularity ratings, was modest, naive, and shy in many respects. My initial inkling of these traits came early in our association when I was working alone with him on a special piece of material. We had labored most of the morning with satisfactory results, and it was now lunch time. Jack stated that instead of ordering room service he'd rather take a walk (he was one of the world's most enthusiastic walkers) to one of the nearby restaurants. Again he chose Lindy's, and he asked me to phone for a reservation while he donned his tie and jacket. As I started to dial the number he said, "Oh, Milt—make the reservation in your name, not mine." Since this was the height of the lunch bunch crunch, I knew that mentioning my name would probably mean nothing to the headwaiter taking phone reservations. I told Jack my thoughts on this before I completed dialing the number. He replied: "Maybe so, Milt, but when you mention that you want the table for Jack Benny it sounds like name-dropping."

At that time I had been with Jack for less than two weeks and didn't know him too well. I wasn't sure whether he was serious or ribbing me, and I wasn't stupid enough to show my ignorance by asking him to explain. Therefore I made the reservations in my name—which, much to my embarrassment, I had to spell five times for the headwaiter.

As we walked to Lindy's, Jack explained that he didn't think it fair to make last-minute reservations in his name and then be given precedence over some poor shnook who had been waiting for a table for half an hour.

As years passed, other examples of his modesty impressed me. For example, it was in 1944, I believe, that a national magazine took a poll to determine who had the best-known voice in America. Jack Benny finished first, followed in order by Franklin D. Roosevelt, Bob Hope, and Bing Crosby.

There was no doubt that Jack's voice, especially the two words with which he opened every radio program, "Hello again," was heard and recognized by more millions every Sunday than any other voice in America. Yet for all the years I knew him, every time Jack called me at home and my wife, Hilda, answered the phone, and Jack simply said, "Hello," and Hilda immediately answered, "Oh, hello, Jack," he was always genuinely amazed that she recognized his voice from the single word "hello." I once explained to Jack that his was the world's most easily identified voice. He answered, "Look, if I said 'hello again,' that's a phrase I always use— but how could she recognize me from one teensy weensy 'hello'?" And he was quite serious about it.

Another example: In the summer of 1970 I was the head writer and script consultant of Lucille Ball's third successful series, *Here's Lucy.* One of the programs we filmed during this period was the memorable show with Elizabeth Taylor and Richard Burton. The script was written by the team of Madelyn Davis and Bob Carroll, but my double duties as script consultant and head writer called for me to be onstage during rehearsals of all episodes so that I could make any changes, cuts, or additions as needed. They had rehearsed this program several times, and then, at the dress rehearsal, Richard Burton did a new piece of business we had not seen before. It got a laugh from the cast and crew, and Miss Taylor asked, "Where did you get that?" Proudly Burton answered, "It's a little thing I picked up from watching Jack Benny."

That night I phoned Jack and told him about the incident, but he didn't believe me. He thought I was just trying to make him feel good by flattering him for old times' sake and said: "You mean Richard Burton actually did a 'take' of mine?"

"Definitely."

"And in front of everybody he admitted that he not only watches me, but copied something I do?"

"Yes. And he seemed quite pleased that he was able to duplicate one of your reactions."

"Aw, come on, Milt, you're kidding me. Richard Burton probably doesn't even know that I exist."

"But, Jack, why shouldn't he know you? The Queen of England probably knows you."

"Well, the Queen should. She's seen my act three times at the London Palladium."

Jack was flattered but still slightly dubious when we concluded our conversation.

Some weeks later Lucille Ball met Jack at a party and repeated the incident to him practically verbatim. Jack called me apologetically to say that it wasn't as though he doubted my word, but he simply couldn't believe that Richard Burton would not only know of him, but would mimic his mannerisms. A trifle exasperated, I said, "Jack, you're one of the biggest stars who ever lived. Why shouldn't Burton know and talk about you?" And Jack answered, "Hell, Milt, he sleeps with Elizabeth Taylor. Why would he waste time thinking of me?"

Before dropping this subject, let me point out that there are other meanings to modesty aside from the opposite of conceit. For example, there is the modesty that prevents a performer from doing any line, or bit of business, which he feels might offend good taste. I remember two incidents in this connection with Jack.

One happened many years ago. It was during the summer and Jack and Mary were vacationing in Europe. At the same time another attempt was to be made to cross the English Channel in the heroic manner of Gertrude Ederle, and once again it was a girl who would endeavor to swim from England to France. As I remember she was quite a comely lass, about seventeen years old, and I believe her name was Shirley May. The big news item concerning her attempt was that she would be an aquatic streaker, swimming *au naturel*. It was reported that all that Shirley May would wear was a coating of Vaseline to protect her from the chill of the water. Jack returned from England prior to her effort, and the actual swim took place several days before we did our first radio show of the season. We had prepared an opening gag that we knew would be a blockbuster, and we had even gotten the network censor to okay it. It was a bit of dialogue between Jack and his announcer, Don Wilson, and it came a few seconds after they greeted each other:

DON

Jack, I understand you just came back from England?

JACK

That's right, Don, I was in England.

DON

You went there for a vacation, huh?

JACK

No, I went there to grease up Shirley May.

At every rehearsal the cast and crew screamed at the line. It was daring in those days, although it would be considered as bland as pablum in these more permissive times. We knew it was sure to garner a big laugh, but during the dress rehearsal Sunday, two

56

hours before air time, Jack suddenly stopped the proceedings and suggested that the gag be deleted. We protested until he explained his reasoning. He said that he was sure it was very funny, and that if Shirley May were a mature woman, he'd do it. However, since she was a teenage girl, he felt that he might in some way embarrass her or hold her up to ridicule. As a result we excised it. This was a prime example not only of Jack's modesty, but of his reticence at getting a big laugh that might embarrass some innocent person.

A final example of this type of modesty, shyness, or whatever you want to call it came at the height of the "feud" between Jack and Fred Allen. It was over a quarter of a century ago and actress Jane Russell was the best-known sex object at the time because of her miraculous mammaries. We gave Jack the following joke: "Yesterday I was very thrilled as I walked down Wilshire Boulevard because suddenly I saw Jane Russell walking toward me. . . . As she got nearer, I realized it was Fred Allen. . . . Gee, those bags under his eyes are terrible."

Jack didn't do the joke on the air for fear of offending listeners. That may seem odd in these days when impotency, menopause, infidelity, homosexuality, alcoholism, and abortion are suitable subjects for entire comedy programs, but Jack wouldn't do it on his program. He did, however, do it at benefits, dinners, and private affairs, and the joke always got a strange reaction. When he'd say the opening lines—"I saw Jane Russell walking toward me. . . . As she got nearer, I realized it was Fred Allen"—this bit, which we thought was the feed line, got a tremendous laugh from the audience. Then when he added the final line, "Gee, those bags under his eyes are terrible," there was an even bigger laugh. Nevertheless, we could never talk Jack into broadcasting the bit.

Jack's attitude toward all things, including humor, seemed very simple at times, but behind this public façade he was quite complex. As the years passed this became more evident, and I, like several other close associates, began to realize it more and more. I doubt if any biographer could capture the various vagaries of his public and private characters, and the countless in-between nuances, in one volume. He was best known as a performer, and this is the facet of Jack Benny that we will examine first.

6
Teamwork

The Jack Benny Show undoubtedly brought more laughter to the world than any other item of entertainment did in this planet's past, or will in the foreseeable future. When you take the number of laughs each of his individual programs garnered, and multiply that by the number of programs Jack did each season, and then further multiply this total by the amount of seasons his show was presented as a regular feature, the total could conceivably be far more than can be handled by your pocket calculator. Add to this the numerous "specials," guest shots, benefits, nightclub, vaudeville, and legitimate presentations, and the other personal appearances he made, and the final result will be astronomical.

True, top television today may reach a larger audience than Jack's radio and TV shows did, but he broadcast on a regular schedule for nearly forty consecutive seasons, and comedy programs no longer enjoy this type of longevity. If a comedy show on the tube runs for four years it is a hit; six years makes it a smash. Anything longer than that is a miracle, and there have only been a handful of such phenomena in TV's short history.

Possibly the record for most comedy shows done on TV by an individual performer is held by Lucille Ball, but the redoubtable redhead had three separate series spanning a total of some twenty years. First came *I Love Lucy,* followed by *The Lucy Show,* and finally *Here's Lucy.* Yet, if we count all three of these series as one continuing show, Lucy did less than half the amount of broadcasts that Jack Benny did.

In radio, a season consisted of thirty-five to thirty-nine new programs. In TV, for over the past decade and a half, the full season consists of twenty-two to twenty-six new programs plus summer reruns.

Radio was a much more casual medium that demanded less of the listener's attention than television, thus making it wear longer and better. Even mildly successful programs on radio ran several seasons. Currently on TV it frequently happens that last season's comedy sensation can be next season's big bore. Today television shows are frequently cancelled and replaced in mid-season, an unheard-of rarity in radio.

If Jack had been born fifty years later and been blessed with his same talent and ability, perhaps he would not have made such a permanent impact on the public. His slow, casual pacing might not have clicked with the modern generation of TV viewers who are accustomed to a more frantic and frenetic type of humor. But Jack's easy, casual approach, neither grating nor bombastic, was perhaps the very thing that made him such a lasting success on the air.

Jack always admitted that the most important ingredients of his show were the cast and crew he so carefully selected and nurtured. No other series in the history of broadcasting gave such enduring, profitable employment to so many performers . . . and writers . . . and technicians. And his cast and crew returned the loyalty and love he gave them. True, there were occasional bruised egos and internal squabbles, but Jack was usually the mediator rather than the perpetrator of any infrequent eruptions. There was never any behind-the-back bellyaching or criticism of his actions or decisions. This was not done blindly or unquestioningly, because any time a member of the cast, or even the least important bit player, felt that there was a flaw in his material, he would bring the matter up immediately, and if, indeed, there was a fault, it was corrected.

His writers, who worked closest with him, argued with him most. However, when a majority of them decided that a routine was right, it usually was. When they and Jack were unanimous in their opinion, it was rarely reversed by any individual member of the cast.

The Jack Benny Show was like an extremely fine precision-made Swiss watch, with each cast member and writer a cog that moved with split-second accuracy and performed to perfection. Broadcasting's version of baseball's Tinker-to-Evers-to-Chance, it was as constant as the earth circling the sun—a unique example of flawless teamwork where the unheard-of temporary faltering of one of its component parts wouldn't visibly affect the whole.

In an analysis of the success of the Jack Benny series, *Time* magazine in its January 6, 1975 issue quoted a more than twenty-year-old complimentary comment from Fred Allen: "Practically all the comedy shows owe their structure to Benny's conceptions. The Benny show was like a 'One Man's Family' in slapstick. He was the first comedian in radio to realize you could get big laughs by ridiculing yourself instead of your stooges."

Allen, as usual, was one hundred percent right. Jack was the butt of all the barbs of his capable cast. His writers endowed him with characteristics diametrically opposed to his real-life personality, and by some miracle of chemistry these all blended into an inseparable oneness. We made him vain, miserly, and overbearing. Yet, no matter what human failing we fastened to his already ample overload of faults and frailties, we kept certain important facts in mind. We made him sympathetic and lovable. Moreover, he had audience identification—possibly more audience identification than any other entertainer ever enjoyed. Practically every viewer or listener saw something of himself, a relative or a friend in the fictional facets of Benny's public personality. They identified with this similarity and loved it. Let's face facts, you can't hate yourself. Other characters on the series were larger than life, but basically Benny was true to it.

The *Time* magazine article continued: "The format was to become a permanent structure. Even today, Benny's influences still echo around the TV channels. Jack's wise-cracking girlfriend—and offstage wife—Mary Livingstone, is the original 'Rhoda.' Don Wilson, the pompous announcer, can be seen in Ted Knight's role on 'The Mary Tyler Moore Show.' The drunken bandleader, Phil Harris, is a hundred-proof version of Ed McMahon, Johnny Carson's sidekick. Rochester, the sardonic Negro valet, is the granddaddy of all the servants, black and white, who have hilariously put down their employers since the invention of the vacuum tube."

Time magazine hit near perfect bull's-eyes in its acutely accurate analysis of the cast members, but it didn't delve into the many nuances hidden beneath the surface. And for some reason it omitted Dennis Day, a vital and frequently instigating factor in plots and premises. Superficially Dennis seemed to be the "kid"—the most vulnerable and least protected of the cast members, and therefore the one Jack could most easily outsmart. However, as with all his other characters, Jack only outmaneuvered Dennis in the early skirmishes. At the end, Dennis, like Mary, Rochester, Phil Harris, and Don Wilson, scored the final victory.

August 1946.

Arriving in New York City, March 1938.

Teaching Jack Dempsey how to play the violin, January 1943.

With Bob Hope, November 1948.

With Mel Blanc (Jack's long suffering, volatile violin instructor, "M'sieu Le Blanc").

With his violin, May 1964.

With Eddie Cantor, March 1948.

With Eddie and Ida Cantor, May 1953.

With his favorite guest stars, Benita and Ronald Colman, December 1950.

Mel Blanc (at the bass) as "The Little Mexican," December 1966.

Going mod with the DeFranco Family, January 24, 1974.

To psychoanalyze the underlying current of comedy in each of their characters would be an almost eternal undertaking. And as all comics and others engaged in the serious business of humor know, when you dissect a joke, gag, or character too thoroughly, you're left with dry dusty words and nothing to laugh at. However, in the next few chapters I will try to touch on each of these tremendous talents and indicate what made them funny in their relationship with Jack and with each other.

7
Mary Livingstone

The lasting popularity of Mary Livingstone on *The Jack Benny Show* was a complete contradiction of the most basic rule in creating comedy programs. For a running character to sustain as a regular member of a successful series, she, or he, must have a clearly defined function in relationship to the star. Edith Bunker is Archie's wife. Harriet was Ozzie's wife. Florida was Maude's maid. Rhoda was Mary Tyler Moore's friend and neighbor. Brenda is now Rhoda's sister. Chico works for The Man. And so it is on all prime-time TV hit programs, but Mary was the exception to the rule. Her reason for being on the Benny broadcasts was even more obscure than Ozzie Nelson's occupation. Only a few radio buffs knew what Ozzie did for a living, and even fewer could tell you what Mary's exact function was on the Benny broadcasts.

Ask any ardent fan who and what Mary Livingstone was on Jack's series and you will get an assortment of answers. However, if you go to the writers who wrote the programs and ask their opinion of Mary's official air status, you could become even more confused.

We writers knew that each member of the cast had a definite duty, which put him, theoretically, under Jack's thumb. Phil Harris was the bandleader, responsible for the music on the show and the behavior of his musicians. Dennis Day was the singer, responsible for singing a song each week (in addition to doing other chores Jack had hidden in clauses in his contract, such as mowing the lawn and running errands). Don Wilson was the announcer, and Jack could chide him and threaten to fire him if he felt the introduction Don gave him at the start of each program wasn't complimentary enough. Rochester was his valet, his major-domo, in charge of his house, chauffeuring him around in his Maxwell, and a hundred other duties which Jack would think of from time to time.

However, Mary fitted into none of these categories. She didn't work for Jack in any given capacity, and yet, every now and then when he felt that her retorts were too insulting, he would remind her that he had taken her out of The May Company where he found her behind a counter selling stockings.

If, in the script, Jack got mad at Mary, he'd get off a rhymed couplet such as:

A candle in The May Company's window is burning bright.
They feel their wandering girl may be coming home tonight.

We did dozens of jokes threatening Mary that she'd have to go back to The May Company for a job because Jack would fire her. But fire her from what? She wasn't his secretary. She wasn't a cast contributor via music, announcing, or singing, as the others were. And, contrary to *Time* magazine, she wasn't his "girlfriend." True, on many programs Jack did date Mary, but he had other "girlfriends" such as Gladys Zybisco (Sara Berner) and the two telephone operators, Mabel Flapsaddle and Gertrude Gearshift (played by Bea Benaderet and Sara Berner; later Sandra Gould replaced Sara).

Excluding Mary, Jack's girlfriends were portrayed as creatures who could easily win "Best of Breed" honors in any kennel club show. They were not simply dogs, they were mongrel mutts. In real life they were attractive, but radio listeners saw with their ears and accepted them as "ugs" because they talked with a Brooklyn, Bronx, or any other laugh-getting accent. They were used on occasions when Jack Benny, through scheming or mistake, would wind up on a double date and go out on the town with a famous and dignified couple like the Ronald Colmans or the Jimmy Stewarts. The crude behavior of Jack's girlfriends would eventually end the evening's gaiety on a harsh but hilarious note. On one such occasion, Jack and Mabel Flapsaddle, played by Bea Benaderet, who went on to become the star of TV's *Petticoat Junction,* were to go out on a date, and Gertrude Gearshift (portrayed by Sara Berner) was asking her what a date was like with Jack. The dialogue went as follows:

MABEL

Last time we was out on a date, he drove me up to Mullholland Drive, parked the car, and we just sat and watched the lights being turned on all over the city.

GERTRUDE

Gee, I didn't think Jack was that romantic.

MABEL

Romantic nothing—he owns stock in the Electric Company . . . Ohhhhh, how he hates it when we go on Daylight Savings Time.

Both of Mabel's lines were big laughs, and we did occasional variations of this type of joke, such as: "Jack drove me up to the top of Mullholland Drive just at dusk." "My, how sentimental." "Sentimental nothing. Jack's idea of a big thrill is watching the sun set over the Bank of America."

So while Jack, at times, did take Mary to social functions on the program, she was not basically Benny's girlfriend. Mary actually had no definable function on the series, yet she was one of its most valuable components because she could most frequently and fearlessly puncture his pomposity. Perhaps because she didn't technically work for Jack on the program, and because she was also an attractive gal whom Jack occasionally dated, she could get away with more frequent and sharper insults than anyone else on the show. They were many, and they were funny. One of the best happened at the opening of a show. The cast was supposed to assemble at Jack's house for a rehearsal. Jack was in a good mood, and as he prepared for his group's arrival, he was singing "You Must Have Been a Beautiful Baby"—except that Jack had personalized and paraphrased the lyrics to fit himself, to wit, "I must have been a beautiful baby." The doorbell rang, and Jack crossed to the door to open it, still singing of his own childish charms via the revised song lyrics. As he opened the door he was singing: "I must have been a beautiful baby," and Mary, on the other side of the door, added, "But, Baby, look at you now." This bit took more time than the average comic would devote to a single gag, but the laugh Mary got on her one-line entrance was well worth it.

Because she had no regular function per se on the show, we created routines for Mary, and one of the most popular, done several times a season, was a letter she read from her mother. Supposedly, Mary's mother lived in Plainfield, New Jersey, together with Mary's spinster sister Babe. Mary's actual sister "Babe," who was quite attractive and, at the time, married to Benny's business manager, Myrt Blum, loved being the butt of our jokes, which portrayed her as a homely man-chaser. One year during the early days of television, our radio program was based on the fact that the entire cast had come over to Jack's home to watch the World Series on TV. Jack suddenly got excited and yelled, "Mary, Mary, look, in the lower corner of the picture. Isn't that your sister Babe?" And Mary answered, "No, Jack, it's Yogi Berra."

When we did these routines, Mary would make her entrance on the program and announce that she had received another note from Mama. Jack would then have a line like, "How nice. And what does 'The Midnight Cowboy' of Plainfield have to say?" Mary would then read the letter to the accompaniment of appropriate remarks from Jack. Here is a composite sample of one of these letters with Jack's comments:

MARY

My darling daughter Mary . . . Everything is fine here in Plainfield except that your sister Babe is very upset because she wasn't selected to go to Atlantic City for the Miss America Bathing Beauty Contest . . . Even though I'm her mother, I must admit that Bertha has the prettiest pair of knees in New Jersey . . . It's a shame they're in the back.

JACK

Yeah . . . lucky for Babe her feet are on backwards or she'd look awful . . .

MARY

Poor Babe never had any luck . . . We thought she finally landed a fellow last week. For seven straight nights a college student took her out.

JACK

Well, a college student.

MARY

But the eighth night he didn't show up. He called and said the initiation was over.

JACK

Poor Babe.

71

MARY

Last year Babe did have a boyfriend named Herman, but he met a very sad end ... He worked for a brewery and fell into a vat of beer.

JACK

And he drowned?

MARY

They saved him from drowning, but he caught pneumonia from everybody trying to blow the foam off him.

(Jack stares at her.)

MARY

That's about all the news so I'll close with fondest regards from your mother, "Cactus Flower" Livingstone ... (*Mary laughs.*)

JACK

What's so funny?

MARY

P.S. Tell Jack that after he spent the night here we found that he had left his toupee and his toothbrush.

JACK

Hmmmmmmm.

MARY

We're mailing them back to him. The one with the handle is the toothbrush.

JACK

I know, *I know*!

A word of explanation about the salutations and signoffs of these letters. Whenever Mary would announce that she had received a note from her mother, Jack would always have a topical description of her. These days he might have said, "Oh, a letter from your mother. What does the 'Maude' of Plainfield have to say?" Or "What does the 'Jaws' of New Jersey have to say?" Or "What does 'The Towering Inferno' of Plainfield have to say?" Jack would always use the name of a current play, movie, radio series, or public figure to describe Mary's mother. And at the end, the signature would be preceded by closing lines like: "From your loving mother, 'The Exorcist' Livingstone," or "From your loving mother, 'Twiggy' Livingstone." These salutations and farewells were always a vital part of these letters and usually got good laughs for the openings and closings of this imaginary correspondence.

In summing up this brief chapter which doesn't do ample justice to Mary or her talents, I must repeat that while Mary seemed to have no actual purpose on the series, she was actually an intrinsic part of the show.

Of course, all of the personnel of the programs figured to some extent in Jack's personal and social activities in addition to their business affiliations. Naturally no one was more important than Mary in this regard, and later in this book another full chapter has been devoted to her private life with Jack.

8
Phil Harris

As mentioned, *Time* magazine analyzed Phil Harris in this way: "The drunken bandleader . . . is a hundred-proof version of Ed McMahon." Merely to dismiss Phil Harris as a drunken bandleader is like calling Einstein that guy who could do arithmetic.

Phil had many facets to his character, as I'm sure Ed McMahon has. His drinking, greatly exaggerated for comedy character, as is true with Dean Martin, Ed McMahon, and others, was a small but vital ingredient that made up the whole.

First of all Phil portrayed a braggart, a bon vivant, a know-it-all boasting a Rhodes scholar's knowledge but having a kindergarten education. He presided over a group of musicians who had all been dishonorably discharged from Alcoholics Anonymous. Phil fancied his singing ability, and in fact, with the possible exception of the long-gone great black entertainer Bert Williams, no one could do certain "folk" songs like Phil.

Phil never just walked on Jack's radio shows as other performers did, with a "hello" salutation of greeting. Phil always made an entrance with a capital "E." In fact, with a capital E,N,T,R,A,N,C,E. He would come on stage and loudly announce himself with egotistical two-line jingles. Here are two typical samples:

The program's been dull, but now Harris is here.
So come on, all you folks, prepare to cheer.

Okay, folks, your troubles are over.
'Cause Harris is here and you're all in clover.

The audiences loved his entrances, his routines, his drinking, and his constant bragging. What in another performer would be grating garrulousness and irritating ego became lovable qualities in Harris.

Also starred was the character of Frank Remley, Phil's guitarist, who had been brought into prominence by almost weekly jokes about him on *The Jack Benny Show*. Remley was an actual person, but on the Phil Harris-Alice Faye series he was portrayed by Elliot Lewis, a valuable member of the Jack Benny cast. Elliot was able to play dozens of different comic characters on Jack's show, but when he became Remley he gave up the other personalities.

Phil's best-known song was "That's What I Like about the South," which boasted a raucous rambling lyric, the only words that could possibly accompany the tune, both of which were Phil's brain-children. "That's What I Like about the South" was the song most requested of him in those days, and is still the most requested nowadays during his frequent nightclub appearances. The lyrics were nonsensical non sequiturs, but audiences loved them and Phil gave them what they loved.

Finally we based almost an entire program on this song. In the script we had Harris announce that he was, once again, going to sing that international favorite, "That's What I Like about the South." Jack remonstrated, remarking that it couldn't be called an international favorite simply because it was as well known in San Diego as it was in Tijuana. Jack continued in this vein, claiming that the lyrics made absolutely no sense, while Phil defended them as both tender and touching. We then had Harris do the song, with Jack interrupting each of its many choruses and demanding an explanation of the meaning. The following is an excerpt from the script of February 29, 1948 (the lyrics are reprinted here with permission from Bullseye Music Inc.):

PHIL

Oh won't you come with me to Alabammy.
Let's go see my dear old mammy.
She's frying eggs and broiling hammy,
And that's what I like about the South.

75

JACK

All right, Phil, all right . . . That I can understand . . . You have a mammy, she lives down in Alabammy, and she's frying ham and eggs . . . Now that's fine . . . that makes sense . . . Continue.

PHIL

There you can make no mistakey,
Where those nerves are never shakey.
You ought to taste that layer cakey,
And that's what I like about the South.

JACK

All right, Phil, all right . . . Hold it . . . That I can understand a tiny bit . . . Somehow your mother added a pinch of baking powder to the ham and eggs and it turned out to be a layer cake.

PHIL

Layer cakey.

JACK

All right, cakey . . . Now go on.

PHIL

Down where they have those pretty queens
They keep on dreaming those dreamy dreams.
Let's sip that absinthe in New Orleans,
And that's what I like about the South.

JACK

Hold it, Phil, hold it.

PHIL

What's the matter?

JACK

Ten seconds ago you were eating ham and eggs in Alabammy, and now you're sipping absinthe in New Orleans.

PHIL

Certainly.

JACK

Well, Phil, answer me this . . . if you're in Alabama . . . how can you sip absinthe in New Orleans?

PHIL

Long straw!

JACK

Well ... all right, Phil, I'll even go along with that ... Now continue.

PHIL

Here come old Bob with all the news,
Box back coat and button shoes,
But he's all caught up with his union dues,
And that's what I like about the South.

JACK

Go on, go on.

PHIL

Here come old Roy down the street.
Oh can't you hear his scuffling feet.
He would rather sleep than eat,
And that's what I like about the South.

JACK

Roy? What happened to *Bob?*

PHIL

Did I tell you about the place called Doo Wah Ditty?
It ain't no town and it ain't no city.

JACK

Hold it, Phil, hold it, hold it ... *I've been waiting for that one!*

PHIL

Huh?

JACK

Phil, I have here a large map of the United States ... Here, look at it
... *Show me one place on it called Doo Wah Ditty* ... I can see Walla
Walla ... Ypsilanti ... Ashtabula ... Tucumcari ... Nacogdoches ...
and even Waxahachie ... but where in the name of Stephen Foster is
Do Wah Ditty?

The program concluded with Jack making a phone call to Rand
McNally and finding, much to his chagrin, that there really was a
town called "Doo Wah Ditty." We used "Doo Wah Ditty" as a running gag through the remainder of that season.

Phil's alleged drinking excesses were merely exaggerations of his
personal life. Phil did drink, and he enjoyed it, but never once did it
cause him to miss a rehearsal or a show. Yet the public loved his
dipsomania and supposed constant imbibing, just as it admires

Dean Martin's "drunkenness." And we had fun with Phil's fondness for booze every chance we could without belaboring it. One of the best lines we ever did was on an opening show where Jack asked Phil how he and Frank Remley spent their summer vacations, and the dialogue went along the following lines:

PHIL

Me and Frankie went to the Swiss Alps.

JACK

Oh, and I know why. That's where they have those big St. Bernard dogs that carry kegs of brandy around their necks looking for people lost in the snow.

PHIL

That's right, Jackson—me and Frankie spent our entire time hunting them.

JACK

Phil ... Phil ... you and Frankie went out hunting St. Bernards?

PHIL

Certainly. They don't always find you, you know.

Another facet of Phil's comedy character was his supposed illiteracy, and an offshoot on this was a line we jestingly put into the script in order to get the censor's reaction. When Jack found out that Phil couldn't read, he said, "Why, Phil, you're illiterate." And Phil angrily retorted, "That's a lie, Jackson—my parents was married." Predictably the censor came flying into the studio, blue pencil poised, and he crossed out the joke—which we weren't going to do anyway. But that was a quarter of a century ago. Today this is tame. As Bob Hope said on one of his shows, "They are now doing things in the movies and on television that I wouldn't do in my bedroom ... even if I could."

Phil's illiteracy, like the shortcomings of every character in the cast, was a frequent topic for humor. We once did a sequence where Jack wanted Phil to write a letter to someone. The dialogue went as follows:

PHIL

Jackson, I can't write no letter.

JACK

But, Phil, I thought you could read and write.

PHIL

Yeah, but I'm a print man.

JACK

A print man?

PHIL

I can only print things. I can't write.

JACK

Well, for goodness' sake, Phil—what do you do when you have to sign a check?

PHIL

The same as you, Jackson. I cry a little.

Phil's alleged illiteracy also gave us many laughs which we called "Jack-Jumps-In-Jokes." The device was simple. In Phil's case, as he pulled the provoking ignorant line, usually a malaprop, Jack would yell his answer immediately before the audience could laugh. Then when the laugh came it was heightened because of the combination of the line itself and Jack's reaction. An excellent example of this occurred when "Sammy the Drummer" (Sam Weiss, a huge, balding, bulky man who was an excellent musician) and his wife were having a baby. Jack asked Phil about the pregnancy's progress and Phil answered, "Oh, she had the baby and they put her in the clink." Puzzled, Jack said, "Phil—they don't put women in the clink because they're having babies." Harris answered, "Don't tell me, Jackson. I visited her, and the sign on the building said, 'C,L,I,N,I,C.'" The split second Phil finished spelling the word, Benny screamed, *"That's clinic!,"* thus fattening Phil's laugh.

So, contrary to *Time* magazine, Phil Harris was more than just "a drunken bandleader." He, too, was a unique original. Phil had a comedy mind that thought in pictures rather than words. Occasionally he would ask permission of the writers and Jack to rephrase a line or joke so it could conjure up a funnier visual image—and ninety-nine percent of the time he was correct.

9
Rochester

The character of "Rochester," whose full cast name was Rochester Van Jones, was scheduled as a one-shot appearance on a program before I joined Jack. Playing the part of a Pullman porter, his gravelly accented voice, timing, and attitude made him an instant hit, and he was held over for a quarter of a century.

"Rochester" was Eddie Anderson, a vaudeville performer of some stature in those days of that dying medium. When he became a regular on the Benny series it revived his career and paved the way for personal appearances, movies, and other rewards. However, Rochester was the most controversial character on the program, for he was a Negro. (In those days it was all right for him to be a Negro. Eventually he became a colored man. Today he is a black.)

Rochester's appearance on *The Jack Benny Show* was relished by the great majority of his race, and in almost direct proportion it was resented by those southerners who still were fighting the Civil War. What they probably resented was his characterization which *Time* magazine (January 6, 1975) dismissed with the brief line: "Rochester, the sardonic Negro valet, is the granddaddy of all the servants, black or white, who have hilariously put down their employers since the invention of the vacuum tube."

And that's exactly what Rochester did—he put Jack down. He was Jack's valet, chauffeur, and general handyman—but when the humor was analyzed, Rochester almost seemed to be the boss and Benny the employee. And in those pre-civil rights days, when almost all other Negroes appearing in any of the media were caricatures rather than characters, this relationship was the cause of many complaints.

Rochester was never disrespectful to Jack by word, deed, or attitude, yet somehow he always bested him in all exchanges. For instance, Rochester was going to a party one night. As he left, Jack admonished him, "Rochester, be sure to come home at a reasonable hour." Rochester politely answered, "Yes, sir. Your reasonable or my reasonable?"

Jack once insisted that his Maxwell looked dirty and suggested that Rochester clean it, a task which Rochester immediately exited to perform. Later in the show Jack figured that Rochester had had more than sufficient time to clean the car, so he went out to see what was happening. He was surprised to see Rochester only about halfway through with his chore, and the reason for the snail's pace was because he was daintily going over the surface of the Maxwell with a damp sponge. Angrily Jack yelled at him, "For heaven's sake, Rochester, why don't you use the garden hose on it?" Rochester answered, "Don't you remember the last time I used the hose on it, Boss? The fenders fell off."

Occasionally Rochester would, through no fault of his own, arouse and antagonize a small percentage of listeners by doing a line or gag that we writers thought was funny. One such incident took place when he was talking with his friend, Roy, who'd occasionally come over to help him with his work, such as it was. On this program Rochester had just returned from New York with Jack and the rest of the cast. The dialogue brought out the fact that Rochester had been across the country dozens of times, and Roy wanted to know what America was really like, as seen through Rochester's well-traveled eyes. We gave him what we thought was a clever line and had Rochester say, "Well, America has Central Avenue [then a celebrated popular street in the ghetto] on the West Coast, and Harlem on the East Coast, and all that garbage in between." The studio audience roared at it, but folks in the Middle West justifiably didn't like their part of the country referred to as "all that garbage in between," and the mailman probably got a double hernia toting in the complaining letters.

They had a right to complain, even though we meant it in good fun. However, we once did a joke that brought a small avalanche of letters for two far-fetched and nit-picking reasons. On this program the cast was supposedly going on a picnic to the beach, with sandwiches, drinks, and everything else supplied by Jack, and various gags came from the cast, such as:

JACK

Dennis, aren't you going swimming?

DENNIS

No. The last time I went swimming a big crowd gathered around me and pointed at me and laughed at me.

JACK

Well, maybe you had a hole in your bathing suit.

DENNIS

Oooooohhhhhh, bathing suit!

At another point in the program Phil Harris was gazing sadly at the ocean. When Jack asked him what was wrong, Phil replied: "What a shame. All that chaser going to waste."

These jokes were pleasant enough, although perhaps tired today, but the best one of the lot was done with Rochester. When Jack noticed that Rochester hadn't gotten into a bathing suit to join the others in an ocean swim, he asked why.

ROCHESTER

Oh, I ain't going into no ocean, Boss . . . I'm afraid the octopussies will get me.

JACK

Rochester, there's no such word as octopussies. The plural of octopus is not octopussies. It's octopi.

ROCHESTER

Don't make no difference, I ain't gonna hang around for more than one anyway.

Now this little exchange gave us several worthwhile laughs, with a big boff when Rochester first said "Octopussies," and a real roof-rattler when he said, "I ain't gonna hang around for more than one anyway." Then the mail started to come in. It was one of the few times that we seemed to get organized complaints from blacks. They had read something into the script—namely that we would not let Rochester swim in the same ocean with white people. On the face of it this was idiotic because in previous years we had gotten batches of bigoted mail from listeners who complained because we had let Rochester dunk himself in the same swimming pool with

82

our lily-white cast. The second complaint came from some blacks who felt that we were ridiculing Rochester's lack of education by showing that he didn't know the plural of octopus. As a matter of fact, Rochester was almost correct when he called them octopussies, because, according to *Webster's New Collegiate Dictionary,* one of the accepted plurals of octopus is "octopuses," a second accepted plural is "octopodes," and the third and least accepted plural is "octopi." We weren't trying to promote racism, subtle or otherwise; we were only trying to get a big laugh, and we did.

In the early days of *The Jack Benny Show,* pre-1943, Rochester did do many stereotype jokes that probably offended his own people. Many of them were funny, but they were of the crap-shooting, gin-drinking, girl-chasing variety. I remember two of them very well. Both concerned the fact that Rochester had lost his week's salary in crap games. In one of these, Jack chided Rochester, saying, "I thought you told me you were going to a literary tea." Rochester replied: "Oh, it was—but somewheres between the literary and the tea, ivory reared its ugly head." The other time Rochester explained losing his salary in a crap game by saying, "Boss, I went down to my lodge meeting, and my fellow lodge members were so happy to see me that they came toward me and greeted me in a circle—on their knees."

Jokes of that insensitive sort tapered off during the war years, and when Jack's new quartet of writers joined him in 1943, such punch lines were at a minimum and soon became non-existent. We never went back to racial humor that might be offensive to any ethnic group—until February 5, 1950.

At that time, we were in New York for a two-week change of scene, and we were to do our broadcasts with a Manhattan flavor and background, but the best laid plans of mice and script writers "gang aft agley." We usually traveled by train in those days, and the trip from Los Angeles to New York was an unusually rough one. We arrived several hours late, tired and cranky. No one was bright-eyed or bushy-tailed, but that was only the start. Jack came down with one of his perennial colds. One of the writers broke a tooth and had to spend several uncomfortable hours in a dental chair. And I was rushed to the hospital for an emergency operation on a strangulated hernia.

It was now Thursday, with only three more days to the broadcast date, and the few remaining healthy members of our staff had written nothing but an introduction and an opening page of jokes. Then Jack's personal secretary, Bert Scott, remembered a script that Jack had done in New York almost exactly ten years ago. A copy of this script was dug up, updated, and shoved in as an emergency measure.

The script concerned Jack trying to find Rochester who had disappeared into Harlem the moment they reached New York. When he called various telephone numbers in Harlem that he found in Rochester's phone book, the answers he got were invariably from charming colored girls who announced things like "Hello, this is the Harlem Gin-Till-You-Spin Club," and each one of these young ladies gave Jack another number where he might reach Rochester. The culmination of this routine came when Jack dialed a final number, and here is the dialogue exactly as it took place:

JACK

Hello?

MAMIE

Hello, Mamie Brown, the sweetest gal in town talking.

JACK

Miss Brown, this is Jack Benny.

MAMIE

Oh-oh.

JACK

I'm trying to get in touch with Rochester. Is he there?

MAMIE

He *was* here.

JACK

Oh ... well do you think he'll come back?

MAMIE

In all modesty, I can *guarantee* that.

JACK

Hmmmm ... Well, when he returns, will you please tell him to call my hotel ... and you can also tell him I'm stopping his salary.

MAMIE

Oh, that ain't gonna bother him. He now *owns* the building that houses the Harlem Social, Benevolent, and Spare Ribs Every Thursday Club.

JACK

Oh, yes, I heard about that. He wins from everybody, doesn't he?

MAMIE

Yeah, when I opened the door and he came in on one knee, I thought it was a proposal.

We had hardly signed off the air when the network's switchboard lit up like a computer gone berserk. Jack, a gentle soul, was amazed at the unfavorable reaction. He remembered that when the material had been done ten years previously it had caused hardly a ripple.

Jack was hurt by the uproar that the rerunning of this routine caused, for he would rather lose laughs than hurt any individual, much less any ethnic group, and he was proud of his record in this regard. For example, some time after World War II, columnist Walter Winchell launched a column crusade against comics who got laughs at the expense of minority groups. Winchell didn't complain about fellows like Sam Levenson, Myron Cohen, Lou Holtz, or any raconteurs who spun stories with Jewish backgrounds or any other ethnic-oriented humorists as long as they didn't ridicule their subjects. He said that there was nothing wrong with racial humor as long as it was performed with love and affection. However, those who got their laughs at the expense of racial minorities by denigrating Italians, Jews, Negroes, and others were on his enemy list. Winchell invented a word, as he was always inventing words, to describe these tasteless comics. He called them "Vomics." However, in his column he made a strong point of the fact that while Jack frequently used Rochester, Kitzle, and members of almost all racial extractions, he treated them with dignity, love, and affection.

Winchell was right!

10
Dennis Day

Dennis Day, the silly, sweet-singing, polite, stupid "kid" on *The Jack Benny Show* was not the only tenor to hold down this job. Over the years, there were at least five other singers on the series. First there were Frank Parker, Michael Bartlett, James Melton, and Kenny Baker. Then another tenor, Larry Stevens, filled in for Dennis Day for two seasons while Dennis saw service in World War II.

I never knew why, but Jack always insisted that his singer be a tenor. Perhaps he felt that their high-pitched voices made them logical candidates for the child-like characters portrayed by Baker, Stevens, and Dennis.

Dennis Day was, if not discovered by Mary Livingstone, at least hired because of her intuition. The show was singerless at the time because the previous tenor, Kenny Baker, was leaving. Auditions were being held for replacements, and agents, knowing what a job as Jack Benny's vocalist could lead to, were avidly submitting their most talented clients. The choices had narrowed down to a precious few—and these few, having proved their musical ability, were now set for interviews. Dennis came into the room to chat with Jack, Mary, and the others. Mary started to question him by saying, "Now, Dennis?" And Dennis said, "Yes, please?" These two words broke Mary up (and while Mary was a good audience, she wasn't the easy mark Jack was). Mary halted the interview and insisted that Dennis be hired on the basis of just those two words. Her instinct in this case proved to be one hundred percent correct. At that time nobody knew that Dennis had uncanny timing for the feed and punch lines of jokes, nor did anyone know that he was possibly one of the best mimics extant.

In the early months of 1944 we played numerous service camps throughout the country. On April 16, 1944, we did our broadcast from an Army base near Stockton, California. On this broadcast we supposedly picked a soldier at random from the ranks. The man we picked was George Hope, Bob's brother, who was actually in the Army and stationed at that camp.

The premise of the program was that George Hope wondered if Jack knew whatever had happened to his brother Bob. At that time Bob was running neck-and-neck with Jack for the number one rating in radio. Jack informed George that his brother Bob was a big radio star whose program could be heard locally every Tuesday at 7:00 P.M. George got an appreciative guffaw from his fellow soldiers when he said, "I wouldn't know—they never let us stay up that late." Then, to show George exactly what Bob was doing, we put on a tabloid version of Hope's radio program. This became my writing assignment, and I never had an easier one. I went through my five years of Bob Hope scripts, pulled out all the big Army jokes, and arranged them into routines. Jack did a truncated Bob Hope "Army type" monologue. Mary Livingstone did jokes typical of Frances Langford, Hope's vocalist. Phil Harris played Vera Vague, a man-chasing girl on the Hope series, and finally Dennis Day came in as the zany Jerry Colonna. While Dennis was imitating Colonna on the air, Jerry's wife Flo, back in Hollywood, got several calls asking her what Jerry was doing in Stockton when he was supposed to be on an East Coast tour of Army camps with the Hope series. Flo Colonna heard the last few minutes, and she, too, was convinced that she was hearing her husband in person. The program was a huge success, with the critics acclaiming Jack for such a perfect rendition of Hope's humor. (Why shouldn't it have been perfect? About ninety percent of the gags we used in writing it were tried and true boffs taken directly from Bob's shows.)

There was a double-barreled aftermath to this incident. First, several radio columnists insisted that we duped, deceived, and deluded the listeners by claiming that Dennis was doing Colonna when in fact we had actually used Colonna himself. These accusations were not only false, but unfair to Dennis Day (though highly complimentary to his impersonation abilities).

The other aftermath had its inception a few minutes after we finished our broadcast. Benny got a person-to-person call from Bob Hope who, with his writers, had heard our version of the Bob Hope program. Hope now wanted to do *his* version of Benny's program, and he asked if Jack would give him free access to his scripts. Of course Jack gave him *carte blanche.*

Unfortunately Bob's version of Benny's broadcast wasn't too successful. In the first place, Hope had heard Jack's version of his show on Sunday, April 16, and he tried to get his version of the Benny show on the air immediately with his very next program, which was Tuesday, April 18, so he and his writers had to rush under terrific pressure. Then, while it was funny for Benny to use Bob's rapid-fire delivery, it wasn't quite so hilarious for Hope to slow down to Jack's leisurely pace. The audience appreciated Phil Harris mincing and swishing his way through the female role of Vera Vague, but didn't quite go for Vera Vague doing Phil's bombastic and alcoholic anecdotes. And, most important, while Jerry Colonna was always fantastic as Jerry Colonna, thus giving Dennis Day a broad canvas on which to paint his verbal impression of Colonna, the reverse didn't hold true. The unique zaniness of Colonna's unusual humor became pallid when he did his "silly kid" imitation of Dennis Day. All in all, Hope's version of Benny's program was somewhat less than successful.

Like all members of Jack's cast, Dennis Day's humor was unique unto himself. It was not a carbon copy of any other cast member's type of comedy. On many radio series of the past and TV programs of the present, the characters are sometimes interchangeable in that a comedy line said by one could just as easily be said by another. However, this was not the case with the regular members of *The Jack Benny Show.* They were not repetitions or extensions of each other. They were originals.

Dennis was the silly kid, the childlike one, but not the fool. He would do seemingly stupid things and then have a certain illogical logic for his behavior. He would accidentally or intentionally drive Jack—and, oddly enough, only Jack—nuts. In fact, Jack complained on one radio program, "That silly kid is gonna drive me crazy. He was over my house to tell me the name of the song he's going to sing on Sunday's show. Then when Dennis left he said, 'So long, Mr. Benny, have a pleasant trip.' I went upstairs to my room and packed two suitcases before I realized I wasn't going anyplace."

Here is a typical example of Dennis' humor:

DENNIS

I bought one of those electric razors and they're fakes. I tried for hours and couldn't get a shave out of mine, and it's brand new.

JACK

Well, Dennis, there may be something wrong with the wiring. Maybe a short-circuit. Did it give off sparks when you plugged it in?

DENNIS

Ooooohhhhhh, plug it in.

Here is another typical example:

DENNIS

I'm in excellent shape. I weigh between 125 and 160 pounds stripped.

JACK

Between 125 and 160 pounds? How come you're not sure of your exact weight?

DENNIS

Before the needle on the scale stopped swinging the druggist came over and made me put my clothes back on.

Another comedy contrivance we used with great success with Dennis was to have him make his entrance voicing an outrageous statement such as: "If I have nothing better to do tomorrow, I'm going to join the Foreign Legion." An excellent example of this comes from the script we did on February 25, 1951:

DENNIS

Would it be all right if I missed rehearsal Saturday?

JACK

I guess so—why?

DENNIS

I'm gonna commit suicide.

JACK

Suicide?

DENNIS

I may miss the broadcast too.

Because of his "silly kid" character, Dennis' line, "I'm gonna commit suicide," was greeted with a loud laugh from the audience. And his quite logical observation, "I may miss the broadcast too," got an even more resounding reception.

Dennis' stupidity always had a smattering of sense. On one program he demanded and received a better contract from Jack. It included a five-dollar-a-week raise and the guarantee that he now could stop his daily mowing of Jack's lawn and perform this chore only once a month. But Dennis was trying to drive a hard bargain. He told Jack that he wanted one more clause in his contract, and he felt that it wasn't too much to ask because almost every person in America had this fringe benefit. Jack said that if the majority of the people had it, then Dennis should certainly get it too, and he asked, "What is it?" Dennis answered, "I want Sundays off." Now you must realize that for as long as anyone could remember Jack Benny did his broadcasts on Sundays, and this made Dennis' demand ludicrous and impossible. Jack's reaction to this request was to fix Dennis with a stare and then quietly say, "Dennis, go home." And just as quietly Dennis said, "Yes, sir." It sounds simple, and it was simple, but because of the mutual impact of their sharply defined characters, it got a tremendous laugh.

Like all cast regulars, Dennis spread his humor over the entire area of the show, as did all the other characters. Mary would have routines with Dennis, Phil, Don, and Rochester, and Phil would have comic exchanges with Rochester, Don Wilson, and everyone else. Frequently the entire cast took part in a group comic exchange. Two excellent examples of this involve Dennis and give at least a partial insight into the inner workings of the mind of the character we created for him.

For the first example, in the early 1950s an elixir, advertised as being only slightly less beneficial than the fountain of youth, found its place on the American market. It was called Hadacol, and was promoted by a Colonel Parker who went on to benefit mankind even more by discovering and managing Elvis Presley. Hadacol was a much advertised and extremely popular remedy—and well it should have been, because its alcoholic content was higher than much of the liquor sold in bars. Maybe Hadacol had a dubious medicinal value, but if you drank enough of it you didn't give a damn how you felt. It was so popular at the time that all comedy programs began doing jokes about it, and we were no exception. On one program Dennis made his entrance several minutes late, but he claimed that he had an excellent excuse, since that morning his uncle had been run over by a truck and was badly injured. The cast sympathized with him until Mary said, "Wait a minute, Dennis. Just as I entered the studio a half hour ago I saw your uncle, and he looked wonderful." Dennis answered, "I know. The truck that ran him over was loaded with Hadacol."

A second example took place on the program of February 4, 1951, when Phil Harris asked Jack to join him in a round of golf.

PHIL

We'll just have a friendly game—ten dollars a hole.

JACK

(gulps nervously) Er . . . no thanks.

PHIL

If you're nervous about the money—make it easy on yourself. We'll play for a buck a hole.

JACK

No, I'd rather not.

DENNIS

I'll play golf with you, Phil, and I'll bet you a hundred dollars a hole.

(Now this was just the feedline, but coming from the supposed simpleton, Dennis Day, whose reputed salary was thirty-five dollars a week, it got a good audience laugh.)

PHIL

What?

JACK

Dennis—how can you bet him a hundred dollars a hole? Phil is a great golfer. He just won an amateur tournament, and you've never played golf before.

DENNIS

I know.

JACK

Well, how do you expect to beat him?

DENNIS

I've been drinking Hadacol.

PHIL

Well, bring it along, Kid—we've got the ice.

This exchange got several laughs, all big ones, and it was based on the divergent characters of the three men—Jack's stinginess and unwillingness to play golf for money, Dennis' childish gullibility in believing the advertisements for Hadacol as a magic potion, and Phil's last line, "Bring it along, Kid—we've got the ice," stemming from Phil's fondness for booze and the almost universal knowledge that Hadacol had a rich alcoholic content.

91

This last point was true in more ways than one. In those days, the simple mention of Hadacol was a "plug." "Plugs" are now supposedly taboo on the TV tube because of FCC rulings, but there are still plenty of them on various programs. In those days mentioning a product through a "plug" usually brought the writers of the show at least one, and sometimes more, cases of booze. Thus from the routine we got good laughs for the show and some bottles of Scotch for ourselves.

I hate to end this essay on Dennis with lines about whiskey because Dennis was practically a teetotaler, and off the air did not act as a silly kid. If he did, he was a precocious kid, because Dennis Day is married and at last count had eleven children. It could be more; I haven't talked to him in over a year.

11
Don Wilson

Don Wilson was with Jack Benny longer than any other cast member with the exception of Mary Livingstone. He was a huge, hefty, jolly man with a wonderful voice that made him one of the top radio announcers of all time. In addition he had a big booming laugh, plus a stomach and bouncy build in keeping with a man who weighed around two hundred and fifty pounds.

All of these assets were a gold mine to the writers, and we added to these physical characteristics a touch of pomposity and frequently flaunted knowledge which, as *Time* magazine rightly said, "can be seen in Ted Knight's role on 'The Mary Tyler Moore Show.'" However, Don was far more intelligent than Ted Baxter as portrayed by Knight, and he irritated Jack because he almost always knew what he was talking about.

Because Rochester was his valet, Dennis a simpleton, Phil an illiterate lush, and Mary a girl with no definite duties, we made Don Wilson the intelligent one. Whenever Jack tried to show off his knowledge and incorrectly quoted an author or messed up a famous date in history, Don would hasten to correct him. Now many times these mistakes were intentional, but often they were simply mistakes on the part of the writers. When an ensuing deluge of mail would inform us that we had broadcast a boo-boo, we would correct it on the following week's program by having Don take Jack to task for it. Jack would try to alibi and avoid being corrected, but Don would persist. Then Jack would threaten him with lines like: "Don ... Don ... Remember ... Confucius say that when big fat announcer try to correct boss who pay him big fat salary, soon boss fire him and big fat salary stop and announcer no longer big fat."

Wilson was always the one to correct Jack when he made errors in history, geography, grammar, or any other subject. One of the best remembered routines occurred when we were entertaining the sailors at a Navy base by doing our broadcast in their auditorium. Jack, in a humorous speech, was listing famed naval heroes, and he said, ". . . and then of course there was Admiral Stephen Decatur, who earned immortality when in the face of overwhelming enemy odds he uttered those fearless words, 'Full speed ahead and "oh fudge" to the torpedoes.' " Mary asked, "Jack—in the middle of a battle, Stephen Decatur said, 'Oh fudge to the torpedoes?' " And Jack answered, "Well, Mary, he wanted to say something stronger but he couldn't because the Shore Patrol was standing next to him."

Now because the actual phrase, "Damn the torpedoes," was so well known, especially by sailors, Jack got a good laugh when he said, "Oh fudge to the torpedoes." The entire audience knew the exact word Jack omitted, and by making it a dainty, almost feminine euphemism in substituting "Oh fudge" for "damn" we got an excellent reaction from our naval audience. Then when he admitted that the quotation was somewhat stronger than the one he quoted, implying the verboten word "damn" was "expletive deleted" because of the presence of the "Shore Patrol," this got an even better reaction because in Navy circles the "Shore Patrol" was fair game for jokes, just as "second lieutenants" were at Army camps.

Then Don Wilson butted into the argument, saying that it wasn't Admiral Stephen Decatur who uttered this immortal phrase but Admiral David Farragut, who said it on August 5, 1864 during the battle of Mobile Bay when one of the battleships in his Union fleet, *The Brooklyn,* was almost blasted out of the water. From his flagship, *The Hartford,* Farragut shouted that memorable encouragement to the damaged *Brooklyn.* (We got this information from the *Encyclopaedia Britannica.)*

Then Phil Harris entered, and Jack, looking for an ally in his fight with the fact-spouting Wilson, asked, "Phil—what naval hero said 'Full speed ahead and you-know-what to the torpedoes'?" Phil answered, "I don't know, Jackson. I musta passed out when the guy said it." Jack now wanted to get out of the argument as gracefully as possible, but Wilson persisted, as he always did in such matters.

When Dennis Day came on the scene, he hardly had a chance to say "Hello" when Jack turned angrily on him and asked, "Dennis, do you know who said 'Full speed ahead and "Phooey" to the torpe-does'?" Dennis answered, "It wasn't me. I get blamed for every-thing around here." Then, as Jack resumed his argument with Wil-son, Dennis added, "And even if I did know, I wouldn't tell—I'm not a snitcher."

This was one of the funniest routines we ever did at a Navy base, and it came about accidentally because one writer claimed Stephen Decatur said it, another thought it was Farragut, a third believed it was Robert Peary, and the fourth disclaimed any knowledge of history, naval or otherwise.

This script argument involved everyone in the cast until Mary took Jack's side and told Don that he ought to give in. Don angrily asked Mary if she ever checked into a history book to see who uttered the famous phrase, and Mary answered, "No—but we've got to take Jack's word. After all, he was there when they said it." This of course turned Jack angrily against Mary, and almost the entire program revolved around the identification of the author of that remark.

When we decided to use the phrase "Full speed ahead and 'Oh fudge' to the torpedoes," we had a wide divergence of opinion as to what American hero said it, and thus we had to do a little research in the *Encyclopaedia Britannica* which credited Farragut with the statement. Then, because we didn't want Jack, who had actually been in the Navy in World War I, to look like a complete idiot, and since we had him crediting the remark to Decatur, we tried to find a famous quote from Stephen Decatur. We did, but unfortunately the censor, who didn't mind us laundering "Damn the torpedoes" to "Oh fudge to the torpedoes," put a firm foot down on our quoting Stephen Decatur. It was Decatur who said, "Our country! In her intercourse with foreign nations, may she always be in the right; but our country, right or wrong." The censor was adamant. In no manner, means, or form, no matter whether it was said by an admi-ral or the President, could we ever use the word "intercourse."

Another example of Don's usage as the most erudite member of the cast came on the programs of November 28 and December 5, 1948.

On the November show we did our annual Thanksgiving pro-gram, but this time the cast members were all guests for dinner at Mary's house, so we dispensed with the usual jokes we had on Thanksgiving dinner shows held at Jack's, such as: "Gosh, Jack, what kind of tweezers did you use to stuff that canary?" At the end of the dinner Jack felt it incumbent on him to say a few serious words about Thanksgiving. In his speech he traced the origin of the holiday back to the day hundreds of years ago when the Pilgrims landed at Cape Cod.

Don Wilson immediately interrupted Jack by correcting him and stating that every schoolchild knew that the Pilgrims landed at Plymouth Rock, not Cape Cod. The festive feast turned into a free-for-all fight, with the main combatants being Don and Jack. Mary tried to act as peacemaker, and in a variation of the gag done during the Admiral Farragut-Stephen Decatur argument she told Don not to argue history with Jack. Don said that he felt he knew his subject because in college he had majored in American history. Mary replied: "I know, Don—but Jack lived through all of it." The program ended with Jack mad at everybody, but not speaking at all to Don.

The following week, in our opening scene, Mary, Phil, and Dennis refreshed the audience's memory by discussing the battle between Jack and Don the preceding week. When Don came in, he was adamant. He knew he was right and wouldn't change his views. Then Jack entered, and his manner was most apologetic. He stated that in the intervening week he had looked through history books, and he found that Don was indeed right, and in front of the cast and our entire listening audience he wanted to apologize to Don.

Wilson accepted Jack's apology graciously, but Jack wanted to make it more flowery, and he added, "Don, through no fault of yours, as the famous author Rudyard Kipling once wrote, 'You have suffered the slings and arrows of outrageous fortune.'" Immediately Don pounced on Jack's literary lapse and pointed out that it was William Shakespeare who had said this, not Kipling. The argument flared up again, and Wilson stomped out (and he was a heavy stomper) indignantly. The other cast members weren't too sure which author had coined the phrase, but Mary said she thought that it was Shakespeare. We then did a "dissolve" or "time lapse" via a musical bridge, and it was supposedly several hours later on the program and the entire cast, minus the departed Don, was going through Shakespeare's works to find out if he had ever written that phrase. Soon they found that it had indeed been created by the Bard of Avon. Shocked and surprised at hearing that once again he was wrong and Wilson was right, Jack seemed truly upset that on two successive weeks he had been involved on the losing side of angry arguments with his announcer. He ended the program by saying, "Well, if Wilson was right both times, there's only one thing left for me to do. I'll call Don up and fire him."

12
The Stooges

"Stooge," as defined in *Webster's New Collegiate Dictionary,* originally referred, in vaudeville, to an actor who, from a seat in the audience, heckled or baited the chief comedian on the stage; hence, a stooge is any actor whose main function is to feed lines to the chief comedian. The second meaning given is to a person who plays a subordinate role to some principal.

To designate Jack Benny's supporting cast (as opposed to his regular stars, Mary, Phil, Rochester, Don, and Dennis) as stooges is to belittle these talented performers and also to correct *Webster's New Collegiate Dictionary.*

Jack had the greatest and most expensive supporting cast of "stooges" in the history of show business, but those stooges hardly fulfilled Webster's definition of them as actors "whose main function is to feed lines to the chief comedian." Jack was, from a prestige and salary standpoint, the main comedian, but he fed the "stooges" the lines, not vice versa. Jack was, in truth, the stooge for all the supporting players who fleshed out the complete cast. And it was they, not he, who got the laughs.

Jack's cast of supporting characters, who were not named in the "opening credits" at the start of each program, included such giants as Mel Blanc, Sheldon Leonard, Bea Benaderet, Sara Berner, Joe Kearns, Verna Felton, Artie Auerbach, Sam Hearn, Frank Nelson, Sandy Gould, Elliot Lewis, Benny Rubin, Doris Singleton, Hy Averback, Veola Vonn, and many others too numerous to list. Not only did these top talents play "single" roles, but they frequently "doubled" and "tripled." As for Mel Blanc, he portrayed such an imposing cast of comedy characters that I know I will inadvertently omit some of his more popular ones. The same will hold true for several other performers.

Mel Blanc

Mel Blanc, who still serves as the voice of such animated cartoon characters as Bugs Bunny, Sylvester the Cat, Tweetie Pie the Canary, and a host of others, was signed to a full-time contract with a regular weekly salary by Jack because he appeared in so many different roles we didn't want to take a chance of losing his services by having him hired to do another conflicting program. Among his roles on the Benny show were Jack's French violin teacher, the voice of the parrot, and the little Mexican, and of course he also did the asthmatic wheezing of the Maxwell's engine as it coughed its way to life. Listing the countless characters done by Blanc and illustrating his roles with excerpts from them would be another Herculean task. Therefore these paragraphs will be confined to the most memorable.

It was Mel's voice that announced at the railroad station: "Train leaving on Track Five for Anaheim, Azusa, and Cuc————amonga." This public address announcement always served to set the scene for the two or three shows we did each season with Jack and the cast taking the train to New York or Chicago. One of the subtle bits of humor that the listeners never truly or really appreciated was that at the railroad station Jack, anxious to get his ticket validated, luggage aboard, and so forth, never once, in all the shows we did, acknowledged hearing the numerous announcements Mel made on the P.A. system. After the first straight announcement all others were jokes with punchlines, but Jack took no notice of them. We also eventually hit upon the device of Mel taking longer and longer pauses in naming the town Cucamonga. Once we set a record by having Mel's voice boom out, "Train now leaving on Track Five for Anaheim, Azusa, and Cuc—" and then we did a full five minutes of routines with other members of the cast before Mel finished that name and over the loudspeaker came the final syllables "amonga," getting a scream and applause from the audience who anticipated its coming but didn't know exactly when it would come.

Mel played the little Mexican, and that was the only name we had for this character. In fact, most of his characters were nameless. As the Mexican, he never uttered more than one word in any sentence. Correction—he never uttered more than one syllable in any sentence. They were delivered by Blanc in flat, expressionless, Mexican-accented tones, and it got so that Jack couldn't look at Mel's face (nor the faces of many other "stooges") when he was delivering his lines. The best illustration of this material is a streamlined version of several routines he did:

JACK

Excuse me, are you waiting for the train?

MEL

Si.

JACK

You're meeting someone on the train?

MEL

Si.

JACK

A relative?

MEL

Si.

JACK

What's your name?

MEL

Cy.

JACK

Cy?

MEL

Si.

JACK

This relative you're waiting for—is it a woman?

MEL

Si.

99

JACK

Your sister?

MEL

Si.

JACK

What's her name?

MEL

Sue.

JACK

Sue?

MEL

Si.

JACK

Does she work?

MEL

Si.

JACK

She has a regular job?

MEL

Si.

JACK

What does she do?

MEL

Sew.

JACK

Sew?

MEL

Si.

As I said, the above is a combination of several routines, but we did endless variations of the same theme, and we got huge laughs—usually the biggest ones from Jack.

Another of Mel's sure-fire routines was when we used him to augment the sound effects of the balky engine of Jack's Maxwell.

Whenever we did a scene where the car was to be used, and Jack was going to be driven someplace by Rochester, he issued the order, "Rochester, please start the engine." That line alone was rewarded by a sizable laugh. Not that the audience found anything funny in the line itself, but all loyal listeners knew what to expect—and they would get it. Rochester would turn the key in the ignition, and we'd hear the mechanical sound of the ancient auto's reluctant motor trying to start. Then Mel would add his efforts to the mechanical sound effects, and Mel was a vocal virtuoso. From his mouth issued sounds never made by mortal man. He actually became the engine of that car, and his asthmatic wheezing and coughing would keep the audience, and of course Jack, in a state of continual laughter. He wheezed, whooped, coughed, choked, snorted, snuffled, and sneezed until we were all mentally praying for him to stop because he brought forth all of these unearthly sounds with one single deep breath, and as his air supply began to fade his face would start to change color, and we worried for his health.

Only once did Mel worry about his own safety. He came into a regular reading and rehearsal on a Saturday and saw, to his dismay, that we had him doing the sound of the Maxwell's motor. He came to the writers and sheepishly said that he didn't know if he'd be able to do it Sunday. He was just getting over an attack of the flu and he still was suffering from a residual effect—a slight case of diarrhea. Therefore, he explained, coughing at that time wouldn't be the smartest thing he ever did. However on Sunday he was never better and he coughed loud enough to register eight on the Richter scale. We don't know how he did it—whether he was following the actor's credo, "The show must go on," or whether he had recovered enough to chance an accident, or whether he owed his perfect performance to liberal doses of Kaopectate.

Mel was originally hired by Jack to do the sound of "Carmichael," a polar bear that appeared on some shows in the late 1930s or early 1940s. It was before my time, and I only remember it dimly. Mel made appearances on the Benny shows every few weeks, just growling like a polar bear. After about six months Jack complimented him on his performance, and Mel timidly said, "Mr. Benny, I can talk too." He was then given lines to read as various characters. However, from 1943 on we developed the many voices and sounds of Mel Blanc as they were heard on the programs.

Like almost all the auxiliary characters on *The Jack Benny Show*, Mel's roles usually originated as "one shots." The writers wrote them in to try them out for one time only, and, sad to relate, many of our comic creations lasted no longer. However, some did catch on and became mainstays in the show's regular cast of characters.

One of these was the French violin teacher, Professor LeBlanc.

101

Mel enacted this part with an almost venomous hatred for Jack's musical ability, or lack of it. As Jack played the musical finger exercises over and over, Mel would keep time by reciting two-line jingles which he delivered with disgust and disdain. Here are a couple of couplets which Mel muttered in rhythm with Jack's violin lessons:

Make the bow strokes a little longer.
How I wish my stomach were stronger.

Shorter notes, make them littler.
This should only happen to Hitler.

Jack would boast that Professor LeBlanc was the perfect violin teacher because "he was tone-deaf and hungry." The violin lessons were always a high spot on the shows, and some of Mel's lines were classics. Once Jack was bragging to him that he started studying the violin while still an infant. Then he pointed to his violin and said that as a child he sometimes used it as a teething ring. He indicated a scarred spot and said, "See, those are my teeth marks." Professor LeBlanc screamed back, "Those could be anybody's."

The high spots of these lessons were the endings. Professor LeBlanc was paid a paltry sum, two dollars for a lesson lasting an hour. The alarm on a clock was set to ring at the end of the hour, and when the bell rang Mel would give an Academy Award performance. He would scream with joy, shouting to the world that his period of penance was over and he was free, *free*, FREE! He would carry on like a man pardoned by the governor just as they were fastening him into the electric chair. Possibly the best of these endings occurred when the alarm rang ending the hour and Mel made his impassioned speech of deliverance entirely in French and exited singing the first four lines of the "Marseillaise."

Mel played the part of Jack's parrot, another scheduled one-shot appearance that became a running character. At first we had the parrot saying the wildest things, but Jack, who was an excellent editor, made us cut down. He had an inviolable rule that the parrot must never say or ad-lib things that it made up. It could only use words that it actually heard someone say. However, since most of the things said about Jack were insulting, there was no shortage of laugh-getting lines for Polly's busy beak.

One radio show we did with the parrot was considered a classic. Mel, as the bird, kept sniffling and squawking in low, depressed tones. The rest of Jack's cast convinced him to take the parrot to a doctor. Jack demurred until he was told to take him to a special doctor, Dr. Hy Averback (played by the actor-director of that name), who was a Ph.D. Jack asked what Ph.D. meant, and Mary told him that it stood for Parrots, Horses, and Dogs. Not only that, she said, but Dr. Averback wasn't an ordinary veterinarian—he was an animal psychiatrist. Jack balked at taking his pet to a psychiatrist and got off the line, "It doesn't seem right taking a parrot to a psychiatrist. The poor little thing will feel so silly lying on a couch on its back with its claws waving in the air." But take him he did, and while they were in the doctor's office, Mel doubled up by being not only the Parrot but the voice of Bugs Bunny.

When Jack first entered the doctor's office, the nurse called the doctor on the intercom and announced that there were two patients waiting to see him, "Jack Benny and Bugs Bunny." Then Mel, as "Bugs," got into an argument with Jack and walked out of the office. A split second later the doctor got his nurse on the intercom and told her to send in both Jack and Bugs, and the nurse answered, "I can't—Benny's here but Bunny's left." It sounds silly, and it was, but we got screams with the line.

Because Mel was so versatile, and also because he was a regular on the payroll, we frequently wrote in minor roles for him, tried to invent new characters, and, best of all from our standpoint, put into the script the most impossible parts for him to portray. We knew they'd never be broadcast, but little "inside" gags like that always made the cast laugh and created a brighter atmosphere at rehearsals. In one bit we wrote we had Jack ask a man something on a street, and in the stage directions we had written the instructions: "Mel answers, using the voice of a Colored, Jewish Fag." Damned if he didn't do it, but it never got on the air. Today it might be suitable for the leading character in a TV situation comedy, but in those days it was taboo.

Once as a gag we wrote, "Jack talks to his goldfish, saying 'Hello, itty bitty fishy,' and Mel, as the goldfish, answers him." If it were television it would have gone on the air, because Mel's face became that of a goldfish.

The most memorable of all of the silly situations with which we tried to trap Mel happened when we did a show where the cast went to the races at Santa Anita. Jack and Mary went down to a paddock to look at the horses prior to the big race. Jack said, "Oh, look, Mary —there's that English horse." Then the stage directions read: "Mel whinnies like an English horse." And he did. Needless to say, Jack wasn't the only one to fall to the floor. Half the writers and cast joined Jack in mass hysteria. It's difficult to describe on the printed page Mel's portrayal of an English horse, but he did a "whinny," and then he added "A-Haw" like a typical caricature version of an elderly English gentleman. We kept the bit in, and it was well worth it. In later years Jack would frequently mention this incident when he appeared on talk and interview shows. (In a recent TV special on early radio Mel recreated his ingenious performance.)

Another important member of Jack's cast of characters was actor-director-writer-producer Sheldon Leonard, whose double first names confused Jack. For some reason Jack always reversed them and constantly referred to him as "Leonard Sheldon." No matter how often he appeared on the program, Jack, who almost always remembered everyone's name, insisted on calling him "Leonard Sheldon." Once, after several years of this, we had written a gangster role into a script and were discussing actors suitable for the part. As a gag one of the writers said, "This part is perfect for Leonard Sheldon." Jack immediately agreed, saying, "You're right! We'll get Sheldon Leonard." This time it was the writers who fell to the floor laughing. We had to explain our hysteria to a puzzled boss, and that week he apologized to an equally puzzled Sheldon Leonard.

When Sheldon made his stage debut, he got rave notices for his role as a hustling Jewish character in Arthur Kober's Catskill comedy, *Having Wonderful Time.* Thus it was only natural when the movies bought this humorous play about a Jewish vacation resort that they sign Shelly to a contract too. However, Sheldon never played in *Having Wonderful Time.* The movies cast such obvious Hebraic types as Douglas Fairbanks, Jr., Ginger Rogers, and Red Skelton. For Sheldon they found a role more in keeping with his ethnic background. They cast him in a Western as an Apache chief.

Sheldon played gangsters in all the Cagney-Robinson-Bogart pictures, as well as a Mexican sheriff with Spencer Tracy and Hedy Lamarr in *Tortilla Flat.* He was versatile and in great demand. Then, when television came, he produced and/or created and/or wrote and/or directed and/or owned and/or acted in such pots of gold as *Make Room for Daddy* (with Danny Thomas), *The Andy Griffith Show, The Dick Van Dyke Show* (with Mary Tyler Moore), *Gomer Pyle, I Spy,* and several others. But until TV ousted radio as an entertainment medium, his main claim to fame was his several annual appearances as the tout on *The Jack Benny Show.*

Jack would meet this racetrack tout at the most unlikely places. At the railroad station he would try to tout Jack off one train and onto another with such racetrack advice as: "Take The Super Chief —it's got a good rail position." "I'm telling you, The Super Chief will beat El Capitan [another famous train] into Chicago by six lengths." "Look, take my word for it, The Super Chief is a sleeper." (Which it was. It had berths, bedrooms, and sleeping compartments, while one of the other trains that Jack asked about was all coach, just seats, no beds or berths.)

At a fruit stand Jack wanted to buy an orange, and Sheldon

touted him onto an apple. At a clothing store where Jack went for a suit, Sheldon touted him off his original choice, one made out of gabardine, and onto a woolen garment. Sheldon delivered his lines out of the side of his mouth and sounded so much like a tout that he was one of the performers Jack couldn't look at during the actual broadcasts.

Sheldon Leonard's tout character caused two minor crises. The first one happened when Jack went to buy a chocolate bar, and at the candy machine Sheldon touted him into buying a pack of Life Savers.

There were supposedly two reasons for network objections to this bit of business. I am not sure that the first one is factual—namely that the owner of Life Savers also owned the ABC network, and the NBC censor took it upon himself to prevent his employer from giving benefits of any kind to a rival. The second, more legitimate complaint was that the words "Life Savers" constituted a "plug," and, after the easy-going early years of gratuitous promotion, the censors would try to delete free plugs for commercial products whether or not the writers were rewarded by a batch of booze.

Jack knew nothing about the plug situation at this time and couldn't have cared less. All he knew was that Sheldon had a great blackout which would be lost by deleting "Life Savers" and substituting, at the censor's suggestion, the words "candy mints." In the routine we had several jokes about different types of candy, all done in jockey jargon. At the end, Jack was supposed to assume Sheldon's side-of-the-mouth delivery and say, "Look, Buddy, you may be touting me onto a very good thing, but I don't like its post position. It's on the rail and could get locked in." Leonard was to respond with a knowing laugh and say: "Don't worry about it getting locked in. Life Saver can get through the hole in the middle." As anyone old enough to remember old-time radio commercials knows, Life Savers were always advertised as the candy with "the hole in the middle." The show did the joke. Sheldon got the laugh. We writers got the booze.

The other incident involving Leonard and his tout character seems ridiculous today, but back in those days it was a *cause célébre*. On many current TV commercials you see the product advertised with a picture of its competitor or competitors, and you are told why the sponsor's brand beats the others, which are now named outright instead of being merely referred to as "Brand X."

In the heyday of radio this would have been heresy, for you couldn't even imply that there was a rival product. If we did a sketch on the Lucky Strike program about the Foreign Legion, you could be sure that the attacking Arabs would be riding horses, donkeys, or dromedaries, but never camels. Like the unicorn, the camel was a non-existent animal on Lucky Strike programs. Conversely, on other cigarette-sponsored programs nobody could ever be "lucky" or go out on "strike." (To digress for a moment in this same vein, W. C. Fields was broadcasting for a cigarette sponsor—I believe it was Camels—and on the air he would always talk about his son Chester. He would tell jokes about getting letters from Chester, and sending gifts to Chester, until an advertising agency executive suddenly realized that this meant that their comic had a son named "Chester Fields." The son ceased to exist, at least on that radio program.)

Anyway, one week the writers had the bright idea of having Jack run out of cigarettes during a rehearsal. He would then walk down the hall to get a pack out of the machine, and the first person he would meet was the tout, Sheldon Leonard. Sheldon would greet him with his well-known opening line, "Pssst, Bud—c'mere a minute." All Jack would have to do would be to cast a stricken look at the audience, which would know that whatever brand of cigarettes Jack named—and naturally it had to be Lucky Strikes—Leonard would try to tout him onto another brand. Experience told us that we had a big laugh right there. Then we figured that when Sheldon asked him where he was going, Jack would try to weasel out of answering. This situation would also be good for laughs. When Jack would eventually be forced into admitting that he was going to the cigarette machine, Sheldon would ask, "What brand are you buying?"—and another helpless look from Benny would insure more audience laughter. Finally Jack would defiantly say that he was going to buy "Lucky Strikes," and the switch would come when Leonard would answer out of the side of his mouth, "A very wise choice." Jack would then angrily answer, "I'm not going to let you talk me out of it," and Leonard would say, "Talk you out of it? Why should I? Luckies are the best." And then, as the tout, he would deliver out of the side of his mouth the Lucky Strike commercial, with the words revised to fit his Runyonesque role as the tout.

All of us, including Jack, felt that this would be a much talked about commercial, and it was—especially in the advertising agency's offices. They talked about it to us loud and clear, saying that Jack was committing the cardinal commercial sin by even implying that there were any other brands of cigarettes in the machine besides Lucky Strikes. The "tout" commercial would have to go. They broke the news to Benny first, and he was furious. He said that he'd call them back after he conferred with his writers. We were equally indignant. Jack called the advertising executives back, but they were adamant. Jack then phoned his sponsor, and, without letting him know about the ad agency's objections, he asked him if we could do this commercial. The sponsor not only loved it but told Jack that he was willing to pay the expense of Sheldon's not niggardly salary.

The way Sheldon did the hard sell on this commercial earned him special kudos from the big brass. It also earned something else. The sponsor never knew that we had encountered trouble trying to do this commercial. Therefore, he sent a laudatory letter to the person he thought responsible for it, and several months later I saw this letter framed in the office of the agency executive who had refused to let us do it.

Artie Auerbach

Mr. Kitzle was portrayed by Artie Auerbach who was originally a successful photographer for the now defunct *Daily Mirror,* a New York tabloid and the flagship for Walter Winchell's column. Despite his profitable and glamorous employment, Artie had a burning desire to get into show business, and his Yiddish-oriented anecdotes made him a hit at private parties. Eventually this led to permanent, although part-time, employment on the Benny series.

Jack's initial meeting with Kitzle took place on the first program of 1946. On that show we told, via flashbacks, how Jack had gone to see the Rose Bowl game. In this scene we had him meet a frankfurter salesman, Mr. Kitzle, who was hawking his hot dogs by singing: "Peekle een the meedle mit da mustard on top."

These were Mr. Kitzle's opening lines on many programs, but the Yiddish-sounding words and melody were not Jewish in origin. John Tackaberry remembered them from his days as a youth in Houston when he had attended sporting events and heard a black man selling hot dogs with his chanted sales pitch.

Eventually Tackaberry was approached by a music publisher who wanted to write a song about it. John told him of the origin of the ditty, but the publisher said that he would take care of all legal clearances. A recording of the song earned Tackaberry a sizable chunk of coin. Not that "Pickle in the Middle" ever made the Hit Parade, but on the flip side of "Pickle" was a song that made the record sell nearly a million copies.

With Mr. Kitzle's routines we used the same philosophy that guided us in Rochester's humor: Don't do any jokes that were specifically "Jewish" jokes or "black" jokes; just do jokes that could be done by any member of the cast, and then have them done by Kitzle or Rochester. True, we deviated from this with Kitzle by giving him occasional opportunities to Judaize some un-Jewish names. He told Jack that on Sunday nights his favorite TV program was "Ed Solomon's Show." His favorite radio program was "Lum and Adler," and his favorite singer was Nat "King" Cohen. But for the most part his jokes could be done with or without accent, and an excellent example is the following exchange which took place when Jack met him as a fellow spectator at a baseball game:

JACK

I didn't know you liked baseball, Mr. Kitzle.

KITZLE

Vy not? Baseball is America's natural sport.

JACK

That's national.

KITZLE

Naturally . . . not only do I like to vatch baseball, but in mine younger days I used to play it.

JACK

You did?

KITZLE

Vould I lie to you? I vas a pitcher. In fact, vunce I pitched a no-hit game.

JACK

That's wonderful. So you pitched a no-hitter. What was the score?

KITZLE

Tventy-six to nothing—ve lost.

JACK

How could you possibly lose twenty-six to nothing? You said you pitched a no-hitter.

KITZLE

I did pitch a no-hitter, but hoo hoo hoo, did I valk them!

Now, excepting for the first few lines, which are based on "Kitzleisms," the rest of the routine is as American as apple pie. And I speak from experience, for years later during my life with Lucy, on a program where Lucy's son met Jim Piersall, the famous baseball player, we did this very same joke, with Lucy bragging to Piersall that in a Little League game her son had pitched a no-hitter. Same lines. Same joke. Same big laugh. And no ethnic accents.

108

Sam Hearn

Sam Hearn's heyday on the Benny broadcasts came before my time. Playing the part of "Shlepperman," he was Jack's first Jewish-accented actor, and a tremendously popular performer. I believe that Jack stopped using him in the late 1930s, and I don't know whether Hitler's horrors had anything to do with terminating the character. However, after the acquisition of Kitzle, Jack met Hearn on the street one day, and Sam said that he'd like to return to the program in some capacity. Jack pointed out that we couldn't use the character of Shlepperman because of Kitzle, and Hearn understood, but he told Jack that he also did a "rube" or "hick" very well.

Characteristically anxious to please an old friend, Jack told us to write a rube routine for Sam, and we did. He clicked so big that he made many appearances on the program. He always greeted Jack as though Benny were a bucolic boob, saying "Hi, Rube," in a rustic high-pitched voice. Supposedly he lived in a vineyard in Calabasas, a suburb of Los Angeles. His humor was rube-oriented, and one of the biggest laughs he ever got was on a TV show when he did a short routine with Jack and casually mentioned that he had to hurry because his wife was waiting for him. Jack said he'd like to meet his wife, and Hearn called out: "Hi, Vi, come out and meet a guy." Onto the stage then stepped a gorgeous, shapely blonde in a low-cut, tight-fitting, form-revealing, beaded gown which caused Jack to do a double-take as the men in the audience wolf-whistled their appreciation. Jack gave her a long, lingering look, taking in every voluptuous curve, and then he asked Hearn in unbelieving tones, "This . . . this is your wife?" Hearn replied: "Yep . . . ain't as much of a rube as you thought I was."

Bea Benaderet, Sara Berner, and Sandra Gould

These three girls were the two telephone operators. Bea and Sara usually played the roles, but Sandy would occasionally fill in if one couldn't make it. Sara and Bea's names were "Mabel Flapsaddle" and "Gertrude Gearshift." (Yes, the names were corny, but in those days the audiences ate them up.) Some characters, like Sheldon Leonard's tout and Sam Hearn's rube, had no names at all, but were simply called "The Tout" and "The Rube," and the same was true of many other recurring regulars on the show. When we did christen a character, we usually went a bit hokey trying to get an audience laugh for the name itself. Occasionally this would lead to complications, the most feared of which was that we might duplicate a living person's name and be sued for invasion of privacy. In this regard the Marx Brothers invented a firm of lawyers whom they called, I think, "Beagle, Beagle, Flywheel, and Shyster." They encountered little trouble referring to this improbable quartet in their theater appearances, but it was taboo on radio because research revealed several lawyers named "Beagle" in addition to five "Flywheels" and three "Shysters."

Therefore, Sara Berner and Bea Benaderet were "Gertrude Gearshift" and "Mabel Flapsaddle," and since their characters were almost interchangeable, so were their names. During the many times we used them, I never knew which was which. I still don't. They supposedly sat at the network's switchboard, and whenever Jack, on stage or from his dressing room, said he had to call somebody, he would pick up the phone and we would "fade" to the two telephone operators. Then we would hear the buzz of a switchboard, and the dialogue always opened with lines similar to the ones in the following two examples:

FIRST GIRL

Oh look, Mr. Benny's line is flashing.

SECOND GIRL

Yeah, I wonder what "Dial M for Money" wants now.

FIRST GIRL

Oh look, Mr. Benny's line is flashing.

SECOND GIRL

Yeah, I wonder what "The Boy with the Green Pockets" wants now.

These lines may be meaningless today, but they were always twists on the titles of currently popular pictures. We did "Dial M for Money" because of a then currently popular movie called *Dial M for Murder,* and "The Boy with the Green Pockets" was used when a picture was released called *The Boy with the Green Hair.*

The two telephone operators would then exchange a page and a half of jokes knocking Jack as a boyfriend (they both went on dates with him), as a comedian, and in every other way. As mentioned, sometimes Sandra Gould filled in for Sara or Bea if one of these two had a conflicting show and couldn't play our program. All three of these girls did additional roles on the series, with Sara playing another of Jack's girlfriends, "Gladys Zybisco," and also a nasal, flat-voiced, off-key, ballad singer on radio whom Jack always tuned in on no matter what program he was trying to get. Sandy Gould also played the part of "Miss Duffy" on *Duffy's Tavern* (one of several actresses who portrayed her), and Bea Benaderet became the star of the TV series *Petticoat Junction*.

Benny Rubin

Benny Rubin played an assortment of roles on the Jack Benny broadcasts, and he is sometimes confused with other actors and the roles they portrayed. Most people think he was the crook who first said "Your money or your life" to Jack. He may have played this part during the several times we repeated the bit, but the first one to do it was Eddie Marr. However, Rubin was the first to play the tout on the program; then an engagement in a legitimate show took him out of town, and this plum fell to Sheldon Leonard who thereafter enacted the role.

Benny Rubin was a big vaudeville star when I was a kid, and only a few months ago I saw some clips of old-time movie newsreels, complete with subtitles. One scene showed a glamorous Hollywood premiere, circa 1926, with a debonair young man getting out of a chauffeured Rolls-Royce, and the subtitle identified him as "Benny Rubin, Famed Vaudeville Comic." When vaudeville disappeared (as Bob Hope once said, "Vaudeville died, and television was the box they buried it in"), Rubin continued in Broadway plays and nightclubs and doing featured parts on radio series.

We used him often, in many ways, and always with great success. One memorable bit was when Jack was at the railroad station and he wanted to get some information about his train's departure. He saw a counter marked "Information" and went over to talk to the man standing behind it. In reading this routine with Rubin, please remember that every one of Rubin's lines was delivered in an increasingly aggravated, irritated tone:

JACK

What track does the Super Chief leave on?

RUBIN

I don't know.

JACK

Well, what time does the Super Chief leave?

RUBIN

I don't know.

111

JACK

Oh. Where can I get my space confirmed on the Super Chief?

RUBIN

I don't know.

JACK

(*mad*) Well, for heaven's sake, if you don't know anything, why are you standing behind this "Information" counter?

RUBIN

Because somebody stole my pants and I can't run around in my underwear.

Verna Felton

Like most radio actresses, Verna Felton was a woman of many voices, but the one we heard most was the one she used as Dennis Day's mother. As timid as Dennis was with Jack, she was his exact opposite. Dennis talked meekly to his boss. Verna brayed at him. She would always ask Jack why he mistreated her talented son, and then would cut off Jack's apologetic answer with a screamed, *"Ehhhhhh, shut up."*

Mary Livingstone once got one of the program's largest laughs (when Jack was explaining his theory of music to opera star Dorothy Kirsten) with a ladylike "Oh, shut up," but Mary's "Oh, shut up" was preceded by a careful buildup to it, and the laugh resulted from the situation. When Verna bellowed, her ear-shattering "Ehhhhh, shut up," the laugh came because of the feeling that she could physically take Jack apart limb by limb. This quality in her character would give us laughs about her even when she wasn't on the show.

Once Dennis said that his mother couldn't come to the program that week because she was at the judo school. Jack said, "I didn't know your mother was studying judo," and Dennis answered, "Not studying, teaching." And though she would fight for her son like a lioness protecting her cubs, she was not above taking a dig at Dennis herself, as the following exchange shows.

VERNA

Now, Dennis, either you behave yourself or your father and I are going to do it again.

JACK

Do what again?

Move away without telling him where.

Frank Nelson

Frank Nelson had a frequent but indefinable role on *The Jack Benny Show*. On different programs he played different parts. In department stores he was a floorwalker, in restaurants a waiter, in supermarkets a salesman, at the railroad station a ticket seller, and so on. However, all of these parts had one common denominator. No matter what or where he was, he was the same character who looked down upon Jack Benny. He never was identified by any name on the show, and he needed no name for identification. The minute Jack addressed him by saying, "Oh, Mister," or "Excuse me, sir," Nelson's long sibilant "Yesssssss" would evoke instant laughter and applause. In the middle of routines with Frank as with other performers, Jack would break up and try to cover this departure from the script by ad-libbing, "Why does he always hate me?" That was a good question, and we could never answer it. But no matter how nice Jack was to him, the character Frank played hated Benny.

Once we did a sketch based on a prison picture, and we employed a popular device where Jack would do narration and tell the story in monologue form over a "filter" mike (a microphone that made the voice sound as though it were coming over a telephone). Then he would use the regular mike when he did dialogue with other characters. In this sketch, called "I Stand Condemned" (a title we used several times a season whenever we did a prison picture parody or sketch where Jack was allegedly the innocent victim of circumstances), the final scene had Jack waiting to be electrocuted at half past five that morning and saying how he dreaded the clock reaching that fatal moment.

Jack continued narrating how he had been caught in this web of circumstances because he was betrayed by "the fickle finger of fate." A split second of silence took place after Jack's overly dramatic reading of this line, and then we heard the voice of Frank Nelson, playing the warden, addressing Jack as though he were inviting his bosom buddy to a party. Frank, his voice oozing good fellowship and happiness, said to Jack, "It's five-thirty. Shall we go?" Jack then dramatically refused to walk the last mile. Cheerfully Nelson said, "Oh, that's all right. We'll bring the electric chair to you." Jack asked, "How can you bring the electric chair all the way over here?" And Nelson happily replied, "We have a long cord."

Veola Vonn

Veola Vonn was a big-busted, beautiful woman who is now married to Frank Nelson. Whenever we needed a "sexpot" on the show, we used her. She not only looked the part but had the voice to match.

In one show Benny visited a psychiatrist who asked Jack to tell about his dreams. Jack started to do so and was interrupted by Veola sexily saying, "Hello, Blue Eyes," after which Jack explained: "I always dream of her." Because of the sensual tones she greeted him with, Jack's explanation about his always dreaming of her was funny to the radio audience, but even funnier to those in the studio watching the broadcast.

Elliot Lewis

Elliot Lewis was one of those fine radio actors who could double in drama and in comedy, and he also narrated the famous album "Manhattan Towers" which sold nearly a million copies. On *The Jack Benny Show* he specialized in two types of roles. He was either cast as a polished gentleman, or as the exact opposite, an uneducated individual we called the "mooley." I don't know how we came to categorize this character as "mooley." It may have been some version of "mule," but many shows used "mooleys," and Elliot was the best of them. For example, Jack was shopping for a bottle of perfume for Mary in a department store, and the salesman who waited on him was a "mooley" done by Elliot. His greeting to Jack was, "Duhhh, can I help youse, huh?" When Jack said he wanted to buy some perfume as a gift, Elliot recited a long list of exotic and sometimes foreign-named perfumes—and with his "mooley" delivery he got a laugh with each one on the list. Finally Jack said, "You're not the type one would expect to find as a perfume salesman. Is this your regular job?" And Elliot answered, "Duuuuhhhh, no. I woik in da fertilizer department, but onest a munt they sends me up here to even t'ings out."

When Lewis performed a role at the opposite end of the spectrum, it was usually in the railroad station sketches, and it always took place in the same way with the same three characters. Jack would be waiting in line to have his ticket and traveling space confirmed by the man in charge, who was always Frank "Yesssssss" Nelson. The moment Frank began to help Jack, an extremely polite and polished gentleman would ask Jack's forgiveness, but since he was in a terrible hurry and would only take a moment, could he go first?

Jack would graciously consent to this. Then Elliot would tell ticket-seller Nelson that because of a traumatic experience he had just gone through, his doctor ordered him to take a trip. It could be anywhere at all, but he had to take a trip.

At this point the scripts would vary, depending on the destination. For example, in one show Nelson said that a train was leaving in ten minutes for Nashville. Lewis sadly replied, "Oh, no, no, I can go to any place but Tennessee." Nelson asked solicitously (this was his character; he was nice to everybody but Jack Benny): "Why can't you go to Tennessee?" Then the dialogue between them went as follows:

LEWIS

You see, I was dancing with my darling!

NELSON

To the Tennessee Waltz?

LEWIS

Yes.

Then Nelson and Lewis went through every single line of the lyrics of that then popular sad song which tells how a man was dancing with his darling to "The Tennessee Waltz" when an old friend he happened to see. He introduced his darling to his old friend, and they became sweethearts, and that's how he lost his darling. Frank and Elliot alternated lines, and we used the lyrics without changing a word, and the audience appreciated every second of it. In one or two spots we tried to have Jack, who was in a hurry, break in and start a sentence, but Nelson always cut off Jack's interruptions with insults which squelched Benny and kept him quiet.

Over the years we did annual or bi-annual versions of this routine whenever the lyrics of a song were about a city or place. Once we did it with Nelson suggesting to Lewis that he take a train to Glocca Morra. Lewis asked, "How are things in Glocca Morra?" and we went right through the entire song with Frank and Elliot alternating lines and Jack impatiently trying to get his train ticket and space confirmed.

We also did this routine with a novelty song called "Istanbul," in which the lyrics mention that it was formerly known as Constantinople. And again Jack stood by helplessly impatient as they went through this song line by line.

115

There were more, many many more, in the cast of auxiliary characters that made the Benny radio and TV shows so memorable. I am thinking of actors like Lou Merrill and John Brown who were frequently used. Of the two old ladies who formed a "Senior Citizens Jack Benny Fan Club." Of Ed Beloin, a former writer, who had a running role as "Mr. Billingsly" a nutty boarder in Jack's house. Of his fast-talking press agent, Steve. Of the crying cab driver he ran into several times. Of his fictitious writer, "Belly Laugh" Barton. Of the two income-tax men who were trying to help Jack reduce his taxes. And of so many others to whom I'll have to write notes of apology for overlooking them.

However, one I can't omit is Joe Kearns who played the part of Ed, keeper of the vault. The vault was supposedly several hundred feet below street level, and Ed had been standing guard over it seemingly for centuries. A joke based on how long he was down there had Jack tell him at the end of World War II, "I have news for you, Ed. The war is over." And Ed answered in his flat delivery, "Oh, how nice. Who won, the North or the South?"

Whenever Jack would announce that he was going to open the safe in the vault, Ed would have a line such as "Shall I gouge my eyes out?" or "Shall I take my Seconal?" And Jack would always say, "No, no, Ed, I trust you." Once, as Jack opened the safe with its ear-shattering, earth-shaking alarm, Ed asked: "How much money are you putting in, Mr. Benny?" Jack answered, "None. This time I'm taking some out." And an amazed Ed said, *"Taking out? My, this is exciting."*

Another performer who must be mentioned is Bob Crosby, although it's difficult to classify him, since he was not a "stooge," nor was he with the series long enough to be considered a true regular.

As television began to make inroads into radio, budgets were cut and casts were trimmed. When we opened our radio series on September 14, 1952, economies had to be exercised. One of them resulted in the reluctant release of Phil Harris. This was all done on the friendliest of terms, and Phil appeared as a guest on many subsequent Jack Benny television shows. However, at this time he was replaced by Bob Crosby.

Bob shared Bing's charm and delivered comedy lines with the usual Crosby aplomb, and in addition he was an excellent musician. Many years previous, before Bing attained the top rungs of the show business ladder of success, Bob had a musical group, "Bob Crosby and His Bob Cats," and today their early recordings are considered collectors' items by jazz aficionados.

A couple of comic incidents involving Crosby stand out. On one

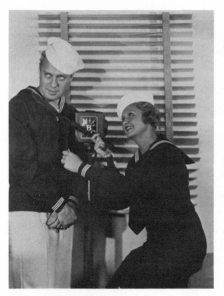

Jack and his first vocalist, Ethel Shutta, August 1932.

Dennis Day's real mother, Mary McNulty, is introduced to Day's radio mother, Verna Felton, December 1939. (Dennis' first program on the Benny show was October 8, 1939.) *Photo by Gene Lester.*

Jack receiving a government award during World War II for making a government bond selling film. With him are its writers Hugh Wedlock, Jr. and Howard Snyder.

A radio rehearsal at Jack's home. (l to r): Marty Spurzel of the Sportsmen Quartet; Larry Stevens, Dennis Day's replacement while Dennis was in the Navy; Mel Blanc; comedienne Sandra Gould; Bert Scott, Jack's personal secretary; a sound man; Mary Livingstone; Phil Harris; Don Wilson; and musical conductor Mahlon Merrick. *Photo by Frank Worth.*

While in the Navy, Dennis Day visited his co-stars (1945): Don Wilson, Phil Harris, Rochester, and Jack.

Jack with Dennis Day, Phil Harris, and Alice Faye, October 1946.

Producer Hilliard Marks, and writers George Balzer, Milt Josefsberg, John Tacka-berry, and Sam Perrin.

Jack and one of his secretaries, Dotty Oh-man, 1961.

Jack with Dennis Day and Margaret Truman, January 1955.

Writers George Balzer, Sam Perrin, Milt Josefsberg, and John Tackaberry going over a script with Jack and singer Tony Martin. *CBS photo by Pierce Grant.*

program he mentioned that he had played golf with his brother who had asked him to give Jack his regards. Dennis asked, "Who's your brother?" Bob answered, "Bing Crosby." Dennis replied: "Name dropper!" The other incident concerned a sketch we were doing in which Bob was portraying a heavy drinker (on almost all radio shows the orchestra leaders and musicians were the drunkards). Jack asked Bob what he was drinking, and Crosby answered "Manischewitz on the rocks." Now Manischewitz is a sacramental wine which was at one time almost exclusively imbibed by Jews, and then only during the week of Passover. But through the wonders of TV advertising, Manischewitz and its greatest rival, Mogen David, now enjoy tremendous year-long popularity among all races, colors, and creeds. Today it's sort of a kosher Ripple. However, back in 1953 this wasn't the case, and we thought it would be funny for Bob to say he was drinking Manischewitz. It was funny, but mainly because Bob couldn't pronounce it. As he said it on the air he stuck in six or seven extra syllables, so that the name came out something like "Manischeveveveveveveitz." For the next six shows we did routines in which Jack tried to teach Bob how to pronounce "Manischewitz."

Perhaps I have dwelled too long on Jack's stable of stooges, but they played a major part in the program's success. Some readers may remember bit players I have inadvertently omitted and they will resent it. Certainly these performers will remember themselves and resent the omission. To all of them, I apologize.

13
The Writers

To attempt an analysis of the Jack Benny broadcasts without devoting some space to his writers would be akin to reciting the story of Noah without mentioning his ark. These writers were an important part of this long-shining beacon in broadcasting. Perhaps we weren't quite as important to the success of the show as Jack thought we were, and we certainly weren't as important as we thought we were, but on a scale of one to ten we registered nine. Jack and his cast were tops, at ten.

Writers come in all ages, religions, creeds, sexes, intermediate sexes, sizes, and temperaments. Moreover, their modes of living and writing styles vary. I know several who can only write from midnight to dawn after everyone else is asleep. There are morning writers and afternoon writers. Also, some write with stereo sets blasting, while others demand deep silence. Some write in shorthand, some in longhand, some use a typewriter, and some can only dictate to secretaries.

There are the pacers, the starers, the sitters, the nibblers, the eaters, the abstainers, the drinkers, and dozens of others. Some can only function in sparsely furnished offices, while others must be surrounded by sybaritic splendor. Some have offices in their homes; others don't feel at home in their homes. Most of them combine incompatible giant-sized egos with nerve-racking insecurity complexes. Ten learned critics could tell a novelist that he has created a masterpiece, but then if his gardener were to say, "I don't like the book too much," the writer's week would be ruined.

Writing is an art and not a science, and as is true in all of the arts, each of us has his own tastes. Perhaps you recall the story of the man who brought a lady friend to a party, and this lady was difficult to describe. Her nose was off-center, her mouth was slit vertically down her face instead of horizontally, one eye was two inches lower than the other, and both of her ears were on the same side of her head. The man introduced this weird woman to a friend whose countenance betrayed his shocked appearance at her bizarre face. Her escort indignantly said to this man, "What's the matter—you don't like Picasso?" In the same vein, what I think is funny you may regard as tragic. It's a matter of taste.

Some writer once remarked "The deadliest enemy of the writer is that first empty page staring him in the face." Dorothy Parker is reputed to have said, "I hate writing. I love having written." When any network or advertising executive criticized one of Fred Allen's scripts, he'd say, "Where were you when the pages were empty?"

Writers don't confine their work exclusively to offices, either at studios or in their homes. A writer's brain is always working. I know of writers who have gotten excellent ideas while playing golf, fishing, walking, watching movies, or even sleeping. I know that my wife Hilda still hasn't forgiven me because once, at a most intimate moment, I broke into wild laughter at a script idea that popped into my head. Not only that, but wives never fully understand their writing husbands' creative habits. A woman can be married to a writer for fifty years and still not understand that when she walks into his office and sees him staring out of a window, he is actually working.

I will try to be as objective as possible about Jack's four writers and the teams they made up. And in discussing the teams I must remind you that if marriages are made in heaven, then collaborations are made in hell. Furthermore, marriage and collaboration have one thing in common—the fact that opposites attract. However, when two writers are paired for better or worse, they are usually more opposite than the partners in a marriage.

Sam Perrin knew Jack the longest. He started his career as a musician and drummer in vaudeville and met Jack while on tour. He impressed Jack with his wit, and when the time came to hire a new staff for the new season starting in the fall of 1943, Sam was given a crack at this prize plum. However, in the summer of 1943, Jack was overseas entertaining our men and women in uniform, and he left the important chore of selecting a new staff to his business manager, Myrt Blum, and his advertising agency-appointed producer, Walter Bunker. These two gentlemen arranged contracts with John Tackaberry, George Balzer, and me, but Perrin felt that he could do better financially by negotiating directly with Jack, so he waited for his return, and as a result of this he missed the first two broadcasts Jack did with his new staff from New York City. At the start, there was also a fourth writer named Cy Howard whom Jack had met in Chicago and hired personally. On the train ride back from New York to Los Angeles, Jack made two confessions to me. First, he said that he was shocked when he returned and found that I was the highest-paid writer hired for his staff when my sole experience was five years with Bob Hope. He half-expected that every joke I wrote would be in Hope's then typical style, starting with lines such as "She was so fat that . . ." or "I wouldn't say she was ugly but . . ." (Let me state for the record that I was Jack's highest-paid writer only until he returned to Hollywood. Then Jack personally concluded contractual negotiations with Perrin, and Sam began earning slightly more than I.) The other confession that Jack made on that train ride to Los Angeles was: "You see, Milt, I understand what makes a writer good for me, and men like Myrt Blum and Walter Bunker who hired you, George, and Tackaberry are businessmen and know nothing about comedy. Yet the three writers they hired are going to work out, and the one I hired [Cy Howard] isn't going to make it." Jack's prediction came true, for Cy Howard left the show after thirteen weeks to become an actor. However, Jack's astuteness in choosing him was eventually proved when Cy Howard became one of radio's most successful comedy creators and producers, with long-running hits like *My Friend Irma* and *Life with Luigi* among his winners. He also wrote what may have been the best Martin and Lewis movie, *That's My Boy,* and recently he directed the critically acclaimed motion picture *Lovers and Other Strangers.*

Despite the fact that Cy Howard made millions in radio, television, and movies, he will probably be best remembered in the legitimate theater for a legendary line he pulled years ago which earned him no money but forever cemented his reputation as a wit. Al Bloomingdale, scion of the famous department store family, was in the process of producing a play that he wanted to bring to Broadway. The play was having serious script trouble during its out-of-town tryout, and Bloomingdale hired Howard to "doctor" the show and make it presentable. Cy sat through one performance and then told Bloomingdale, "Take my advice: close the show and keep the store open nights." This line alone should be sufficient to indicate that Jack wasn't too wrong in selecting Cy Howard as one of the humorists he wanted to write his programs.

Sam Perrin was a much more seasoned comedy writer than I was when we became members of Jack's staff. My only experience had been with the Bob Hope program, but Sam had worked on several shows. As a matter of fact he had worked on *The Jack Benny Show* prior to 1943, but friction between him and Bill Morrow, one of Benny's best writers, caused Sam to leave. Ironically, later on this same exact conflict arose between Perrin and me, and I wanted to leave but Jack wouldn't let me.

Sam had written such radio shows as *Screen Guild Presents* and *The Tommy Riggs and Betty Lou Show.* The latter was a pleasant piece of fluff with Tommy, a ventriloquist, acting as the voice of Betty Lou, a female version of Charlie McCarthy. Around this time Perrin picked a protégé named George Balzer. Prior to teaming with Perrin, George, one of the few native-born California comedy writers, drove a delivery truck for his father's Van Nuys laundry service which specialized in diapers. I can assure you that Balzer was the butt of every obvious joke concerning the contents of diapers compared to the contents of his scripts.

Both were excellent writers, with Balzer having a special flair for "wild" humor. They collaborated exceedingly well, but their personalities were completely different. Balzer was an excellent and conservative businessman, while Sam was always looking for sure-fire investments such as uranium mines.

During the years we all worked together, each writer admired certain contributions of his competitors, and on a multi-writer show even your own collaborator was occasionally your competitor. To list all the great gags and bits Sam contributed to the success of the shows would fill volumes—and the same holds true for each of the writers.

I will however tell two of Sam's gags which were among my favorites. One had nothing to do with the script. We were traveling, playing Army camps, during the late war years, and the accommodations we got on trains were something less than luxurious. However, since you needed a priority rating to travel at all, we couldn't really complain. On this train trip there was a shortage of berths, and Jack knew that Sam and our producer, Hilliard Marks (Mary Livingstone's brother), had shared a berth on a previous trip. Jack asked Sam if he would mind doubling up in a berth with Hilliard again. Sam said, "I don't mind, Jack, but I must admit that for the little pleasure I get out of it, it's not worth it."

The script line of Sam's that I want to quote perfectly expresses, at least in my opinion, the essence of Jack Benny's character. In the script Mary had heard that Jack was underpaying his writers and she tried to persuade him to be more generous. Here is Jack's reply, written by Perrin: "Mary, I'll tell you why I won't give my writers a raise. Years ago I had a writer with very bad eyes. He came to me in tears. He said, 'Mr. Benny, my eyes are so bad that I'll go blind if I don't get a pair of glasses.' I took pity on him, loaned him the money, he went to an optometrist, got himself a pair of glasses, read his contract with me, and quit. So go be nice to people."

And before leaving Sam, let me relate the greatest bit of unconscious humor that ever took place at a script session. One day Jack came in very excited, saying, "Fellows, I know how we can all get a week off and go to Palm Springs. I looked at the show we did about the Easter Parade two years ago, and it could fit this Easter without changing a word."

In those days, every Easter we would do a show where the orchestra would play "Easter Parade" and Jack would walk down Wilshire Boulevard, meet the various characters in his cast, do short routines with them, and then walk on humming the music, until he met the next member of the cast.

The thought of a full week off—and, as usual, at full salary—delighted us. We began to bolster Jack's enthusiasm by telling him that the Easter Parade show two years ago was great. We reminded him how funny Mary's routine was, that Phil Harris' bit was sensational, that Dennis was never better, and how Rochester got screams. Jack, who originated the idea, was at last fully convinced, and he decided to call his sponsor and inform him of his decision.

At this point Sam Perrin threw in what he thought would be the final clincher and said, "And Jack, we get a tremendous break. Easter falls on Sunday again this year." Jack wasn't the only one to fall on the floor that day—but we got the week off.

Sam's collaborator, George Balzer, was the least likely man for him to write with. Sam and George had vastly different personalities but their conflicts were kept to a minimum, except when it came to religion. Sam, born into the Jewish faith, claimed to be an atheist, while George was a devout Catholic. It was this fact that caused us to kid him, leading to a blowup on one occasion.

The incident occurred on an Easter Sunday, but on this occasion we were broadcasting the program live. George was a little late that day because he had been to Mass. As usual we met at noon for a cast reading, and then the writers and Jack adjourned to our office to make the final cuts and changes before going on the air. One of the writers in the group had put two Mercurochrome-stained Band-Aids on his hands—one across each palm. He kept them hidden during the cast reading, but when Jack and the writers were in their private session he made no attempt to hide them. Soon someone spotted the red-stained Band-Aids on his palms and asked, "Hey, what happened?" And the writer replied seriously: "I don't know. I woke up this morning and my palms were bleeding." Everyone laughed but George, who said, "That's not funny, it's blasphemy," and walked out of the meeting.

The third member of our troop was John Tackaberry, a Texan in word and manner. Tackaberry (automatically nicknamed Tack) and I didn't join the program as a team of collaborators like George and Sam, but as separate entities. For the first couple of years we each worked independently. Then at Jack's suggestion we joined forces, and for eight or nine years we wrote as a team.

Tackaberry waged a noble war against the anti-black, anti-Jewish prejudices he had picked up in his less than liberal youth. He idolized Jack, as we all did, and oddly enough he formed a fast friendship with Rochester despite the fact that Rochester would never play the title role in any "Blondie" movie. At the end of our first season when we disbanded for the long summer vacation, Tackaberry went back home to Houston for several weeks. When we got together to resume writing for the fall, we spent the first hour or so recounting our vacation adventures.

Then Tack said, "Milt, you would have been real proud of me the way I acted down there. I was at a big barbecue one night and some bigot began making anti-Semitic remarks. I jumped up and yelled, 'Look, I want everybody here to know that I make my living writing for Jack Benny and Rochester, and I never met two finer people, so while I'm here I ain't gonna stand for anybody making any nasty remarks about the niggers or kikes.' " He was sincerely proud of his conversion to liberalism.

The final member of the quartet is the author. I was born, raised, and educated in Brooklyn, and I took night courses in advertising and journalism at CCNY. I couldn't attend any other college because I had to try to earn a buck which wasn't easy in those Depression days. I began sending contributions to Broadway columnists such as Mark Hellinger and Walter Winchell. This eventually led to a job with a Broadway press agent, and soon I opened my own public relations office. I hired a fellow named Jack Rose to help me. After he left, he went on to achieve much fame, most recently as the co-screenwriter of the award-winning comedy, *A Touch of Class,* with Mel Frank, who also directed and produced this brilliant comedy. When Jack Rose left, I hired another young man, Mel Shavelson, and he was with me for two weeks when I was given a chance to land Bob Hope—about to start a new radio series in September 1938—as a publicity account. One of my ideas was to write a weekly letter on a topical subject from Bob Hope to be sent to all the radio editors. Shavelson and I wrote a sample letter which we submitted to Hope's manager, James L. Saphier. He immediately called and said our letter was far funnier than any of the scripts he had received from writing applicants for Mr. Hope's staff. We were signed and went to Hollywood where we worked together for five years with Bob, and then I joined Jack Benny, while my collaborator Mel Shavelson decided to try writing for the movies. Since then he has written and/or directed and/or produced, or any combination of these three, either alone or in collaboration, many notable movies, including *The Seven Little Foys, Cast a Giant Shadow, Houseboat,* and *Yours, Mine and Ours.* In addition to this, Shavelson has written two books and a Broadway play, and he achieved the highest honor his peers could confer on him when he was elected President of The Writers Guild of America several years ago. I knew the talent this man had because when I hired him his starting salary was supposed to be twelve dollars, but before I paid him for the first week, I immediately raised it way up to fifteen dollars.

One small anecdote before getting off the subject of press agents. When I went from Hope to Benny I had achieved some sort of fame among my former colleagues in the publicity business. Thus whenever I returned to New York, I always arranged lunches with them to show that I hadn't gone Hollywood—and possibly to gloat in my new-found status.

On one of these occasions I lunched with David O. Alber, a press agent for whom I worked briefly, sending jokes credited to his clients to the Broadway columnists. But now I was considered a solid success, since I had five years with Hope behind me and was currently in my third season with Jack Benny. We reminisced, and Dave informed me that he had just hired another young man to perform my former chores for him. "The kid is clever," Dave said, "but he's no Milt Josefsberg."

Dave was right. The kid was no Milt Josefsberg. He was Woody Allen, who I think is one of the two funniest living comedians and writers.

In 1950 it was decided that Jack would continue with his radio series but also take on the added task of television. In order not to overwork his writers, Jack hired an extra team, Al Gordon and Hal Goldman. Because they were years younger than the rest of us, and since they were newcomers, they were always referred to as "the Kids." Like all of us they grew rich, old, and gray in Jack's service, but we still referred to them as "The Kids."

Jack was a guest star on a *Here's Lucy* show that I wrote in 1971, and we were having lunch together. At that time all of his ex-writers were gainfully employed, and Jack said to me, "I'm glad everybody is doing well—especially 'The Kids.'" I laughed at this and said, "Jack, their hair is almost white now. Why do you still call them 'The Kids'?" And Jack said, "Because they're too young to be called 'The Old Farts.'"

In this lengthy description of the writers, I am only concentrating on those who worked with me or during my period of employment. Ed Beloin and Bill Morrow preceded us, and Harry Conn and Al Boasberg preceded them. They all had a hand on the typewriters that created Jack's crystal-clear comedy character, and I and the others are deeply grateful to them for their major contributions.

The last team of writers I'll list knew Jack the longest, starting with him in April 1936, and then writing the series with Beloin and Morrow for another full season. They were Howard Snyder and Hugh Wedlock, Jr. If ever a team of collaborators had divergent opinions and opposite modes of life, it was these two. Howard Snyder was Jewish, but outside of his business associates I don't think he had a single Jewish friend or knew a word of Yiddish. Hughie Wedlock was Irish, and I don't think he had a single Gentile friend, since he socialized exclusively with Jews. During our early acquaintance Hughie was talking to me and threw in a couple of Yiddish phrases which I didn't understand, and he had to explain them to me.

I said, "Hughie, how come you use so much Yiddish?"

And he said, "Hell, Milt, how else can you express yourself?"

Hughie would always break up Jack and me because of his penchant for making up Jewish jokes. One Jewish New Year he sent Jack a "Happy Easter" card with a note saying, "Dear Jack, I tried to get you a Jewish New Year's card, but this is the best I could do in my Gentile neighborhood."

That same Jewish New Year he called me and asked me what year it was. I said it was 5734.

Hughie said, "Damn it, for the next three months I know I'll still be dating my checks 5733."

Anyway, those are, or were, the writers—the fellows who every week sat down at their typewriters and saw the defiant blank page staring back at them. And it's a tribute to all of them (myself included) that we filled those blank pages with better than average material which, in the hands of the incomparable cast, became what will probably be remembered as the longest running and most consistently intelligent comedy show of all time.

To the average reader this achievement may fall into the "So what?" category, but our peers in the profession admired our efforts, and I'll illustrate this with a true but little known story.

In the late 1940s the ratings for the Jack Benny radio show were always at or near the top, and it made no difference whether those ratings were compiled by Hooper, Crosley, Neilsen, or Arbitron. On the West Coast we hit the air live at 4:00 P.M. on Sundays, and for the benefit of the many listeners who might be out of the house, the program was rebroadcast at nine at night. On one of these nights a party was being held that included the leading literary lights of the country. At one minute before 9:00 P.M., writer Moss Hart, whose comedy exploits both on his own and in collaboration with the fabulous George S. Kaufman are legendary, unobtrusively sneaked out of the crowded room and hurried to another one where he knew there was a radio. When he entered this room he was surprised to see that the radio was already turned on to Jack Benny's station, and waiting to hear it was a fellow writer and one of his few equals, Norman Krasna. Krasna, like Hart and Kaufman, was a giant in the comedy field. His screenplays had been nominated for several Academy Awards and he had won a coveted Oscar for the movie *Princess O'Rourke*. In addition, he, like Hart, had dozens of glittering Broadway hits to his credit.

Krasna and Hart sat glued to the radio for the next half-hour laughing loudly at every quip pulled by Jack and the members of his cast. The show ended with Don Wilson giving the closing credits, including the writers' names. As Hart turned off the radio, he turned to Krasna and said, "You know, we're lucky to be getting five thousand dollars a week doing movies; we could never write shows like Jack's week after week."

There was actually a fifth writer on our staff—Jack Benny himself. Jack was probably the greatest editor of comedy material in the business, and he sat in with us for many hours each week as we tried to edit and polish the script.

During these sessions he was not our boss. He claimed that he was merely one of the writers and that his opinion should carry no more weight than any other writer's. If Jack and one writer wanted a routine or situation to go in one direction, and the three others wanted to take a different tack, the majority ruled and the decision would go against Jack.

Once Jack wanted a scene to go one way but his four writers were unanimously against him. Jack was adamant, and for nearly an hour he insisted that it be done his way. Then George Balzer switched to Jack's side. Benny said, "So you finally decided I'm right, George." Balzer answered, "No, Jack, I figured that we *four* writers could be wrong." Jack did a take, then laughed hysterically and gave in. The routine was done the way the writers wanted it.

In the days of radio when a gag fell flat it was a standard ad-lib for the comedian to say, "That's the last time that writer works for me." Come to think of it, this line still provokes laughter on TV.

Jack always did the opposite. Once he heard someone (I believe it was playwright Norman Krasna) say, "I need you like a moose needs a hatrack." Jack thought the line so clever that he asked the author's permission to use it on one of his broadcasts. We worked it in so that when Phil Harris boasted with his customary cockiness,

130

"You need me, Jackson," Jack answered, "Phil, I need you like a moose needs a hatrack."

The audience reacted with a smashing silence. There was not a single snicker or an audible chuckle. Phil started to read his next line, but Jack stopped him and talked to the audience—and remember, this was during the time when every broadcast was done live. Jack said, "Folks, during my many years on the air, that's the *only* joke I ever put in a script. Not my writers. Me. One solitary joke I put in and nobody in the entire audience laughed. Now I'm going to give you one more chance."

He repeated the line, "Phil, I need you like a moose needs a hatrack." The audience, which had laughed at Jack's explanation, now applauded the line. Jack scolded them in mock exasperation, "I don't want applause, I want laughter. Now one more time ... Phil, I need you like a moose needs a hatrack." This time the audience laughed.

When the show was over the writers got the idea of making it the premise of our next program, provided that Jack didn't feel our story line held him up to ridicule. The plot was quite simple. We wanted Jack to complain to each member of his cast that the writers were mad at him for ruining their wonderful script by putting in his lousy joke.

We told the idea to Jack, and he loved it. We not only based our next show on that idea, but we kept Jack defending the line "I need you like a moose needs a hatrack" for many weeks until it became somewhat of a national catch phrase.

That was a quarter of a century ago. In the late 1960s, prior to the price rise in sugar, that industry was fighting the erosion of its profits caused by the increasing popularity of diet sodas, and part of the campaign featured institutional ads in magazines extolling the energy-giving food value of sugar. One of these full-page advertisements showed a picture of an athletic nine-year-old boy engaged in some sport, and the caption under it read, "He needs a sugar-free drink like a moose needs a hatrack."

I received a copy of the ad in the mail from Jack. He attached a note to it, saying, "See, Milt, I know when a line is great. It's just that I was ahead of my time. Jack."

A short time later, on February 15, 1969, the National Academy of Television Arts and Sciences tendered a ball in honor of Jack's seventy-fifth birthday with the cute gimmick of the tickets selling for thirty-nine dollars each. There was the usual star-studded dais, including Bob Hope, Johnny Carson, and George Burns. After all the speeches were over—most of the roast variety, but not too scatological because it wasn't a stag affair—Johnny Carson presented Jack with a handsome plaque commemorating the event. Jack was given a standing ovation when he accepted it. When the applause stopped, he looked at the plaque and said, "I need another plaque like a moose. . . ." He never finished the sentence. The audience remembered his line of many years ago and rewarded him with the biggest single laugh in an evening of tremendous hilarity. Afterward Jack said smugly, "I always knew that line was funny. I waited nearly twenty-five years, but I finally got my laugh."

Jack's relationship with his writers was known by all the creators of comedy, and they envied us, particularly because he never interfered with any of our activities and gave us free rein in almost all matters. One of these is worthy of special mention because, although it still exists to a small degree, it is largely forgotten.

In my early days in radio we frequently did jokes that mentioned commercial products, and at that time we not only didn't get gifts, but we actually had to procure permission in advance from the advertising agency to make any reference to the item. One such joke was done during a Bob Hope monologue in 1940. Bob said, "Three weeks ago I mentioned Martha Washington candy on my program, and they sent me a ten-pound box of goodies as a gift. Two weeks ago I mentioned Kodak, and they sent me a free camera. Last week I decided to press my luck and I mentioned Cadillac, and sure enough, on the way home I got hit by one."

The line was greeted with a large laugh, but no gifts came to any of the writers, or anyone else, from the three products mentioned. Yet during my sojourn with Hope and my first few years with Jack, we writers kept kidding commercial products the same way we'd do material on any topical subject, movie, or book.

Then, in the mid-1940s, plugs became a big business as public relations men discovered a new El Dorado and dug deep. When a radio show mentioned their clients' products, the P.R.'s would send a gift of liquor to the writers. The usual payment was a case of liquor, but in many instances the rewards were larger, depending on the rating of the show and the importance of the mention. Since *The Jack Benny Show* was usually in the top three, we writers were liberally supplied with liquor.

As mentioned, we saw nothing wrong in receiving gifts for writing about the same products we had been using as past program targets for our humor. However, one writer on another show was morally indignant at what he felt was a prostitution of our art, and he vowed that no product would ever receive free advertising on his show. This boomeranged when the comic he was working for heard all his peers poking fun at seemingly topical subjects while his program lagged behind the times. Therefore the comic began to do plugs, and his writer's morality wasn't sufficiently high enough for him to reject the accompanying rewards.

On our show we were not indiscriminate, for we set certain standards. The joke containing the "plug" must be at least as funny, if not funnier, than the rest of the script. Also, we would never accept money for giving gratuitous publicity, just gifts. This may be petty nit-picking, but we felt that it was more honorable. Finally, we would never do a "reverse" plug—one that derided or injured a rival product or business. For instance, at one time when the freight train tycoons were suffering setbacks because the trucking industry began getting a larger share of business, a P.R. man tried to get the various programs to make disparaging remarks about trucks and truck drivers. He even invented a word, "Mackophobia," which supposedly meant "fear of being hit by a truck," and promised that if we would have a member of our cast just utter and explain this word during a broadcast, we would receive twenty-five hundred dollars. We turned the deal down, and I believe every other show did likewise because I never heard "Mackophobia" mentioned on any broadcast.

Eventually our listeners became aware of this little racket, and they quickly jumped to the false conclusion that every time a comedian mentioned a commercial product, lavish gifts were forthcoming. This wasn't true, but the public's knowledge of the situation led to a memorable moment on one of our broadcasts. It happened during a show where the action took place in Jack's home. It was supposedly late at night and he was getting ready to retire for the evening. The dialogue went as follows:

ROCHESTER

It's kind of chilly. Do you want me to turn up the heat?

JACK

No, just turn on my General Electric blanket.

ROCHESTER

But, Boss, you don't have a General Electric blanket.

JACK

I have now.

The audience laughed knowingly when Jack merely mentioned "General Electric blanket," and they howled at his punch line, "I have now." They felt they were in on an inside joke. Oddly enough, we had selected "General Electric" specifically because we felt that the company would not respond to the mention. However, the day after the broadcast we were contacted by a General Electric representative, and all the people connected with the show—cast, crew, and writers—received free blankets for every bed in their homes.

Plugs frequently gave us the biggest laughs on the show. One incident occurred when an enterprising P.R. man was publicizing the paper plate industry. As a promotional gimmick he invented "National Save a Wife Week" which fostered the idea of using paper plates, thus giving your wife time off from the drudgery of dishwashing. Just mentioning "National Save a Wife Week" was a plug. During our dress rehearsal that Sunday, Jack was dissatisfied with the opening joke in a routine where Rochester was serving him breakfast. As we were trying to think of a suitable substitute, I said that a great feed line would be to have Jack sit down and say, "Rochester, how come you're serving breakfast on paper plates?" Rochester would then answer, "Because this is 'National Save a Wife Week.'" Jack, always an easy laugher, thought this was hilarious and wanted to put it in the script immediately. However, the other writers weren't so sure of the laugh-provoking possibility of this simple statement and we tried to get a topper. Finally George Balzer came up with two great additional lines, as follows

JACK

What has "National Save a Wife Week" got to do with you?

ROCHESTER

Boss, anyone whose contract reads "Till death do us part" fits in that category.

This four-line routine was one of the high spots of the program. Jack was right in gauging the value of Rochester's first line because it got more than an average audience reaction. However, Rochester's "Till death do us part" punch line garnered an almost ear-shattering laugh.

Practically every comic in radio quickly became aware of the proximity of laughs and liquor when a trade name was mentioned. The writers usually informed their bosses, not so much out of honesty, but because of self-preservation. They realized that the men they worked for were of above average intelligence and would soon start wondering why week after week they kept telling jokes about Bulova watches, Schwinn bicycles, Bendix washing machines, and other such products.

The comics never objected. Jack simply admonished us to keep it within reason and to make sure that the joke containing the freebie was funny. Some of the comedians declared themselves equal partners with their writers, and they weren't above ad-libbing a few plugs during the broadcast for their private benefit. One famed funny-man informed his writing staff during the middle of one December that on their Christmas shopping show (an annual standby of all programs) all product mentions were taboo. The writers figured that this restriction came as a result of a memo from the sponsor or the network, but at the first reading of the script that week everything became clear. The comic had written a lengthy joke concerning the many Christmas gifts he'd have to buy for his cast and crew. This single gag contained twenty-nine brand names, each of which was a plug. Santa Claus came a little early to the comedian that year, and one of his cars had to be parked in the driveway because his garage looked like an overstocked liquor store.

Only once during my lengthy tenure did Jack benefit from this broadcasting gold mine, and it was the writers who suggested it, not Jack. During a rewrite session we heard Jack tell his secretary to call a department store and find out the prices of television sets, since he wanted to give one as a gift to a less well-to-do friend. We told Jack to hold off his purchase while we tried to think of how we could get one gratis. We did it on the very next broadcast. The program was one where Jack dreamed that he was married to Mary, and that they had a daughter Joan, who by a not too unusual coincidence was played by their daughter Joan. In one scene she had a boyfriend visit her, and they were sitting in the living room. Joan pointed to a picture of Jack on the television set and proudly said: "Daddy was in the Navy." The boy commented, "Gosh, he was an admiral." Joan replied, "No, that's the television set." Joan got her laugh and Jack got a free TV set from Admiral.

Plugs were frowned upon by the networks, but as long as they got big laughs there was no way of curtailing them. However, after the big quiz scandals in the 1950s, stringent rules were enforced and no plugs were permitted. The weekly salary checks given to writers, performers, and "prop" men (who would occasionally furnish sets in TV shows with easily identifiable products such as Coca-Cola bottles) bore the legend, "By signing this check the endorser vows that he received no remuneration in gifts, cash, or kind, for advertising any product other than the sponsors'." The warning went on to remind you that you could be fined or given a jail term or both for violation of this oath.

In recent years most programs have abandoned this loyalty oath. However, because reruns might be sponsored by rival manufacturers, the writers censor themselves. Some comedy shows still do mention commercial products, but few writers try to capitalize on them. No merchandise or gifts are given to them. The laughs we get are sufficient rewards, and television scripting assignments are so rare, and so richly remunerative, that the writers avoid the risks.

14
Jack's Favorite Jokes

Jack Benny undoubtedly told more jokes than any other comedian in the history of the world. If you are interested in statistics, he broadcast on a regular weekly basis (twice a week his first year) from 1932 to 1965. Then, after discontinuing his regularly scheduled series, he starred in several one-hour TV specials each season, and he made countless guest appearances with other stars, including at least one a season with Lucille Ball. He was a frequent visitor on talk shows and was no stranger to the nightclub circuit. For all of these he had original topical material prepared, even if it was for a charity dinner or private party.

For thirty-three uninterrupted years he did a half hour of comedy each week, averaging thirty-eight programs a season, and on each show he and his cast got an average of sixty laughs. If you include his one-hour television specials, guest shots on other programs, and personal appearances in theaters, nightclubs, and elsewhere, this comes to well over one hundred thousand jokes.

To ask a man his favorite few in that vast number is tantamount to having him choose the prettiest snowflake in a blizzard. However, newspaper columnists, magazine interviewers, and hosts on talk shows invariably asked Jack to name his favorite jokes, and

Jack always answered as though it were the first time he had been asked to do so. His list unfailingly included three or four favorites, but others were added and discarded as his memory dictated.

On June 16, 1969, Hank Grant (a noted radio commentator and the columnist for the trade paper *The Hollywood Reporter*) printed such a list. A few days after Jack passed away, Mr. Grant reprinted the column. I have received permission from Hank and *The Hollywood Reporter* to publish it in this chapter with Jack's original comments as they first appeared in Grant's column.

(When Jack Benny agreed to do a guest column for me, little did he know then what tremendous reaction it would receive. Portions of it were reprinted in newspapers across the country and Benny laughingly told me, "Gee, if I'd known that my first byline [he claimed it was his first and only one in anecdotal style] would be so popular, I could have sold it for a fortune; you got it free!" And Benny did not use a ghost writer or a press agent. He wrote every word himself in painstaking longhand. Benny said he was prouder of that column than anything he'd ever written, adding: "Everybody I talk to has read the darn thing! Of course, I have, too, a hundred times!" It is only fitting that we reprint his column as a memorial. I am sure he would have approved. . . . Hank Grant)

About twenty years ago on one of my programs I did a gag that got a terrific amount of nationwide publicity and is still getting it whenever a columnist discusses the great jokes of the past. The gag, which supposedly got the longest laugh that I have ever received in radio or television, was:

HOLDUP MAN

Your money or your life.

JACK

(Long pause—in fact one of my longest)

HOLDUP MAN

Quit stalling—I said your money or your life.

JACK

I'M THINKING IT OVER!

* * * * * *

Now here's another one we did that was good for a twenty-second audience reaction (and that's a long time):

MARY

Jack, why don't you stop being so stingy?

137

JACK

Mary, I'm not stingy, and you know it!

MARY

You're not, eh? . . . Last year when you were going to have your appendix removed, you wanted Rochester to do it.

JACK

I DID NOT. I merely asked him if he knew how.

* * * * * *

Now here's one, Hank, that I distinctly recall as being about as good a laugh as I could possibly desire. Rochester was raving about a new girlfriend and telling me how beautiful she was:

JACK

Well, Rochester, I've never heard you rave that much about any girl. Tell me, how beautiful is she?

ROCHESTER

Do you want me to describe her to you?

JACK

Yes.

ROCHESTER

MR. BENNY—DID YOU EVER SEE A HERSHEY BAR WITH ALL THE ALMONDS IN THE RIGHT PLACES?

* * * * * *

Here's one we did on television. The scene was my dressing room. Rochester had just taken a quarter out of my pants' pocket to tip a Western Union boy. About a minute later I entered and picked up my trousers to put them on. As I held my trousers in front of me, I "weighed" them for a couple of seconds. Then I turned to Rochester and said: "ROCHESTER, WHO TOOK A QUARTER OUT OF MY PANTS' POCKET?" This was about a fifteen-second scream.

* * * * * *

Here's another one. Mel Blanc played the part of my French violin teacher who was always disgusted with my tone and technique. During one of my lessons, the following episode took place:

JACK

Professor LeBlanc—do you think you can ever make a good violinist out of me?

MEL

I do not know. How old are you?

JACK

Why?

MEL

HOW MUCH TIME HAVE WE LEFT?

* * * * * *

Mary Livingstone got a laugh with *only three words.* She got it through her delivery in a very funny situation. Dorothy Kirsten and Don Wilson were discussing different operas.

DON

Oh, Miss Kirsten, I wanted to tell you that I saw you in "Madame Butterfly" Wednesday afternoon and I thought your performance was simply magnificent.

KIRSTEN

Well, that's awfully kind of you, Mr. Wilson, but who could help singing Puccini? It's so expressive—particularly the last act starting with the allegro vivacissimo.

DON

Well, that's being very modest, Miss Kirsten, but not every singer has the necessary bel canto and flexibility or the range to cope with the high tessitura of that first act.

KIRSTEN

Well, Mr. Wilson, didn't you think in the aria "Un Bel Di Vedremo" that the strings played the con molto exceptionally fine, with great sostenendo?

JACK

Well—I thought . . .

MARY

OH, SHUT UP.

Now, Hank, because of this very humorous situation, Mary's simple three words—"Oh, Shut Up"—practically stopped the show. If I had to choose only one bit as being the funniest, that's the one I would have to pick.

* * * * * *

The jokes listed by Jack in Grant's column are certainly among his favorites. During all interviews he invariably listed "Your Money or Your Life," because no reporter ever failed to ask about it. He also seldom failed to mention "Oh, shut up" and "Who took a quarter out of my pants' pocket?" The others in the list rated high in his private popularity poll, but here are some others of which he was especially fond.

There was one routine we used that had no punchline but got nearly a minute of continuous laughter from the audience. In the script Jack had to make a long distance phone call from Los Angeles to New York, and for plot purposes he made it on a public pay telephone. When he told the operator the number that he wanted in New York, she said, "That will be two dollars and fifty cents. Please deposit ten quarters." Jack asked, with a tinge of tears in his voice, "Ten quarters?" And the operator said, "Yes, sir. Deposit ten quarters." Jack said, "Yes, ma'am. Here they are." First we heard the sound of a quarter dropping into the coin slot of the pay phone and then the sound of a second quarter dropping in. As we heard the sound of the third quarter being deposited, very softly we heard the mournful notes of "Taps" being played on a bugle. The audience got the gag immediately and started screaming. The rest of the routine consisted of Jack dropping his quarters into the pay phone as a full chorus of "Taps" was played. There was no punch line in the accepted style of jokes, but the audience howled with delight as the bugler blew "Taps" from beginning to end. When Jack put in the last quarter, as the final notes of "Taps" faded away, there was spontaneous applause. This routine may not read as funny as some of the above gags, but it gave Jack as long and loud a laugh as anything he ever did.

* * * * * *

Another memorable moment had Jack and Rochester driving up to the studio gate. The guard shot at them and Jack said, "Don't you recognize me? I'm Jack Benny. I made a movie here at Warner Brothers—*The Horn Blows at Midnight*. Didn't you see it?" And the guard answered, "See it? I directed it."

* * * * * *

When we first started using Ronald and Benita Colman, the contrast between their dignified way of life compared to their alleged next-door neighbor, Jack Benny, gave us a fertile field for harvesting laughs. One of the biggest, and most simple, came in one of the very first shows on which we used the Colmans. They were discussing, with obvious distaste, the weird happenings that always seemed to be taking place at Benny's home next door—and the even weirder people who participated in them. On this particular program Colman was practically delivering a soliloquy on the short-comings of Jack and his cast, and as he ranted, Benita was munching on an apple. Finally Colman said, "And that Phil Harris' orchestra! Have you ever seen any of his musicians?" Very plaintively Benita said, "Please, Ronnie, not while I'm eating."

This joke is well over a quarter of a century old and has been repeated by numerous comics numerous times in numerous ways, but I'll wager that it never got the laugh it got when Benita Colman uttered the line so pleadingly.

* * * * * *

The Colmans always gave us superior programs, particularly because of the contrast between their dignity and Jack Benny's idiosyncrasies. We once did a series of jokes on a single show where Jack had come over to the Colmans, believing that he had been invited. Dennis Day, being an excellent mimic, was egged on by Phil Harris to phone Jack, imitate Colman's voice, and invite Jack to the party. At the party Colman was indignant that Benny was there, but Jack never realized that he was unwelcome and uninvited. He thought that he had been personally asked to come by Colman himself. Ronnie tried every ruse to rid himself of his unwelcome guest, and we had a couple of excellent laughs from the two following bits. They were discussing King Arthur and his Round Table, and Colman asked Jack what he thought of Sir Galahad. Jack answered, "Oh, he was a good knight." Ronnie shouted "Good night" and tried to usher Jack out. Then Ronnie turned the conversation to the stock market and asked Jack what he thought of R.C.A.'s stock. Jack answered, "R.C.A.? That's a good buy." Colman immediately yelled "Goodbye" and tried to shove Jack out of the door. We eventually used a couple of other versions of this gag, but those were the two that paid off most profitably.

* * * * * *

On one program we dramatized Jack Benny's biography, with George Jessel acting as narrator. Via this device we had Jessel do several monologue jokes describing Jack's childhood, and one of those jokes always remained among Jack's favorites. Jessel said: "In his youth Jack wasn't an only child. Jack had a younger sister named Florence. Today he has an older sister named Florence."

* * * * * *

In his opening monologue on one of his last TV specials, Jack decried the fact that almost anything appearing on television for sixty minutes or longer was called a "special." "I don't like programs being called specials," Jack said. "To me a special is when coffee goes from ninety-eight cents a pound to forty-nine cents."

* * * * * *

One show had Jack and Mary shopping in a department store, and Mary stopped at the cosmetics counter to purchase some perfume. After the salesgirl wrapped it, Mary opened her purse to pay for it. Jack suddenly inhaled deeply and said "Ooohh, that's a heavenly aroma. What is that I smell?" And Mary answered, "Money!"

* * * * * *

Jack also loved the follow-up snapper on the above joke. When Mary handed her a twenty dollar bill to pay for her perfume, the salesgirl rang it up, and we heard the unmistakable sound of a cash register. Jack happily whispered, "Listen, Mary, they're playing my song."

* * * * * *

On one occasion Jack returned home from the studio and was greeted by Rochester. Then Jack asked if there were any messages. "Yes, sir," said Rochester. "Your dentist and your barber called." "What did they say?" asked Jack. Rochester answered, "Both gave me the same message—you can pick 'em up tomorrow."

* * * * * *

Jack's taste in what should or shouldn't be aired on the program sometimes set standards in sophistication and subtlety. On the other hand he could "fall in love" with the most outrageous and outlandish puns. Two of these will suffice as examples.

The first occurred on an occasion when we had Barbara Stanwyck as a guest star. The proximity of Christmas turned the topic of conversation toward the holiday, and Jack broke the audience, and mostly himself, up, when he innocently asked Miss Stanwyck, "Do you believe in Santa, Barbara?" (On the West Coast, because Santa Barbara is a famed resort town an hour away from Los Angeles, this was a natural for a large laugh. In New York, I have a hunch that it would have gotten a small snicker.)

The second example occurred during a sketch when we had Gregory Ratoff, Irene Dunne, and Vincent Price as guests. The plot revolved around the fact that Jack wanted Ratoff to cast him in a particular role. Jack said, "I'm a good actor, I have box office appeal and I'll work cheap. I'll beat Vincent's Price."

* * * * * *

On that same show with Vincent Price, Irene Dunne, and Gregory Ratoff, there were two other jokes that Jack loved. When he

142

pleaded with Ratoff to let him supplant Vincent in the picture Ratoff was casting, the dialogue went like this:

RATOFF

Jack, you work in radio, don't you?

JACK

Yes.

RATOFF

You also appear in television?

JACK

Yes.

RATOFF

And you also act in nightclubs?

JACK

Yes.

RATOFF

Then please, let somebody else make a buck!

There then followed a beautifully written bit of business. In trying to convince Ratoff to use him instead of Vincent Price, Jack said, "Look, Mr. Ratoff, why don't you have me and Vincent compete for the part, and you can decide who is the best actor?" Price not only objected to this, but he coolly corrected Benny's grammar by saying, "You mean *better* actor, not *best*. If three or more were competing, then *best* would be correct. But since only two of us are involved, you should use the comparative, and *better* is correct. Not *best* actor, but *better* actor. I therefore suggest that before you think of competing with me for an acting assignment, it might be well if you first learned to speak English." At this point, to preserve peace, Irene Dunne served coffee. Ratoff and Price turned the beverage down, and only Jack and Miss Dunne drank it. Jack took one sip and then announced appreciatively, "This is the *better* coffee I ever tasted." Price screamed at him, "You mean the *best* coffee." And Jack screamed right back at him, "There are only *two* of us drinking it! Make up your mind!"

* * * * * *

While in a department store during one of our annual Christmas shopping shows, Jack complained to Mary that he couldn't think of

143

any gift to get for his new secretary. "And," he added, "it must be something special, because this secretary is special. She's tall, blonde, and beautiful, and has one of the greatest shapes I've ever seen. She's friendly and willing and able. She's the only secretary I ever had who's cheerful and cooperative and willing to work nights." Mary suggested, "Why don't you buy her a Scrabble set?" And Jack answered, "No, Mary, she can't spell."

* * * * * *

On one program a Western Union boy, riding a bicycle, delivered a telegram, and Jack gave him a tip. The boy's surprise and elation was so great that he said, "Gee, Mr. Benny. A whole dollar." Dazed by this generosity, he departed. A few seconds later the boy returned and sheepishly explained, "I forgot my bicycle." Jack snapped at the kid, "You didn't forget it. I bought it." Then he added, "I hate people who make deals and don't stick to them."

* * * * * *

In one script Jack was playing golf, with the ubiquitous Rochester acting as his caddy. During the game Benny lost a ball, and despite many minutes spent searching, they never found it. Jack finished his eighteen holes, and as he was driving home, he said, "Rochester, maybe we ought to go back to the golf course and look for my ball some more." Rochester replied: "We're never gonna find it. Why don't you give up?" Jack said angrily: "Give up? Give up? Rochester, supposing Columbus gave up? He never would have discovered America. Then what would have happened?" Rochester answered: "We'd be looking for that ball in Spain, Boss."

* * * * * *

Mel Blanc, as Professor LeBlanc, complained after one violin lesson that Jack hadn't paid him. Jack said, "Oh, how thoughtless of me, Professor. Have a chair." LeBlanc answered, "No, no, no! I had a chair last time. This time I want money."

* * * * * *

Prior to a scene when he was going to descend to the lower depths where his vault was located, Jack remembered that this happened to be the birthday of Ed, the keeper of the vault, so he brought him a present. When he reached the bottom of the tunnel where the vault was, Jack made a little ceremony of presenting the birthday gift to Ed, who lived in the vault six hundred feet below ground. Ed took it and said, "Oh thank you, Mr. Benny. I've always wanted a kite."

* * * * * *

On one program Jack was bragging that he had lunched with Edgar Bergen. Phil Harris said, "Yeah, I heard about you eating with Bergen. You even picked up the check yourself." Jack replied: "Yes, and that's the last time I'll ever eat with a ventriloquist."

* * * * * *

When we shifted our radio show from NBC to CBS, it was well publicized that the move was initiated or consummated by the head of that network, William Paley. On our initial show on CBS, Phil Harris greeted Jack by saying, "Well, if it isn't Paley's Comic."

* * * * * *

During one show the cast was discussing a bit of then current news about astronomers expecting the appearance of a small comet in the skies. Don Wilson asked: "Jack, did you ever see Haley's Comet?" And Mary answered, "Twice!"

* * * * * *

Once Rochester informed Jack that he had broken up with his girlfriend because she was now going out with another guy on account of his money. Jack asked, "Oh, does he have a lot of money?" And Rochester answered, "No, but he has *some*."

* * * * * *

In burlesquing the plot of the motion picture *Gaslight,* Jack, as the villainous husband, tried to make his wife, portrayed by Barbara Stanwyck, think she was going crazy by moving furniture around, by making the lights in the house grow dimmer and brighter, and also by turning pictures and other things upside down. During a tense dramatic moment in this comedy, Jack yelled at Barbara, "You're going crazy! Crazy, crazy, crazy!" Then Barbara began to whimper and cry, and through her sobs she said, "It's you who are doing these things. You turned the table upside down. You turned the chairs upside down. You turned the pictures upside down. Yesterday I made an upside down cake and you turned it right side up."

* * * * * *

We once did a very different type of television sketch where Jack's home was burglarized while he slept through the entire event. The burglars were frustrated in their attempts to get money or valuables out of Benny's home. Everything was booby-trapped,

including the safe. When they opened the safe they found themselves face-to-face with the head of a huge, live, snarling Bengal
tiger. This frightened them so much that they tried to rush out of
the house via the window through which they entered. However
the window was now locked, and there was a sign on it saying, "To
exit, please deposit 25 cents."

The sketch was unique because the star on the show, Jack Benny,
slept through the entire routine while the mystified burglars
(played by Mel Blanc and Benny Rubin) got every single laugh in
the sketch. Jack just lay in his bed, eyes closed, pretending to sleep.

The next scene showed Jack waking up in the morning and realizing that he had been visited by burglars. He picked up the telephone, dialed Information, mentioned that he had been robbed, and
said that he wanted the telephone number of the police station. The
operator said, "The number is Hollywood 9, 9 . . ." Jack interrupted
her by saying, "No, no, I want to call the Beverly Hills police station." And the operator answered, "I'm sorry, sir, but that's an
unlisted number." The program concluded with this big laugh
caused by both the unseen telephone operator's line and the expression on Jack's face.

* * * * * *

Selecting the top ten of the hundreds of thousands of Jack's jokes
is an invitation to debates with all those who had their own favorites. The ones I have mentioned I know ranked highest in Jack's
own opinion. And of them all, the most quoted and famous, which
was cited in almost every obituary on Jack, was "Your money or
your life." Every interviewer on television, radio, or the printed
media asked him about its origin, and despite the wide publicity it
has received, it bears repeating here.

The joke was first aired on the radio program of March 28, 1948. It
was actually created accidentally, and John Tackaberry and I happened to be the midwives. We were writing a program where Jack
was supposed to have borrowed Ronald Colman's Oscar and then a
crook stole it from him. This was to lead to programs on subsequent
weeks when we'd do shows with other Academy Award winners as
guest stars, with Jack borrowing each one's Oscar and returning it
to the preceding week's guest—but always leaving him one Oscar
behind.

As we started to write the scene with the holdup man, I paced the
floor while Tackaberry reclined on the sofa. We threw a few tenta-
tive lines at each other, none worthy of discussion. Then I thought
of a funny feed line but couldn't get a suitable punch to finish it. I
told this to "Tack," saying, "Suppose we have the crook pull the
classic threat on Jack, 'Your money or your life.' Jack will get

screams just staring at the crook and the audience—and if we get a good snapper on it, it'll be great."

Tackaberry seemingly ignored me. I kept thinking of lines and discarding them as mediocre or worse. Finally one line seemed better than the rest, and I threw it at him, half-confidently: "Look, John, the crook says, 'Your money or your life,' and Jack stares at him and then at the audience, and then the crook repeats it and says, 'Come on, you heard me—your money or your life?' and Jack says, 'You mean I have a choice?' "

Now frankly that wasn't too bad an answer, but Tackaberry made no comment, good or bad. I got angry and yelled, "Dammit, if you don't like my lines, throw a couple of your own. Don't just lay there on your fat butt daydreaming. There's got to be a great answer to 'Your money or your life.' "

In reply, Tackaberry angrily snapped at me, "I'm thinking it over."

In a split second we were both hysterical. We knew we could never top that.

In almost every interview since that joke was first broadcast, Jack would always be asked about its origin. And since we had told him about it, he related the story on practically every talk show on the air: Johnny Carson's, Merv Griffin's, Jack Paar's, and all the others.

Shortly before he passed away I was discussing this joke with Jack, and I told him that I had what I thought was a funny idea. I suggested that the next time he was on a talk show and was asked what writer or writers wrote the joke "Your money or your life" and the subsequent punch line "I'm thinking it over," Jack should stare at his interviewer and say, "What writers? Nobody wrote it. That was an incident from real life."

Jack got hysterical at this, and it was the last time I ever made him fall to the floor—and in a new suit yet. Then he said, "Milt, it's very, very funny, but I couldn't do that. It might sound as if I didn't want to give my writers credit."

That was Jack—always giving credit where credit was due, even if it meant losing a big laugh.

15
The Way Jack Worked

While the cast, crew, writers, and technicians were important and integral parts of the program's success, the ever-present motivating force behind it all was Jack Benny himself. No other star in broadcasting paid more attention to each and every detail, no matter how minute, than he did.

Supposedly, he lacked a sense of humor and couldn't construct comedy, but he worked with his writers constantly. True, they completed the first rough drafts without him, but he was always in attendance when the script was polished and cut prior to the first rehearsal reading by the cast. Then, after each of the repeated rehearsals and readings, he served as a fifth writer.

Casting was not a chore left to the devices and whims of a producer, director, or agency executive. No other star was as careful in molding the auxiliary characters to be portrayed or in selecting the performers to play these roles. On rare occasions, he would cast a needy actor or friend for a very minor role, but when it was a vital routine, he disregarded personal feelings and financial needs. He always went first class.

He was the unquestionable boss, but no dictator, and he respected every craftsman connected with his series. Sound men, technicians, and musicians had their say, but his was the final word. Yet there was an admirable flexibility about him. He could be wild about a routine, gag, or bit of business, but if even just one writer in the group questioned its value or humor, he would engage us all in a serious debate concerning its merits. However, he was rarely shaken from a script decision if he and the writers unanimously backed it. No performer or group of performers was likely to change his mind, though he would discuss it with them and the writers. If his script staff stood firm, so did he.

In the days of radio and the embryonic television years, most name-comics owned the shows on which they starred. Today the number of series owned and operated by the stars keeps diminishing. Years ago the star was the show. Today, the show is the star.

In the past, the Bennys, Hopes, Allens, Berles, Burnses, Ozzies, Fibbers, and Skeltons had the final word regarding their radio programs, and those who converted to television continued to do so. And the newcomers who were making names for themselves on the tube, such as Lucille Ball, Sid Caesar, Martin and Lewis, and Jackie Gleason, were the stars of their shows, dominating them and devoting much time to developing the programs, but no one was as conscientious as Jack.

In the next few chapters, I will attempt to give illustrations and examples of how Jack worked, and how he compared in this respect with his peers. These habits of his went into the making of Jack as both a person and a personality.

16
Jack Vs. the Other Comedians

Because I wrote for both Jack Benny and Bob Hope I have been often asked to compare the Jack Benny series to Bob Hope's programs. However, comparisons are usually odious, and in this instance they are definitely difficult. My loyalties lay with both of them, and so did my respect. Each was vastly different from the other, yet very much the same. Therefore the following opinions are merely that—opinions—and personal opinions at that.

In the early and mid-1940s, Jack's almost constant ranking as the "Number One Comic" of the airwaves was seriously challenged and often topped by Bob Hope. In that era the country was concentrating on its war effort, and the tempo of the times had speeded up. Hope certainly had speed. From his earliest radio series—and he had several before he began to click in a big way—he used a Gatling gun delivery. We writers with Bob tried to write our gag lines as short as possible, and we quipped that anyone who knew how to work in funny punctuation would rule the roost.

On the other hand, Jack maintained his leisurely pacing even though his ratings were threatened and occasionally bested by Hope's fast frenetic funnies. For example, at that time Henry J. Kaiser, who eventually went on to smaller things as the producer of the Kaiser-Frazer cars, was our most publicized supplier of war material—mainly ships. Hope once did a monologue about the speed and efficiency of Kaiser's shipbuilding. One of the lines went: "I dropped my cigarette lighter. Before I could pick it up, they had put a keel and decks on it, hit it over the top with a bottle of champagne, and it was halfway to Guadalcanal with a load of Sherman tanks." Two or three other similar gags rounded out the routine on Henry Kaiser's shipbuilding speed, and then Hope grasshoppered his monologue to another topical subject for several more quick quips. He would advise his audience, "Laugh first, figure them out later."

Conversely, if Jack Benny and his cast visited the Kaiser shipyards they would do practically an entire show describing the visit and each cast member's experience and/or surprise at the rapidity with which the ships went from the construction of the keel to the final launching. Jack would have a very funny show, but with his casual pace his entire program would have approximately sixty laughs. Hope would concentrate half that many gags in the first four minutes of his opening monologue, and the rest of his show would zoom along with the seeming speed of light.

They were both masters of timing and almost without equal in delivering a punch line or acting as a stooge or straight man for their various cast members. Jack could milk a laugh with a stare, but Bob was no mean mugger himself. A certain electricity charged the air and the applause usually culminated in standing ovations when either of them stepped on the stage. Hope's receptions eventually became louder and more spontaneous at the initial entrance, but they ran a dead heat in audience appreciation during their performances and at their exits.

The main difference I could discern between them was that Hope was comparable to the brilliant star of a Broadway revue—a Ziegfeld production where he did specialties, sketches, and monologues with no connective thread—while Benny, on the other hand, starred in carefully constructed comedies, miniature plays with each line a laugh in itself, and yet a build-up for something to come later on. Such an analysis would seem to indicate that Jack was the superior actor of the two. Yet when it came to movies, Hope scored smash after smash, sometimes solo, but frequently aided and abetted by his "Road" partner, Bing Crosby. On the other hand, Jack made several pictures which got rave reviews, but his movie success did not approach Bob's. Yet basically, to a large extent, both Bob and Jack portrayed extensions of their radio characters on the screen.

This prelude has been wordy, but it was a necessity if we wish to furnish an accurate comparison of Jack with other comics. Bob's career, in many ways, ran parallel to Jack's, especially in his attitude to writers. Unfortunately this has not always been true of all comedians.

When Dean Martin and Jerry Lewis scored the biggest success on TV since Milton Berle became "Uncle Miltie," they were extremely lucky to sign two bright young comedy writers named Norman Lear and Ed Simmons. Ed Simmons has had numerous excellent credits since then and is currently the head writer on what is probably the best of the variety offerings on the air, *The Carol Burnett Show.* Norman Lear, in collaboration with Bud Yorkin, has made a monetary liar out of Newton Minow who once referred to television as "a vast wasteland." Lear has the alchemist's touch and has turned this waste into gold. Lear and Yorkin started dominating the TV tube with their precedent-shattering *All in the Family,* which quickly begat *Maude,* which in turn begat *Good Times* (starring Maude's maid, Florida). Then *All in the Family* also begat *The Jeffersons,* and somewhere along the way the Lear-Yorkin combine managed to find time to conceive *Sanford and Son.*

Now in addition to all these imposing credits, both Lear and Simmons have movie credits and other achievements, any of which would be sufficient glory for a lesser writer. However, back in the early 1950s they were just breaking in, and they had attached their wagon to Martin and Lewis. They got a glorious ride, and in many ways the wagon pushed the stars.

This eventually led to their departure from the highly successful series. Their salary as writers kept rising until they were being paid the startling sum of ten thousand four hundred dollars for each program, thus making them the then highest paid two-man team in television. Norman and Ed enjoyed this status, but they realized that success in the industry is ephemeral and can be a one-time thing, because you can have an unbroken string of successes, but you're only as good as your last show. Therefore, they reputedly hired a press agent to exploit their achievements. All of this seemed to irritate Jerry Lewis. One day, according to Arthur Marx's incisive biography of Martin and Lewis, *Everybody Loves Somebody Sometime (Especially Himself),* Lewis suddenly lost his temper while sitting in producer Ernie Glucksman's office, "picked up the telephone, dialed Simmons' and Lear's press agent, and screeched into the mouthpiece, 'This is Jerry Lewis. I have a hot news item for you. Simmons and Lear are fired.'" And he wasn't kidding.

Shock waves rippled through the industry where the slogan seemed to be: "Never tamper with success." From a legal standpoint it was known that Simmons and Lear had an ironclad contract, and even though Dean and Jerry hastily hired a new battery of writers, four this time, Ed and Norman had to be paid ten thousand four hundred dollars for every script they turned in, even if those scripts were eventually consigned to the wastebasket—which they were.

The story of the scripting schism startled the entire industry. Everyone was amazed, but none more so than Jack Benny and his writers. We couldn't comprehend this case of the dog being upset because the tail wagged. Benny always lavished praise on his writers in private and in print. And during my five years with Bob Hope, prior to going to work for Jack, I frequently heard Bob extol his writers. The same was true of Lucille Ball and most of the top comedy performers.

Most, but not all. Many comics like Jack Benny made major contributions to their scripts but rarely took credit. Some, however, insisted on their names being listed on the credit crawls as a full-fledged member of the writing staff. Prominent among these was Red Skelton.

Red is a complex personality who has often been the subject of conjecture and gossip among his peers. There is no doubt that he did make contributions to his program material, but whether it was sufficient to entitle him to writing credit, and thus to sharing writing residuals on reruns, is debatable. One incident, based upon his claim for credit, has become a legend in the industry.

Red was making an appearance on one of the late-night talk shows, and as his contribution he performed several pantomime vignettes, for which he received thunderous and well-deserved applause. When he seated himself next to the host for the usual chit-chat and banter, he was asked how he got the ideas for these routines. A beatific glow brightened the comic's countenance as he gazed heavenward and said, in effect, "I don't know. I get up to perform and God tells me what to do."

Some of Red's writers saw this particular program, and while they didn't deny that the Almighty may have had something to do with Skelton's performance, they didn't recall Him being in the room when they sweated out the routines on their typewriters. Since they received no cash when Red repeated routines, they felt that they should at least be credited with originating them.

The writers registered their objections with a CBS executive, and he in turn conveyed them to the comic. However, Skelton ignored their complaints, telling an interviewer that his writers were so egotistical that they demanded top billing over God.

In his book *The Funny Men*, an analysis of sixteen top comics at the time of its publication (1956) by Steve Allen (a pretty funny man himself), Steve quotes Jack in one of his rare, seemingly immodest moments as saying: "I may not be the world's greatest comedian, but I think I am at least one of its most successful performers. And I have an explanation for this success. I work closely with my writers, who are darn good ones. I act mainly as their editor, *but my writers are everything.*" (The italics are mine.)

Leaving the subject of writers for the moment, let's go on to further comparisons between Jack and other comedians, beginning with Milton Berle. Berle is brash and bombastic, while Jack was always soft-spoken and mild-mannered. Berle became "Mr. Television" because, among other comic gimmicks, he mugged outrageously, while Jack was the master of the quiet stare or the hurt look, and an expressive monosyllabic "Well!" or "Hmmmmm" was all he needed to convey his feelings.

I am in no way denigrating Milton, a man who was very kind and generous to me, when I reveal these things. In his recently published autobiography, *Milton Berle,* written with Haskel Frankel, Berle discusses this facet of his humor frankly and openly. He tells how, after a smashingly successful multi-year run on the *Texaco Star Theatre,* he began a new series in which it was decided that instead of being simply a variety show devoid of continuity, he would follow a format in which he had a regular cast of characters in a loosely connected type of situation comedy. He started with a new staff of writers headed by the talented Goodman Ace. Goody was an erudite man, a one-time drama critic, and also the star of his own radio show, *Easy Aces,* with his wife Jane. Additionally, Berle was fond of him as both a man and a talent.

In his book, Milton tells of his squeamishness in breaking away from his old format, but he writes of Goody with the respect Ace deserves, even though Milton wasn't too happy with his efforts. Berle says, "I drove him a little crazy by always telling him he had to make the jokes more 'lappy.' In time Goody came to me and confessed he didn't know what the hell I was talking about when I used the word 'lappy.' " "Then," writes Uncle Miltie, "I explained that the jokes had to be laid in the audience's *lap.*" Hence "lappy." That was Berle's style—the pie in the face, the pratfall, the seltzer squirt, the walking on his ankles, the blacked-out teeth, the outrageous costumes. And for Berle's type of humor it was most effective. I'm sure that even the most sophisticated viewers were more than occasionally broken up by Berle's "lappy" routines.

On the other hand, Benny's approach was almost the antithesis. I first realized this during my early weeks in his employ. We needed a line for a situation, and all the writers kept offering their efforts. Finally I threw one gag that broke him up, and I felt smugly self-satisfied. When he stopped laughing, he said, "Okay, fellows, let's try to get that line." I said, "Jack, I thought you liked the line I threw. You even laughed at it." "I did," he explained. Then he added, almost apologetically, "But, Milt, that's a *joke!*"

Jack said the word "joke" as though he were afraid that the gods of comedy were going to wash out his mouth with soap. And although Jack did innumerable jokes, they were usually based on the strong characters of his cast. The other writers and I soon learned that if we had an out-and-out joke, we had better clothe it in the character of one of the cast members before we offered it to Jack.

On several occasions we had bits of humor that were extremely subtle, and the writers, including Jack, argued whether the humor was too obscure and whether perhaps these quips might benefit if we broadened them. I shall offer a few examples of this here to illustrate Jack's craftsmanship.

Jack occasionally—once or twice a season—called on the excellent team of Hugh Wedlock and Howard Snyder to write a script and take the pressure off us. One such script they wrote was a takeoff on the one-woman radio playlet, so ably performed by Agnes Moorehead, entitled *Sorry, Wrong Number*. In this brief tour de force, a woman, via crossed telephone wires, overhears a plot to murder her, and the entire action of the show concerns her futile efforts to phone various people who might help her.

The playlet was so popular that it was repeated several times on the air. Wedlock and Snyder wrote a great parody on it where Jack, trying to reach his sponsor on the phone, gets cut in on a crossed wire where he hears his sponsor's voice say, "Well, if you feel he's been with us too long, let him go." Jack immediately jumps to the conclusion that he is the subject of the discussion and that his contract is about to be terminated. He frantically tries to phone anyone who might possibly help him. After several calls, Jack suddenly gets a thought and says to himself, "I ought to call my agent. This is something my agent should be doing for me. After all, why am I paying him his nine percent?"

In the rewrite session this line, a perfect example of pure character humor, caused a long discussion. Some of the writers thought that the average listener wasn't familiar with agents. Another thought that nine percent wasn't funny, explaining that a tightwad like Jack would cut his agent's commission at least in half to five percent. Jack ended the discussion by saying, "Fellows, it's enough that I'm chiseling one lousy percent from my agent's commission. Nine percent almost makes it sound as though I'm taking ten percent of his ten percent. Five percent is too blunt and broad. I'd rather get a chuckle with nine percent than a big boff with five percent." Therefore, he did it on the air as nine percent, and he got not a chuckle, but a big, beautiful boff.

As another example, Jack used to do informal monologues on his radio shows in contrast to the more traditional ones with which Bob Hope opens every program. Bob comes out, stands stage center, and tells several minutes of very funny jokes about anything that's topical at the time. Jack occasionally opened his TV hour specials this way, but on radio he did monologues in an informal manner. He'd be walking down the street, the soundman would furnish appropriate noises of traffic, footsteps, birds, etc., and as Jack walked he would talk to himself about the neighbors, whose houses he was passing, and any other suitable subject. On this particular program the plot premise was based on the fact that the preceding night Jack had thrown a party for his cast, and they were all angry at him because he didn't have a television set. (They were comparatively new then.) Thus, in the script, Jack was walking to a store to inquire about the price of a TV set. John Tackaberry wrote the routine with me and we had what we thought were two good gags, but felt we needed a third. The lines we had Jack say, as he walked, were: "I don't know why everyone got so mad at me because we couldn't watch television. When I invited them I felt sure we'd all watch television. How was I to know that Ronald Colman would pull down his shade. . . . Gee, Claudette Colbert's house looks nice since she had it painted, but I can't understand why a big star like her doesn't get those dirty curtains in her windows cleaned. Especially since this month I'm having a special, three for a dollar." Then we added another line. We had Jack say, "I think when I get to the TV store, I may buy a new phonograph record. The gang keeps complaining that they're tired of dancing to 'Cohen on the Telephone.'" Now the first two jokes in the "monologue" were joint efforts, but the third one was exclusively mine. I take credit for it not out of ego, but because Tackaberry didn't know what I was talking about when I threw the line. Frankly, the reason I remembered the record was because when I was a pre-kindergarten kid, my dad had a phonograph store, and I would listen to customers in the store playing "Cohen on the Telephone," possibly the first comedy record ever made, and certainly one of the earliest successes in this field.

Born in Australia and raised in Texas, Tackaberry was an Episcopalian and he had never heard of the record in which a Yiddish-accented man named Cohen tries to get his landlord on the telephone to register a complaint. The record was a one-way monologue starting with Cohen explaining to his landlord, in a thick Yiddish accent, "This is your new tenant Cohen. . . . Your *new tenant* Cohen. . . . No, no—not *Lieutenant* Cohen." It may sound trite and tired today, but in those days it was Neil Simon, and from hearing the record over and over in Pop's store, I could recite it nearly verbatim at the age of four. My mom nipped my talent for elocution in the bud because I was imitating Cohen's accent, and she didn't want it to happen that any of her American-born children "should talk like greenhorns."

I was amazed that Tackaberry had never even heard of the record, and I asked him as a special favor to let me include the line in the script, if only for Jack's amusement. On simple matters like this, we always were amiable, since no single short line could hurt a script. The gag stayed in our first draft for Jack's approval.

When we had our reading on Friday, Jack Benny hit the floor when he read the joke. With his usual enthusiasm, he turned to the others, saying, "Isn't that great!" Sam Perrin, older than I was by several years, and also Jewish, agreed. However Sam's collaborator, George Balzer, the youngest of the writing quartet and a devout Catholic, said, "Jack, I don't know what it means." Also our script secretary, Jeanette Eymann, much younger than any of us, confessed that she failed to understand the humor of it. Jack then said a line he often used during these script conferences: "If we can't devote fifteen seconds in a half-hour program for our own amusement, we're in the wrong business."

Then one of the writers suggested that the lines be changed to: "I may buy a new phonograph record. The gang keeps complaining that they're tired of dancing to that old comedy record, 'Cohen on the Telephone.'" Jack made a face and said, "If I have to lay it out for them by saying 'that old comedy record,' I'd rather not do it." The argument continued for a few more minutes until Jack suddenly came up with an excellent bit of logic. He said, "Fellows, let's suppose that there never was a record called 'Cohen on the Telephone.' The title sounds funny, and the mere fact that I would have a record called 'Cohen on the Telephone' should get a laugh."

Jack did the joke on the program the following Sunday. It got a nice laugh—much bigger than a chuckle, but smaller than a boff. Whether the audience laughed because they remembered the record or because the title sounded funny, I'll never know. But I do know that when we finished the program and Jack came offstage there was a person-to-person call from New York for Jack from famed composer Cole Porter who was confined to a hospital with leg injuries. According to Jack, Porter said to him, "You owe me the price of setting both legs in casts. That joke about 'Cohen on the Telephone' made me laugh so hard that I fell out of bed." To a sophisticated man like Cole Porter who was old enough to remember the famed recording, the fact that Jack, with his miserly reputation, would make his cast dance while he played this ancient comedy routine on his phonograph was the epitome of hilarious humor. That phone call from Cole, plus the reaction that the line got from the audience, made it all worthwhile to Jack.

The final example I will offer of Jack going for the subtle, rather than broader and more sure-fire humor, concerns the Yiddish-flavored Mr. Kitzle.

On one radio show we were doing a favorite formula program

with Jack and the cast taking the train to New York. Mel Blanc's announcements, with appropriate funny endings, came booming over the public address system: "Train leaving on Track Five for Anaheim, Azusa, and Cuc-------amonga." Jack ran into Sheldon Leonard as the tout, Frank Nelson (Yesssssss) as the ticket seller, and all the old reliables. Finally he met Mr. Kitzle. They exchanged greetings and expressed surprise at seeing each other. Then Jack asked him where he was going. Kitzle answered that he wasn't going anywhere but was just there to meet his son who was coming home from college. Jack asked "What college?" and Kitzle, in his thick Yiddish accent, answered, "Southern Methodist." The answer had caused a debate among the writers. Wouldn't Notre Dame be funnier? Wouldn't the audience get it quicker if Kitzle's answer was "Texas Christian"? Now both of these answers, I'm sure, would have gotten an excellent response, but Jack turned them down on the grounds that they were too obvious. He said: " 'Texas Christian' lays it on the line too broadly. It says Christian. So does 'Notre Dame.' 'Southern Methodist' is a bit more subtle. It takes a split second to realize that Methodist means Christian." It stayed Southern Methodist, and the line was received with a long laugh and loud applause.

With all due respect to Milton Berle, Jack never made the jokes "lappy."

17
Jack's Sense of Humor

After Jack and his first writer, Harry Conn, parted company some forty years ago, Conn dismissed his ex-boss' creative ability saying "Jack Benny couldn't ad-lib a belch after a Hungarian dinner," a put-down which had more humor than fact in it. Nevertheless, it remains one of the most denigrating oft-quoted canards in show business. Like so many critical cracks of the past, it probably would have been long forgotten except that it was quoted too frequently. And the man who quoted it most often was Jack Benny himself.

Jack loved this libelous line. He thought it was brilliant and true. Brilliant it was; true it wasn't. The format of his program, almost a situation comedy, gave him little opportunity to deviate from the script during a broadcast. And even when he did ad-lib, it was usually about his inability to ad-lib.

The best known example of this occurred when he was a guest star on a Fred Allen radio show, and Fred suddenly abandoned the script and speared Benny with several extemporaneous barbs. After the third one Jack turned on Fred and snapped, "You wouldn't dare talk to me like that if my writers were here."

Jack made hundreds of appearances on the talk shows hosted by Johnny Carson, Jack Paar, Joey Bishop, Merv Griffin, Dick Cavett,

Mike Wallace, Dinah Shore, "Kup," and many others. He never went on these programs with prepared material, but handled all questions asked him, no matter how unusual, or personal, with a remarkably high and humorous batting average. Yet the legend persists that he lacked a sense of humor.

For some unfathomable reason Jack actually believed that he had no or little sense of humor. He'd publicly pull quips like, "If somebody sneezes, I'll need at least two writers to help me ad-lib 'Gesundheit.' "

He'd also make up jokes about what a miser he was, thus lending life to another legend. Jack explained it to me once by saying, "It's the easiest subject there is. The public has been educated to it for all these years and if I say something about being cheap, they are so accustomed to laugh at lines like these that mine need only be mildly amusing and still get a good laugh." That's a pretty sound analysis of a comedic angle by a man who allegedly lacked a sense of humor.

Jack didn't simply have a sense of humor. He actually had two definite senses of humor. He was doubtlessly the best editor and judge of material that the comedy world ever knew. He had an unerring instinct for what was funny, and how to use it to make him funnier. And, he had unfailing faith in his ability, and every one of his writers respected it. An incident indicative of this happened because of a headline event in the international financial world.

The theme of that Sunday's show had been set, and the writing of the script was divided at what we considered mid-point between the two teams. Balzer and Perrin took one half; Tackaberry and I took the other. While we were writing our assignments the newspapers suddenly ran big headlines concerning the fact that England had devalued the pound.

Radio writers knew that if the audience realized the humor was as current as the daily headlines, they would appreciate the lines more. So it was only natural that when England devalued the pound, and both teams of writers were working on their halves of the script, each section would have a reference to this event. John Tackaberry and I had a scene where Rochester was being helped with his housework by his friend, Roy. Roy asked Rochester if Mr. Benny was as eccentric as he had heard, and Rochester answered: "Even more so. He still does things that I don't understand. After all the years I've been with him, this week for some strange reason he started paying me my salary in English pounds." While Tackaberry and I dismissed this devaluation situation with a single line, Perrin and Balzer wrote a routine where Don Wilson, our rotund, obese announcer claimed that he now only weighed 150 pounds because England devalued the pound. George and Sam had written four funny pages on this situation and it represented Don Wilson's entire performance on that particular program.

Tackaberry and I realized that if our joke was cut, it needn't even be replaced because we had written a sufficiently long and funny routine with Rochester. We suggested cutting out our joke since we couldn't do both it and the Don Wilson routine. While we loved topical humor, we never knowingly belabored it. If Jack decided to retain our gag, this meant we would have to write a completely new routine for Don Wilson. Our writing rivals immediately concurred with our suggestion, and they admitted to Jack that our line was definitely funny, but so was their four-page routine. Jack, however, wouldn't listen to us.

I believe this was one of the few times that Jack went against the combined efforts of his four writers. He launched his logical attack against Tackaberry and me. He said, "Fellows, evidently you thought it was very funny or you wouldn't have put it in the script." We couldn't deny this. Then he turned to Perrin and Balzer and said, "Even though you've made your material topical, basically it's another 'Don Wilson Fat' routine, and we do jokes about Wilson's weight almost every other program." Sam and George admitted this. "So," Jack said, "let's stop stalling and write another spot for Don."

We did this, and I don't remember what we did for Don, but I do know that Rochester's line, "This week he started paying me my salary in English pounds," was greeted by loud laughter plus applause from the appreciative audience. In the following days we received many clippings from critics' reviews proclaiming the gag as the funniest one done on the devaluation of the pound.

While Jack's judgment and sense of humor in editing scripts was impeccable, his personal sense of humor, and by that I mean the gags he pulled, ranged from childishly corny to ultra sophisticated. Here are some examples:

Sam and Peggy Perrin once threw a party for the cast and writers. It was a casual affair, and everybody was there when we noticed the obvious absence of Jack and Mary. The Perrins began to worry that the Bennys had forgotten the date, or worse yet, decided not to attend. Then the doorbell rang. Sam opened the door and got hysterical. Standing in the doorway stood Jack Benny, every inch the society man wearing top hat, white tie, gloves, tailcoat, and Bermuda shorts. He made an entrance like a leading man in a Noël Coward comedy. He entered, closed the door without a word, then slowly and elegantly removed his gloves finger by finger without uttering one word. Then he announced in an overly exaggerated English accent, "My darling wife, Marrrrrrry, wouldn't ac-

161

company me because she inferred that I was a bit of a *schmuck!*"
Mary came in a few minutes later, but all through the evening Jack
talked in affected English tones, and kept breaking everybody up,
most of all himself.

* * * * * *

Early in Jack's radio career he began to out-rank the then ruler
of the rating roost, Eddie Cantor. They were on the air on different
nights and Cantor claimed that Jack had an unfair advantage because Benny broadcast on Sunday, and Eddie did his show on a
weekday. And because of this, Cantor did an unprecedented thing.
He convinced his sponsor and network to put his program on Sundays, with his time slot opposite Benny's. That way, he stated, both
comics would be in direct competition with each other, and the public would decide which was the more popular. The date of the first
face-to-face broadcast was publicized so much that there were fist
fights in families over which comic they would listen to, and the
situation caused a couple of divorces. I listened to Benny, and that
week, his first one opposed by Eddie Cantor's program, Jack did a
show with a sketch based on pirates. The blackout of Benny's
broadcast had him captured by the pirates and he was about to
meet his doom in the customary manner of execution by pirates. He
was to walk the plank. As we heard his footsteps walking the plank
the pirate leader asked him if he had any last words and Jack said,
"Yes. I wonder what Eddie Cantor's doing now."

This was a shocking statement because in those early days it was
unthinkable to mention a rival program or even network. Jack's
writers at the time had a different blackout for the show, and half
kidding, half seriously, Jack told them, "Wouldn't it be funny if I
could get away with saying, 'I wonder what Eddie Cantor's doing
now'?" The writers howled at Jack's line, and they loved the audac-
ity of it. Encouraged by their attitude Jack quickly got the consent
of both his network and sponsor and did one of the smartest lines
ever heard on radio.

(P.S. The one-to-one confrontation between the Benny and Cantor shows lasted just a few short weeks with Jack outdistancing
Eddie badly. In fact, Cantor's ratings in his weekday time slot were
always excellent, but bucking Benny they were less than mediocre.
Cantor got out of the situation gracefully via a press statement
saying, "It's unfair to ask the American public to choose between
two of their favorites, and since Jack Benny had the Sunday time
slot first, I'll return to my former weekday time.")

* * * * * *

When Jimmy Cagney was cast in the lead of *Yankee Doodle*

Dandy, for which he won the Academy Award, Jack made up a joke which he told frequently. He said that he went to Jack L. Warner, head of Warner Bros. and producer of the picture, and complained that he, and not Cagney, should get the part. Then, Benny said, Mr. Warner looked me in the eye and said, "Jack, this picture is based on the life of George M. Co*han.* If it was Co*hen,* you'd get the part."

* * * * * *

Prior to the season starting in September, 1943, Jack's radio programs were written by the incomparable team of Bill Morrow and Ed Beloin. Bill, a jovial balding bachelor, loved liquor. And although I have heard the story from Ed Beloin personally, as well as several other sources, I'll quote it directly from Maurice Zolotow's *Cosmopolitan* magazine treatise.

> Once, Benny and his writers were on the Sante Fe Chief to do several broadcasts in Chicago and New York. Morrow had installed himself in the club car and was getting stiff. Just before dinner, Benny found a seat in the club car and watched with incredulous eyes as his writer sponged up one slug after another. Suddenly, Morrow, who was at the bar, started to prance toward Jack, lost his balance and fell flat on the floor with a heavy thud. Then he slowly pulled himself up. He rubbed his face. He lurched to the bar. He promptly ordered himself another drink.
>
> "I'm glad you did that, Bill," Benny called out. "I'm glad you got up on your feet and went right back to that bar like a man. Otherwise you'd always have been afraid to take a drink."

* * * * * *

A few years after I left Jack Benny I became the Head Writer and Script Consultant on Lucille Ball's *The Lucy Show*—not to be confused with her earlier series, *I Love Lucy,* or her last series, *Here's Lucy.* Television is a transitory trade and for a writer to remain with a situation comedy series for more than one year is a rarity. Two years is a career. Three years or longer is a miracle. (It may sound like bragging, possibly because it is, but my personal record of having spent seven years with Bob Hope, twelve years with Jack Benny, and eight years with Lucille Ball is a record for longevity in a field of quick turnovers.) At any rate, after eight years with Lucy, I left her under the most amiable conditions.

When I did leave Lucy it was a newsworthy subject for the Hollywood trade papers, and both *Daily Variety* and the *Hollywood Reporter* carried stories. Both news items were flatteringly long, telling of my triple hyphenate function with Miss Ball as "Script Consultant-Head Writer-Writer," and also mentioning the fact that I had created her current format. The news stories then told of my future plans and past achievements in broadcasting. But the gist of both stories was the fact that I left Lucy after *eight* years. The evening of the day these news items appeared in print I received a telegram from Mr. Benny. All it said was, "What's the matter, Milt, can't you hold a job? Jack Benny."

* * * * * *

One Christmas the writers were completely stumped as to what to give Jack as a gift. It's rough to pick a present for a man who receives so much. We finally got a bright idea that we thought Jack would appreciate. We bought him a gross of golf balls, each one stamped, "Jack Benny, Age 39." Jack was delighted with the gift, and his various golfing companions grabbed them so fast as souvenirs that Jack immediately ordered another gross. Jack's logic was, "I'm such a lousy golfer that I usually lose two or three balls during each nine holes I play. Now some people are going to find those balls eventually. When they pick up the ball and see it marked, 'Jack Benny, Age 39,' they're bound to think it's funny, so I'll be getting laughs even when I'm not there."

* * * * * *

Corbett Monica, a youthful nightclub and TV comic, told me of the following incident: He was at Joey Bishop's home one day and Joey had just received an offer to host a nighttime talk show for one year in Australia. The offer included a lavish salary and Bishop didn't know whether to accept it or not. Corbett knew that Joey was on friendly terms with Jack and suggested that Bishop call Benny for advice, and he did. Jack listened to Joey's dilemma and then said, "Joey, one year is too long for you to be away from America. Your fans are liable to forget you and no matter how much money the job pays, it's not worth it." Joey agreed with him, thanked him and hung up. One minute later Bishop's phone rang. It was Benny who asked, "Joey, what's the name of the agent who books that show?"

* * * * * *

Sometime during 1944 the newspapers carried a humorous story concerning the fact that President Franklin D. Roosevelt would try to relax under the terrible strain of the war years by occasionally playing poker with some friends. The news item mentioned that F.D.R. usually played for low stakes with four or five of his most intimate acquaintances, and once in a while one of them would bring along a trusted friend to participate. During this particular poker game, when the chips were cashed in, it turned out that the President lost exactly $20 and the friend of one of his friends won

Jack and Fred Allen in a friendly pose, 1944.

Bob Hope with Benny writers Al Gordon and Hal Goldman at a 1954 rehearsal.

Bob trying to break into the Benny vault. *Photo courtesy of Graphic Photo Service.*

Jack breaks up Hope, November 16, 1970.

Jack and Marilyn Monroe during her guest appearance on his TV show (1953-54 season).

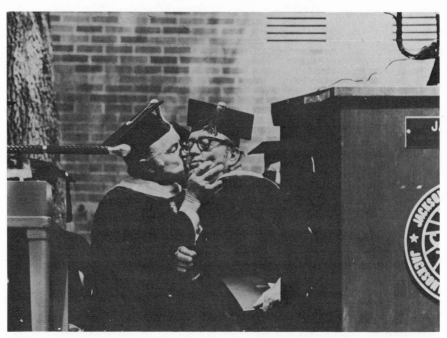

Bob bussing Benny as both men were awarded honorary degrees by Jacksonville University, April 6, 1972. *Photo courtesy of Bob Hope.*

Jack reacts as Phyllis Diller mugs on an October 1966 special.

that amount. President Roosevelt extracted a twenty dollar bill and handed it to the winner. This gentleman timidly asked F.D.R. if he would autograph the $20 bill because it was his intention to have it framed and never spend it. Roosevelt took the $20 bill back and said, "In that case, I'll give you a check." And he did.

When Jack read the story in the newspaper he clipped it out, pasted it to a sheet of his personal stationery, and sent it to the President with a note saying, "Stop stealing my character." Roosevelt, busy, harassed, and a seriously sick man, took the time to send Jack back the note on which he had personally scribbled, "I was here first."

Now Jack's reaction to the President saving money, and the note that he sent F.D.R. certainly weren't the funniest things he ever did. But he had enough of a sense of humor to enjoy the situation and see something of himself in Roosevelt's action. Appreciation of something funny is usually absent in a man without a sense of humor, and Jack's constant laughing at the clowning of other comics assuredly affirms this appreciation. And the appreciation went so far as to make Jack try to get his writers and other intimates to enjoy anything he felt noteworthy in the field of humor. In her *I Love Lucy* series, Lucille Ball and Desi Arnaz once had William Holden as a guest star in an episode which Jack saw, and thought was the funniest thing TV ever offered. When he found out that not one of his four writers had seen it, he arranged for a special showing of the program for us. He was right. It was, and still is, one of the funniest programs ever to be seen on the tube. And you'll have to take my word for it because much to my regret it was written prior to my joining Miss Ball, and I resent the fact that it was so funny without my having anything to do with it.

Unlike others in the entertainment field Jack was absolutely devoid of jealousy. If he saw something funny, like the William Holden appearance on *I Love Lucy,* he wanted everybody to see it. And if he heard something funny he hastened to repeat it, always giving credit to the original source. Although almost all of broadcasting's historians say that Jack's "Your Money or Your Life" bit was the funniest single joke in the history of broadcasting, Jack loved another joke on a rival program so much that he once said, "I'd have given ten thousand dollars if I had done that joke." It was on the old *Duffy's Tavern* radio show. Actor Ed Gardner played the part of Archie the bartender, who worked in the Tavern. One day he was complaining to a customer that his boss, Mr. Duffy, who never made an appearance on the program, wouldn't give him a raise because he was cheap and stingy. The customer said, "Why does Duffy keep saving all his money? Doesn't he know he can't take it with him?" And Archie came up with the immortal line, "If Duffy can't take it with him, Duffy ain't going to go."

By nature Jack was not an envious man, but more than once I heard him say, "Gee, I wish I had done that gag." He had probably pulled more memorable jokes than anyone else in history but it still bothered him that a joke which was so much in his character was done by someone else.

While Benny obviously prided himself as a performer, he never tried to masquerade as a humorist or wit. Yet he unmistakably and frequently got laughs with his own remarks in addition to the lines his writers fashioned for him.

18
Chutzpah

Chutzpah is one of those Yiddish words that is rapidly becoming a part of the American idiom. Literally, *chutzpah* means nerve—real and unmitigated nerve. The story that best illustrates *chutzpah* tells of a man who in a moment of anger kills both his mother and his father. Then when he is brought to trial he pleads with the court, saying, "Judge, have mercy on me, I'm an orphan." That's *chutzpah*.

For Jack Benny to appear as soloist with world-famous philharmonic orchestras, to play duets with violin virtuoso Isaac Stern, to even appear on the same stage with world-renowned musical conductors and to charge the audience double and triple the ordinary prices for these concerts—that's *chutzpah*.

Jack's initial entrance on the stage of these concerts was also *chutzpah*. The fact that he appeared there at all was *chutzpah*, but his entrance was double *chutzpah*. For those who never had the pleasure—and it was a pleasure—of seeing Jack perform in concert, let me describe it.

The orchestra would play the opening overture. Then the house lights, already dim, would go almost completely dark. From the side of the stage Jack would enter, corresponding in exact detail to everyone's mental image of what a great violinist should look like. He always wore white tie and tails. A spotlight would brighten the darkened stage and shine on nobody but Jack as he took that long walk from the side of the stage to the center. He would acknowledge the thundering applause like a veteran of a thousand perfectly performed concerts. With that oft-imitated but never equaled gait of his, he would slowly stroll to the podium, evincing a slight, sophisticated, knowing smile that customarily plays over the lips of the true virtuoso.

The spotlight concentrates its brightness as it grows steadily smaller, accentuating the blueness of his eyes. He reaches center stage. A nod of his head acknowledges the audience's applause. The concert master, or conductor, taps twice with his baton for silence. An expectant stillness fills the huge auditorium. Then the light in the concert hall brightens. The conductor lets his baton descend in the downbeat, and the hundred or more musicians start the overture. On cue, oozing confidence, Jack lifts his violin with his left hand to gently place it under his chin; then he raises his right hand to start caressing the strings with his bow. But his right hand is empty. *It has no bow.* Jack murmurs an apologetic "Ooops, I forgot my bow," and then in front of the thousands of music lovers who paid exorbitant prices to hear him play, he embarrassedly walks the full length of that football field-size stage to get his bow, never once running, or even hurrying—and then once again, bow now in hand, walks slowly back to center stage.

Jack displayed *chutzpah* in many of his routines on the air. His famed talks with his sponsor where he kept repeating the single word, "But," would go on for over two minutes occasionally, and these bits would be the high spots of the programs.

The classic example of Jack's *chutzpah* is illustrated by one of his best-remembered openings. We opened the program by announcing to the audience that we were going to take them on a free sight-seeing bus tour through the swank residential area of beautiful Beverly Hills. Then the program started with the sound of a bus motor starting up, and we heard the voices of the various passengers, all played by Benny's group of high-priced stooges, while the driver of the bus pointed out the homes of high-priced celebrities. We had the driver say, "Ladies and gentlemen, we are passing the home of W. C. Fields. I call your attention to the swimming pool in front of the house. W. C. Fields is the only man in Beverly Hills to have a swimming pool in his front yard." Then a passenger asked, "Why are those green marbles floating in the pool?" And the driver answered, "Those are olives."

Then the sound of the bus faded to the background to fit in a joke between a newly-married couple who were happy to be enjoying this free bus ride on their honeymoon. After that the driver announced: "On the left, ladies and gentlemen, you will see the home of Phil Harris and Alice Faye." Then we did what in professional parlance is known as a fade. The sound of the bus faded completely away and we supposedly were in the home of Alice Faye and Phil Harris who did some dialogue about Phil returning to Jack Benny's program that day. Their routine ran three minutes or so, and we faded back to the sound of the bus driving along, and the driver announced to the sight-seeing tourists: "I call your attention to that clump of trees on the right, folks. Behind those trees is the house of Orson Welles. Mr. Welles' home was designed by Mr. Welles. It was decorated by Mr. Welles. It was furnished by Mr. Welles. The trees were planted by God."

Next the driver said, "Again on your right I call your attention to the small white bungalow. Dennis Day and his mother live there." Again we did a fade, and we found ourselves, via the miracle of radio's imagination, in Dennis Day's home. His mother did her customary insults such as: "And Dennis, this season I don't want you going down to the trolley car anymore. If Mr. Benny wants to squeeze the last drop out of his toothpaste tube, let him put it on the trolley tracks himself." There were a few more jokes between Dennis and his mother, and finally she told him that she'd like to hear the song he was going to sing on the show that evening because she didn't want to listen to a full half-hour of "that skinflint" just to hear "the only good thing on it, your song." After Dennis sang his song, the audience applauded, and when they stopped we heard the sound of the bus, and once again we had the illusion that we were taking a free sight-seeing tour.

After another joke by some passenger in the car, the driver announced, "That white house on the corner belongs to Mr. and Mrs. Don Wilson. It's the only house on the block with a sunken living room. It became a sunken living room the first time Don stepped into it." Again the bus sounds died away and we were in the Wilson home, where Don was asking his wife to coach him in his rendition of the Lucky Strike commercial. Don made a slight, intentional mistake, and his wife said, "Maybe you'll do it better if you hear me do it first." She read it, with appropriate and humorous remarks from Don, and thus we had found another novel way to sell the sponsor's cigarettes.

Back on the bus again, after a few more jokes between the passengers, we once again heard the driver's voice as he announced: "The blue house on the left belongs to Mary Livingstone." The sound of the bus faded away and we were in Mary's house where she was preparing to go to the studio to rehearse for the opening program. We did about three or four minutes of dialogue, mostly in which Mary told her maid about how tough it was working for a man like Jack.

At the conclusion of Mary's material we again heard the sound of the bus and then some more jokes from the driver and passengers, and also from the honeymoon couple who wondered whether they'd be having as much fun back in their hotel room as they were enjoying this free bus ride.

The program had nearly run out of time when the bus driver said, "We are now passing the home of Jack Benny," and at this point Jack spoke his very first line, which was: "Stop the bus, driver, here's where I get off."

The scream and applause this got was unbelievable. The studio audience had been wondering what had happened to our star. They knew that Jack was supposed to be on the program, because in the fifteen-minute warm-up before we began the broadcast, all of the participants were introduced, and Jack got his usual introduction, told several of his standard warm-up jokes, and played a short passage on his violin.

In television it would have been difficult to do this joke because we would have to have had Jack hidden, either reading a newspaper or squatting down in his seat. Both of these devices would have been a case of "cheating" the audience, because on a sight-seeing bus everybody is supposed to be sitting upright, looking through the windows and taking pictures of the sights they deem worthwhile. But we were able to do this in radio, and we wound up with as much praise as any program ever got.

Jack's entire appearance on that show lasted four minutes, which he shared with Rochester, and Rochester, as usual, got the lion's share of the laughs.

The critical acclaim we got for both the quality and daring of the program was amazing. One prominent critic wrote, "Jack Benny didn't make his appearance on the show that bears his name until the final four minutes, but that's all this master comedian needed. In just four minutes he proved he was the star of the show."

The following week we opened the show by reading excerpts of this critic's column, and Don Wilson introduced Jack, after reading the pertinent passages of the review, by saying, "So now, ladies and gentlemen, I give you our four-minute star, Jack Benny."

I don't think we'll ever see such examples of show-biz *chutzpah* again!

174

19
Censorship and Fluffs

Bob Hope was right when he said that Jack Benny had taste. Jack was neither prim nor prissy, and we occasionally did a risqué routine, but it was done in such a way that only those over the age of adolescence would understand it—and we did it only if it was extremely clever and funny. Smut for the sake of a few extra easy laughs was not Benny's bag.

Despite this we had countless scrapes with the censors, and in these earlier, more innocent days the censors were stricter even though the material was far more bland. For instance, on rare occasions you were allowed to say "hell" on a dramatic show, but it was verboten in comedy. Also, under no conditions were you permitted to make a reference to a rival network. This once caused a complaint from Fred Allen which became a classic. Fred said, "NBC denies the existence of hell and CBS, though not necessarily in that order."

We also had some classic combats with the censors, and some of them were completely pointless. For instance, in one sketch where Jack was a college student, we used the device where Jack would act as the narrator, speaking through the filter mike, to set the scene, and then he and the other performers would do their dialogue on the regular microphones. At this point in the sketch Jack was describing his meeting with the campus queen. He said, "Then *she* came into the room. You could tell she was the campus queen because she was wearing seventeen fraternity pins. No sweater, just pins."

Now the actress who played the part of the campus queen was Veola Vonn who, as I mentioned elsewhere, was built. To give you an idea of her build, if you walked into a room and Raquel Welch was standing next to Veola, you'd push Raquel aside and say, "Excuse me, sir, I want to talk to the girl." But in writing about her entrance for the college sketch, her figure didn't figure in our thoughts. We just thought it was a funny line: "She was wearing seventeen fraternity pins. No sweater, just pins."

Our censor must have worked hours with a tape measure because he came screaming into the studio saying that the joke was dirty. Seventeen small fraternity pins couldn't possibly cover all of Miss Vonn's frontage. To appease the censor we offered to change the number to one hundred and seventeen fraternity pins, but it was still no go. He claimed that number of pins was still too few to cover the view. How he arrived at his final figure we'll never know, but he insisted that we say three hundred and fifty fraternity pins. We quickly acquiesced because we didn't feel it would affect the line in any way—but it did. It got the biggest, dirtiest laugh of the year, because the audience evidently figured that we said she was wearing three hundred and fifty fraternity pins because we wanted to show how big her bosom was, and only a girl with a build like that could carry all those pins.

Despite the fact that this was the era of radio and only a few thousand people ever saw Miss Vonn perform, compared to the many millions who heard her, her bust measurements caused another conflict with the censor.

We did many sketches on the Benny broadcasts, and most of them were our versions of famous movies, plays, and novels. On one occasion we decided to do a "Klondike" show, using the frozen North with its howling winds and freezing weather as the basis of our humor, and perform our version of Robert W. Service's famous poem, *The Shooting of Dan McGrew*. As in all sketches of this type, we had Jack do narration and then we went into dramatization. However, on this show Jack's narration was simply the recitation of the four-line stanzas of the poem, with each quatrain furthering our story line. We didn't tamper with Mr. Service's poem, and after the big shoot-out ending of the sketch, Jack recited the final lines:

Pitched on his head and pumped full of lead
Was dangerous Dan McGrew,
While the man from the creeks lay clutched
To the breast of the Lady that's known as Lou.

Now while this may not have been Shakespeare or even Rod Mc-Kuen, it has been a part of our literary folklore for over half a century, and we quoted the last line exactly as it was written. However, because Veola Vonn played "The Lady That's Known As Lou," we had to alter the final sentence to read, "clutched in the arms of the lady that's known as Lou."

Censors sometimes blue-penciled our scripts with good reason, but occasionally we couldn't figure out how their minds, if any, worked. On one show we were doing a Wild West sketch. The script called for the sound of a buffalo stampede, and one of the cast members was to yell, "Look out everybody—it's a buffalo stampede." We got our script back from the censor, where it was always sent immediately after being mimeographed to receive what was called "Official Continuity Acceptance," and the censor had attached a very interesting note. He called our attention to the earth-shaking fact that at that particular time, in that exact location in America, there were no buffaloes. There were only bison. Therefore, we would be misleading our millions of listeners if we were to say that it was a buffalo stampede. It's lucky for the censor who brought us this historic news that John Wayne wasn't our guest or the Duke might have put a bullet through his head.

We finally made this man feel that he had done his duty to all of those millions listening out in radio land when we said that we would keep the line, "It's a buffalo stampede," but that we would make our sound-effects men give us the sound of a bison stampede. He left, looking at us in a peculiar manner, but that's the way we did it.

Sometimes we'd put in stage directions that were only instructions for the performers. Once we hired an actress to play a prim old maid, and in her directions we had the words: "She speaks in the voice of a virgin prune." Now even though no one outside of our cast, which got a chuckle at this impossible voice description, would ever see or hear this line, the censor objected. The word "virgin" could never in any manner, shape, or form be used in a radio script.

Any joke with a sexual connotation was a red flag waved in front of the bull-like censors. They'd rush in to destroy anything that even implied that there were two sexes.

On one show Mary Livingstone was talking to her maid, played by Doris Singleton and portrayed by her as a fun-loving, man-hungry girl. Mary was discussing this facet of her character with her, and Doris said, "You're right, Miss Livingstone. Do you know what my favorite dream is?" "No," said Mary, "what is it?" Doris answered, "I dream that I'm a bar of soap in the Brooklyn Dodgers' shower room."

We expected a visit from the censor on this, and we weren't disappointed. He described in anatomical detail the various places a bar of soap might touch members of a baseball team taking showers. We didn't expect to win this argument, and thus we were ready with a still funny but somewhat more acceptable version of the line. Miss Singleton ended up saying: "I dream that I'm a Dixie Cup in the Brooklyn Dodgers' locker room." It got a nice laugh, but not as big as we would have had with the original version.

We once did a script where Don Wilson urgently had to see Jack about the commercial. Going to his home, he was informed by Rochester that the boss was upstairs taking a bath. We then did a fade to Jack's bathroom where Jack was lolling in the tub, and suddenly we heard Jack say, "Well, I think I'll start scrubbing my toesies." There was a short pause and we heard Jack recite, "This little piggy went to market, this little piggy—ehh, I think I'm getting too old for that."

After that we did another joke about Jack playing with his rubber duck. (In those days no comedian ever took a bath without his rubber duck.) Then there was a knock on the door, and in answer to Jack's "Who's there?" Wilson announced himself and said it was urgent that he talk to him.

Jack told him to come in, and we heard the sound of the door opening, Don entering, the door closing, and Jack saying cordially, "Come on in, Don. Make yourself comfortable. Sit down." That did it. A corps of censors came down and described us as dirty old men trying to corrupt the country because in the bathroom there was only one place that a man could sit down. What really killed me was that the head censor couldn't bring himself to utter the word "toilet." He said, "The only place Don could sit down is on the potty." We pointed out that many bathrooms have extra chairs in them and that the tub could have a wide side, but it was all to no avail. Finally one of the writers said sarcastically: "Look, suppose we have Jack say, 'Don, make yourself comfortable—put down the cover and sit down.'" The head censor—or "potty man," as we now thought of him—got mad and said, "That's dirty!"

Possibly our greatest argument with the censor on the Jack Benny series came when we did our version of the MGM movie *King Solomon's Mines*. This adventure picture with an African locale starred Deborah Kerr, and Miss Kerr also appeared in our version. When we started writing it we had so much fun that we did something that was a rarity for us—we made a "two-parter" out of the sketch. These shows were aired on January 7 and 14, 1951. In the second show, Jack, as the Great White Hunter, is guiding Miss Kerr through darkest Africa searching for King Solomon's mines, when suddenly they are captured by cannibals. Jack said, "Don't panic, Deborah, I'll amuse them. I'll tell them a limerick. They love those." Then Jack recited:

There was a galoom from Nuwaga,
Who oola magana tomaga,
He aga noo wad,
Nakowa kasad,
And booga lanoya karaga.

When Jack completed reciting this pure gibberish limerick, the actors cast as cannibals all laughed. Then the dialogue went as follows:

JACK

It worked, it worked. They've gone.

DEBORAH

That's wonderful. What was the limerick?

JACK

(shyly) Oh, I can't tell you. It's dirty.

When the CBS censor read this he wanted us to delete it from the sequence of the script even though we assured him that the words had no meaning in any language, living or dead. He said that it didn't matter. As far as he was concerned, all limericks were dirty, and our punch line only emphasized the fact that it was a pornographic poem.

At this point Miss Kerr gave the censor a withering look, and in tones to match she said, "Oh, really now!" That did more than all our arguments. The limerick stayed in the script and was rewarded with laughter and applause, and Jack's apologetic refusal to translate it to Deborah got another big laugh.

Because sometimes censors could snip a quip that offended their taste but no one else's, writers took defensive measures to protect their material. They reworded punch lines, obfuscated them, left out key words, and transposed words so that they appeared to be innocent. Then, on the air, the comic would do the punch line correctly, and since it was live, nothing could be done by way of punishment except the threat to cut you off the air next time.

When we writers had a line we liked that we were afraid the censor would blue-pencil, our favorite device was to write two or three really risqué jokes into the script. Then when the censor came down to argue with us, we'd bargain with him and give in on all the risqué ones we wrote as a camouflaging diversionary tactic, but as a concession we'd ask to be allowed to keep in the one we really wanted.

This gimmick once backfired on the Benny bunch. We had one gag that we thought the censor would excise, and to save it we stuck two blue gags in the script. I don't remember the second one, but the first one I clearly recall. We had Jack going for a medical examination and walking down a long hallway in a building exclusively used for doctors' offices. As he passed each doorway he read off the medical men's names and specialties—and the line went like this: "Let's see ... Dr. Eyman, Eye Doctor ... Dr. Earlich, Ear Doctor ... Dr. Footer, Foot Doctor ... Doctor *Ballzer*????" Now, possibly because we had a writer named George Balzer on the staff, the censor read no double meaning in the gag, nor did he ask us to excise the second double-entendre line we had slipped in, and, best of all, he made no mention of the line that we wanted to keep. Then at rehearsal we read the script as it was written and the cast howled at our two dirty jokes, but even though they had the censor okay, we removed them ourselves.

Possibly the classic outwitting of a censor was done by Jack Douglas who used to write for TV but has now gone honest and become an author and frequent guest on late-night talk shows. In his radio-writing days, Jack was creating gags for the Jimmy Durante-Garry Moore series at the time Jane Russell was being touted for her outstanding talents.

On this show Durante told Moore that he had a date with Jane Russell. Moore asked Jimmy, "*The* Jane Russell?" Jimmy assured him he went out with *the* Jane Russell. Moore said he doubted that Jimmy had a date with *the* Jane Russell. They kept repeating her name, and after each line there was a music cue: "Timpani." Now this seems like clean-enough dialogue, so it was never questioned. However, the timpani, as any music lover knows, is a double drum instrument, and it was resoundingly struck twice every time the lady's name was mentioned, so on the air we heard "Jane Russell, *Boom, Boom.*" Her name was used several times in this innocent-appearing dialogue, but every time you heard Jane Russell you heard *Boom Boom.* It was one of radio's funniest bits, and certainly a most resourceful ruse in outsmarting the censor.

For one of his TV shows—I believe it was an hour-long special—I brought Jack a special bit of business that I thought was quite funny, and he concurred. However, when we put it in the script, the censor cut it out. It was a simple bit that would have been all the more funny because Benny was then in his seventies.

According to the script, Jack would pick up a copy of *Playboy* magazine, open it to its well-known centerfold section, and extend it to its full length. He would then look at what the audience knew was a large, sensuous picture of a gorgeous, almost nude girl. He would stare at it wistfully and longingly for several seconds and then begin to sing "The Impossible Dream."

Now anyone with the slightest writing knowledge would realize that just having Jack pull out the *Playboy* centerfold and letting him stare at it would be good for several seconds of laughs, and singing "The Impossible Dream" would be a worthwhile topper to this situation. However, this time we lost the fight with the censor despite Jack's ardent arguments, and the bit was cut out of the script.

Let me digress here for a moment in an attempt to bury once and for all an erroneous legend that has continued to live for nearly forty years. During the days of radio, if a comic insisted on telling his studio audience a verboten quip, the censor would sit in the control room, and when the performers started on the offending bit of bawdiness, the censor would press a button cutting him off the air, and the audience would hear nothing but silence for fifteen or twenty seconds. That was the extreme punishment for saying naughty no-no's. Today, because almost every comedy program is filmed or taped in advance, the unapproved words are simply "bleeped" from the performance.

During one of the many times we broadcast from Palm Springs, something went wrong with our direct connection to Los Angeles which then fed the program to the entire network. Maybe the wire went dead or an inefficient engineer pulled the plug for several seconds before he rectified his mistake. However, the listeners, accustomed to the fact that a "cut-off" during a program meant that something bawdy had been broadcast, deluged us, the network, and radio columnists with letters of inquiry. A few printed explanations quickly scotched any rumors of ribaldry, and let me add that Jack was *never* cut off the air for using questionable material.

Jack once did a cleaned-up version of a current dirty gag, but there were no repercussions. This joke went as follows: "Did you hear about the guy who died while making love? It took the mortician three days to wipe the smile off his face." During the week I heard it, we were writing a routine where Jack Benny met Sam Hearn, the rube character who worked at a winery in Calabasas. Jack asked him how things were, and Hearn answered, "Had a tragedy there. Man fell into a vat of wine and drowned." Jack said, "That's terrible," and Hearn answered, "Yep. Took the mortician three days to wipe the smile off his face."

It was a funny gag. Unfortunately our censor was not as square as he seemed. He had heard the original version of the story, and came down with his freshly sharpened blue pencil. After a ten-minute argument, we convinced him to let the bit stay in the script.

After all, we explained, if the dirty version never existed, then our clean version of it was funny and inoffensive. And if some few listeners had heard the original censorable story, how could we further offend them, since they had already been subjected to the story?

Therefore we did the gag, and the audience reacted nicely. But as the laugh died down, the members of the orchestra, who heard every unmentionable joke as soon as it was created, recognized our cleverness in cleaning it up, and they reacted with what we called "The Double Dirty Laugh." This is a second, knowing, different-sounding guffaw which follows the first normal reaction. Their raucous acknowledgment of the fact that "they knew" broke Jack up, and fortunately Sam Hearn ad-libbed "Yep, does sound funny even though it's tragic. Nice way to go, though." From that time on Jack requested that we clean up no more jokes for his program, and we rarely had censor trouble, at least in regard to taste or questionable material.

The last time I ever had a hassle with a censor involving Jack Benny was when he was a guest star on a *Here's Lucy* program for Lucille Ball's 1971 season. In the script which I wrote with Ray Singer, Jack has been reminiscing about the women in his life. Suddenly he looks at his wristwatch, realizes that it's very late, and tells Lucy that he and a friend of his have a date with two chicks.

As he said this, the doorbell rang, and Jack opened it, admitting George Burns who was making a surprise cameo appearance. Jack welcomed George, said that he'd be ready to leave in a minute, and asked what time they were supposed to pick up the girls. George told Jack he'd already picked them up and called out, "Trixie, Ginger, come on in." Lucy reacted when Trixie and Ginger walked in, because they were two of the cutest eighty-year-old ladies our casting department could hire.

Their appearance and Lucy's reaction was good for a big laugh. Then one of these octogenarians said, "We're sorry we're late, Jack, but we had to stop and pick up the pill." Lucy, in wide-eyed surprise, asked, "The pill?" And George Burns answered, "Yes, the one that keeps us awake." Then George, Jack, and the two old ladies exited.

Believe it or not, we had censor trouble—and not just the usual phone call this time, but a personal visit from the head censor who claimed that our joke about "the pill" would corrupt every person past the age of puberty. Lucy said, "For heaven's sake, if anyone knows what purpose the pill serves, then just looking at the four of them"—and she pointed to Jack, George, and the two "girls"— "makes the viewer realize that not one of them is under seventy-five years old, and they don't need the pill." At which Burns said to Lucy, "I don't think you have to waste money on it either." We all were laughing at this—all of us, that is, except the censor.

At this point Jack resorted to the type of logic I've mentioned earlier in this chapter. "Look," he said to the censor, "if a viewer hears this dialogue and *knows* about the pill, then that person also knows we're way past the age when we need it, so we can't corrupt them. On the other hand, those who know nothing about the pill have seen or heard ads and commercials for 'No Doz' which is used to keep you awake, and it's funny that four people like us would go on a date and have to take a pill to keep us awake for the evening."

I don't know whether Jack's logic swayed the censor, or whether he was a bit in awe of the formidable three B's—Ball, Benny, and Burns—but he let us do it. The mere mention of "the pill" by the eighty-year-old lady got a worthwhile whoop from the audience, and George's blackout line got an even bigger laugh plus applause.

This "indecent infraction" of censorship brought us a total of forty letters. Thirty-seven of them said that it was a pleasure seeing the three big stars on together and that the blackout line was very funny. The other three condemned us for our lewdness. One letter was signed "Former Fan," the second was signed "Disgusted Viewer," and the third complained that she watched the show with her entire family, and it was signed, "Indignantly yours, Mother of Twelve."

The censor could control all within his purview, but he was completely impotent when it came to on-the-air fluffs. For that matter so were the writers.

On the Benny show we had more than our share of fluffs, and we almost always put them to good use afterward. These were legitimate muffs and mistakes that had not been planned beforehand, and most of them were committed by Don Wilson and Mary Livingstone.

Mary figured in a great fluff. In the script Jack was driving down to Palm Springs with Rochester and had some trouble with the car. When Mary appeared she was supposed to ask what was wrong with the Maxwell, and Jack, defending his jalopy as always, was to ask, "What makes you think there's anything wrong with it?" Mary's answer was to be, "When I walked past the service station I saw it up on the grease rack." Now this was just the feedline to a joke, but I don't remember what the joke was because we never got to it and it was never broadcast. Mary read her line, "When I walked past the service station I saw it up on the *grass reek*." The audience howled and Jack reacted, but Mary didn't change her expression because her mind heard her say the words exactly as they were in her script, "grease rack." Not till Jack began to break up and half-hysterically say *"Grass reek?"* did it dawn on Mary what had happened. Then she began to laugh. Now Mary has two laughs —a stage "prop" laugh which we'd have her use frequently on the air, and her real laugh which is slightly heavier and heartier. And this time she laughed her heartiest, which naturally broke Jack up, and his contagious laughter spread to the audience.

The following week we had Jack take Mary to task for not only fluffing the line but using a combination of words like *grass reek* that no one had ever heard before. Again Mary defended herself and said that the phrase she uttered was a very common one. In fact, she said, it had appeared in a news item in that day's paper which she had clipped out and brought along as proof. Jack skeptically suggested that he didn't believe what she was saying, and Mary said, "Okay, I'll read it to you." Then she read the following news item: "Yesterday morning a skunk ran across Dr. Smith's lawn, and gee, did that *grass reek*." The audience, always anxious to see Jack humbled, howled at this, and we made reference to it in several subsequent scripts.

Don Wilson made more than one mistake, and the unfortunate thing is that Don, as an announcer, usually made them at the top of his lung capacity. Our sponsor, Lucky Strike, always kept trying extra added slogans to augment their "LS/MFT" and "They're So Round, So Firm, So Fully Packed" and the chant of the tobacco auctioneer which always ended, "Sold American." The new slogan for selling our cigarettes was "Be Happy—Go Lucky." We tried to work this in comedically as often as possible, but each of our commercials began and ended with Don Wilson saying, "So remember, 'Be Happy—Go Lucky!'" All went well until the broadcast when he said, "Be Lucky—Go Happy." As I mentioned, Mary was unaware of her slip of the tongue when she said "grass reek" instead of "grease rack." Now, not only didn't Don realize what he said, but Jack wasn't sure what he had heard, so he automatically departed from the script and asked, "Don, did you say, 'Be Lucky—Go Happy'?" And Don, not knowing what was bothering Jack, answered, "Yes, Jack, I said, 'Be Lucky—Go Happy.'" They stared at each other momentarily, and then they practically fell on each other, shaking with uncontrollable laughter.

The following week, as I remember, a strange voice, not Don Wilson's, did the opening announcement of *The Jack Benny Show*. When the members of the cast entered individually, they inquired, "Where's Don?" Jack said, "He's in that room." The audience heard the sound effects of the cast member walking and a door opening, and through the open door, in cadence, Don could be heard repeating the phrase, "Be *Happy*—Go *Lucky*, Be *Happy*—Go *Lucky*." We did this bit with every member of the cast, and each time the door was opened, Don was heard repeating the phrase, "Be *Happy*—Go *Lucky*." And each time we got a big laugh.

Radio had such an immediacy to it, something TV lacks, that sometimes we didn't even wait for the following week to correct or capitalize on a mistake. If it happened early enough in the program, and an appropriate spot was found later in the script, we'd change it while we were on the air. When veterans of the radio era gather and reminisce, one such situation stands out. It happened when Jack was supposed to get into a political argument with Don Wilson, and, as usual, Don was to stick to his guns because he had a full fund of facts. The clincher came when Jack asked Wilson why he was so sure he was right, and Don was to answer with firm finality, "Because I read it in Drew Pearson's column." And because this was to terminate the debate, Don was to deliver it with more emphasis than any of his other dialogue. But what he boomed out was, "I read it in *Dreer Pooson's* column." Jack repeated "*Dreer Pooson*," the audience laughed and the show went on.

As I said, however, it happened in the opening lines of the show. The program was to end with a scene where Jack went to a swanky hotel to meet someone. And prior to entering the hotel, Jack was to talk to the doorman played by his always encountered archenemy, Frank Nelson, who hated Jack in every role that he played. In this scene Nelson was the doorman at the hotel and Jack was to open the conversation by asking, "Excuse me, are you the doorman?" And Nelson would sneeringly say, "Well, who do you think I am in this red uniform—Nelson Eddy?" (For those readers too young to remember, Nelson Eddy was a wooden-visaged actor who sang beautifully, usually opposite Jeanette MacDonald, and it seemed that in every other picture he was cast as a member of the Canadian Royal Mounted Police whose red uniforms look so splendid in Technicolor.) This hotel-doorman scene took place a full fifteen minutes after Don tongue-twisted Drew Pearson's name into "Dreer Pooson." Jack, a completely unsuspecting *shnook,* now approached Frank Nelson and asked, "Excuse me, are you the doorman?" and Nelson shattered Jack's composure when he answered, "Well, who do you think I am, *Dreer Pooson?*" The new answer not only undid Jack, but it had the same hysterical effect on the cast, crew, and musicians, all of whom had heard Frank rehearse the regular written line about "Nelson Eddy," and all of them thought "Dreer Pooson" was an ad-lib on his part.

What actually happened was that when Don made his fluff the

writers, listening to the program's proceedings in the control booth, got the happy idea of changing Frank's line. We quickly motioned to him where he was sitting on stage waiting his turn. We got him into the booth, suggested our change, and he immediately penciled in our new line.

20
Expensive Jokes

In the cost-conscious field of entertainment, where every dollar must more than pay for itself, the most damaging and derogatory remark that can be made about an actor, writer, director, or producer is: "He went over the budget." If there is an Eleventh Commandment in Hollywood, it is: "Thou Shalt Not Spend Too Much Or Thou Wilt Go Over Thy Budget."

This dates back to the old nickelodeon days of Hollywood when a more ambitious than usual producer wanted to go out of town to far-away Lake Tahoe to get authenticity for some forest scenes he was supposed to film. He suggested this expensive trek to the studio head who uttered those immortal words, "A tree is a tree, a rock is a rock, go shoot it in Griffith Park."

In the old-time entertainment field most of those in charge had the attitude that "a penny saved is a dollar earned," and their credo was: "Don't make it good, make it fast." There were notable exceptions to this penny-pinching attitude, but economy was the rule, not the exception. Fortunately all of the comics for whom I poured out my creative juices were more interested in making it good than making a buck—and Jack Benny was among them.

Jack always got and paid for the best, and because of this attitude the writers felt that anything that would reward us with a good laugh would be worth any expense. This eventually led to Jack doing one of the longest and certainly most expensive gags in radio history. Moreover, he repeated it several times, even though each reuse cost him a small fortune.

Jack first did this gag on his radio show of January 18, 1953. According to the script, Jack and Mary are at an auction and engaging in a conversation while the auctioneer is simultaneously conducting his spiel and various participants are shouting out their bids for these items.

As the auction progresses the auctioneer proudly announces that the next item will be a much-sought-after work of art—an umbrella stand made out of the leg of an elephant personally shot by the maharaja of some fictional Indian principality we had invented. Jack is amazed that anyone would want an umbrella stand, especially such a grisly one made from the leg of a defunct pachyderm. He is even more amazed and voluble when in the rear an old lady opens with a bid for one hundred dollars. Jack whispers to Mary: "That's the most ridiculous thing I've ever heard of ... offering that much money for a worthless piece of ugly junk." The bidding continues higher and Jack keeps whispering to Mary about how stupid the people are. Mary then changes the subject, and she whispers to Jack that she met Bob Hope the previous night and that Bob seemed upset because Jack hadn't sent him his check for appearing on his program the previous week. All the time that they are having this conversation—which runs nearly two pages—there isn't a single funny line or laugh in the script. The bidding continues and Mary and Jack keep whispering until Mary says that Hope had expected to receive his regular guest fee for appearing on Jack's show. Jack inquiries: "What is Bob's regular guest fee?" Mary whispers: "Five thousand dollars." Jack shouts: "FIVE THOUSAND DOLLARS!" And the auctioneer says, "Sold to the man who just bid five thousand dollars." The resulting scream lasted forty seconds.

As I have said, this was possibly the longest and most expensive joke ever done in the history of radio, mainly because of the quality of the cast. The auctioneer was played by Hy Averback, who went on to become a famous director. The old lady was played by Bea Benaderet. One of the men who was bidding for the elephant's leg was played by Benny Rubin, who portrayed many characters on Jack's show. The audience had never before waited so long for a laugh, and they were giggling nervously, knowing that something had to happen, and when the auctioneer said, "Sold to the man who just bid five thousand dollars," there was a fantastic scream. Everyone in the routine was a top-salaried performer.

By an odd coincidence Jack also participated in the most expensive single joke ever done on TV, only this time it was on Lucille Ball's *Here's Lucy* program. And I'm happy to state that the radiant redhead spent money just as freely as Jack to get quality into her programs.

In this 1967-68 episode, which I wrote with Ray Singer, and which eventually won us an Emmy nomination for comedy writing, Lucy was working for a bank, and they wanted to get Jack Benny's bank account. The plot revolved around the fact that Lucy's boss, Mr. Mooney (Gale Gordon), had to get up some gimmicks to boost the bank's business. Lucy suggested that if they could advertise that Jack Benny, known for saving his money in his own private vault, had put his funds in their bank, it would be an excellent endorsement and advertising gimmick.

Lucy visited Jack and played on his emotions by saying that she wanted to earn extra money to pay for her nephew's violin lessons. Finally, Jack promised Lucy that he would put his money in Mooney's bank if they could build a safer and stronger vault than he had in his basement. Lucy agreed to do this, and creating the new vault with its many gimmicks and special effects cost a small fortune. And then, because we needed a wild blackout to top everything else, we came up with a device that cost more than any other single-usage gag in TV comedy.

The entrance to the vault was protected by an electronic eye which triggered a "guillotine" that would split asunder any unlawful trespasser. Next the intruder would be confronted by a tribe of tomahawk-tossing Indians, and then a huge gorilla. Then came a deep stream filled with piranha fish—and their voracious appetite was illustrated when a huge ham was dipped into the water and after several seconds of turbulence an empty bone was withdrawn. To get safely over the stream Jack and Lucy had to walk over the backs of snapping turtles which appeared on signal.

All of these devices formed a highly expensive obstacle course leading to the vault. Then between them and the vault itself was a stretch of twelve to fifteen feet which seemed to Jack to be ordinary ground. Lucy then took him by the hand and started to walk toward their goal, and what seemed to be solid earth turned out to be quicksand. Although the entire set was costly, the quicksand into which Jack and Lucy sank up to their necks hit the jackpot.

Here is how the gag was done. On the stage where Lucy filmed her shows before a live audience at Paramount Studios, there was a six-foot square, five-foot deep hole in the stage floor. When not needed, this hole was covered with thick boards so that it was solid like the rest of the stage. On the occasions when it was necessary for various gags, the boards were removed and the hole was readied for whatever crazy piece of business the writers concocted in the name of comedy.

For the quicksand routine we had to build a small special elevator in this hole. The floor around it was raised about a foot via a small sloping wall, and the entire area was then filled with lukewarm water. Then this small lake was covered with a dark sawdust-like material, a couple of inches thick, which floated on the surface, giving it the appearance of solid ground. As Lucy and Jack walked into this pit, the slightly sloping walls made them seem to sink. When they reached the "elevator hole" they stood still, the machinery was turned on, the elevator went down, and they slowly began to sink from view. Though the hole was five feet deep, the elevator could only descend about four feet, because of the machinery we had installed. When Lucy and Jack felt the elevator stop as it reached bottom, they were almost shoulder high in the gooey mixture, but now they slowly bent their knees, giving the further illusion that they were going to disappear into a bottomless pit.

The quicksand effect cost many thousands of dollars, going well into five figures, but the audience reaction made it worth all the money. When the audience had left at the completion of the show, and Lucy and Jack had showered and changed, we stood around discussing the wildness of the bit and the enthusiasm of the audience's reaction. Then Jack said, "One thing about Milt—he doesn't mind spending money." And Lucy quickly added, "Yes, as long as it's not his." Then she hugged and kissed me and added, "Milt, I don't mind how expensive a gag is as long as it gets a good laugh—but please watch it next time."

Jack and Lucy, September 27, 1967, sinking in a quicksand moat guarding a vault. This was the most expensive gag in TV history.

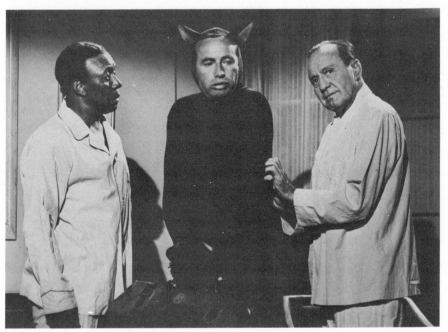

Jack and Rochester apprehend "Cat Burglar" Joey Bishop.

Lucille Ball watches Johnny Carson imitate the well-known expression of Jack on a March 1968 special.

Jack and Lucy, 1969.

Jack with Lucy and John Wayne.

Dean Martin mimics one of Jack's famous expressions on Jack's January 1973 special.

21
Jack's Favorite Routine

Although Jack Benny was a veteran of vaudeville and had appeared on Broadway in several musicals, he rarely played nightclubs until late in his career. He still would make personal appearances at theaters during his radio era, but he only played the top ones, such as the prestige-packed Palladium in London. The English audiences loved him there.

However, in the late 1950s Jack began to listen to the overtures of the lush Las Vegas gambling palaces, and finally they made him the proverbial "offer he couldn't refuse"—he would be paid a higher salary than any star ever to appear there. That record has since been shattered, but at the time it was amazingly astronomical.

When Jack made these Las Vegas appearances his usual act consisted of some small talk and an attempt at a serious violin solo, backed by a group of the most disreputable musicians ever to wander out on a stage. They were dressed in cast-off clothing from the Hatfields and McCoys, and Jack had named them "The Beverly Hillbillies" long before the TV show of that name came into existence. Jack, dressed in overalls, straw hat, and appropriate accessories, was the leader of the orchestra. One of the specialty acts connected with "The Beverly Hillbillies" was an eight- or nine-year-old gal whom Jack would introduce as "Mah featured soloist and mah wife." It eventually turned out that the little girl was a child prodigy, a violin virtuoso, and when she played, either solo or in a duet with Jack, the looks of envy and hatred he aimed at this little girl always broke up the audiences.

Jack did several other routines in his nightclub act, and of course what the audience wanted to see and hear most was Jack himself—"in one" is the theatrical expression—just standing center stage, reminiscing, and regaling them with stories and anecdotes. Jack wasn't a "one liner" man. One-liners, as the phrase so "cleverly" describes them, are a series of one-line quick jokes, and Henny Youngman is an acknowledged master of this genre. Bob Hope did a rapid-fire monologue of one-liners at the start of every radio and TV program he ever hosted, as did many other comedians, including Milton Berle—but they would also augment their acts with skits, sketches, and routines involving other performers. However, when Jack would appear "in one" he preferred to become a raconteur in the manner of Danny Thomas who has so many stock stories that it's difficult for him to try out new material because his audiences keep shouting for their old favorites.

Jack was scheduled to play Las Vegas and Harrah's at Lake Tahoe during his air hiatus in the early 1960s, and he hired me to write some routines for him. Now writing nightclub material for Jack is not as easy as preparing his weekly shows, since you must invent a complete miniature plot, premise, or story with a suitable smash blackout. In preparing several of these for Jack I simply wrote skeleton outlines because it would have been a waste of time to labor long hours making the beginning and middle funny if he had no faith in the ending. I showed these outlines to Jack, and he liked a couple of them, one in particular. I left him the original copy of his favorite because I knew he liked to edit and reword ideas to fit his own inimitable style. I'll admit that I am one of the world's greatest authorities on Jack Benny's style, but Jack himself was the greatest.

We made an appointment to meet again in three days when I would bring him the first fleshed-out draft of this anecdote. In the meantime while I'd be working, Jack would be flying up to Las Vegas where his best friend, George Burns, was getting ready to begin a two-week appearance at one of the pleasure palaces the following night.

I don't have a copy of the original half-page outline of this material I wrote, nor do I have the final version that he eventually used for years. What I do have is a reprint of it which appeared in *Weekly Variety*. It is longer than the original blueprint for the piece, and shorter than the finished effort. It went as follows (and now I am quoting from *Weekly Variety*):

"I always have problems working in gambling casinos," says Jack, "like the other night. After I did my second show it was too late for me to eat, too early to go to bed, and as far as gambling is concerned, let's not be ridiculous. I quit gambling after I lost my last bet. Whoever figured that Truman would beat Dewey? . . . Having nothing to do after the last show I just sat around the bar noticing how cheap people were. Really cheap. Would you believe I sat at that bar for over two hours and nobody offered to buy me a drink. . . . So I bought my own, Mogen David on the rocks. . . . Then a very attractive blonde sat down next to me. I wouldn't say she was beautiful, but she'd certainly get whistles on a windy day. . . . She was very attractive and looked vaguely familiar, so when she smiled at me, naturally I smiled back. Then she asked me if I'd like to join her in a martini, and I said, 'Do you think there's room enough in that little glass for both of us?' *(Jack does high-pitched laugh.)* You see, I *can* ad-lib. . . . Anyway this girl and I had a couple of drinks, and one thing led to another and, well . . . you know how those things are . . .? Maybe you know, but I don't. . . . Finally she said it was noisy and crowded at the bar and we'd find things quieter and cozier if we went to her room. . . . Well!!!!! I was shocked!!!! I went, but I was shocked. . . . When we got to her room she told me to make myself at home while she slipped into something more comfortable. *(Jack does high-pitched giggle again.)* While she was out of the room I sat on the sofa, loosened my tie, and thought those few serious thoughts that every married man thinks of at a time like this: What my wife doesn't know won't hurt her. . . . Then I began wrestling with my conscience, and I'm kind of proud to admit it. You know, that's the first wrestling match I ever won. . . . After all, when you've lived a good clean life for thirty-nine years, your conscience is so out of condition it's a pushover. . . . At this point the girl came back into the room. She was wearing the most gorgeous black negligee I ever saw. She dimmed down the lights, turned on some soft romantic music, then held her arms toward me so we could dance. As we danced she snuggled close and asked me if I'd like to kiss her and naturally I said I would. And then she said, 'Before you kiss me, I'll have to take off my wig.' I was stunned and asked, 'Take off your wig?' And she said, 'Yes, I'm Allen Funt and you're on Candid Camera.' . . . Well, the the wig came off, and sure enough it was Allen Funt, and was I startled! I was so surprised I could hardly finish the dance."

That's the routine, a bit shorter than Jack used to do it on night-club floors and in theaters, but three times as long as the bare outline I gave him. I told him I'd work on the idea and put in some extra "Bennyisms" while he went to attend George Burns' premiere in Las Vegas. However, two things worried Jack. First, he wanted to know if Allen Funt and *Candid Camera* were well enough known to the general public. I assured him that they were, although I didn't have the heart to tell him that at the moment Funt's *Candid Camera* was rising high in the ratings race and had climbed past Jack's program in the weekly popularity polls. Jack's second worry was whether we'd need legal permission from Funt to do this routine, and whether there was anything in it that might possibly offend him. I assured him that there would be nothing in it to which Allen could object, and that in fact it would probably flatter him to have a man of Jack's importance doing a routine about him. Furthermore, although I felt that we had no legal responsibility to obtain Funt's permission, if for some reason it turned out that we did need it, I was confident that I could get it on a personal basis because when we were kids Allen and I lived in adjoining apartment houses in Brooklyn, and my first boyhood crush was on Allen's beautiful sister Dorothy. (When the routine I wrote gained fame and Funt heard of it, he sent Jack a warm personal letter of thanks, and also a note congratulating me on having written it.)

So, feeling happy that Jack was pleased with the idea, I went home to fill it out and punch it up. The preceding printed version you read contains much of this subsequent work.

Two mornings later I got a person-to-person phone call from Jack Benny, and the telephone operator told me as she announced the call, "I don't believe it's really Jack Benny because he's not calling collect." On the other end of the line I could hear Jack screaming with laughter at the fact that a telephone operator could "top" him.

Jack got on the phone and with his usual enthusiasm opened the conversation by saying, "Milt, isn't that the funniest telephone operator you ever heard?" Then he continued by telling me the purpose of his call. He said, "Last night George Burns opened here, and Milt, he was the most fantastic sensation." He then spent several minutes raving about Burns' big hit, and he added, "When George finished his show, he introduced me from the audience and they applauded. George stopped them by saying, 'Don't applaud him or he'll want to come up here and perform.' Well, they applauded louder and George made me get up on stage. I wasn't prepared, but I had read the Allen Funt routine a couple of times, and even though I didn't know it perfectly I figured I might try it on George's audience, and Milt, I want to tell you that this is possibly the greatest piece of material ever written."

Jack continued, "I'm only sorry you weren't here to hear it, Milt, because it set the world's record for long, loud laughs."

I was flattered, but then I reminded Jack that I had been working on the routine for the past two days and I had added enough to it to make it run a little over four minutes in length. Jack said, "Milt, last night it ran six minutes." I was surprised at this because the less than a page of material I had given him should have taken no longer than a minute or two to perform at the most, and I asked him how come it had run so long. Jack started explaining, modestly at first, "Well, George warmed up the audience with his show which was so great that they were in a laughing mood. Then, the situation of me picking up a girl was so funny that every little pause I took, or stare I gave, plus a few lines I ad-libbed, all got screams from the audience."

Two days later he returned to Los Angeles and we finished the routine as it is printed in this chapter—and let me make it clear that at least a couple of the laugh lines were those ad-libbed by Jack when he had tried it out a few nights earlier.

Jack was scheduled to start his nightclub tour playing Harrah's in Lake Tahoe the following week. The morning after he opened I got another call from Jack.

Jack was more enthusiastic than ever. This time he told me that he had done the routine at both shows at Harrah's the night before, and he apologized for not calling me to report between the dinner show and the late show. He said the first show was the best he had ever done in his entire career, but the second show was much better. Then he added in a teasing voice, "Milt, I cheated you. I underpaid you for that routine." The fact was that, as usual, he had rewarded me more than generously. Jack invited me to fly up to Tahoe with my wife Hilda as his guests to see the show and spend a few days with him, but I was working on another series at the time and couldn't take the time off.

Jack called me almost every day from Lake Tahoe to tell me that the reception the routine got every night surpassed the excellent way it was received the night before—and he would sometimes add, "Oh boy, did I underpay you for that routine."

After a week or so he phoned me, all excited. George Burns had finished his engagement in Vegas and flown to Tahoe to catch Jack's show. George caught both the dinner and late performance, and then he told Jack that he thought he had a funnier finish for the routine. Jack told it to me: "You know how the routine ends with my saying, 'The wig came off, and sure enough it was Allen Funt. I was so surprised I could hardly finish the dance!' Well, George suggests that I say, 'The wig came off, and sure enough it was Allen Funt, and I was so startled that I left. I didn't feel too bad leaving because I figured I saved fifty dollars.'" Now that was George's suggestion for the finish, and a funny one. Moreover, George was a top comic with more experience in comedy than anyone else except for Jack himself. And in addition to that, George was Jack's best friend. Yet Jack wouldn't change a line in my routine without checking with me first. (This was not a tribute to me. He treated all his writers identically.)

I thought it over for a few seconds and then answered, "Jack, George's idea is very funny—perhaps funnier than the blackout you have now. But one thing bothers me. During the entire routine you are an innocent man who is not on the prowl for a girl. The most you hope for through the entire bit is to spend an hour or so talking and dancing with an attractive girl. If you do the ending about saving fifty dollars, then from the moment you met this girl you took her for a hooker and you were out for. . . ." At this point Jack interrupted me: "Oh my God, Milt, you're so right. I change from an innocent shnook to a dirty old man." Then I added, "Jack, maybe you could try George's ending at one of the late shows when there are no children in. . . ." Again Jack interrupted me saying, "No, no. No matter how funny it is, this new ending gives an entirely new connotation to the whole routine."

The next time I heard from Jack was when he called me from London. He was playing the Palladium and had been there a week, and he apologized for not calling sooner. When he arrived in London, he found out that *Candid Camera* was a favorite TV show there. Therefore he did the routine at the Palladium, and the English theatergoers liked it even more than the American audiences. "And," Jack added apologetically, "the reason I didn't call you sooner was because I wanted to see the royal family's reaction to the routine. Milt, you'd be thrilled if you saw how the Queen of England and all the other members of her entourage screamed and applauded your jokes." Then he closed with his now-perennial ending, "Gee, Milt, did I underpay you for that routine."

After he had hung up and I was coming down to earth again I thought to myself, "Gee, people have loved it in Las Vegas and laughed at it in Tahoe, and in London the Queen and the royal family screamed and applauded it—and I have never yet heard Jack do the routine before an audience."

Several months passed and I was awakened one morning by a phone call from a friend and occasional collaborator, Al Schwartz, who asked me if I had seen the Jack Paar program the previous night. When I said I hadn't seen it, he informed me that Paar told his audience that he had seen Jack Benny do one of the funniest nightclub routines he had ever witnessed, and because he felt that Benny would be too bashful to broadcast a slightly blue bit, he would give his version of what Benny did. Then Paar had done the entire routine, trying at the same time to mimic the mannerisms and stares of Benny. Schwartz told me that Paar had gotten lots of laughs with it. I greeted this news with mixed emotions. I was happy that Paar thought it was so excellent, and unhappy because I got neither cash nor credit. And not only that, but now almost all of America, as well as London, the largest city in England, had seen my material performed, but I hadn't.

Three mornings later I got phone calls from several people asking me if I had seen the previous night's Paar show, and again my answer was no. They told me that Jack, who was in New York from where Paar's programs emanated, had made an unscheduled appearance on the program. Jack, I was told, had put on his pouting act, pretended he was hurt, and announced his unhappiness that a few nights earlier Paar had performed his favorite routine. He had come on the Paar program at this time, he said, to show the audience how the routine *really* should be done, provided that the audience would like to see it. The audience began to applaud loudly, led by Paar who knew a good thing even though he realized that he would be the butt of several gags. Jack then did the act, and everyone told me that he was magnificent, that he had milked every laugh line in the routine to the greatest possible extent, and that he had finished to a standing ovation, again led by Paar. Jack then walked back to his seat next to the host and said in semi-swishy tones: "There, *that's* how it should be done." Paar again led a standing ovation for Benny who pretended not to be mollified.

So again the routine had been broadcast, and again I had missed it. Now I began to watch Paar's program every night, but the only other reference to the bit was the following night when Bob Hope was a guest. Hope commented on the fact that he had seen both Benny and Paar do the routine, and he said, "That's what amazes me about Benny. He takes a one-line joke and makes a career out of it."

Several months later I was signed to write a one-hour television special starring, among others, Jack Benny. When we met at the first rehearsal Jack told everybody about the fabulously funny routine I had prepared for him and how well he had done with it. Then I broke the news to Jack that I had never seen him perform it. Jack thought for a moment and then said, "Well, you'll see it this week. When we film the show, I'll come out in advance and warm up the audience by doing it for you and the gang. But don't expect any extra money for it."

On the night we were to film the show, I was sitting in the booth feeling nervous but pleasantly excited. Jack was introduced, got his usual applause, and told a couple of short jokes to get the viewers in a laughing mood. Then he said, "Ladies and gentlemen. One of the writers of tonight's program is a man who wrote my radio and television shows for dozens of years. Recently he wrote one of the greatest nightclub routines in history, and due to circumstances beyond his control—which means I never paid him for the material —he's never seen me do it. Tonight he's sitting in the sponsor's booth, and I am dedicating this performance to him, so for his sake, not mine, laugh at it. Here it is."

Then Jack proceeded to do an entirely different routine!

After he said the first few lines, I realized that he wasn't per-forming the "Candid Camera" bit but was doing something else—in fact, something I hadn't even written. For one of the few times in our association, Jack had turned the tables on me and made me fall on the floor helpless with laughter. When he finished, he walked offstage to thunderous applause, and a moment or two later the phone in the sponsor's booth rang. It was Jack calling me. I got on the phone, and all he said was, "Don't tell me I haven't got a sense of humor!" And he hung up.

They then proceeded to film the one-hour television special. Now these specials are not filmed in one continuous stretch, but usually in several sequences lasting from a few minutes to nine or ten minutes long. (They can't run any longer because the cameras only hold about ten minutes' worth of film.) Thus when we make a show like this there are several breaks while cameras are reloaded, new scenes are set up, and old sets are removed. During these breaks, the comics come onstage and clown around so that the audience will not "cool" off. At the second break that evening Jack walked on-stage and, grinning like a schoolboy who had pulled a prank, told the audience what he had done to me. He then proceeded to do the routine, and possibly because he had the audience so captivated by then, or perhaps because his delivery was better than his usually perfect performance, he was even more brilliant than ever that night. He finished to a standing ovation, and then, much to my embarrassment and delight, he yelled "Author, Author," and I came onstage and took a bow with the audience giving me an ovation.

When we had finished filming the show that night, Jack thanked all those who were connected with it for their cooperation. Then he took me aside and very seriously thanked me for having given him a truly great piece of material. He said that he knew he frequently kidded me about underpaying me for it and that he wanted to give me a bonus. I told him that I had a big enough bonus in the knowl-edge that every time he performed that piece, he thought of me. I said that just having him think kindly of me was important to me, and also that the many phone calls plus the tribute he paid me that night, and calling "Author, Author," all added up to more than sufficient compensation. Jack continued to insist that he wanted to give me a check as a bonus. I said, "No, Jack, I'd feel better if you don't." And, quick as a hair trigger, he replied, "Well gee, Milt, if your health is concerned, forget it."

22
Jack and the Critics

While Broadway drama critics, movie critics, and book critics serve a useful purpose and wield tremendous power and influence, the radio critic was about as important as being a dance director at Forest Lawn Cemetery.

When radio was done live there was little likelihood that any critic could hear this program in advance and thus warn the listeners against it, or urge them to tune in the show. And unlike television programs, there were no reruns during the heyday of radio if the initial broadcast was missed.

Television critics today are more important than their earlier radio counterparts because almost everything on the tube today is filmed or taped weeks in advance, and critics are usually allowed to view these offerings ahead of their broadcast dates and thereby give their readers an inkling of what they have in store for them. The radio critic had no such advantage and thus far less power. It is true that the constant carping of a critic could do some damage to a comic, but more probably to his ego than to his ratings. Nevertheless, most of the stars tried to maintain cordial relations with the radio critics and to pretend affection even where none actually existed.

In the case of Jack Benny, he had reason to like reviewers because they always liked him. At least most of them did. One who didn't was a lady named Harriet Van Horne who served as columnist and critic on the *New York World-Telegram and Sun*. I remember clearly that I had written my first program with the other members of Benny's new team of writers for his 1943 seasonal debut on October 10 with a show emanating from New York. On Monday, October 11, I rushed out and bought up all the newspapers to see what they had to say about us. We knew that Jack's revamping of his writing staff would make the critics pay a little more attention to us than to those other regular series starting their new seasons. I was pleased because the write-ups ranged from good to raves, except for Miss Van Horne who dismissed us with a few lines implying that it was the usual boring Benny broadcast.

We were elated at all the other comments, but Miss Van Horne's casual dismissal of the program as something second-class upset us. However, Jack wasn't fazed. He said, "Fellows, I'll never get a good review from her. She insists that once she set up an interview with me, and not only didn't I come, but I didn't have the decency to call her and break the appointment." Then he told us that he had no recollection of the incident, but when he found out that she was angry, he wrote a note explaining this, and when it wasn't answered, he tried to call her personally but couldn't get her, and she never called back.

As I got to know Jack better, I realized that he was telling the truth. He was fanatic about punctuality, and if he thought he was going to be late he would call the person in question or the restaurant to leave an apologetic message, explaining why he was tardy.

Fred Allen once told me that he was supposed to meet Jack at some restaurant for lunch at 12:30, and Jack called him and said, "Fred, take your time. I may be as much as five minutes late." Fred smiled, and then he added, "I didn't follow his instructions and take my time. I had to rush like crazy because I was going to be ten minutes late."

Oddly enough our next experience with Miss Van Horne also involved Fred Allen who was one of her favorites, and who was the guest star on the opening show of our second season, October 1, 1944. This was a momentous program because after many years of saying J,E,L,L,O, Jack was now going to start saying LS/MFT, LS/MFT, since his sponsor was no longer General Foods but the American Tobacco Company. The plot of the program was simple, and it was based on what seemed to be the truth. We hinged our action on the fact that Jack was nervous about pleasing his new sponsor, and during the first half of the show he mentioned several times to the members of his cast that he had a noon appointment with the sponsor and didn't want to be late. There were several jokes about plugging the new product, and at one point Don Wilson was reminded that Luckies didn't come in six delicious flavors.

Everyone kept advising Jack not to be so nervous, which only made him more jittery. Finally he left the house and arrived at his sponsor's office a half-hour early. The secretary informed him that Mr. Riggio, the sponsor, had someone else in his office, but she would notify him that Jack was waiting.

The scene now switched to Mr. Riggio's office, and when the secretary informed him on the intercom that Mr. Benny was waiting in the outer office, he told her to tell Jack to wait a few minutes because he was in conference. Then he clicked off the intercom and said, "I'm sorry for the interruption—now what were you saying?" And we heard the unmistakable tones of Fred Allen nasally knifing Jack by saying, "You're making a big mistake in hiring Benny."

The studio audience greeted Allen's surprise appearance with laughter and applause. For several minutes Fred ripped Jack apart to his sponsor. Then when the sponsor felt that he had to call Jack in, there was no way for Fred to go out without Jack seeing him, so he hid in the closet.

Jack came in and did all his standard nervous bits, including the high giggle, the nervous laugh, and getting his sponsor's name mixed up by talking too fast. Naturally he told the sponsor how lucky he was to get him instead of a has-been like Fred Allen.

Finally Fred came out of the closet to defend himself, Jack accused Fred of stabbing him in the back, and we wound up with a crackling exchange of insults, which was neither new nor unique, but what the listeners always wanted of Allen and Benny.

The audience reaction was good, and the newspaper reviews were unanimous in rating the show anywhere from good to great—unanimous, that is, until we received a copy of Miss Van Horne's review. She crucified us. As I recall, words like "contrived," "flat," "belabored," and "dull" were some of the nicer things she said about us. She gave us only one small compliment when she remarked that the show was saved from being a total loss by the appearance of Fred Allen in the last half. And, she continued, Mr. Allen's many ad-libs were the only good laughs on the program that opening night.

Now a line like that last one was both unfair and unfounded. How could this lady, three thousand miles away, know what was written in the script and what, if anything, Fred threw in? It so happened that we had a tight script, and we finished "on the button," which meant that everything was timed exactly right so that we went off the air precisely when we were scheduled to do so. Perhaps because Fred may have felt that Jack was nervous with a first show for a new sponsor, he kept his unwritten remarks to a minimum. In point of fact, he only ad-libbed three things.

Fred was with us when we saw the review, and he was disturbed. He, like everyone else, especially our new advertising agency and sponsor, was delighted not only with the high rating but also with the excellent reviews and reaction we got. Fred told Jack that he was going to phone Miss Van Horne and set her straight on his contribution to the show. However, Jack asked him not to do so, since he didn't want it to seem as though he had put Allen up to it.

What Fred did do was drop her a note with a copy of her column. I saw the note, and as nearly as I can remember, he wrote, in his usual lower case typing, "i only ad-libbed three things on that jack benny show. two of them landed on the floor and broke and you could have made an omelet out of them big enough to feed all of arizona. the third got a snicker so miniscule in size that it would have been crushed to death on the abbott and costello show. sincerely yours, fred allen."

As far as I know, the note was never acknowledged by Miss Van Horne privately or in print.

Needless to say, not all the bad reviews we got were undeserved. We had our share of bad shows, but I'm vain enough to think that even our weak ones had at least a few minutes of humor.

Once Jack got a review from an out-of-town paper where the critic must have majored in vocabulary because it contained a word "exacerbates" that none of his writers had remembered hearing before. Jack looked it up in the dictionary and became hysterical. He said, "Hey, we've got to use this in one of our shows." And it was used.

The review, as I remember it, said, "I am among the first to acknowledge the supremacy of Jack Benny's television shows, but at times they have a tendency to exacerbate." On the next TV program, Jack proudly read the review to Rochester, and he pronounced the last word slowly, syllable by syllable. Then he went to the dictionary and started turning the pages until he found the word. After reading the definition to himself, he said, "Gee, Rochester, do you know that ex-ac-er-bate means to irritate." Thus, instead of brooding over an uncomplimentary review, he turned it into a good routine on his show.

Jack never resented bad reviews if he felt that they were justified, constructive, and based on intelligent reasoning, even though he disagreed with that reasoning. To substantiate this, let me cite an interesting incident that took place in February 1947. We were at Palm Springs for relaxation and a change of scene for a couple of broadcasts. While we were there, one of us bought a copy of *Esquire*. That particular issue contained an essay on radio humor written by a well-known critic, Gilbert Seldes. In his article, Seldes said that unfortunately almost all of radio humor was based on insult.

It so happened that Seldes was also in Palm Springs during our sojourn there. After a staff meeting, he was surprised to get a phone call from Jack, not berating him for his mild blast, but asking him if he wanted to appear on Jack's show as a guest star to defend his published sentiments.

Seldes agreed, and in his book *The Public Arts* (Simon & Schuster, 1956) he discusses his debut as a "comedian" on Benny's broadcast and admits that the writers for the program (Sam Perrin, Milt Josefsberg, George Balzer, and John Tackaberry) "accomplished the miracle of making me seem very funny indeed." He then goes on to mention that his guest appearance was brought about by the paragraph he had written for *Esquire* protesting that "virtually all air comedy [came down] to jokes about Jolson's age, Benny's miserliness, and a few other insults."

Seldes goes on to write that Benny and the cast started his sequence by calling attention to the fact that he objected to so many insults in comedy. We then proceeded to play a brief scene showing how the program would sound if no insults were used. Everyone was so sweet that the best way to describe it is by recalling Oscar Levant's acid comment: "I never watch Dinah Shore's show. I'm a diabetic."

According to Seldes, "The dialogue assigned me was brief and bright and, at one or two moments, insanely funny." We made this short sketch nauseatingly saccharine, and wound up with Seldes getting big laughs by insulting everybody on the show. As he writes, "My exit line was an insult to Benny which left him apparently defeated."

Thus, as we have shown, Jack took the bad reviews with the good, and he made capital of them on these two occasions. Oddly enough, in view of Seldes' complaints, we used only insulting reviews as program material, for we knew that "nice is nice, but nasty is funny." Jack put these two derogatory reviews to excellent use, showing that insults, in their place, are a much needed ingredient in comedy.

Possibly the strangest thing that ever happened in the history of the Benny show, and perhaps any show in the history of broadcasting, began with a very complimentary review of our Sunday night program in critic John Crosby's column for the *New York Herald Tribune*. I've been fortunate to have worked almost my entire career with three of the top and most popular performers in show business, and, due more to their talents than my own, I have basked in the warmth of hundreds of great notices. However, none was more glowing than the tribute John Crosby paid to Jack and his writers. He devoted his entire column to telling the world that it was an amazing coincidence that the world's greatest comedian had hired the world's four greatest writers. Each of us felt like a reincarnation of Mark Twain, only wittier. Friends called me from New York, and I tried to accept their collective kudos with an almost shy nonchalance. One columnist even printed an excerpt from the column, saying, "The reason Jack Benny and his writers are walking ten feet tall is because of the unbelievable compliments John Crosby's column heaped upon them." We all felt that John Crosby was unquestionably the most knowledgeable of all critics and the epitome of erudition.

A few days later, Jack received a personal note from John Crosby in New York. Crosby also enclosed a clipping of the column with the notation: "In case you haven't seen it." (Hadn't seen it? Jack and every one of us had been sent copies via air mail special delivery letters from friends and relatives in New York. We carried copies in our wallets, temporarily evicting our children's pictures. We even boasted that we would have the words tattooed on various parts of our anatomy, and one of us said that he was putting a codicil in his will to make sure that it was engraved on his tombstone.)

Crosby's note said that he admired the script so much, he would be delighted if Jack would send him a copy so that he could keep it among his treasured trophies. Jack not only sent it to him, but also a lovely note of thanks for himself and on our behalf.

One week later John Crosby wrote another column in which he referred to the ecstatic review he had given to the show the week before. He told his readers he was so impressed with the program that he had sent for a copy of the script. He had now read it and found it flat, turgid, belabored, and contrived, and to prove his point, he reprinted two pages from the script.

Now Jack Benny's scripts did not normally read as funny as the scripts of comics who went in more for jokes than for character. Jack's scripts were slower, and each laugh was carefully built on the preceding one which was laid as a foundation for the overall effect of the whole show.

However, Mr. Crosby picked out two of the funniest pages we had ever written. They not only were funny when performed but also funny when read, and we got dozens of calls telling us how hilarious they thought Crosby's excerpts were and asking "What's the inside story?"

There was no inside story. Mr. Crosby wrote that just inserting a "Hmmmm" or "Well" and the repeated usage of the single word "But...but...but..." do not a writer make.

We writers were furious. We wanted to take out ads in the trade papers and print the two columns side by side and ask, "Which John Crosby knows what the hell he's talking about?"

Jack talked us out of this. However he couldn't stop us from replacing the Crosby columns in our wallets with the beautiful pictures of our beautiful children or from calling up the tattoo artist and breaking our appointments. Needless to say, I also phoned my lawyer and had a certain codicil removed from my will.

23
Fabulous Guest Stars

One of the advantages of working on a big-time, high-budget show like Jack Benny's was getting to meet so many interesting people. During the nearly five hundred programs I worked on for Jack, more than half of the shows had guest stars. We had practically every important motion picture actress or actor on the program. Jack played host to mayors, governors, and even ex-President Harry Truman. We had police chiefs, movie producers, directors, musicians, composers, network presidents and vice presidents, authors, and song writers. We made comedians out of columnists like Louella Parsons, Walter Winchell, and Ed Sullivan, and we had every type of athlete perform. We did a prizefight show with Joe Louis, who read his lines in such a flat, funny, dead-pan fashion that we immediately booked him back for the following week's program. We fooled around with football by having Notre Dame's coach, Frank Leahy, as a guest. We gagged about golf with Ben Hogan, and Leo "Lippy" Durocher represented baseball on several of our programs.

We got all these celebrities to appear for two main reasons. First, Jack paid top money. Second, they knew that Jack would see to it that they would get the best material possible, and that, unlike some other comedians, he would play straight for them instead of vice versa.

In all the years I was with *The Jack Benny Show,* we were only turned down by one movie star—The King, Clark Gable, who told Jack he was afraid that he might actually become physically ill if he appeared on a live radio show. He said that if he made a fluff or read a line badly, he was afraid he'd be so shaken up that he might be unable to continue. Jack tried to tell him that once he read his first line on the air, the audience reaction would be so great that he'd breeze through the rest of the show. And Gable said, "Yes, Jack, but I might very well throw up waiting to do that first line."

The idea we had for Clark Gable's appearance seemed like a fun-filled gimmick. It was to start with Jack's sponsor informing him at the opening of the script that he must get Gable as a guest star. When approached, Clark would agree to appear, but only if he received the then astronomical salary of ten thousand dollars. Naturally Jack would be aggravated at having to pay this high fee, but at the same time he would be afraid that if he didn't produce Gable, his sponsor might even cancel his contract. Therefore he would reluctantly agree to pay this small fortune, but he would tell his cast members, "I'll get my money's worth." Then the script would be written with numerous "interruption" bits, and Jack would have Gable play all these unimportant menial roles.

For example, Clark would be the attendant in the parking lot who would ask Jack, "Shall I park your car, Mr. Benny, or do you want it to fall apart right here?" Next he would come into the studio as a Western Union boy and say, "I have a wire for Jack Benny from Fred Allen." Jack would say, "I haven't got my glasses. You read it for me." And Gable would answer, "It's not the kind of wire you read—it's the kind you twist around your neck."

Gable would then come in as a new sound effects man and try out some funny sounds with Jack; next he would be the network censor objecting to Jack saying "heck" in the script because everyone knew that "heck" meant another four-letter word beginning with "he--." Jack would defiantly say to Gable, "Look, censor, what'll you do if I don't change it?" and Gable would then paraphrase his famous farewell as Rhett Butler to Scarlett O'Hara and say, "Frankly, my dear, I don't give a *darn.*"

We also planned to have Gable come in as an engineer to test the microphone by talking into it and repeating the usual phrase, "1,2,3,4, testing," and to use a falsetto voice while playing a script girl or secretary. Finally after making him play a dozen or so "extra" roles, Gable was supposed to angrily quit, and Benny would happily tell his cast that he had obeyed his sponsor's wishes, and not only that, he had saved the ten thousand dollar guest fee because he wouldn't have to pay it since Gable walked off the show. At this point we planned to end the show by having Gable return and say in his so easily recognized voice, "I'm Mr. Smith, Clark Gable's lawyer, and he's suing you for a million dollars for holding him up to public ridicule."

It was an excellent idea for a Benny broadcast, but it never came off because of "The King's" mike fright. We tried to think of some other star who could substitute for Gable, but Jack told us that it had to be Clark or no one. To my knowledge he was the only star who ever turned down a guest appearance on the show, and whenever he saw Jack after that, he would apologetically say that he knew it was a great idea, but he just couldn't bring himself to do a live comedy broadcast.

Writing guest appearances for big-name stars was easy. Most of them had well-defined characters on the screen, and we built our situations around the images they had built. When we had Bing Crosby, we would take advantage of his relaxed easy delivery, and would work in a song, preferably a comedic one. We used him on one show as a member of a new quartet Jack was supposedly auditioning to replace The Sportsmen, who sang many of our commercials with special lyrics. Of course, a Milton Berle would lead us into a broader type of comedy, while dramatic actresses like Ingrid Bergman and Barbara Stanwyck would participate in shows where we would take advantage of their forte. The real challenge came when you had a celebrity in a field other than entertainment, and some of these provided us with unforgettable incidents.

One was the governor who walked on stage with his fly open. Fortunately this was radio. And also fortunately it happened in the pre-broadcast warm-up so there was no sudden shout, scream, or laugh from an audience seeing something they weren't supposed to. Of course, if it had taken place during our broadcast it might have been interesting. He could have been one of the first politicians to be exposed on the air.

The date was May 10, 1953, and we were doing our broadcast from San Francisco where Jack was making a concert-type personal appearance at a local theater. (Oh yes, the opening act that Jack hired to round out a bill, including singer Giselle McKenzie, was a practically unknown performer named Sammy Davis, Jr.) The guest on our radio program was Lieutenant Governor Goodwin Knight, who later became governor of California.

Don Wilson started our customary warm-up fifteen minutes before air time by introducing Dennis Day, Rochester, Phil Harris, Mary Livingstone, and then Jack Benny. After the customary standard warm-up banter, Jack brought out our special guest, Goodwin Knight. The Lieutenant Governor walked out on stage, acknowledged his applause, and then sat down waiting for the broadcast to begin.

There were nine or ten people in the booth including the engineer, producer, writers, and our secretary, Jeanette Eymann. Suddenly the normally low-volume talk that went on in the control room was broken by a sharp feminine gasp. Jenny had spotted the open fly on Goodwin Knight's pants.

We had just two minutes to air time, and we wanted to warn the governor of his potential embarrassment—but how do you tell a governor his fly is open?

We tried to catch the eye of one of the members of our cast, but they were all busy giving their lines in the script a last minute once-over. We didn't think it would be smart to announce over the intercom system, for the entire studio audience to hear, "Hey, Guv, the stable's open." We decided the most tactful way was to bring him a note, as if he were receiving a message concerning the show. We wrote on the back of a page of script in large letters, "Dear Sir, your fly is open, but we'll still vote for you. The writers." Then we decided he might get flustered or think it was a joke, so we cut out the last part and just sent the vital first six words.

We folded it over, got an usher, and made him rush out on the stage. He handed the note to the governor with less than a minute before air time. Goodwin Knight's reaction to the note when he read it made us all realize that he would go from Lieutenant Governor to Governor and maybe to President some day.

He read the note and acted as though it contained a message saying that a dear friend was behind him waiting to greet him. Knight smiled, stood up, turned his back to the audience, waved a friendly greeting to a non-existent buddy with one hand while the the other pulled up the offending zipper, and he seated himself with the look of a man who had done nothing more than say "hello" to an old buddy. It was all done in one graceful, flowing, continuous movement and no one on the stage knew about the incident until later.

When the show was finished, the Lieutenant Governor gleefully told the cast what had happened. Then he added to Benny, "You know, Jack, I could have ruined both of our careers if I stood up with my pants open as the orchestra started the opening bars of your theme song, 'Can It Be the Breeze That Fills the Trees [With Rare and Magic Perfume]? Oh No, It Isn't the Breeze, It's Love in Bloom.'" And that was probably the first and only time Governor Goodwin Knight made a great comedian fall to the floor in hysterics.

Possibly the most polished political figure we ever had on was California's Governor Earl Warren on May 20, 1945. He was a delightful man, and he read his lines much better than many professional performers.

At that time Governor Warren was being discussed as a strong possibility to receive the next Republican nomination for the presidency. The writers mentioned this to him and as a gag we gave him a slogan if he did run for the nation's highest office. The slogan was:

When you go to the polls in forty-eight,
Remember the kid from the Golden Gate.

Warren smiled, asked us to repeat it, and jotted it down in a notebook. One of us asked, "You wouldn't really use a slogan like that, would you?" He smiled and said, "No, but I'm going to get a lot of laughs with it at parties."

In the script we had one memorable joke, with Jack, in his usual position of trying to brag about his expertise in another man's domain, telling the governor that he knew plenty about politics because he had a very important friend in politics, Edward Flynn. Warren reacted on hearing the name and asked Jack, "Do you mean Edward J. Flynn?" Jack, in tones both proud and smug, said, "Yes. Do you know him?" And Warren answered, "I should. He's my chauffeur." It was the biggest laugh on the show.

Guest stars were welcome breaks in the regular routine of writing weekly shows, and some of our more memorable moments, both on and off the air, were provided by the biggest names in and out of the entertainment field.

While almost all of them provided the show with a welcome lift, one of those we looked forward to with especially eager anticipation was Isaac Stern, the violin virtuoso. Jack admired, and openly envied, all the great violinists, but I believe that from a friendship as well as talent standpoint his favorite was Isaac Stern. (Incidentally, I believe it was Stern who was responsible for Jack making his famous appearances with philharmonic orchestras that eventually raised so many millions of dollars for those financially troubled groups.)

Whenever we had Stern as a guest we would insert at the appropriate spot in the script the words "Isaac Stern Does Musical Number Here." Then, when the cast readings were finished, the proceedings never varied. It was a set piece like an ancient Kabuki play where no line of dialogue or action has been changed for centuries. Stern would ask Jack if there was any particular musical composition he preferred, and Jack would defer to Isaac's judgment. Isaac would name three or four selections and Jack would seem to think them over, giving each consideration. Finally he would solemnly say, "Maybe I'd be able to choose better if I heard them." Then the great virtuoso would give a private concert for Jack and his group, and eventually they would confer and agree on one number. Afterward Stern would say, "You always do this, Jack. You know well in advance what you want me to play, and yet you make me give a private command performance for you." Jack would invariably laugh hysterically, nodding in agreement to Stern's accurate accusation. Yet the next time Isaac Stern was booked as a guest star on the show, they would go through the same routine as though it had never happened before.

Two-time Academy Award winner Ingrid Bergman unintentionally supplied us with a hilarious moment during rehearsal, and this was the only occasion I can recall when Jack stifled his laughter, doing so in order not to embarrass the great dramatic actress.

The incident stemmed from the well-known fact that Jack didn't meet the success in movies that he did in radio and TV. He had made some excellent movies, and in its extremely complimentary obituary on Benny, *Time* magazine (January 6, 1975) said, "Cast as the Polish ham actor in Ernst Lubitsch's wartime comedy, *To Be Or Not To Be*, the comedian gave one of the screen's classic performances." However, although he was singled out for critical acclaim by virtually all reviews of this picture, as well as for several others, including *Charley's Aunt* and *George Washington Slept Here*, he is best remembered for a mediocre movie, *The Horn Blows at Midnight*.

In his customary self-demeaning way, Jack constantly poked fun at this picture, and it became one of the program's most consistent running gags. Long after the film was out of release we constantly quipped about it as one of Hollywood's most egregious efforts. Finally, after many years of panning the picture, we had Miss Bergman as a guest on one of our radio programs.

In the midst of a coffee break during rehearsal, Miss Bergman began to tell Jack how much she admired him as a comedian and what a consummate showman he was. Jack basked in the warmth of Miss Bergman's ardent praise until she added in all earnestness, "Jack, no other comedian but you would have had the foresight to purposely make a bad movie like *The Horn Blows at Midnight* so you'd have a subject to talk about on your radio shows." Her obvious sincerity and admiration filled Jack with mixed emotions, and he almost choked on the laughter he swallowed. Later, when she left to get dressed for the broadcast, Benny turned to us and said, "I didn't have the heart to tell her that I didn't make that movie stink on purpose."

Possibly the most popular and consistently funny guest stars on the Benny broadcasts were Ronald and Benita Colman. Their numerous appearances with Jack eventually enabled them to get their own program, the witty and erudite *Halls of Ivy*, and their British dignity and reserve provided a rich counterpoint to the buffoonery of Benny and his cast.

When we wrote the first script for the Colmans, we originally had no intention of having Benita appear with her husband. Although an actress, she was hardly known to listeners in America, and her comedic abilities were an unknown quality. Thus it would have been safer, and cheaper, to hire an experienced and inexpensive radio actress for the then minor role of Ronald Colman's wife.

Jack, however, was always a stickler for realism, and he was the one who decided that Benita Colman might possibly play the part of Benita Colman. It was one of his more fortuitous decisions, because not only did she lend more realism and publicity value to the part, but her sense of comedy and timing was so instinctively impeccable that she immediately became as important to the programs as her far better known husband.

At the start we treated the Colmans with the deference they deserved, but after a couple of shows we were all on a first-name basis, for they were very warm and down-to-earth human beings. As part of a program based on Halloween we had written a script where Ronnie and Benita were surprised, but not really too much so, that Jack had disguised himself as a kid and gone around cadging goodies via the traditional "Trick or Treat" gambit. Colman, in his usual disdainful tones when talking about Jack, related how he had answered the door to a series of impatient, insistent rings.

COLMAN

Imagine my reaction when I saw this . . . this *shnook* dressed as Little Bo Peep.

BENITA

Jack wore a "Little Bo Peep Costume"?

COLMAN

Yes . . . Then like an ill-mannered eight-year-old, he recited the following poem:

"Give me some candy,
Some cake or some pie,
'Cause if you don't do it,
I'll 'pit in your eye."

Then he curtsied and his toupee fell off.

Now there was something about this last line, or the one that followed it, which bothered Colman. When we finished reading the script he said, "Jack, exactly what is my motivation in saying this line?" Now the theater and television nowadays are loaded with actors, mainly dramatic actors, who studied Stanislavski's "method" of acting and who must know the motivation behind every word they utter. In radio comedy this was seldom if ever important. Therefore, Jack was not only surprised but a bit puzzled when Ronnie asked, "Jack, exactly what is my motivation in saying this line?" Jack thought for a split second and then answered, "Ronnie, I think your motivation is to get the biggest frigging laugh you can."

The cast and crew laughed at this, and Colman chuckled with the rest of us, but subconsciously he was still bothered, so he persisted: "Really, Jack, I would like to know—what is my real motivation in saying this line?" At which point his wife Benita answered him in her so well-groomed and clipped, cultured tones, "Ronnie dear, you heard him. Your motivation is to get the biggest frigging laugh you can." And he did.

Possibly Jack's favorite non-actor guest star was Sam Goldwyn who at the time was one of Hollywood's true living legends.

Jack was fond of Sam and delighted in occasionally telling stories about him. One concerned the renowned "yes men" in the industry who keep their high-paying positions by agreeing with the boss on everything and anything. Goldwyn was in a meeting with some of his executives, a few of whom fell into this category. It was many years ago before the air in Los Angeles turned to smog and you could breathe it without feeling it as a tangible thing. Visibility in those days was amazing, and even today, on a rare clear late afternoon, a Western sunset is a thing of breathtaking beauty.

This conference wore on, lasting for several hours. Suddenly Goldwyn rose from his chair, walked to the window, and said, "Never in my life did I ever see such a glorious sunset." The others in the room went to the window to share their employer's enthusiasm, and one "yes man" said, "Isn't it wonderful that a big man like Sam Goldwyn takes time out to admire a little thing like a sunset!"

Jack liked Sam so much that he had him as a guest star several times. Two of these appearances were memorable—one because we kidded him about a famed Goldwynism, and the other because he surprised us all by doing the unexpected—unexpected, that is, from anyone but him—on our radio show.

The first occasion took place on April 6, 1947. A short time before this, the Academy Awards had been broadcast and famed composer Hoagy Carmichael had won an Oscar nomination for having written the best song of the year, "Ole Buttermilk Sky." The award for the best song had been presented to the recipient by Sam Goldwyn who also had the task of announcing the names of the nominees to the large listening public. However, instead of saying "Hoagy," he introduced him as "Hugo" Carmichael.

When Jack heard the broadcast, he immediately got the idea for our next program to have two guest stars, Sam Goldwyn and

"Hugo" Carmichael. It was a simple scene to write, and when both Jack and Hoagy kidded Goldwyn about saying "Hugo," Sam pretended to be indignant and said that he might occasionally make a mistake and mispronounce a word, but that he never got mixed up on the name of a famous person.

Jack said, "Okay, Sam, we'll take your word for it that you never mispronounced the name of a celebrity. Now tell us, what's the next picture you're going to make?" And Goldwyn replied that he was having a screenplay prepared, based on the novel *Les Miserables*, by that famous French author, Victor Hoagy.

It was a funny bit, and since nearly every listener to our show had heard his boo-boo on the Academy Awards broadcast and also read about it subsequently in the newspapers, they were all familiar with the situation and our program was well received.

However, from Goldwyn's reaction to the blackout line when he first read it at our Saturday rehearsal, we should have had an indication of what was to come the following year. Sam didn't want to do the joke about the famous French writer Victor "Hoagy," not because he was afraid that it would make him seem ignorant, but because, as he explained to Jack, he had no intention of making a film based on *Les Miserables*. The Victor "Hoagy" line was the perfect payoff to the whole program, but Goldwyn was adamant. He wanted us to use the name of the picture he was actually producing —not for the publicity value, but merely because he wanted to tell the truth.

We solved this crisis by changing the lines. Originally the script had him say, "The next picture I'm going to make is. . . ." We switched this line so that Sam said: "I'm having a screenplay prepared. . . ." His logic was that this could be true because often a producer has a script prepared but never gets around to making a movie out of it. By saying that he was having a script prepared rather than that he was actually making a movie, he felt that he would not be lying to the public.

If we had only learned our lesson from this episode about his integrity, which was evident in every movie he made, we would not have had the famed incident that took place one year later on our broadcast of April 18, 1948.

Our show emanated from Palm Springs that Sunday, and in it we did our almost annual version of a sketch we called "Murder at The Racquet Club." As a special guest on this program we had Charles Farrell, a famous star of early movies, who had wisely invested his money in The Racquet Club, a popular tennis resort in Palm Springs.

Every time Jack, who played the chief of police, ran into Farrell during the sketch, the actor would identify himself by saying, "I'm Charles Farrell, star of *Seventh Heaven*." For those too young to remember, *Seventh Heaven* was an excellent movie that *The New York Times* had chosen as one of the ten best pictures of 1927, and Farrell had co-starred in it with Janet Gaynor. However, by now it was twenty years old, and his constant repetition of the line, "I'm Charles Farrell, star of *Seventh Heaven*," began to build into big laughs.

We frequently had several important stars make cameo guest appearances on our shows from Palm Springs. They showed up a half-hour before we did our broadcast, ran over their lines which usually amounted to twenty or thirty seconds of dialogue, and then got a big reaction from the audience when they made their surprise appearance.

One of the guest stars that week was Frank Sinatra, who identified himself as a friend of Charlie Farrell, star of *Seventh Heaven*. A few minutes later, Police Chief Benny, investigating a murder, wanted to interrogate Frank again, but Jack was told that the singer wasn't there anymore. Jack was indignant, saying he had given orders that no suspect was supposed to leave, and he was told, "Sinatra didn't want to leave; he got carried away by the five o'clock breeze to Banning." This was a double gag, the first based on Sinatra's much-joked-about thinness, and the second, slightly esoteric, deriving its humor from the fact that starting in the late afternoon a strong wind usually whips through Palm Springs toward the nearby town of Banning.

In his quest to solve the murder at The Racquet Club, Benny cross-examined several equally important celebrities, all of whom made some remark about Charles Farrell, the star of *Seventh Heaven*. And toward the end of the list of surprise stars we had written in Sam Goldwyn. When Jack asked him where he was at the time of the murder, Goldwyn's answer in the script read, "I was in my room hating myself because I didn't produce *Seventh Heaven*."

Now this was in 1948, and at that time Sam Goldwyn had won Academy Awards for the best picture in 1939, *Wuthering Heights*, and the best picture of 1946, *The Best Years of Our Lives*, the only producer to that date to win two such Oscars. We thought it would be funny for a man with this impressive record, plus numerous other memorable pictures, to say that he hated himself because he didn't produce *Seventh Heaven*, which, although a fair picture, had been made over twenty years earlier and was now practically forgotten.

Goldwyn made his entrance on the program and received as big an ovation from our studio audience as any of the stars who were on it. However, when Jack asked him where he was at the time of the murder, Sam ad-libbed, "I was in my room hating myself because I didn't produce *Gone with the Wind*."

Posing as a reluctant Santa Claus, December 1936.

Training for a prize fight with Fred Allen, 1939.

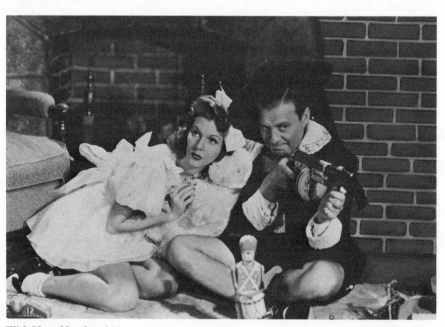

With Mary Martin, 1941.

With Rochester in Paramount's 1940 *Buck Benny Rides Again*.

With Ann Sheridan, 1942.

As Gracie Allen with George Burns at a "Friars Frolic" in the late 1940s. *Photo by Frank Worth.*

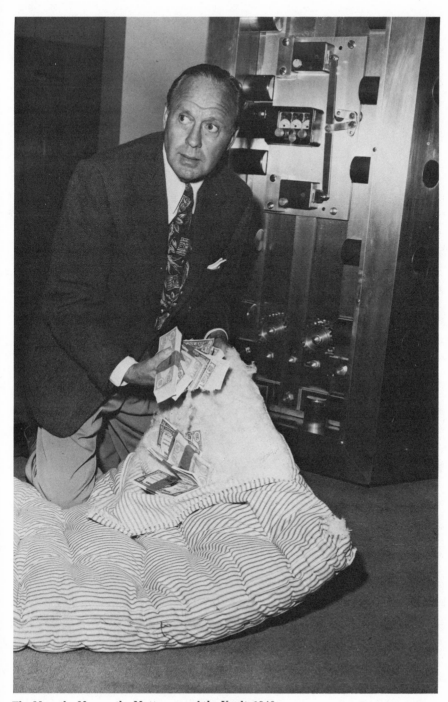

The Man, the Money, the Mattress, and the Vault, 1948.

As Ben Hur in a Milton Berle TV special, 1959, with Lawrence Harvey, Milton Berle, Kirk Douglas, and Charlton Heston.

As a hippie for the NBC special, *Jack Benny's New Look.*

As a sultan being weighed to receive his weight in gold, 1964.

As a hillbilly, October 1964, with fellow hillbillies Connie Francis and Don Wilson.

As a Bert Parksian beauty contest MC, on his December 1966 NBC special.

With fellow Roman statue George Burns, on his January 24, 1974 *Jack Benny's Second Farewell Special.*

It was one of the few times I've seen Jack's blue eyes almost pop out of his head as he stared at Sam in open-mouthed wonder. The line made no sense at all. *Seventh Heaven* was supposed to be the topper on a running gag. *Gone with the Wind* came out of left field, and the audience didn't laugh or even giggle. There was no reaction at all, except, as we could see from the control room, for some puzzled expressions on some faces. Meanwhile, we writers were all indignantly asking each other who the hell the idiot was who had changed that line, but we all pleaded "not guilty," and in our hearts we knew that none of us would make so important a script change without consulting the other three or Jack himself.

When the show was over and the audience had departed, we gathered around Jack who was thanking all the guests for their appearances and performances. He saved Sam for the last, and when he asked Goldwyn why he had said *Gone with the Wind* instead of *Seventh Heaven,* the producer gave what he felt was a perfectly logical explanation. He said, "Jack I've produced so many pictures better than *Seventh Heaven* that I don't care who made it. The only picture I didn't make which I wish I did was *Gone with the Wind,* so that's what I said because that would be funnier than *Seventh Heaven.*"

And for the rest of his life Sam Goldwyn probably thought that he was right, because his explanation reduced Jack to a quivering heap on the floor.

24

The Personal Side of Jack

Jack probably had more friends and fewer enemies than anyone else in the entertainment business, a clique-like colony known for its mercurial changes of opinions and affections. He exuded affection and, like a magnet, attracted it. In 1973, when an interviewer questioned him about his legion of friends, Jack answered, half-seriously, half-quipping, "When you live as long as I have, you get to meet and like a lot more people."

Strolling the streets of any city, or, for that matter, any country, with Jack was a unique experience. In the more metropolitan areas he couldn't walk ten steps without being greeted by someone, and his greeting usually matched the other person's effusiveness. And as they exchanged pleasantries, his mind would be groping through his many memories, trying to recall if he was chatting with some long forgotten friend, or somebody in show business, or just a fan anxious for an autograph.

Because nature hadn't equipped him with the computer-like mind of a Milton Berle or Bob Hope, both of whom have instant and almost total recall of thousands of faces (and jokes), Jack tried harder. If indeed it was an obscure acquaintance with some tenuous ancient claim to friendship, and Jack recalled his name or possibly his occupation, his joy was usually greater than that of the surprised greeter. On the other hand, if the person was just a fan or admirer who felt that he actually knew Jack from having seen or heard him so many times via movies, radio, and TV, he was equally pleasant. He would patiently answer the same banal questions again and again and laugh at their jokes which he had heard thousands of times.

Jack defended his attitude toward these time-consuming interruptions, and his reasoning, an indication of his character, pursued the following lines: "I love walking, and I'm not going to give it up for anything. Also, I have enough ham in me to be flattered by being recognized. And what's so valuable about my time that I should worry about wasting it in pleasant conversation? After all, most people are nice, and if they take the time to talk to me, the least I can do is return the favor. And this way there is no chance of my offending someone I knew long ago."

Jack's fans traded quips with him on the street and he laughed at their jokes, usually based on his broadcasting image of the stereotyped skinflint. Endless autograph-seekers, thrusting their pens and papers at him, would say, "Make sure you're not signing a blank check." And he would laugh, as though he had never heard that crack before.

Jack's friends—varying in degrees of intimacy from men he truly loved, like George Burns who knew him for over half a century, to those he had met a scant few times—probably numbered in the thousands.

As time passed, until he was more than twice his admitted age of thirty-nine, Jack's circle of friends was an ever-widening one that encompassed the widely divergent ends of society's spectrum. His writers were fortunate enough to meet many of these famed personages on a business basis through his radio and television shows. A substantial percentage of them were constantly in his company, or at least were around him so frequently that to some small degree we considered them our friends too.

The next few chapters are devoted to those friends of his whom I knew through association or osmosis. There were many people who considered themselves close to Jack—and who probably were—whom I met only briefly or casually, and therefore I have only devoted a brief sentence or paragraph to them. Others through ignorance or oversight were inadvertently omitted.

As has often been noted in these pages and because George Burns was his closest, longest-lasting, and most intimate friend, we will start with him.

25
Jack and George Burns

Jack Benny and George Burns were the Damon and Pythias of show business. Fate created their characters and personalities so that they would blend perfectly, not so much in a theatrical sense but in their offstage relationships. George loved to entertain and Jack loved to laugh. This made for a healthy and happy friendship. At parties George would entertain the minute he was asked—and frequently when he wasn't asked. And all the guests at a party, though they numbered in the hundreds, knew that while Burns was clowning in front of all of them, he was performing for one person only—Jack Benny!

I guess the best-known story about Benny and Burns concerns the time when they were walking along Broadway and George told Jack that he had no sense of humor, which Jack stoutly denied. George then bet Jack five dollars that he would do something so corny that not even a feeble-minded fool would laugh at it, yet Jack would break up. Jack dared him to do it. George simply took his cigar, opened the breast pocket of Jack's jacket, and flicked his cigar ashes into it, and Jack collapsed right on the sidewalk in an hysterical heap.

When Jack met Mary he acted like most normal young men in love—he wanted his best girl to meet his best friend. Jack and

George were then on layoff periods between vaudeville tours and living at one of those hotels catering to the profession—any profession. Jack picked Mary up in a cab and then had the driver take them to the hotel where George was waiting. When they got out of the cab, Jack tried to be a courtly gentleman in the best Emily Post tradition and introduced them in formal fashion. "Mary," he said, "may I present my best friend, George Burns. George, may I present my fiancée, Mary Livingstone." Mary said a friendly hello, but George looked her over appraisingly for several seconds and then said in a side-of-the-mouth whisper that was intentionally loud enough for Mary to hear, "Gee, Jack, she's even nicer than the one you've got stashed in your room." Even though Mary was still practically a teenager, she had an excellent sense of humor, and while she may have subconsciously suspected that Burns' statement was true, she laughed at it.

From the first Mary "dug" George's sense of humor and they got along famously—and so did Gracie and Mary when they met. The Bennys and Burnses were a famed Hollywood quartet, and they were never afflicted with any of the petty bickerings you hear or read of in the gossip columns.

George had one favorite prank that he played on Jack numerous times, but usually when he was booked into variety theaters on the West Coast and Jack was back East. He would phone Benny person-to-person at about midnight, his time, thus waking Jack up because it was 3:00 A.M. on the Atlantic side of the continent. George would apologize, but tell Jack that he and some other performers on the same bill with him were involved in a heated argument about an act or performer, and Jack, as an expert, should be able to settle the debate. For instance, he'd ask, "Jack, in the act 'The Two Black Crows,' did they bill themselves as 'Moran and Mack' or 'Mack and Moran'? Jack, groggy from being roused from a deep sleep, would think a moment and then say, "Well, George, they usually billed them...." And Burns would hang up on Jack in mid-sentence. Now it cost George several dollars in phone bills for pulling a prank like this, but he did it frequently because he could visualize Benny bellowing in bed doubled up with laughter. As a matter of fact, Jack told us, once he laughed so long and loud that the hotel house detective tapped on his door to make sure he wasn't sharing his bed with any forbidden females. Jack said, "I told the house dick I didn't have a girl in my room, and if he had had any sense of humor he would have said, 'Okay, then get that laugh out of your room.'"

George played this same simple practical joke in a predictable variety of ways which never failed to break Jack up. Jack reminisced about this during an appearance on Johnny Carson's show on April 22, 1968. Carson's programs were still emanating from New

York at that time, and Jack was in town because he was making one of his rare New York nightclub appearances at the Empire Room of the Waldorf-Astoria.

On that evening's show, Jack gleefully recalled the many instances when Burns had insulted him, and he then added that prior to his opening at the Waldorf he had received a hysterically funny telegram from George. Laughing at the mere thought of it, Jack took the telegram out of his pocket and proceeded to read it to Carson and his audience. It took him several seconds to get the first words out because he was so convulsed. Then Jack said, "In the first place George starts this telegram with the word 'Dear'—and then he's got a Jewish word which I wouldn't *dare* repeat. . . . How he got it into the telegram I'll never know."

The New York studio audience, a large percentage of them Jewish, laughed as they made calculated guesses about what the actual Yiddish obscenity was. Then Jack added: "George got away with it because he probably had a *goy* [Gentile] operator." The word which Jack refused to read was *schmuck*, and eventually Jack told us that Burns got it past the Western Union people by telling them that it was Benny's Jewish name.

The program proceeded with Jack reading the rest of the telegram. He continued in a giggle-choked voice: " 'Dear So and So. You've been in show business all your life. You've played fairs, vaudeville, radio, concerts, television, theaters, and finally nightclubs, the Waldorf. Get wise to yourself. If you haven't made it by now, why don't you quit? . . . And that bit you do after each joke where you stand and look at the audience and cross your hands and hold on to your wrists, the audience thinks you're timing a joke but I happen to know that at your age, you're taking your pulse.' "

That line got a robust reception from the audience, and then Jack resumed reading; but first he added, "Now George has got another word I can't repeat. And here's where he stopped in the middle of a telegram. He says: 'I'm sorry I can't be there for your opening, but if you're still there tomorrow, let me know. . . . Now disregard everything I said because I'd really like to get serious. . . .' And, he quit. The telegram ends."

Carson asked, "That's it?"

And Jack answered, "That's the end of the wire. He hung up on me in the middle of a telegram."

Carson and the audience laughed, but no one laughed louder or longer than Jack. That laughter may have been at the current incident, but it was probably fueled by the many memories of similar pranks played by George over nearly half a century.

Perhaps no high-priced entertainer ever devoted more time and effort aimed at making one man laugh than George did—and perhaps no other man met with more success. No affair was too solemn, somber, or dignified for Burns to seek Benny out and try to break him up—and succeed.

One time the Bennys and Burnses attended a swanky soiree given by a major movie mogul. This was to be more than a formal sit-down dinner, for after dining the group was to be entertained with a musicale, the highlight of which would be a concert of songs sung by Jeanette MacDonald.

After the meal was finished and seats were arranged for the few hundred guests fortunate enough to be invited to this magnificent party, George sauntered over to Jack and began chatting with him. He started by casually observing that this wasn't the typical type of Hollywood social gathering but more like a society affair worthy of the bluebloods' famed 400. He pointed out how every man in attendance was impeccably dressed in white tie and tails, or at least a tuxedo, and that the women were wearing gowns that were obviously exclusive and expensive creations. Most important of all, he said, no low-brow buffoons were present, and also the entertainment scheduled was fitting for the occasion. There would be no corny comedian doing cliché jokes, and no popular songwriter sitting at the piano doing the usual "and-then-I-wrote—" repertoire of his hit tunes. This was class. This was elegance.

"And Jack," cautioned George, "I hope your behavior is in keeping with the company here." Jack protested mildly that his manners were always good. George hushed him, told him not to raise his voice, and continued: "I know you usually behave well, Jack, but you have a habit of laughing at anything, even if it's not funny. Now, for instance, Jeanette MacDonald is one of the world's greatest singers, and it would be embarrassing if you started to giggle when she performs." This upset Jack a bit and he said to George, "I know enough about music to appreciate a serious singer." George said, "Good, I just wanted to make sure."

Soon the guests were being seated and the Bennys and Burnses were in the very first row. Miss MacDonald was introduced and applauded by those chosen few who were to get a private concert of operetta arias from a voice known throughout the world. The orchestra ran through an arpeggio, and as this was happening, George leaned over to Jack and whispered, "Remember, don't laugh." Miss MacDonald hit her first note which immediately stopped being a solo and became a duet as Jack's loud laughter joined it. Embarrassed, but still shrilling an almost maniacal laugh, Jack rushed out of the room. Everyone stared after him in surprise, and nobody's face bore a more amazed, innocent look than George's.

Once Benny and Burns took a trip together, and they shared a hotel suite consisting of two bedrooms separated by a living room. They were sitting in the living room at midnight, sipping a nocturnal brandy to help them sleep better, when Jack complained that he knew this would be one of those nights he'd suffer from insomnia. George told him to try another half-shot of brandy as a soporific. They both did this and then adjourned to their separate bedrooms. Despite his earlier predictions Jack quickly fell into a sound sleep. Over two hours passed, and then his bedroom door opened and the light flashed on, awakening Jack to the sight of a pajama-clad Burns carrying a deck of cards. Jack started to ask if anything were amiss, but George held his finger to his lips for silence. Then he mixed the cards in a mysterious fashion, shuffled them, cut them, and held out the deck to Jack, saying, "Here, pick a card." Jack picked a card, and as he was looking at it, George started to leave the room. Jack called after him, "George, what about the card?" George said, "Put it under your pillow. It will help you sleep better." Then he turned out the light and left. Needless to say, Jack didn't sleep better. He hardly slept at all.

It frequently happened that when Jack and George were scheduled to appear at the same benefit or roast and it was convenient to do so, they'd drive to the theater or hall together so that they could enjoy each other's company. George always did the driving because they both feared what might happen if Jack were at the wheel when George said something funny. At the very least, auto insurance rates would definitely have skyrocketed all over California.

On one occasion when they went to a rehearsal in separate cars, Jack finished working first and left a few minutes before George did. He was driving along Wilshire Boulevard in his usual leisurely manner, when suddenly Burns' car drove up alongside of his. Burns opened his window and yelled to Jack to pull over to the curb because he had something important to tell him. Jack found an empty space along the curb, pulled into it, and parked, but Burns just kept driving along and never looked back. Jack said that he started to pull out into traffic again, but he began to laugh so hard that he was afraid of an accident—either driving or urinary. He had to turn off his ignition, get out of the car, and walk around the block until he felt he had gained sufficient control of himself to drive home.

Because of their early days in vaudeville, both the Bennys and the Burnses led nomadic existences until they had established themselves in the comfortable upper brackets of broadcasting. Then both couples bought permanent homes in Beverly Hills, and while the four of them were extremely popular and went to many major parties, sometimes separately, what they enjoyed most was each other's company.

But one year in June, when all big-time radio went off the air and summer replacements were substituting for them, George and Gracie took a three-month trip without the Bennys. I don't know why they took this trip alone. Maybe it was a vacation; perhaps it was to promote their program.

Jack missed George during that summer, and in the last weeks he was literally counting the days until he came home. One afternoon he was playing golf at Hillcrest in a foursome. As they teed off on the eighteenth and final hole, a figure was seen racing toward them from the clubhouse. The members of the foursome, plus their two caddies, strained their eyes, and suddenly they all recognized the running man as the returned George Burns. The length of the hole was several hundred yards. Seeing George running eagerly toward him filled Jack with energy and he forsook his game companions and started to run forward to greet the approaching Burns. At their meeting point Jack yelled some warm welcome and stopped running in order to give George an affectionate masculine embrace. But Burns ignored Jack's outstretched arms and continued running toward the other members of Jack's group. When he reached the remaining players, he ignored them too. Instead he embraced Jack's colored caddy and began to regale this bewildered young man with all the details of his trip.

During the several minutes it took to complete this final hole, George would converse with no one but the caddy. The effect of this on Jack's game of golf was disastrous. Jack wasn't a great golfer like Bob Hope or Dean Martin, but he played better than the average duffer. However, as he told us, "On this hole I took a fourteen, and I think that I cheated a couple to strokes to get it."

The attempts at practical jokes on each other weren't one-sided, but the resultant laughter usually was, since something always went awry with Jack's efforts to break George up. While George could, and did, reduce Jack to a quivering helpless hysterical mass by the simple and childish trick of pasting long green pieces of paper on his upper eyelids to make them look several inches long, Jack would go through elaborate and sometimes expensive endeavors to get a rise out of George but he was always doomed to failure.

For example, during their early vaudeville days George and Jack were living on different floors of the same hotel. One day Jack picked up the phone, asked the operator to connect him with Burns, and then, using a highly dramatic and nervous voice, begged George to rush right down to his room, saying that it was an extreme emergency that couldn't be discussed on the phone. George said he was on his way and hung up. Jack smiled to himself at this because now he was ready for his big joke. He was already stark naked. Now he put a lampshade on his head, took a round ashtray and held it in his right hand like a discus, and thus posed in the center of the room, nude, in his version of a Grecian statue.

Within minutes there was an urgent knocking on his door, and Jack, fighting to keep himself from laughing at his own cleverness, said, "Come in, the door's open." The door opened, and in walked— the maid. She gave a frightened scream at the sight of this nude nut and ran yelling from the room. Then George entered to find an embarrassed Jack trying to modestly cover himself with a lamp- shade and an ashtray.

George then told Jack that something in his tone of voice on the phone gave him a hint that Jack was planning a practical joke. Therefore, when he got to Jack's floor he searched for the room maid, found her, and told her it was imperative that she go into Jack's room and help him because he had a hunch that the man in the room wanted to commit suicide.

The most elaborate and expensive prank perpetrated by Jack on George also didn't turn out the way he expected it to, and it seems odd that this man who could almost uncannily choose and edit ex- cellent material for his radio and TV programs usually missed the mark when it came to personal humor. This incident had its origin when Jack Benny first played the Palladium many years ago. Jack claimed that when an English audience loved you, it became an intimate, intense personal affair.

After Jack's second or third triumph—and they were triumphs— at the Palladium, he began insisting that his pals, George and Gra- cie, make an appearance there. They agreed, were quickly signed for an engagement, and flew to England several days ahead of their opening to get used to the climate and the people, examine the theater, and have sufficient time for rehearsals. And now Jack pro- ceeded with "Operation Surprise."

Jack flew to England, his trip shrouded in as much secrecy as that of a courier carrying plans for an atomic weapon. Not one word appeared in the press that he was leaving, and Jack just casually mentioned to us that he wouldn't see us for a few days, not even wishing to tell us, his trusted writers, of his destination, for he didn't want anyone to have the slightest inkling of his big gag.

He arrived in London the day that Burns and Allen were set to open at the Palladium. One of the executives of the theater, the only man in on Jack's private plans, had rented him an apartment adjacent to George and Gracie's. When the Burnses returned to their apartment that night, after scoring a smash hit in their Lon- don debut, a party was being held in their honor. At the height of the party, their telephone rang, and an English phone operator at the hotel, who also was informed of the practical joke, asked for George Burns. When he got on, she said, "Please hold the wire. I have a person-to-person call from a Mr. Jack Benny, in Beverly Hills, California, U.S.A."

While George was anxiously clasping the phone to his ear, Jack sneaked into the apartment, tiptoed up behind Burns, and said, "Hello, George." George turned around, saw Jack, and was so shocked and surprised that he burst into tears.

Indignantly, Jack said to the other guests, who were touched by this tearful evidence of strong friendship, "How do you like that? I spend thousands of dollars on a practical joke to break him up, and instead of getting a laugh, I make him cry." Then he turned on Burns and in mock anger asked, "Why didn't you laugh?"

George, who by now had recovered from his emotional outburst, said, "Well, Jack, when you said, 'Hello, George,' you read it wrong." So Jack spent a small fortune to get a rise out of George, and instead he himself wound up on the floor in his usual state of hysteria.

On February 13, 1975, just one day before Valentine's Day, which would have seen Jack hit the age of eighty-one, the trade papers in Hollywood had a news item of interest to the movie-making colony. The following is a direct quote from *The Hollywood Reporter:*

BURNS JOINING
'SUNSHINE BOYS'

George Burns will star with Walter Matthau in Neil Simon's *The Sunshine Boys.* Burns will take over the role slated originally for the late Jack Benny, Burns' life-long friend.

I know it sounds corny, but I think that Jack would have wanted it that way.

26
Jack and Fred Allen

No biographical book on Jack Benny would be complete without a chapter on Fred Allen and their famous "feud." Unfortunately this is the main reason that their names are linked together in the history of radio. I say "unfortunately" because so strongly were the feelings expressed in that feud that even today there are many people who think that it was an earnest Hatfield and McCoy affair and that the two comics actually disliked each other.

Nothing could be further from the truth. Jack and Fred were friends and admirers of each other's ability not only before the feud, but dating back to the days when both of them were breaking into broadcasting. They met frequently when their paths crossed on their theatrical tours. Both were generous and helpful to others, and since their styles were unique, even rival professional jesters were fond of them because they had nothing to fear in the form of comic competition.

When they were both radio stars they frequently appeared on each other's shows, and even though they lived on opposite coasts they kept in touch through phone calls and letters. Jack would always let us read Fred's notes, typed in that easily identified lower case lettering. Fred was fond of creating picturesque phrases, and Jack knew that we'd enjoy them. Also, as he once pointed out to us, he hoped that some line in the letters would trigger a comic response from one of us that Jack could include in his answers to Allen.

One of Fred's phrases in a letter to Jack concerned a radio show which he felt was the epitome of corniness. The line, as near as I can recall it, went, "It's amazing how each week they mulch the maize to reach such monumental heights."

Occasionally a line that Fred sent Jack in a note would wind up as a gag on his radio show. I remember that once, when he was obviously trying to amuse Jack, he wrote about an invented uncle of his who was a famed hunter, but his trophies differed from the usual ones. "Instead of mounting the heads of the animals on the walls, he mounted the rear ends. Why, when you enter Uncle Wilbur's den, you feel like you're overtaking a herd." Some months later, Allen did this gag with Titus Moody on Fred's famed "Allen's Alley," and the audience appreciated the humor as much as I did.

The Benny-Allen feud, which gave listeners loads of laughs, lasted about twenty years. It started as an accident. Jack often said, "If Fred and I had gotten together and planned a feud for publicity purposes, it never would have worked that well." According to *The Big Broadcast* (Viking Press, 1972), by Frank Buxton and Bill Owen, "The feud started on Fred Allen's broadcast of December 30, 1936. As a guest on that show Fred had a young violin prodigy, 10-year-old Stuart Canin, who gave an excellent rendition of Schubert's 'The Bee.' [Although *The Big Broadcast* says that the young violinist played Schubert's "The Bee," I am almost positive that the number played was Rimski-Korsakov's "Flight of the Bumblebee."] In complimenting the kid on his performance, Allen ad-libbed: 'A certain alleged violinist should hang his head in shame.'" That started it. On his next program Jack made some disparaging remark about Fred, and the feud was on.

They ribbed each other on at least several programs a season, but it seemed to happen more often. In the mid-1940s, when a radio critic wrote that he was tired of their mutual insults, he followed this column up with one a week later saying that he had received hundreds of letters about this item, and he was honest enough to admit that the mail was running practically one hundred percent against him. However, because Benny and Allen were afraid of wearing out a good thing, their exchanges were more on a monthly basis than a weekly one.

Perhaps Allen's best known, and cleverest, verbal slam was based on a true happening when, in order to honor their most noted son, Waukegan planted a tree in Jack Benny's honor. Evidently no one in Waukegan had a green thumb because the tree soon died. Fred announced this sad event on the air by saying: "Everyone wonders why the tree they planted in Benny's honor died. It's very simple. How can a tree live in Waukegan when the sap's out in Hollywood?"

On one program Fred kept knocking Benny, and Portland Hoffa came to Jack's defense, saying, "Fred, even you have to admit that Jack's popular. He has a large following." Fred answered, "Look closer, Portland. That large following is all Benny . . . and it would be even larger if he didn't wear a girdle."

When Jack's daughter Joan got married, Fred said, "The reason Jack Benny is looking so sad these days is because he's not only losing a daughter, he's also losing a deduction."

One year Jack was elected honorary chairman of The March of Dimes campaign. Allen commented on this event by saying, "So Jack is now the chairman of 'The March of Dimes.' The dime hasn't been made that could march past Benny."

Early in Rochester's career he became the hottest member of the cast. (All members of Jack's cast enjoyed this flash of fame at the start, mainly due to their newness and novelty; then they settled down to the enduring popularity which brought them the solid foundation leading to their long-lasting careers.) At any rate Rochester was at the height of his popularity and Allen quipped, "Jack Benny is spending all his spare time in the sun in Palm Springs getting as tanned as possible so people will mistake him for Rochester."

Jack didn't let Fred get away unscathed. Once while Christmas shopping for Allen he sighed discouragedly. "It's so hard getting a Christmas present for Fred Allen. What can you get for a man who has nothing?"

On another occasion Jack was informed that Milton Berle was set to be Fred Allen's guest star. Jack said, "Now there's a combination. Allen and Berle. That's like two Abbotts and no Costello."

When *The Caine Mutiny* by Herman Wouk was published in 1951, that novel quickly skyrocketed to the top of the best-seller lists. On one of Jack's programs Don Wilson pointed out the fact that Wouk started his literary career by writing for Fred Allen. Then Don said, "But Wouk left Allen to join the Navy and go to war." Jack sneered, "The coward."

On another occasion Jack topped Fred and his studio audience (although not the outside listeners) by committing one of comedy's corniest capers—he dropped his pants. It was during one of our almost annual visits to New York for a change of broadcasting locale, and as always Jack and Fred were scheduled to exchange guest appearances. From past experiences we knew that on the Allen show Fred would start ad-libbing and Jack, mainly because he'd be reduced to a quivering, helpless, laughing target, would be no match for Allen's wit.

At that time Jack was broadcasting for Lucky Strike cigarettes, and everyone who listened to radio was painfully aware of the endless rapid repetition of their slogan in those days: "LS/MFT . . . LS/MFT." You heard it again and again on several top shows and dozens of spot announcements, and Benny's broadcasts, like all others sponsored by the American Tobacco Company, assaulted your ears with "LS/MFT" till you wanted to upchuck. It was because of this background that Jack and his writers got together and cooked up a practical joke that succeeded in startling the unflappable Allen.

Jack guested on Fred's show and all went smoothly until the program was half over. At that point Fred followed his usual custom of departing from the written word and ad-libbing with his usual wit. Suddenly he was startled by an unusually loud hysterical scream of appreciation from the audience before he had reached the punch line of one of his barbs. Unknown to him, while reading some of his extemporaneous remarks which he frequently penciled in on the marginal spaces of his scripts, Jack Benny had dropped his pants. When Fred finally looked at Jack to see if he was responsible for the outburst, he did a shocked take when he saw that Jack's trousers were at less than half mast. However, what he wasn't able to see at first was plainly visible from the audience's point of view. In extra-large and bright red embroidered letters on the right leg of Jack's white boxer shorts were "L.S." and on the left leg were "M.F.T."

Allen broke up, and was even more convulsed when Benny said, "Fred, I don't need writers. My underwear can out ad-lib you."

Afterward Allen told us that this was the biggest single laugh he had ever gotten on any of his broadcasts, including the time that he had a trained bird—an eagle I believe—as a gag guest. During the program the bird gave an unmistakable critical opinion of radio by deserting the stage, flying around the studio, and bombarding the audience with several mementos of his visit.

The Benny-Allen feud ended with the advent of television. For some strange reason Fred never had a hit series on TV, and Jack felt that it would be unfair to keep poking fun at Fred on his shows when Allen couldn't retaliate. However, their friendship continued, and their personal regard for each other was very deep. Whenever Fred was in Hollywood or Jack was in New York, they would spend as much time with each other as their unbelievably busy schedules would allow.

Jack's writing staff also admired Allen as both a talent and a person. We had heard rumors that although Fred hired high-priced writers, he frequently rewrote most of their efforts. Although well paid, their egos were obviously crushed by this. However, whenever he was a guest on Jack's broadcasts, his alterations were minor. He seldom did massive rewrites on shows where he was a guest star. This was out of respect for his host comedian. And because of Allen's admiration for Jack, he did even less changing on his show than on other programs.

During the dozen years I was writing the Benny broadcasts they must have exchanged guest appearances at least a score of times. When Jack was scheduled to be on Fred's program, most of Jack's writers would attend the rehearsals, even though we had nothing to do with the scripts. In addition to being fun, it was educational. And when the situation was reversed and Allen was Jack's guest star, we looked forward to working with him. Fred sat in on our rewriting sessions, and during those weeks we felt that we should be paying Jack for the privilege instead of being paid.

Like Jack, Fred stopped being a star and became a writer during those sessions. He always bowed to our judgment, claiming that we were the best authorities on the Jack Benny character, and he didn't tamper much with our efforts. He accepted what we wrote unquestioningly, probably because he knew that since Jack sat in with us on creating the program, the script reflected his judgment, and he respected, even revered, Jack's editorial ability. Of course, Fred would write a couple of ad-libs into his script on almost every appearance, but our material remained practically intact. Occasionally he'd ask permission—that's right, Fred Allen asked permission—to change the wording of a joke in order to make it sound more like him, but he never changed the actual humor content.

At rewrite sessions he and Jack would sit around and discuss old times, old friends, and old occurrences, and even though we knew that this would slow down our writing and make us late for any appointments, we listened like schoolboys seated at the feet of great teachers—which they were. Our wives automatically knew that when we had Allen on the program and we went to Saturday's reading and rehearsal, we wouldn't be home for early appointments or dinners.

I first met Fred during my initial two weeks with Jack in the fall of 1943. Fred casually said to me, "Milt, the next time you're in town, socially or on business, give me a buzz and we can try to have a quick lunch together." This sort of invitation is extended by almost every celebrity appearing as a guest star on a big-time program. Then, as now, it was nothing more than an industry formality, a code phrase for bidding a fond farewell, and nobody ever took up the invitation.

In 1944 *The Jack Benny Show* went to New York for a pair of programs. We had been there almost a week when one night, after attending a show, I returned to my hotel and found a message from

Fred with his phone number and a request that I call him. Since he was scheduled to appear on our second New York show and had already received the script, I assumed that he wanted to discuss some dialogue changes. I was wrong. When I talked to him he seemed genuinely hurt that I hadn't called him when I hit town. (This wasn't due to my great charm or charisma. Fred was fond of writers, loved talking with them, and liked to spend time with them.)

I wound up having dinner at his home the following night with his wife Portland and my fellow writer John Tackaberry. The meal was cooked by Portland herself, and she also did the dishes. We spent one of the most enjoyable evenings ever, with Fred discoursing on radio, other comics, human nature, and, most of all, Benny, whom I found he truly loved. I also discovered one other thing that night—never to admire anything belonging to Fred. In preparing pre-dinner drinks, Fred had used a portable hand-turned ice crusher, and Tackaberry admired this ice crusher device. Not to be unmannerly, although I had, and still have, a total ignorance of liquor and ways of serving it, I also expressed admiration for the gadget.

Two weeks later, back in Los Angeles, I received a package containing a replica of this ice crusher. I sent a letter of thanks to Portland and Fred, and with it I sent along a delicacy I had discovered on the West Coast: a couple of cans of smoked sturgeon. My tiny token thank-you gift was acknowledged with a humorous note saying that since he lived in New York, noted for its sturgeon, I was carrying canned coals to Newcastle. And with this note he sent an automatic letter opener. I answered Fred's note and sent back an equally useless, inexpensive household appliance. The exchange of letters and gifts continued for several months, and when I mentioned the incident to Jack, he said, "You might as well quit, Milt. No matter what you send Fred by way of thanks, he'll send you something to show that he wanted to give you a gift with no thought of reimbursement." Thus I finally stopped the seemingly never-to-end exchange.

One of the most memorable days in my entire life happened on a sunny afternoon when I was walking along Broadway with Fred and Jack. What happened during that short stroll was enjoyable, unforgettable, and unbelievable. We were stopped literally dozens of times, mainly by fans who recognized either or both of them, but occasionally by former vaudeville and variety actors who knew them. Fred would always shake hands when saying goodbye, and he seemed to secretly slip something into their hands. Later Jack told me that Allen kept four separate pockets in his suit filled with currency. One was loaded with dollar bills, a second contained fives, tens were in the third, and the fourth was filled with twenties. Fred had an army of out-of-luck performers who could always count on him for a handout of one sort or another. Jack told me, "The *schnorrers* [Yiddish for a man who will beg every chance he gets, even though he is working, but will whine to wheedle a little something extra from a benefactor] get dollar bills. Those Fred isn't sure about receive fivers. If a man is down on his luck but seemingly making no attempt to better himself, he gets a ten spot. But if a man is deserving and keeps trying to work, but the breaks are against him, Fred gives him a twenty dollar bill."

Jack also had his army of unfortunates—former writers, actors, or people who felt that Jack should help them. And Jack did. He sent countless checks to the unemployed luckless ones he had known when he himself was less prosperous. What he did most often with unemployed performers was to have us write a bit part into the script for them. The salary they received was fairly substantial and came directly out of Jack's profits because he owned the show. "But that way," Jack explained, "they feel like they're earning the money and it's not a handout." Then, obeying the compulsion he always had to stay in his miserly character, even in real life, he would add, "And besides, that way it's deductible."

During our walk down Broadway we were also stopped by old show business friends who now had some sort of job and wanted nothing more than the assurance that both of these greats remembered them. Jack and Fred amazed me by recalling not only their acts, but also the various theaters they had appeared at together. One man, though, will always stick in my mind. (I've changed his name so as not to embarrass him, should he still be alive.) Neither Jack nor Fred seemed to recognize this gentleman who proudly informed them: "I was Fido, The Human Dog." Then he went into his act. He *actually* became a dog. He barked, whined, cried, whimpered, begged, and cavorted as though he were truly a dog. He did this for about five minutes, and he wound up his performance by standing on his neck, shoulder, and one ear and gave the impression of a dog performing a trick. The crowd, which kept increasing as he kept performing, applauded, as did we three, and he acknowledged this reception with a bow. I applauded less enthusiastically than the others because I was afraid he was going to do an encore—and I moved away from him every time he lifted one of his legs.

Jack and Fred immediately asserted that they remembered him and that they were still impressed now, as they always had been, by his amazing uncanny canine ability. The man proudly dusted himself off, asking nothing but a handshake from two fellow artists.

As we left him, Jack, who was always honest, said, "Gee, Fred, to tell the truth, I don't remember him at all." Fred said, "I seem to

remember him, but I think I have him mixed up with Rin Tin Tin."
Then another crowd gathered as Benny fell to the sidewalk, and I
almost joined him.

Though from a dramatic and comedic standpoint the dog-man
was a good "finishing act" to our walk, it was not the main attraction. The crowning climax came when he passed the Capitol
Theatre on Broadway and two typical ten-year-old New York
street-smartened boys passed us walking in the opposite direction.
One of them kept going, but the other looked at Jack and Fred,
knowing he had seen them before. To continue his inspection, he
had to walk backward to keep pace with our forward motion. Suddenly recognition dawned on the kid's grimy face, and in a dulcet
Brooklyn accent he shrieked to his disappearing companion, "Hey,
Hoibie, it's Jack Benny and Fred Allen." "Hoibie" came rushing
back to us, and a crowd started to gather.

Fred then went into a funny philosophical monologue. He looked
at the kid and said, "You had to tell *Hoibie*, didn't you? Would
Hoibie have told you? The world is full of *Hoibies* who keep things to
themselves, but you had to tell *Hoibie*. Maybe you think that *Hoibie*
will grow up and become a millionaire and give you a job. Not *Hoibie. Hoibie* will forget this ever happened." For over two minutes
Fred kept up this mock scolding of the boy, much to his delight, and
also Hoibie's. The crowd kept laughing, and Jack helplessly held on
to me for support. Never once did Allen say anything derogatory or
insulting to the kid, who stood there smiling, not in the least
embarrassed.

Then, when Fred seemed finished, the boy asked: "Would youse
two give autographs to me and Hoibie?" Fred started anew, "Again
you're doing something for *Hoibie*. In all the time I've known you
I've never heard of *Hoibie* doing anything for you. Mark my words,
son, fifty years from today you'll come to him for a favor and *Hoibie*
will turn you down cold."

I've known other comics who might have been funnier than Fred,
but none who were sharper or more erudite. He didn't *try* to say
clever things; he was a completely natural wit.

Because they lived near each other on the West Coast, Jack was
probably friendlier with George Burns than with Fred Allen. But I
believe the person whom Jack most admired as a man and as a
comedian was Fred Allen.

As I've written time and again, Jack was an "easy laugher," but
he was a "hard crier." If and when Jack cried, he kept his grief to
himself. It was a private emotion. I only saw Jack really break
down and cry twice. Once was when he heard of Franklin D. Roosevelt's death, and the second time was when he got the news that
Fred Allen had passed away and left this a less happy world.

27
Jack and Danny Kaye

There is a reflected joy and glory in helping some young talent along the road to success, as I discovered during my years of working and associating with Jack Benny.

Jack was never afraid of competition. In fact he encouraged it and actually seemed to thrive on it. Whenever he found a young performer with comic ability, he became a one-man rooting section and press agent.

When Judy Holliday scored her Broadway success in *Born Yesterday,* Jack went to see her in the play five times in a two-week period, and he spent the rest of the two weeks raving about her rare talents. When he announced to us at a writing session that he was going to see *Born Yesterday* a fifth time, one of the writers quipped, "What's the matter, Jack? Didn't you understand it the first four times?" Jack laughed at this remark, but then in dead seriousness he said, "Fellows, it's an education to any comic to watch Judy Holliday perform. She can give us all lessons in timing."

Now at this time Jack, the seasoned old pro, was the acknowledged master of timing in show business. Every review he got, whether or not the critic liked the content, was sure to compliment Jack on his incomparable timing. Yet Jack went to see the Judy Holliday show again and again, each time raving about the newcomer's timing and talents.

Years ago Jack flew to Las Vegas because he was preparing a short theater tour and needed an act to round out the show he was to present. I, among others, told him of an amazing group we had seen, "The Will Mastin Trio, Featuring Sammy Davis, Jr." Jack went, saw the act, signed them for his show, and became one of Sammy's biggest boosters. And when Sammy suffered the tragic auto accident that resulted in the loss of an eye, Jack was among the many friends who journeyed to that hospital between Los Angeles and Las Vegas to comfort Davis.

However, Jack went with an added mission. He knew that I had gone through life, since the age of nine, virtually blind in my right eye, and while it has occasionally bothered me, it is no great hindrance (outside of the obsessive fear of a future accident to my good eye). Jack wanted to tell Sammy not to worry, because he had a writer who had been blind in one eye all his life, and he got along fine.

After returning from the hospital, Jack told me that he felt this psychological boost helped Sammy's morale. At that time I was the only one available that Jack could use as a single-orbed example because Moshe Dayan and Peter Falk hadn't burst on the scene yet. In fact, at one time my main claim to fame was that, with the exception of Sammy Davis, Jr., I was probably the world's funniest one-eyed Jew.

Jack pushed the careers of almost all the young talent he came in contact with. When Dean Martin and Jerry Lewis hit Hollywood, he became their greatest booster, and I know that on the day it was announced that this team was splitting up, Jack was heartbroken, as though two of his dearest friends had gotten a divorce.

But of all the people he discovered or helped, I think Jack was fondest and proudest of Danny Kaye who had begun to be talked about on Broadway when he appeared as a new and distinctly different comic at a posh, high-priced New York nightclub, La Martinique, around 1940.

At one of his first appearances there, Danny's timing was nearly thrown off by a man in the audience—and Danny's timing is sometimes the essence of his entire act. He does one number where he rattles off the unpronounceable names of seemingly thousands of famed Russian composers in slightly less than a minute, and his gibberish-like "git-gat-giddle" songs are masterpieces that demand the split-second accuracy of an electronic timepiece. On this night he was performing these numbers, and a man sitting out in the darkened vastness of the nightclub was laughing throughout his entire act, causing his precise pronounciations to be a fraction off so that the audience couldn't catch the full comedic impact of his efforts. And not only was this man laughing, but he was also pounding the table like Joe Louis mauling Max Schmeling.

Because of the bright spotlight on his face while he was onstage and also because of the dimness of the nightclub, Danny Kaye couldn't see who the offender was. When he finished his act to the usual thunderous applause, he stepped offstage and angrily asked, "Who's the drunken butter and egg man who kept laughing in the wrong places?" When he was told that it was Jack Benny, he was momentarily upset but then sighed with relief and said, "Thank goodness no one told me in advance that he was in the audience. I would have been nervous."

Then the stage manager asked Danny if he would like to meet Jack. Danny said he'd love to, but he didn't want to impose. The stage manager laughed and said that Jack had told him that he'd like to meet Kaye if it wasn't imposing.

They met, and that became the start of a permanent mutual admiration society. Almost everyone knows from talk shows and the other media how Jack Benny was George Burns' "patsy." What is not quite so well known is that Benny was also Danny's "patsy," but in a different way.

While Jack thought that George Burns was the greatest comedian in the world, he thought that Danny Kaye was the greatest everything in the world. He once said, "If Danny set his mind to playing golf, he'd be another Ben Hogan. If he seriously tried to be an opera singer, he'd run Enrico Caruso a close second." And Jack was one of the first to extol Danny's virtues as a chef in the Escoffier tradition, which is strange because Danny's most widely known culinary coups are not French, but of the Chinese variety. Today he supposedly is one of the world's best cooks and leading authorities on Chinese food.

Jack also raved about Danny's ability as a private plane pilot. He once told us, "The only non-professional pilot I'd ever fly with is Danny Kaye, because he is so perfect and knows so much that if we were flying to Hawaii, and he heard that a leaf was falling into the Grand Canyon because of a wind over there, he'd know exactly the speed, direction, and velocity of that wind and every other breeze within ten miles of us."

Danny appreciated and prized Jack's admiration for his assorted abilities, and he reciprocated by announcing at every interview that Jack Benny was not just the greatest comic he knew, but the greatest man he had ever met. In addition, he tried to repay him, either consciously or subconsciously, in the only manner he knew how—by making the man who loved to laugh so much laugh some more.

Unlike Burns, Danny was not one of Jack's constant companions. Perhaps this was due to the disparity in their ages, or maybe the Bennys and the Kayes didn't collectively create that great chemistry the Bennys had with the Burnses that melded them into an almost inseparable quartet. However, Danny tried to make Jack laugh whenever he could.

When George Burns entertained at social functions he performed in front of the entire party, although he was aiming his act exclusively at Jack. Danny resorted to different tactics. He never acted or performed his usual stage routines or pieces at parties for Benny's sole pleasure. If Benny laughed with the crowd, which he did, that was a bonus, but Danny performed a little *shtick* which he had created exclusively for Jack.

At all social events he went to great lengths to see that he was seated beside or directly opposite Jack at the dinner table. Then he would never address a word directly to Jack, but all his actions were for Jack alone. He would fork a piece of food and jam it into his nose, ear, or eye—anyplace but his mouth. He would partake in no conversations, but would rapidly swivel his head with that wonderful mobile face and lean forward in every and any direction that a conversation was taking place and pretend to listen attentively. And he ate with the precision of an automaton that was programmed to dispose of everything on the plate in an exact order and sequence. For instance, he would have his plate filled with steak, french fried potatoes, peas, and fried onions, and add a generous dash of ketchup on the side; in addition, he would always have a piece of bread handy. Then, like a wind-up toy or robot, he would start eating. First he'd cut a piece of steak, then dip it in the ketchup, then bring it to his mouth. Next he would fork a potato, bathe it in the ketchup, and mouth it. Then a forkful of peas would join the potato and steak in his mouth, followed by some onions he would shovel in. Finally a piece of bread dipped in the gravy would be jammed in his already overcrowded mouth. Then, and only then, would Danny elaborately start to slowly masticate this conglomeration with increasing speed, and he would finally make several deep swallows before he'd repeat this unvarying routine, with the food always taken in the same exact order: first the steak, then the potato, both liberally covered with ketchup, and finally the peas, onions, bread, and gravy.

As he neared the end of his repast Danny was meticulous in cutting the steak into smaller or larger pieces and eating tinier or greater forkfuls of the other items so that he would end with one complete sweep of the entire plate, giving his final forkful a bit of everything—and leaving his plate absolutely devoid of the least particle of anything.

Jack, who would be seated next to or opposite him, couldn't keep his eyes off him, and he would giggle and half-choke at these antics, but Danny never seemed to be aware of Jack's presence as he made his circular, never-varying rounds of the different foods on his plate.

Danny had one other device that he used solely for Jack's benefit. When he talked to him at parties, he wasn't Danny Kaye. Rather he assumed the character of a meek little Jewish man named "Mr. Kaplan" who was in the clothing business. He invented an entire family for Mr. Kaplan, a business involving a partner, and all the trials and tribulations of a struggling dress manufacturer.

At party after party Danny would sadly narrate in slight Yiddish accents the difficulties that he, Mr. Kaplan, was having. It was like a one-man soap opera, and it reached its climax one night when Danny, as Mr. Kaplan, began telling Jack that he never would have had the strength to go on if God in his goodness hadn't blessed him with the greatest business partner in history, Mr. Mandelbaum. According to "Kaplan," Mandelbaum was a prince. Mandelbaum was a godsend. Mandelbaum was a pillar of strength for him to lean on. Mandelbaum was someone he could tell his troubles to and get comfort and solace from his thoughtful, compassionate advice. "And," added Danny/Kaplan, "would you believe it, but this morning my accountant went over the books, and he tells me that this angel among men, this heaven-sent partner, this benefactor to whom I actually owe my life, has been monkeying with the accounts and stealing five dollars a week from the business." At this point Jack went along with the story and said to Danny, "Well, Mr. Kaplan, I imagine you got so mad that you fired the accountant!" "No," said Kaplan/Danny, "I'm suing Mandelbaum for every dime that crook has got."

It was another floor-faller for Jack, and the unfortunate thing is that it was the end of Mr. Kaplan's career as well as his life, a fact that actually disturbed Jack a bit because, as he told us, "I got to know Kaplan and his family and I liked them very much. Now I have a feeling I'll miss them like old friends."

28
Jack and Mary Livingstone

Earlier in this book you were told about Mary as an actress. What follows is an attempt to analyze Jack and Mary's relationship as man and wife, as people rather than performers, although these roles frequently overlapped. These conclusions are drawn from over thirty years of observing her and Jack, including the dozen years I worked with her several times a week at rehearsals, and at writing sessions at the Benny home, and meeting her occasionally at social functions.

To a large extent, Mary was and is an extremely private person. I doubt if any of her best friends knew her as well as even a casual acquaintance knew her husband.

Jack and Mary were, to many, a study in contrasts and contradictions. When they were married on January 14, 1927, Jack was a month shy of his thirty-third birthday. He was a well-known headliner sporting the sophisticated patina of show business, and via vaudeville he had crossed the country numerous times and had dallied in those quick casual romances that former variety performers discuss so nostalgically.

Conversely, Mary was barely out of her teens, lived at home with her family, had few boyfriends, was working at a comparatively mundane job as a stocking saleslady in a department store, and enjoyed the lifestyle you would expect of a girl in the late 1920s.

Despite all this, Mary seemed to be the worldly one, while Jack came across as the naive innocent, and this seemingly strange reversal of roles continued through the years. If there were any changes, Mary became more knowing, but Jack remained pleasantly the same.

Jack was sociable; Mary was social. Jack was outgoing, and friends with everybody. Maybe Mary wasn't snobbish, but she was selective. On many occasions Jack would show up at parties alone, Mary preferring to spend the evening alone at home. Conclusion-jumpers immediately decided that Mary wouldn't go to a party unless it was hosted and attended by celebrities and stars of the top magnitude. This wasn't totally true. If one of the writers, a member of the cast, or anyone connected with the show invited the Bennys to a social event, she would frequently attend, although the people present might not be members of what the movie colony's social set designates as the stellar "A" group. Yet frequently she would reject an invitation to a superstar's soiree if she wasn't in the mood. Jack, however, would go everyplace.

Jack was gregarious by nature. He liked to be among crowds of friends. He didn't attend these social gatherings because of a desire to be seen or heard. Unlike most other comedians, he wasn't always "on." He went to see and hear—not to be the performer, but the audience.

There were certain parties that were obligatory for Mary to attend because to remain away would be to offend some important person, such as a sponsor or a network executive. To Jack it didn't matter if he was the guest of a top echelon executive or some former vaudeville star who was now no longer a "name." Jack enjoyed attending parties.

Jack was seen so frequently without Mary that it gave rise to rumors that there were rifts in their marriage. Jack laughed these off by saying, "Hell, here in Hollywood, if a guy goes to the men's room alone, the columnists print that he and his wife are seeing their lawyers."

Neither Mary nor Jack cultivated people for financial benefits. True, they made most of their friends through the business, but not for business. When they entertained at their home, they invited people they liked for themselves, not for their connections. They were friendly with some of the newspaper columnists who ladled out the Hollywood news to the gossip-hungry world, and these reporters were invited to the Benny home. However, others, who worked for powerful newspaper syndicates, were ignored.

Once they had a lavish dinner party, and the noted movie colony chronicler Hedda Hopper was not asked to attend. Miss Hopper subsequently got snide revenge by writing a second-hand account of the soiree, saying, in effect, "The hostess [Mary Livingstone] went up to her room three times during the evening to change. Not her clothes. Her jewelry."

Where Miss Hopper got her information, no one knows, because the incident never happened. Hedda based her hearsay gossip on other gossip—namely, that Mary was extravagant. Maybe she was, but "extravagant" is a hard word to define. To a pauper who is hungry for bread, an ice cream cone is extravagant. To a multi-millionaire, a Rolls-Royce is merely a means of transportation.

Mary worked on Jack's show for most of her life, and like every other member of the organization she was generously rewarded for her efforts. Add her substantial income to the fact that her husband was one of the highest paid entertainers in the world, and it's obvious that Mary had no financial worries. She did with money what she felt should be done. She enjoyed it. She spent it. And from the viewpoint of those closest to her, she spent it sensibly rather than flauntingly. She loved quality clothes, so she dressed well, but not flashily or ostentatiously. And she wasn't the type to wear an expensive dress once and discard it. She got good use from her gowns. She had fur coats, but no more than anyone else in her position as a performer and the wife of an upper bracket headliner. The jewelry she preferred was the costume type, and while it was always exquisitely made, she didn't go in for oversized, eye-dazzling diamonds.

When Mary and Jack were preparing to move into the mansion on North Roxbury Drive where they lived for so many years, they hired one of the best-known interior decorators in Beverly Hills to do the entire house. When the wallpaper, drapes, and carpets were installed, the Bennys went on an inspection tour of the premises before settling on the furniture. Mary glanced around, shook her head negatively, and over fifteen thousand dollars worth of carpeting, wallpaper, drapes, and curtains wound up as an almost total loss and had to be replaced with something more suitable to Mary's tastes.

Certainly this sounds extravagant, but the home cost more than a quarter of a million dollars, and that was over thirty years ago. At that price, you don't want the accessories to spoil your enjoyment. And Jack uttered not a single syllable of dissent because he was happy if Mary was happy.

Mary also liked art and antiques but she wasn't a zealous collector who considered her acquisitions as her main interest in life. She made her purchases casually and impulsively.

During a script-writing session at the Benny house, one of her acquisitions arrived. It was an antique cobbler's bench, and most of us—the writers, a secretary, and the servants who helped the delivery men bring it in—had never seen one. For those not familiar with this now much sought after collector's item, let me tell you that it is not the most impressive or beautiful *objet d'art*. It was, as the name implies, a bench used years ago by cobblers. This specimen was made of scarred, nicked wood of an indeterminate original color. It had a couple of sections of scratched semi-taut leather where the ancient shoemakers kept their tacks and tools. To antique experts, the more dilapidated the bench is, the greater the value. This particular one was suitably shabby and looked as though it had lost a battle with a pride of sharp-clawed lions. We all stared at it in silence, until finally Jack said, "Let me tell you something, fellows. You've got to be awfully rich or awfully poor to have one of these things in your house." But Mary loved it, so Jack liked it, or at least he acted as though he did. He loved his "Dollface" and she could do no wrong.

Possibly no one other than Jack and Mary can speak with any authority on the sex life they shared. Occasionally rumors were heard of extramarital dalliances, but their intimates dismissed them for what they were—rumors. There was no doubt that they loved each other, with Jack being the more demonstrative of the two. They were both attractive people and probably had frequent opportunities for extramarital affairs but these, if any, were subjects for guessing and gossip, with no concrete evidence to back the suppositions.

At one time, several years ago, Jack decided to write his autobiography—one of those "By Jack Benny, As Told To . . ." histories. A highly reputable writer spent many months with Jack gathering background material, and he then wrote an excellent first draft. Mary read the draft and allegedly rejected the manuscript because in it Jack unabashedly discussed several romances that he had prior to meeting Mary. They were typical show-biz brief encounters, but Mary didn't want Jack to admit in print that others had shared his favors first.

During the entire time I knew them, I never heard a harsh word said by Jack to Mary. However, she would occasionally snap an insult at him. These were probably not launched with the intention of hurting her husband, for they seemed to be only an extension of the character she played on his program—the brash, bright, flip gal who always tore Jack down.

Yet once we writers witnessed an embarrassing incident where one of Mary's remarks, which may have been made with no more rancor than the rest of them, touched a sensitive sore spot. It happened in early June 1944, at the end of our first season together. World War II was still raging, and Jack was going overseas to entertain our troops during the show's summer hiatus. The Allied armies were in North Africa and had just invaded the European continent, and Benny, like Bob Hope and others, would follow them and entertain our fighting men.

Because there was always the remote chance of some of these performers being captured by the enemy and facing the accusation of being spies, they wore Army uniforms rather than civilian clothes. And because the Geneva Convention, or some other civilized agreement to make war more humane, stipulated that a captured commissioned officer was to be accorded favored treatment not given to an ordinary soldier, these entertainers wore officers' uniforms. These were rarely Government Issue. The stars usually had them specially fitted.

Jack went to one of the most exclusive tailors in town and had a uniform made to his measurements. He took the trouble of going through three fittings, and then, like a boy expecting his first Scout uniform, he couldn't wait for it.

We were working with him at his house when it was delivered. Mary was in one of the other rooms, and evidently he had kept the uniform a secret from her. He excused himself, went into a bathroom, changed, stepped out, and preened himself before us, like Clark Kent exiting from a telephone booth as Superman. When we all assured him, and in complete honesty, that he looked like a matinee idol, he called out to Mary, "Oh, Doll, come in here for a moment. I want to show you something."

As Mary entered the room, Jack snapped a brisk military salute and asked, "Well, Doll, how do I look?" Mary answered, "Like a big *schmuck*," turned, and left the room.

It was the only time I ever saw Jack seem hurt by one of Mary's jibes. His expression changed, and every vestige of color drained from his face. Then he forced a feeble smile as he addressed us and said, "That's Mary, always joking."

He excused himself for a few minutes to change back into his civvies. During his absence we whispered about the incident, giving Mary the benefit of the doubt and assuming that she meant it solely as a joke. But when Jack returned and we tried to resume writing, nothing seemed funny to any of us, and we soon called it quits for the day. No reference was ever again made by any of us to this incident.

As the years passed, we realized that Jack was frequently the butt for Mary's squelches in private as well as public. Rather than resenting them, however, Jack relished repeating Mary's barbs at his expense.

One incident he related several times concerned his admitted limited knowledge of any topics other than show business and vaudeville. On these subjects he was somewhat of an expert, but when the talk turned to anything with which he wasn't too familiar, he rarely participated in the conversation, although he listened avidly, as always.

Once, at a Hollywood party, he found himself in a group consisting of Jimmy Stewart, Henry Fonda, and Gregory Peck. While this trio discussed politics, Jack was quietly attentive, and he continued to remain silent as the talk turned to piloting private airplanes, something the other three were interested in. Then they began to discuss world affairs, and again Jack didn't utter a word.

At this point Mary joined the group and Henry Fonda, kidding Jack, pointed to him and observed, "He never opens his mouth."

Mary said, "Just start talking about Van and Schenck [the vaudeville team] and he'll never stop."

To Jack, flippancies like this, when uttered by his "Doll," were the epitome of brilliant repartee. There were some who privately disagreed with Jack and thought that Mary was merely making these remarks as a natural extension of the character she portrayed on the program. Others felt that these insults indicated insecurity on Mary's part, and that she was trying to compensate for the fact that while she was Jack's wife, she didn't share top billing on his broadcasts as in the case of other husband and wife teams like Burns and Allen, Ozzie and Harriet, and Fibber McGee and Molly. None of the ladies on these shows constantly made cracks at their husbands' expense off the air—but, then, they didn't do it on the air either. The nearest any of them came to it was Molly's mild reprimands of "T'ain't funny, McGee."

Mary was in the peculiar position of being both a performer and the wife of the boss. She didn't play the part of Jack's wife, nor was she a co-star on an equal footing, but she was a power to contend with. However, while she definitely had personal likes and dislikes among the cast and the writers, she never let these affect her professional attitude toward any of the members of the team. To her the program came first; then came her personal preferences, if any.

This didn't always hold true on radio shows starring or featuring husband-wife combinations. Occasionally a wife would let her spouse know of her distaste for an individual connected with the program, and this disaffection eventually rubbed off on the boss. On one well-known occasion, a member of the writing staff of a show got into a beef with the wife of the comic. Later, while lunching with his fellow writers, he tried to justify his position, and, bravely whistling in the dark, he also sought to give the impression that he wasn't worried about the situation. "After all," he said, "she's just another actress on the program. What if she is his wife—she doesn't have any more to say about the show than any other performer." Then one of his co-writers silenced him by remarking, "Oh, yes she does. She has her say during the wee horizontal hours of the night."

Maybe Mary did have Jack's ear occasionally during the "wee horizontal hours" of the night, but to my knowledge this pillow talk was never used to grind any personal axe.

Oddly enough, Mary was responsible, indirectly, for Jack losing his first, and possibly best, writer—Harry Conn who created the famed format that Jack used during his entire broadcasting career.

In the early days of radio, while other comics relied on out-and-out jokes and sketches, Conn supplied the show with humor based on the characters of Jack and the rest of the cast. This was to be Benny's perpetual trademark, and a major reason for his enduring popularity.

If we are to be completely accurate, Al Boasberg actually was Jack Benny's first radio writer, but he supplied Jack with individual jokes lacking continuity or character during Benny's initial broadcasts when he acted as a master of ceremonies doing little more than introducing various singers and other performers. Boasberg continued to furnish Jack with laugh lines for his scripts as long as he lived. However, Conn was the first writer to establish Jack's cast as believable, if larger than life, characters.

At the time, in the early and mid-1930s, Conn was the highest paid writer in the industry, receiving well into four figures for his funny lines in Jack's behalf. In those days of low taxes and deflation prices, this was an easy road to riches. As the star of the show, Jack, of course, earned more. This didn't seem to bother Conn too much, but it evidently rankled his wife. She is supposed to have felt that her husband spent the entire week hunched over his typewriter, suffering in solitude, while Jack relaxed and merely read the lines Conn created, and thus gained increasing fame and fortune which more properly belonged to her husband.

Several times she complained about what was, to her, a highly unfair situation. The culmination came one night when the Conns were at a party and the Bennys arrived. Mary was wearing an expensive new fur coat. Everyone at the affair admired it, and as the compliments subsided, Mrs. Conn allegedly said, "My husband's brains paid for that coat." That was Conn's last season on the series.

Whether Mary was actually the moving force behind the Benny-Conn split, I never knew as a certainty. I do know that whenever Conn's name was mentioned, Jack spoke of him with great respect and moderate affection. I never heard Mary speak of Conn at all.

On leaving Jack, Conn convinced CBS that it was his material rather than Benny's performance that had made the program so popular. CBS therefore hired Harry Conn to write a show starring Harry Conn, but it didn't last a full season. Conn then tried his hand at creating comedy for other stars, such as Eddie Cantor, but for some unknown reason he had the Midas touch only with Jack Benny. Toward the end of his life he had lost most of his money and was unemployed. It was typical of Jack to lend a helping hand, although not through a handout. Jack bought sketches and skits from Conn for which he paid substantial sums, but only rarely were we able to work any of the material into our scripts.

In all matters concerning the program, Mary behaved no differently than any other member of the cast. During rehearsals she joined in any open discussion as to the advisability of keeping or cutting a routine or joke. Like the other supporting performers, she would occasionally object to a specific line we gave her, and Jack would either delete it or let it remain, as he saw fit.

Once we had written a routine where she was telling Jack about the love life of her sister, Babe. She told Jack that Babe had a new boyfriend, an undertaker. Then she added, "But he's very progressive; he's the only undertaker in town with a convertible hearse."

Jack acted surprised and asked, "A convertible hearse?"

And Mary answered, "Yes, his slogan is, 'Get a Little Brown, Before We Lower You Down.'"

Mary winced when she read this at our first rehearsal, despite the fact that the cast and crew gave these lines an excellent laugh reaction. She asked that it be deleted but was voted down by the overwhelming majority of those present. She did the line on the show, and it got so loud a laugh from the audience that the routine was repeated twice in subsequent years. Each time it appeared in the script she again voiced her displeasure, and each time she was overruled. Judging from the huge hysterical roar she got the three times that she did the bit, there was nothing in her performance to indicate to the audience that she found the routine personally repugnant.

The only complaint we ever heard Jack register against Mary was her lack of infatuation with show business. Mary seemed almost completely devoid of any desire to be a performer, much less a star, while Jack felt, and rightly so, that she was an important part of the radio show. Mary had no ham in her character, and when she'd occasionally ask for a week off, we would write her out of the script.

She was frequently nervous and apprehensive prior to a program. More than once she became ill with a cold or some other minor ailment on the actual day of the show or the day before it. We then would write a few quick explanatory lines in the script and have a glamor girl like Alice Faye or Barbara Stanwyck fill in for her. And at least a couple of times a season, immediately after completing a show, Mary would walk offstage and collapse in a dead faint. It may have been psychosomatic, but not even doctors were too familiar with that all-encompassing word in those days. Whatever it was, it never affected her during an actual broadcast, but within seconds after we signed off the air, Mary would sometimes simultaneously sign off by passing out cold.

It was a frightening sight the first few times I witnessed it, but after several occurrences, while I still felt badly, neither I nor anyone else was too alarmed. Our sympathies seemed to lie more with Jack who always acted frantic as though this could be "the big one."

We quickly learned not to crowd around but to see that she had ample air while Jack cradled her prostrate form with one arm, and with the other made fanning motions or patted her cheeks, all the while whispering softly to her. Soon she would regain consciousness (psychosomatic or not, she *was* in a temporary state of suspended animation) and get up without showing the slightest sign of any after-effect.

It was one of these fainting incidents that once caused Jack to lose his temper in public, an exceedingly rare occurrence for him. We had just finished a program which was broadcast from an auditorium in Palm Springs. It was a very warm April day, and the hall we used as a studio wasn't air-conditioned. One hundred and five degrees would be a conservative estimate of the temperature onstage.

As soon as we concluded the program, we all rushed for the exits to get some fresh, if not cool, air. We never knew whether it was the air, or the brilliant sunshine, or just a psychosomatic reaction, but the moment Mary came outside, she keeled over and collapsed like a puppet with its supporting strings slashed. New dress and all, she fell face-first into the dust and sand which accumulate in that desert spa when the breezes blow as they do constantly in the late afternoons.

Jack immediately knelt beside her, automatically administering to her needs. The rest of us, from years of experience, stepped back to give her air as he tried to revive her.

Suddenly a well-dressed middle-aged lady officiously pushed through the surrounding circle and imperiously ordered everyone out of her way. We quickly moved so as not to impede her progress. From her manner we figured that she was a doctor, or at least a nurse. She knelt beside Jack, who was still trying to revive Mary, and, opening her purse, whipped out a pen and piece of paper and said, "Mr. Benny, can I have your autograph?"

We were all too startled and stunned to react. This seemed like

Jack and Mary, November 1934.

Jack, Mary, and their daughter, Joan, January 1936.

Jack and Mary, May 1938.

Jack and Mary at Grand Central Station, December 1938.

Celebrating their 13th wedding anniversary, January 1940.

Jack, Joan, and Mary, January 1940.

Jack and Mary, January 1942.

Jack with Joan in the early 1940s. *Photo by Gene Lester.*

George Burns, Gracie Allen, Jack Benny, Mary Livingstone, and Joan Benny. *Photo courtesy of Wagner-International Photos, Inc.*

Jack and Mary, 1970.

Jack and Mary, 1970.

some crazy script situation that we might consider and eventually discard as too unbelievable. Jack's blue eyes blazed as he tried to control himself, and then he angrily answered, "Lady, can't you see my wife has fainted? This is no time to ask for my autograph."

The lady rose indignantly and retorted with the classic cliché: "That's very impolite of you. We're your fans. We made you and we can break you."

Two of us stepped forward to lead this thoughtless intruder away before the already incredible incident developed into something far worse. As we reached her, Jack gritted his teeth and said in an overly polite low voice, "Lady, as soon as my wife snaps out of this faint, you can ask me for my autograph. Then I'll tell you to . . . [expletive deleted] yourself."

Shocked at this mildly spoken reply, the lady left indignantly as we all laughed loudly and nervously.

At this moment Mary regained consciousness with no ill effects other than the surprise she showed at hearing the group laughing. Puzzled and a bit petulant, she asked, "What is this? I pass out and everybody laughs as though it's a big joke."

Jack, relieved at her recovery, ad-libbed, "Doll, you pulled the funniest falling down faint we ever saw."

Mary pressed the point, and finally Jack told her what had actually happened. Mary thought it over momentarily and then said, "Jack, you should have given her the autograph. I'm only your wife, but a fan is a fan."

I haven't seen Mary since Jack left us. I called her twice and sent a condolence note, but received no response other than a formally printed card. There's no doubt that she took Jack's death hard, but shortly afterward she went to Frank Sinatra's home in Palm Springs for a few weeks of rest and recovery. She also hosted a small wedding reception in honor of Merle Oberon, and attended several intimate parties and large charity affairs during February and March 1975.

To some it seems odd, but she is now attending many of those social functions that she avoided when Jack was alive.

Perhaps she's trying to forget.

Or remember.

29

A Pair of Jacks— Benny and Paar

Jack Benny, like so many other big men in various fields, always went out of his way to help newcomers. If he could find, encourage, and develop talent of any sort, it was a source of joy to him. This is one of the reasons that Johnny Carson adored him, and every time Jack appeared on Johnny's show you could almost *feel* this admiration seeping through the tube. As mentioned previously Jack also gave Sammy Davis, Jr., Danny Kaye, and others a big boost up the ladder of success, and he was practically the discoverer of Jack Paar.

In the days of radio the longer-lasting programs—and heaven knows they lasted much longer than they do in television—would usually do thirty-nine shows from mid-September to mid-June, and then be off the air for thirteen weeks. During those thirteen weeks the morning glories of the airwaves flourished—the summer replacements. Many a summer replacement seemed to attract big listening audiences and get rave reviews from radio columnists during the hot months, but when they went up against the big league competition in the fall and winter, they wilted and were soon forgotten.

Television has reruns with only an occasional summer replacement, but in the days of radio no one ever heard of reruns. Summer replacements were so commonplace that jokes were made about them. In fact one that we did took place on an opening show when, as was customary on such programs, everybody asked, "What did you do during the summer?" Jack was discussing vacations with Phil Harris and inquired, "What did Sammy the drummer do?" And Phil answered, "Sammy was Willie Sutton's summer replacement." (Willie Sutton was one of the most notorious bank robbers of the era.)

In the heyday of radio, when a star was as important as Jack Benny, he could frequently have a say as to what his summer replacement would be. No comic wanted some somber dramatic show filling his time slot for fear that it would drive off his loyal fans.

Jack rarely interfered with the advertising agency's suggestions for his summer replacements, but whenever he made a suggestion they respected his wishes. And as we approached June in 1947 and were looking forward to a three-month hiatus, Jack became interested in a young comedian named Jack Paar. He thought that Paar was bright, breezy, clever, and witty, and he decided that he wanted to have him do a summer replacement show in his time slot. Not only that, but he wanted his own production company to produce the Paar series. And to provide a little insurance as far as material was concerned, Jack worked out a deal with his writers where each of us would serve Paar's program in an advisory capacity for a period of four weeks. (Benny only did thirty-six broadcasts that season, and Paar would do sixteen, and that made the arithmetic easy.)

In those days it was customary for the Jack Benny series to do the final two broadcasts each season from New York, and it was an annual custom to have Fred Allen as a guest on the final show. Benny didn't want to deviate from this formula, but he also wanted Jack Paar on the final show to introduce to his listeners so that he could ask them to tune in the following week to Paar's program.

We wrote a show that was as good, or bad, as our usual "farewell till fall" programs, and it had one scene in which Jack and Fred Allen both complimented the young newcomer, Paar. When we finished our first rehearsal on Sunday, Benny began to worry—and, if I haven't already mentioned it elsewhere, Benny was the greatest worrier in the business. On one occasion we tried to reassure him that we had taken care of every possible contingency and he had absolutely nothing to worry about, and he said, "I know, that's what worries me."

But on this Sunday he had a legitimate reason for worrying, for he remembered Fred Allen's penchant for putting in punch lines where none existed before, and Fred's frequent acidulous ad-libs could be devastating. Jack worried that something unforeseen might happen to make the inexperienced Paar a target for Allen's arrows. This, thought Benny, might upset Paar and cause him to make a bad impression on the listeners.

Never one to beat around the bush, Benny broached the subject to Fred while we were in our final writing and cutting session before going on the air. Allen, a gentle and gracious man despite the honed edge of his air image, immediately set Jack's mind at rest, and he even pulled some funny quip along the lines of: "With you around, Jack, whom else do I need to poke fun at?"

The program went on the air and was well received by those in the studio, and the spot with Benny, Allen, and Paar evoked a favorable audience reaction. Twice during the bit Fred started to ad-lib something aimed at Paar, but he quickly turned it so that Benny was the butt of the jokes. Not only that, but Paar got off two ad-libs at Allen's expense, and instead of Fred retaliating, he again concentrated his barbs on Benny. All in all it was an excellent show that served the dual purpose of saying farewell to our listeners for the summer and launching the Jack Paar program that was to replace us.

The following Sunday Jack Paar did his first program as our summer replacement. Even at that early date he showed signs of the temperament that became so evident on his television talk show and may have been one of the reasons for his huge success. I won't dwell on the daily difficulties of Mr. Paar, except to note that he hired and fired more writers during his first few weeks than Jack Benny used in his entire lifetime. One of the writers who started with Paar, and who, I believe, was instrumental in discovering him and bringing him to Benny's attention, was a huge, in fact immense, man called "Fat" Larry Marks. This was to distinguish him from a more normally built writer also named Larry Marks. It is possible that their surnames were spelled differently—I just don't remember—but they were pronounced exactly the same. A conservative estimate of "Fat" Larry's weight at that time would be three hundred and fifty to four hundred pounds.

At any rate, Jack Paar's program flourished while his relations with his writers deteriorated. At one script session the squabbling became so intense that Paar is reported to have said, "Writers are the cheapest commodity in the business. I can buy and sell you guys by the pound." And "Fat" Larry supposedly answered, "Not me, you can't," and walked off the show.

June passed into July, and soon it was the start of August, and the only summer replacement show that had made a favorable impact on the public that year was Jack Paar's. It was so good, in fact, that *Time* magazine ran a piece about Paar and his program, interviewing him at greater length and giving him more space than

Time usually devoted to newcomers. And in this article Paar was quoted as saying (and this is not a direct quote, but as near as I can recall after more than a quarter of a century): "I intend to bring a much needed fresh approach to radio humor. I don't want to do any 'old hat' comedy of the type that's being done by Fred Allen and Jack Benny."

A few days after this appeared in print, Benny received a letter from Fred Allen. Jack opened the envelope, and it contained nothing but the page from *Time* magazine with Jack Paar's quote underlined and a note scribbled by Fred across the page saying, "Dear Jack: I'm so happy that you told me not to make any ad-libs at the expense of this nice kid. F.A."

Despite this seeming ingratitude on the part of Paar—I believe he apologized and said that he was misquoted—Jack always admired his brashness and humor. When Paar first started to climb to the big time with his late-night NBC talk shows, Jack Benny was a frequent guest. Two of these guest appearances are worth writing about. One has already been detailed in an earlier chapter. The other occurred during the famous Jack Paar-Ed Sullivan feud.

There had been several "feuds" between major stars on the air, but most of those, like the weekly verbal vituperation heaped on each other by Benny and Allen, found no ill-will between the participants. The antagonists simply insulted each other on their programs, and this, they hoped, would stimulate fans into listening to get a vicarious thrill from the supposed argument. Certainly Fred Allen reaped a rating harvest from this gimmick one season when his program was on the air on Sunday nights an hour or so after *The Jack Benny Show*. Radio buffs would listen to Jack, and whenever Jack took a derogatory dig at Fred, many of them would make a mental note to tune in to Fred Allen later on and hear his answer. Fred had the big advantage because of this time difference, and that very evening he usually had a couple of snappers to zing back at Benny's earlier lines. However, off the air, Benny and Allen were the best of friends. This was definitely not the case with Ed Sullivan and Jack Paar.

From the advantage of this point in time, retrospection shows that, as is true in most arguments, there was a right and wrong on each side. It began because Ed Sullivan would pay guest stars large fees, sometimes ten thousand dollars or more, for a single shot on his variety hour. Then those same stars would casually drop in on Paar's nightly, less formal, show, sit for a while, chat with Paar, and sometimes wind up doing the same routine they had performed, or were going to perform, on Sullivan's show. What griped Ed was that he was paying thousands of dollars per appearance while all Paar's program paid was union scale, three hundred and twenty dollars.

Irked by this obvious discrepancy in remuneration, Sullivan let it be known that those stars who appeared with Paar would not be welcome on his show. Naturally this ukase in turn irritated Paar, especially when several stars, fearful of losing large salaries from Sullivan, cancelled their scheduled appearances with Paar. The daily press played it up, and each of the combatants made uncomplimentary statements about the other to the delight of non-participants in the industry. Gags were printed in the papers, and some comics jested about the situation on their own programs, but to the belligerents this was no joking matter. This state of affairs had been going on for some time, perhaps for several weeks, when Jack Benny appeared on the Jack Paar show.

Paar gave Benny his usual and sincere laudatory introduction, the orchestra sounded the strains of "Love in Bloom," and Benny made his appearance. While the audience applauded wildly, Benny bowed, and he then took the guest of honor's seat, next to Paar. Paar smiled and relaxed a little, knowing that he had a reliable guest who would fill a large part of his nightly ninety minutes with laughs and humor. But Jack was serious that night.

I watched the program as I watched almost every Benny broadcast, even when I wasn't on his regular weekly staff. Some friends say that I did this out of loyalty or love, and though these were certainly underlying reasons, my main purpose was purely selfish —to enjoy a performer who never failed to entertain me.

I don't know how he started that night, but I can't remember him telling jokes or striving for laughs. He was quite serious, which was unusual. However, the charm of the Paar show, like that of his able successor, Johnny Carson, and all other successful talk shows, was in its spontaneity. And that night Jack Benny did something unique—unique, that is, for anyone else in show business, but if you knew Benny, really knew him, afterward you'd say, "I had a hunch he'd do something like that."

Like what?

Like this: Practically his first statement after the usual salutation was, "Why are you and Ed Sullivan acting so foolishly?" Paar was so startled by this remark that he was visibly shaken and had no time to utter a single sentence of defense or protest. Benny now talked directly to the audience: "Can you imagine," he said, "Jack Paar and Ed Sullivan, two of television's biggest and best stars, are mad at each other like a couple of kids." Perhaps my mind is trying to rewrite my memory, but I believe a childish tone crept into Benny's voice as he said this sentence.

Paar tried to interject a few words in order to change the direction that the conversation was taking, but Benny wouldn't let him. The audience listened attentively in silence, and I leaned forward in my chair, caught up in the situation. I knew of Paar's mercurial moods through personal experience, and the entire nation knew of them because at least once, in a fit of pique, he walked off his own show right in the middle of the program. Yet for some reason—and I suspect it was the great respect and love he had for Jack Benny—he held himself in check.

Jack continued with words to this effect: "Gee, with all the trouble in this world, why should two nice guys like you and Sullivan be fighting? You want to hate somebody? Hate Hitler! Hate Eichmann!"

The audience broke into loud and long spontaneous applause, preventing Paar from saying anything. However the audience was obviously on Benny's side, and, smart showman that Paar was, he did seem to show contrition. In fairness to him it must be said that Benny may have breached a broadcasting rule of etiquette by surprising Paar in bringing up so private and personal a subject.

Benny's attitude was not one of anger, but more of sorrow. He, the guest, then reversed the tables and began to interview the host. He asked, "Tell me, who is the performer you give most of the credit to for discovering you and helping you get where you are today?"

Paar relaxed a bit, evidently figuring that the public chastisement was over. He smiled and said: "Jack, I've said it before and I'll say it again. You were practically my discoverer. You gave me my first big break. You're responsible for whatever success I have today."

Benny then said, "So it's probably a fact that if I hadn't been around to discover you, you wouldn't be a big star today."

Paar modestly tried to say that he wasn't a big star, but he agreed that Benny was responsible for the fact that he was in his current prominent position.

Then Benny leaned over and said in confidence, to Parr and his several million viewers: "Well, I've got news for you. I was discovered and given my very first chance on radio by Ed Sullivan. So you're mad at the man who discovered the man who discovered you. If it wasn't for Ed Sullivan you wouldn't be here today."

The audience laughed and applauded, and Paar smiled at Benny's far-fetched logic. But it was true that Jack Benny had made his first air appearance in New York in 1931 on a local radio show hosted by Ed Sullivan.

The dialogue between the two Jacks now took on the appeasing tones of a family quarrel being patched up. Benny reminded Paar that when his daughter Randy had wanted almost unobtainable tickets for The Beatles' appearance on the Ed Sullivan show, despite the bad blood between her father and Sullivan she wrote Ed a note, and the priceless tickets were immediately forthcoming.

Before Jack left that night he extracted a promise from Paar that he would make up with Sullivan, provided that Sullivan would meet him halfway. Jack said, "Leave Ed to me." Sullivan realized that Benny's unusual appearance on Paar's program had made an impact on the public; furthermore, he, too, was fed up with the foolish feud, and eventually the two stars resumed their friendship.

I had lunch with Jack some weeks after this incident, and I immediately asked him if he had planned this ploy prior to appearing on the program. He thought for a moment and then said, "I honestly don't know. I guess that deep down inside of me I was thinking of doing it because you know how I'm always upset when two people I like are on the outs with each other." I knew this to be true because I had witnessed Jack's peacemaking efforts on previous occasions. However, I was still amazed at the chance he took by opening up this sensitive wound in public. I said, "Jack, weren't you taking an awful chance putting an unpredictable man like Paar on the spot like that?" Jack smiled and said, "Milt, what could he do to me? Punch me in the nose? I'm old enough to be his father! I guess I am sort of a father image to him. And come to think of it, I walk like his mother." Then Jack gave vent to that high-pitched phony falsetto laugh he always uses for comedic effect and added, "And they say I can't ad-lib."

30
Some Personal Traits

In the Japanese motion picture *Rashomon,* several people give their own versions of a crime they witnessed. None of them seems to be lying or even distorting the truth, but as each tells what he believes actually happened, the audience views several entirely different accounts of the same simple occurrence.

In writing a biography of any sort, the reader usually gets most of the facts plus the writer's personal feelings, regardless of how objective he may be. For example, currently there are a dozen or so books about Judy Garland. Each publisher asserts that his offering is the best, with the most complete and factual portrait of the diminutive singer who captured the movie-going public's heart in adolescence, and then shocked it in later life. There is no doubt that each of these authors portrayed Judy via the various truths as he or she gathered and interpreted them. And it follows that each of these biographies reflects its writer's personal opinions, either consciously or subliminally.

There eventually will be several books about Jack Benny. Most of them will be written by people closely associated with him. Each will create an image of Benny based on the material that he or she was personally privy to. My own knowledge of Jack covers an extremely broad scope, and yet I realize that I, like all the others, will not completely capture the man. However, the following collection of "Bennyana" should go far to fleshing out the complex private and public image of the man.

The Show Mustn't Go On

Every branch of show business has given birth to superstitions and traditions. You must never whistle in a dressing room . . . and you don't throw your hat on a bed . . . and instead of wishing a performer luck when he starts a new show, it's considered good taste to tell him: "Break a leg."

Possibly the strongest, and certainly the best known, of these traditions is "The Show Must Go On." Yet this was one saying that Jack, who was steeped in show business, scoffed at and claimed was ridiculous. He'd say, "Sure, if you have a slight cold or a minor sprained ankle, the show should go on. But must the show go on if, God forbid, your wife or child is undergoing a serious operation at the time? Some people say it's good for you, that it takes your mind off whatever's happening. I wouldn't want my mind taken off it at a time like that. What's more important, my loved ones' lives or doing a show?"

If any member of the cast was ill, Jack made that person stay home and rest, and with all the great performers we had, giving each of them an extra joke or two would easily take up the slack. In fact, Jack himself was written out of one show when he had some polyps removed from his throat.

Jack also violated this supposedly holy, and yet foolish, custom on a couple of other occasions. The first-time happened prior to my association with Jack. In late 1941 he had made the movie *To Be Or Not To Be* with Carole Lombard, who was then married to Clark Gable. As soon as the filming was finished, Miss Lombard went on a war bond selling tour and met an early, sudden death in a plane crash on January 16, 1942. Jack Benny was so shaken up by this tragedy that he immediately announced he would not do his show the following Sunday. He felt that he couldn't go on the air and be funny immediately after the untimely and tragic death of his beautiful co-star and friend. An emergency program filled his time slot, featuring music and songs by Dennis Day.

On the second of these occasions I was with Jack in Palm Springs on April 12, 1945. We were in a bungalow at the Deep Well Hotel writing our show which was to emanate from that resort city on Sunday, April 15. We were all relaxed, as we usually were when we were down there, and the script was coming along fast and fine. Possibly we were all laughing a little longer and heartier at our mutual efforts in hopes of finishing early and getting in some sunshine and swimming before the sun slid behind the mountains and changed the climate from tropical to Arctic. Suddenly, someone came into our room and broke the news to us that Franklin Delano Roosevelt had died.

I remember our reactions vividly. Not a single word was said. Jack stood up, and with tears streaming down his cheeks he walked outside. A moment later I left the bungalow. My eyes too were filled with tears, and this, together with the change from the lamp-lit room to the brilliant blinding sunshine, made it difficult for me to see clearly, but I observed Jack walking toward the desert, away from the swimming pool, play area, and other bungalows.

In less than a minute all four writers and our secretary at that time, Jane Tucker, had exited from the room, and each walked away alone and stood in solitude. Not one of us spoke to, or looked at, anyone else. We must have presented a strange sight: five men and one woman, all crying, and not one trying to comfort the others.

After several minutes we seemed drawn together as though our mutual grief had turned into a magnet. Then our secretary, Janie, timidly asked if we were going to resume writing the program. Benny, still crying, asked, "What program?" Jane answered: "Sunday's show—the one we were just working on." Jack said grimly, "We're not doing any show this Sunday."

With the exception of Jack himself canceling his show at the time of Carole Lombard's death, no precedent-setting situation like this had ever happened to any of us before in the short history of commercial broadcasting. One of the writers said, "But Jack, suppose the network and the sponsor insist that the show must go on?"

Jack angrily retorted, "Then let them put their own show on. Mine will not go on the air."

The network and sponsor contacted Jack on their own a few hours later, telling him that all commercial broadcasting would cease for a week in memory of F.D.R. This also happened in 1963 when President John F. Kennedy was assassinated, but by then they had a sad precedent to follow that had been started in 1945. And while no network broadcast any commercials or entertainment programs for a full week in 1963, there were no losses sustained by the stars or producers, since by that time almost all television shows were on film, and they were simply shown at a later date. Any and all losses were borne by the networks.

However, in the days of radio, Jack's gesture in immediately canceling his show could have been a costly one. The guest stars, cast, crew, and writers would have had to be paid, and if the network or sponsor wouldn't have agreed with Jack's decision, he would have suffered a large financial loss. Arrangements were finally made with NBC and his sponsor so that it cost Jack a minimal amount of money, if any at all, but he had no way of knowing this at the moment he made his decision.

We all knew from his attitude on that mournful day, April 12, 1945, that even if it cost him a huge amount personally and involved legal difficulties that could result in the show's cancellation, Jack would not adhere to the unwritten law of the theater, "The Show Must Go On."

Politics

When I first met Jack he didn't have an avid interest in politics. From what I gathered, he seemed to be a Democrat. Three of the writers were also Democrats, and one of them, as he said, "leaned toward being a Republican."

Jack was slightly naive when it came to politics, and in those days comics or comedy shows tried to be impartial with their humor, since the sponsors and the networks would become concerned if all your quips lambasted one political party and favored the other.

In radio we had to be circumspect or we'd be deluged with hundreds of letters. As a matter of fact, every time we did a joke about Franklin Roosevelt or his wife Eleanor, we'd increase our weekly mail. Half the messages would call us lousy Republicans for always criticizing the Roosevelts; the other half would call us stinking Democrats for always praising them. Moreover, the almost evenly divided critical letters were about the same joke.

The first presidential election that took place when I was working for Jack Benny was F.D.R. vs. Tom Dewey. From all the discussions it seemed that Jack was going to vote for Roosevelt, but then a week or so before the election he came into the office and said he had changed his mind and would cast his ballot for Dewey.

The trio of writers who were Roosevelt-backers began to cross-examine him, for we wanted to know the reason for his sudden switch. He told us that he had been at a party the night before and was convinced by such astute political experts as Lela Rogers and her daughter Ginger that Dewey was the better man. Now I don't want to rehash old differences, but the political inclinations of Mrs. Rogers and her daughter Ginger can be best summed up with a wisecrack that was then popular: "I don't understand how Ginger Rogers can be such a wonderful dancer when she has two right feet."

We asked Jack just what it was that Lela and Ginger Rogers had told him that caused him to become pro-Dewey. Jack turned to me and said, "Milt, you come from New York, and you know that any man who can be a successful governor of that state should make a good President. And you've got to admit that Tom Dewey was a damn good governor."

"You're absolutely right, Jack," I said. "Dewey was almost as good as Al Smith, but nowhere near as good as Franklin D. Roosevelt."

Jack was speechless with a peculiar expression on his face for a few seconds, and then, half-laughingly, he said, "Oh my God, I forgot that Roosevelt had been governor of New York."

Jack voted for Roosevelt again that year.

Jack and the Unions

Jack must have belonged to as many trade unions and guilds as anyone, and he respected all of them. Moreover, in his role as an employer, he paid far above the union scale minimum.

During the days of radio, Hollywood writers did not have one strong organization. Instead, they were divided into two factions, The Screenwriters' Guild and The Radio Writers' Guild, each a separate entity and neither one assured of the other's support in case of a strike. And in the late 1940s, it seemed that The Radio Writers' Guild was going to stage a walkout against the networks because certain writers of new programs and other shows were allegedly receiving sub-standard wages.

The elite in The Radio Writers' Guild were the comedy writers. Almost every comedy show paid its writers several times the minimum scale, and on *The Jack Benny Show* our remuneration was upward of a dozen times the minimum.

The newspapers treated the strike as a source of humor. They printed stories about the impending walkout sprinkled with lines like "Jack Benny's writers are striking for Rolls-Royces instead of their crummy Cadillacs," "Bob Hope's writers want larger swimming pools," and "Red Skelton's writers want maids for their maids." Because the comedy shows then, as now, were the most popular ones on the air, it was only natural for them to become the targets for the newspapers' barbs.

We writers on Jack's staff had a meeting and decided to tell him that while we had everything we could possibly want, if our guild called a strike we could not scab. We would have to—reluctantly, it's true—stop working. We jointly told him this, adding lamely, "We hope our going out on strike won't cause any hard feelings."

Jack looked at us, smiled, and said to his quartet of writers, "If there's a strike, the *five* of us are going to walk out." Although not a member of the guild, Jack considered himself a writer.

Fortunately there was no strike and we didn't have to walk out. Frankly, I think that if there had been a strike and we didn't join our fellow writers on the picket lines, he would have lost respect for us.

Religion

Jack couldn't be considered a religious man as far as following the strict tenets of Judaism. He belonged to the Wilshire Temple but he seldom attended services, even on the High Holy Days. He didn't observe the dietary laws, but today many Jews, especially those who are Reform and Conservative rather than Orthodox, do not do so either.

Herman Wouk, the author of such best-selling books as *The Caine Mutiny* and *Marjorie Morningstar*, is one of the few Jews in the industry who adheres not only to the well-known "Ten Commandments," but also to the more than six hundred other, lesser known, commandments that a religious Jew must follow.

When Herman came to Hollywood in an advisory capacity while they were filming *The Caine Mutiny,* he told me: "I gave my agent a tough assignment. I told him he had to rent me a four-bedroom house in Beverly Hills within walking distance of an Orthodox synagogue." (An Orthodox Jew may not ride in a car on the Sabbath or on Yom Kippur.)

But if Jack wasn't a good Jew according to the book, he was a good man. He was proud of his heritage, but not boastful. He appeared at almost every Jewish benefit—not to mention benefits for other religions and all charitable causes. When Israel was declared an independent nation in 1948 and the Arab countries immediately launched the first of many wars to obliterate this small country, many fund-raising drives were held, and Jack acted as master of ceremonies at these affairs whenever possible, sometimes at several in one day.

There is an old Yiddish joke which goes: "The Jews are a very argumentative people. The only thing you can get two Jews to agree upon is what a third Jew should give to charity." Jack gave generously to charity, all charities, and those who knew the size of his donations agreed that he had given more than enough.

While he never emphasized his Jewishness, he certainly never denied it. One incident that stands out in my mind was the time we were scheduled to do our regular Sunday broadcast in Los Angeles at 4:00 P.M. All Jewish holidays start at sundown, and sundown that Sunday would mark the start of the most solemn and holiest of holidays, Yom Kippur, the Day of Atonement. The day before the

281

broadcast Jack told me that he felt very badly that although on the West Coast the sun wouldn't have set yet, it certainly would be down and it would be dark on the East Coast where we were heard from 7:00 to 7:30 P.M.

He said, "Milt, I wouldn't want people to think I'm desecrating this holiday by working on it." I smiled and pointed out to Jack that he had nothing to worry about. Since it would be sundown in New York and the East Coast, all the Jews living there would be in their temples praying, and they wouldn't know that he was on the air.

Jack shook his head and answered, "I wasn't thinking of the Jews, Milt. I wouldn't like the Gentiles to think I didn't respect my religion."

He had a very valid point, and therefore we inserted an innocuous line in the script—some small joke which hinged on the fact that there is a three-hour time difference between both coasts of our country, and how amazing it was that it was broad daylight here in California, and yet back East it was already evening. Jack was content with that—and he was right in wanting this line inserted.

Jack's Home

When I first went to work for Jack, he lived in a beautiful, large, expensive house in Beverly Hills. We visited his home frequently for business reasons, and we'd meet with him there occasionally for script sessions if he had a cold; otherwise we worked at his office.

We attended a couple of social gatherings a year with Mary and Jack as our hosts. However, these were mainly for the cast and writers. He occasionally had a few other people there, but we knew that the Bennys entertained the people they considered "friends" rather than members of the show on other occasions.

Jack was probably the least handy home-owner in history. If he managed to replace a burned-out light bulb without calling an electrician, he considered himself a genius. This inbred ineptitude was the indirect cause of the embarrassing occasion when he spewed a mouthful of coffee over playwright George S. Kaufman. They were having lunch in Sardi's renowned restaurant when Jack mentioned how anything the least bit mechanical frustrated him, and as an example he said, "I can't even screw an electric bulb into its socket." Then, as Benny started to sip his coffee, Kaufman replied, "Jack, I haven't even figured out the hammer yet." Kaufman, brilliant as he was, also hadn't figured out that it was courting sartorial suicide to say anything funny to Jack while his mouth was filled with food, solid or liquid. Benny's roar of laughter was instantaneous, and coffee was sprayed for several feet, with Kaufman getting his fair share.

One day we were in his bedroom on the second floor of his Roxbury Drive mansion. We were working there because Jack had the start of one of those frequent colds to which he was so susceptible. I felt rather warm and so did the other writers, but no one wanted to mention it because we thought that perhaps the room was overheated at his doctor's suggestion. Finally Jack pushed his covers aside and said, "How can you guys stand it? It's so hot in here." We agreed and asked him why he didn't turn the temperature down. He sheepishly admitted that he didn't know how. One of the writers walked over to the thermostat control, turned it down, and said, "Jack, that's all you have to do."

Jack, who had lived in this more than a quarter-million-dollar mansion for several years, looked pleasantly surprised and said, "Oh, so that's what that's for." Then he told us that he never knew what that gadget, as he called it, was doing in his room. We asked him why he didn't call his butler or one of the maids and ask about it. He answered sheepishly, "First of all, I hate to bother anybody, and in the second place, I don't want them to know what a big *schmuck* their boss is."

Loyalty

While I, and others, have written about Jack's loyalty to his writers, that loyalty was extended to all of his employees. When I joined him his script secretary was a young lady named Miss Jane Tucker. She had already been with Jack for several years at the time, and she remained for two more years, after which she left to get married. She was replaced by Miss Jeanette Eyman, who not only was his script secretary for the remainder of his career, but also used to appear on his programs several times a year doing small parts and thus adding to her income.

In addition to his script secretaries, Jack had a permanent personal secretary named Bert Scott who had served Jack Warner in the same capacity for sixteen years and remained with Benny for another thirty years.

Jack also had a combination companion and valet, Ned Miller, who was with him for over twenty years. But then loyalty was something you'd expect from a Hollywood star who married just once and stayed with the same wife, his beloved "Dollface" Mary, for over forty-seven years.

For over forty years the mere mention of Jack Benny's name conjured mental pictures of misers, skinflints, and shrewdness in saving a buck. As in the case of all his other traits, the private Jack Benny was vastly different than the public one. It's well known, as I've often said, that Jack was the most generous boss in the business. He gave lavish gifts, and if at luncheon or dinner you tried to pick up the check, he'd regard it as a personal insult.

Several times during the twelve years that I worked on his staff and the twenty or so years that followed my departure from his stable of writers, I had occasion to consummate business deals for my services with him. If the transaction transpired directly between the two of us, there was never the slightest argument over financial arrangements. Jack knew each of his employees' worth, and as long as a person didn't have an exaggerated sense of his own value, they arrived at an agreement quite quickly.

Stars always seem embarrassed at printed reports of their alleged wealth—usually because those reports are greatly exaggerated, and also because they want to have their fans think of them as their equals so that the public can have empathy for them.

Several years ago a magazine devoted to show business printed an article on the world's richest stars, starting with the poor people who had only amassed from ten to twenty-five million dollars, and reaching the heights with one man who is reputed to be worth from two hundred and fifty to five hundred million dollars—Bob Hope. Among the names of those wealthy Hollywoodites were listed such people as Fred MacMurray, Lawrence Welk, and Lucille Ball. Jack Benny's name was not among them.

Amassing money seemed to have no appeal for Jack. Certainly it was nice to have, but he had all he needed, and he wasn't going to use all his energies earning a vast fortune for the sake of wealth alone. He didn't avoid work, but frequently it seemed that he got more pleasure out of a non-paying fund-raising concert appearance with a financially troubled symphony orchestra than playing a nightclub or fair where he'd earn a six-figure salary for an engagement of a few weeks. Jack raised nearly ten million dollars for these worthy causes, and if you add to this all the benefit appearances he made for various charities, you can see that he might have earned several more millions if he had charged for these services.

The only time I ever saw Jack upset about finances involved what for him was a trivial amount. At that time Jack had his clothes made by one of the town's most exclusive tailors, and although he had excellent taste in clothes, he was never really known as one of Hollywood's best-dressed men.

Jack was having his suits fashioned for him at a price of around three hundred dollars each, in the days when the best men's tailors were making suits to order for the biggest stars at approximately one hundred dollars less. One day, while he was being measured for suits of three different materials he had selected, his eye lit on a bolt of some special material that looked soft, luxurious, and beautiful. Upon inquiring, he was informed that this was not for suits, but topcoats. (I believe it was vicuna, before that material was made vulgar as a result of a pre-Watergate Washington scandal.) Jack immediately insisted that such a topcoat be made out of it for him.

Several weeks later, after a couple of more fittings, Jack went to collect the finished suits and coat, and he was shocked to find that while the three suits cost a total of nine hundred dollars, the cost for the coat alone exceeded this figure. Since he never spent more than three hundred dollars on any garment, he was angry, asserting his feeling that he should have been informed that this material was so expensive.

The manager said, "Mr. Benny, you seemed to want it, and I figured a man in your income bracket wouldn't even want to discuss its cost." Jack replied with his opinion that even if a man was a billionaire and something he was ordering was priced at more than three times what he usually spent for the same article of attire, he had a right to know. The man immediately offered to cut his price by thirty percent and then by half, but Jack wouldn't accept this discount, since he felt that a deal was a deal. He took the coat, and when he wore it, it looked well worth the price, but it received less use than any other similar garment in his extensive wardrobe. He once confided to me, "It burns me up because every time I wear it, I feel like a stupid *schmuck*—and I guess the fact that this subconsciously stops me from wearing it makes me an even bigger *schmuck*, but I don't enjoy it." We rarely, if ever, saw him wearing it.

Jack was financially independent for most of his life, and certainly from the time he reached stardom, or close to it, in vaudeville.

Despite the fact that he was earning important money long before Bob Hope began building his financial empire, Jack's net worth was nowhere near that of Bob's. Because of my long and deep relationships with both men, I probably knew them better than any other person, and I have often been asked by curious—actually, nosy—acquaintances the reason for the vast monetary discrepancy between them. I don't know all the facts, but here they are to the best of my knowledge.

Hope is alleged, via various magazine articles in such accepted

285

authoritative sources as *Time* and *Look*, to have amassed an unbelievable fortune of from two hundred and fifty to five hundred million dollars. Whenever Bob reads such an estimate of his wealth, he cracks lines like, "I wish they'd stop printing such stories about all the dough I have. Whenever my wife Dolores reads one of them, she runs out into our backyard and starts digging up the place again."

I cannot speak with factual authority on the amounts of their fortunes, but during my many years with them I did notice some examples of why there was such a disparity in their wealth. Hope is an astute businessman, a gambler, a take-a-chance-guy. When he began to see his salary soar, he invested wisely and well. Only his accountants and business managers know how much land he bought in the booming San Fernando Valley and other areas that were soon to become valuable. He spread his money around, and he was blessed with the Midas touch. Moreover, Bob was never reluctant to do anything for a buck as long as it was legal, honest, and not demeaning.

In short, Hope was an investor, and perhaps even a speculator, although a sophisticated one. Conversely, Benny's business advisors were perhaps too conservative at a time when, because of income tax benefits, he could afford to gamble. On one occasion, Jack jokingly told us that his advisors were so careful and conservative that if he wanted to buy one hundred shares of AT&T (the traditional stock of widows and orphans), his managers would not only investigate the solidity of that company, but would also check its records back to Alexander Graham Bell and make sure that they found no trace of scandal in Bell's life before they'd let Benny risk a few dollars in AT&T.

It was because of this background that I was probably more shocked than anyone else when I read, several months prior to his passing, that Jack, along with numerous other show business greats, had been bilked in a fraudulent oil drilling deal.

Jack Benny on Jack Benny

Practically every comedian and alleged authority on humor has theorized and given reasons for Jack's long-lasting love affair with the public. We writers discussed this with Jack several times, and he had various thoughts on the subject.

I think the best analysis Benny ever made of himself was in an interview he gave to Larry Wilde, an author and comedian of excellent repute. Larry printed this in a book called *The Great Comedians*, published by Citadel Press in 1968. During this interview, Larry asked Jack, "What qualities are required [of a comedian],

Mary and Jack aboard the *Normandie*, August 1937, with John Royal, Mr. and Mrs. Jack Pearl, and Mr. and Mrs. Ed Sullivan.

Jack and Robert Taylor at a baseball game in the early 1940s. *Photo by Frank Worth.*

Jack and Thomas E. Dewey, June 1941.

Jean Parker selling Jack a batch of tickets at a fund-raising affair in 1942. *Photo courtesy of the Hedda Hopper Collection.*

Stars of 1944. Seated: Jimmy Durante, Ginny Simms, Nelson Eddy. Standing: Dinah Shore, Fred Allen, Frances Langford, Ed "Duffy's Tavern" Gardner, Jack. *Photo by Gene Lester.*

At a Friars stag dinner, 1950. Jack's friends include George Raft, Eddie Fisher, Frank Sinatra, and George Jessel.

Jack with Vice President Richard M. Nixon in 1959. Standing: Milton Berle, George Burns, and Eddie Fisher.

Jack going over script with President Harry Truman prior to the program in 1959.

This quintet harmonized in the early 1960s. Seated: Jack and Danny Thomas. Standing: songwriter Harry Ruby, producer Lou Edelman, and Sheldon Leonard.

At the Friars Club: Jack, George Jessel, director Mervyn LeRoy, and George Burns. *Photo by Frank Worth.*

With Bishop Fulton Sheen and Milton Berle at the Friars roast for Berle, September 1969.

With Spiro Agnew and Ed Sullivan, September 1969, at the Friars roast for Milton Berle.

Milton Berle, Jack, Rosalind Russell, and Frank Sinatra, 1972.

At movie pioneer Adolph Zukor's 100th birthday, 1973. Jack, Jack Warner, George Jessel, and Barbara Stanwyck.

other than being able to make people laugh?" Here is Jack's answer:

"In the first place, to become real successful, your public must like you very much. They must have a feeling like: 'Gee, I like this fella'— 'I wish he was a good friend of mine'—'I wish he was a relative.'

"You see, it's like a radio or TV show—if they like you, you may think sometimes that you are doing a bad show and you're not at all. But if they don't like you, you cannot do a good show. Of course we had great schools in those days—vaudeville and burlesque which you haven't got today. That's why I give all the new comedians a lot of credit for making it as quickly as they do and actually getting big laughs. For instance, I can walk on stage and if I want to feel secure I can open up with a couple of stingy jokes and everybody screams. Well, a lot of comedians who haven't got those characterizations have to make good as comedians, not as institutions—household words. Not that I'm bragging that I'm an institution, I'm just trying to explain."

Personally I think that in so short a space, this is as good a critique of Jack Benny's attitude toward humor as can be made, and since it came from that very source it is extremely accurate, but I must differ with one point.

Jack said he was not an institution. He was, and still is.

31
Other Intimates

Aside from those we have mentioned, there were many others who, for such divergent reasons as business, kinship, or friendship, were extremely close to Jack Benny. In this chapter we shall offer some thumbnail descriptions of their relationships.

Joan Benny

First, of course, we must mention his daughter Joan—not his "adopted" daughter Joan, but his daughter Joan. Never once, in all the time I knew him, did I ever hear Jack refer to Joan as being adopted. He would have been happy if no one had ever used this adjective in referring to her, but the newspapers and magazines seemed to make a point of it.

When I first met Mary and Jack's daughter, she was a pretty, well-behaved, ladylike little girl about eight years old. Mary and Jack adored her, and if we were busy with a script conference at his home when she returned from school, he would always excuse himself for several minutes to greet her with a fatherly kiss and a chat on how her day went.

One sunny afternoon we worked in Jack's backyard, and it had the biggest swimming pool I've ever seen in a private home. It was also all tile. Most pools are made of cement or gunnite and painted over with a light-blue special waterproof material. Only at the very top of the pool is there a border of two and a half or three inch square tiles because they are very expensive. Jack's pool was done entirely in tile, and small tiles at that. It looked like a mosaic work of art. And at the deep end of the pool there was a design made out of tiny tiles, mostly green with some red ones, which had been inlaid at great expense. It resembled an octopus, except that it had no head or face, yet it seemed to move in a lifelike way when the surface of the water shimmered.

Afterward I learned the story behind this unusual tile decoration. Originally it had in fact actually been an octopus, complete with eyes and mouth, and it gave the pool a unique appearance. However, the first time little Joan dove down to the bottom and looked at it, it frightened her and she climbed out of the pool almost in tears. Despite the advice of many friends that she would get used to it, Jack ordered the pool to be drained immediately and had the octopus redesigned so that it looked like an eight-petaled water lily. It cost Jack many thousands of dollars for the alterations, but Joan was able to use the pool without waiting to get over her fear, and this made Jack happy.

One day Mervyn LeRoy gave Jack tickets to his box at the Hollywood Park Race Track. Since Jack knew that I occasionally liked to place a small bet on the horses, he invited me to be his guest, and Joan, who was now eleven or twelve, accompanied us. This turned out to be a never-forgotten experience for me for a couple of reasons. First, Mervyn LeRoy was one of the founders of Hollywood Park, and his box at that time was in the clubhouse, at a corner, and jutted out directly over the finish line. There were no other seats that could compare to these. Secondly, when you go to the races with a man like Jack Benny, every horse owner, trainer, or smart bettor with access to special wire services and privately paid early morning clockers tries to give him the winners.

Among us we had three programs, and these were marked for us, at different times, by the most knowledgeable people in the so-called Sport of Kings. However, their first place selections were rarely unanimous, and while our cards were marked with the winners of all of the first six races, we didn't always make the correct selection.

Joan would study the three marked programs and then make a

two dollar "place" or "show" bet. (I had to go to the window and make the bet for her because she was too young, and Jack and I decided that having him place two dollar show bets on heavy favorites might make it seem that his radio reputation for miserliness wasn't a joke after all.)

Joan had won five of her six wagers, but betting "place" or "show" on favorites doesn't pay much money, so she was about four dollars ahead. I was betting two dollars across the board on the second or third favorites and had a couple of wins and a second, so I was about twelve dollars ahead. Jack was betting fives or tens, to win, on the first or second favorites and had the worst luck of our trio. He was about fifty dollars behind.

Now we came to the seventh and feature race. Mervyn LeRoy, who was wandering from box to box, came over to Jack and said that he had his own horse entered in this race, and from what Mervyn's trainer had told him, plus all the charts and forms, it should win.

Evidently everybody at the track thought so too, because the horse—I believe its name was "Aviatrix"—received a huge play on the "tote" boards and was an odds-on favorite. LeRoy told Jack that if he bet sixty dollars to win on Aviatrix and the horse won, he would recoup his fifty dollar loss and wind up even for the day. Then Mervyn went on to another box to sit with some other friends.

When he left Jack wondered aloud whether he should follow his advice. Joan said, "Daddy, if the horse wins, you'll only break even, but if he doesn't come in first, you'll be losing over a hundred dollars, and that's a lot of money."

Jack then asked me for my opinion, and I told him I agreed with Joan. I also pointed out that LeRoy's horse was such an overwhelming betting favorite now that the odds on the second and third favorites were disproportionately high, and therefore I was going to bet two dollars on each of them across the board. Joan played them both to show, while Jack decided to ignore LeRoy's advice and bet five dollars across the board on the same two horses.

I was lucky in that race because the two horses I picked wound up in a photo finish, and the one with slightly higher odds was the eventual winner. When we cashed our tickets in, Joan was nearly ten dollars ahead, I was about fifty dollars to the good, and Jack, who would have ended up losing one hundred and ten dollars had he bet on Aviatrix, was now a few dollars ahead.

As we drove home from the track, Joan was excited about her good fortune, but her father cautioned her that the next time she could lose instead of win. He wound up this little lecture by saying, "For example, Mervyn LeRoy knows everything, and he was wrong. Yet Milt was right and he doesn't know anything."

Before I could figure out whether this was an insult or a compliment, Joan indignantly said, "Daddy, that's not nice, saying Milt doesn't know anything."

Jack tried to explain to his daughter and apologize to me at the same time by saying, "Joan, I was only talking about horses. Mervyn LeRoy owns the racetrack and a stable of thoroughbreds. I only meant that he knows more about racing than Milt does."

And Joan answered, "Not today he didn't." Jack started to laugh (and so did I), and he had to pull his car over to the side of the road until he felt that his laughing wouldn't interfere with his driving.

Unfortunately Joan has not found the happiness her parents did in marriage. She has been married three times, and her first wedding, to Seth Baker, was one of Hollywood's—or, rather, Beverly Hills'—most exclusive social events. It was held in the Crystal Room of the fashionable Beverly Hills Hotel, and more major stars, studio owners, network presidents, and other assorted celebrities were seen that night than at any affair since Hollywood's early days.

The press, of course, made the soiree sound even more glamorous for their readers, and on the following morning the *Los Angeles Times* had a headline saying, "Jack Benny's Daughter Married in $25,000 Affair." The *Los Angeles Examiner*, which was still in existence then, headlined its story, "Benny Spends $50,000 on Daughter's Wedding."

That morning Jack was awakened by a phone call from Eddie Cantor who asked, "Did you read either of the morning papers yet?" Jack answered that he hadn't seen them, and Cantor said, "Well, do yourself a favor and just read the *Times*. You'll save $25,000."

Jack rarely discussed his daughter's triple trip to the altar, but he was deliriously happy with the four grandchildren Joan gave him. He delighted in taking his oldest grandson to the Los Angeles Dodger baseball games, where he maintained a season box, and he acted like any other proud grandpa during these outings. He once said, "I don't want to spoil the boy rotten, but I think I'm entitled to spoil him a little."

The last time Jack spoke to me about Joan was a couple of years ago, shortly before her thirty-eighth birthday. Jack mentioned the impending event, and then his eyes lit up as he said, "Gee, in just two more years I'll be thirty-nine, and I'll have a forty-year-old daughter."

I haven't seen Joan too often since her first marriage. However I, like millions of others, did get a glimpse of her on May 19, 1975, when she graciously accepted the Emmy that was posthumously awarded to Jack. Her mother was not visible, and I must assume that she did not attend.

One night around 1952 we were taping a radio show at the CBS studios on Sunset Boulevard. In those days Jack was doing thirty-nine radio shows plus several TV programs each season, and we were permitted to transcribe our radio shows in advance of the air dates. We usually did this at night, and after our dress rehearsal we would go out for dinner prior to the program.

On this particular night we were eating in an Italian restaurant on Gower Street when in walked a scrawny-looking soldier in uniform. As he approached us, we all recognized Frank Sinatra who was shooting late on a movie he was making at Columbia Pictures.

Sinatra's career, which had put him in the superstar category only a few years earlier, was now at a low ebb, and he only got this part in the picture because he practically begged Harry Cohn, the head of Columbia Pictures, for the part. Also, he was willing to work cheap, and for his role in this movie he was to receive only a tiny fraction of his former salary.

Since Sinatra was alone, Jack invited him to join us for dinner, and he did so. We all knew that the picture Frank was making was *From Here to Eternity,* based on James Jones' best-seller. And we were all familiar with the fact that this could possibly be his last career chance because he had accepted the role for the paltry (compared to what he used to earn) sum of ten thousand dollars for what would be at least eight weeks of work.

We all knew Frank slightly because of his several appearances on the Benny series, and we were all rooting for his success. Through most of the meal he talked about his part as "Maggio" and how he felt, from the moment he read the book, that in many ways the character was really an extension of himself. He just hoped that the public would accept him in this dramatic non-singing role. Jack asked him if he would like to make an appearance on the program, at the show's top salary for guest stars. Frank thanked Jack, but said that he wanted to do nothing but concentrate on the mood of Maggio. He finished dinner and hurried off because he had to rush back to his studio.

After he left, Jack began speaking of Sinatra, using the extravagant compliments he always overindulged in when discussing a friend. Jack said to the group of us, "I'll tell you quite honestly—he's convinced me that he *is* Maggio. I'll bet he not only gets good reviews in the picture, but there's an outside possibility he might even be nominated for an Oscar." And on this occasion, like many others, Jack was right. Sinatra was not only nominated for an Academy Award, but he won the Oscar for best supporting actor with his portrayal of Maggio.

Jack wasn't a close friend of Frank's when the bobby-sox brigade first zoomed the crooner into fame. Their close association blossomed years later when Sinatra suffered the first of his several career setbacks. It bloomed through the later years, and they grew closer with the passage of time. As was usually the case with Jack and his fellow stars, a mutual admiration society developed, and Jack was one of Frank's staunchest defenders no matter which of the various scrapes Sinatra was embroiled in at the moment.

Their affection started initially because of their professional contacts and broadened when they found themselves neighbors in the coterie of celebrities who bought winter homes in Palm Springs. It was there that Frank honored Jack with a lavish party celebrating his seventy-eighth birthday.

Only once did I hear Jack make a disparaging remark about Sinatra, and it was really a mild, even rueful jest. After Frank's brief retirement ended, his comeback was heralded with the slogan, "Old Blue Eyes Is Back." Jack said, "I wonder why he calls himself that. I was 'Old Blue Eyes' before he wore his first bow tie."

Groucho Marx

Jack's admiration for Groucho Marx as a comic and a wit was great indeed, but his personal feelings were slightly different. He once carefully emphasized that he liked Groucho but couldn't warm up to him, and oddly the reasons for his admiration and lack of warmth were caused by the same characteristic—Groucho's caustic wit.

The moustached comic could be devastatingly funny on any subject, and Jack felt that this was a fault. Groucho considered no subject to be immune from his quick quips, but Jack had greater sensitivity and winced occasionally when Marx took pot shots at certain sacred cows. For example, he felt that loved ones and tragedies were not meant to be the source of laughter.

Many years ago a typical Groucho story was related with relish as an example of his humor. The leering comic was traveling by train from Los Angeles to New York, sharing a compartment on one of the luxury Pullman cars with his daughter. The child was then eight or nine, and she was sleeping in the upper berth while Groucho occupied the lower.

Somewhere in the vast wasteland regions that separate Los Angeles from Kansas, the little girl began to suffer severe pains in the abdomen that were suspiciously symptomatic of an appendicitis attack. An eminent surgeon in Wichita or some other sizable city along the route was contacted via telegram, and his advice was to apply ice packs, eat light foods sparingly, and move the child as little as possible.

After several hours the train made an unscheduled stop at the doctor's home town, and he hurried aboard and was rushed to the Marx compartment. However, he was extremely short, and when he had to reach up to examine the girl in her upper berth, some delay was incurred while they brought a bench for him to stand on. As the doctor was clambering up, Groucho ad-libbed to the gathered sympathetic porters and conductors, "Next time either get her a lower berth or a taller doctor."

Since the child suffered no ill effects, eventually the anecdote was gleefully told and retold. I was with Jack when someone started to tell it to him. Jack had already heard it, and he coldly interrupted the raconteur by saying, "I don't think it's funny for a man to make jokes while his child is suffering."

In 1944 we had Groucho as a guest star on our radio show. On Saturday we had our regular cast reading, and by the time we were halfway through with the script, gloom had gripped the studio. Groucho was reading his part with all the enthusiasm of a priest administering the last rites—and we were rapidly coming to the conclusion that the last rites were exactly what the script needed. Groucho's reading was flat and toneless and done almost in a whisper. In fact, his whole performance was more of a mumble than a reading. Finally Jack stopped the proceedings and said in slightly testy tones, "Groucho, we hold these readings to see if the cast can laugh at the script." Groucho answered, "On my show we hold these readings to see if the cast can read."

Groucho then apologized and said that he usually wasn't good at "cold" readings, and this was the first time he had even seen the script. Could Jack give him twenty minutes or so to familiarize himself with his part and then resume the reading? Jack agreed to this, and Groucho went into one of the dressing rooms to study his lines. During those twenty minutes Jack began to worry that Groucho might not like the script, that Groucho might not like the studio, that Groucho might not like the way he was treated, and finally that Groucho might not like him. (Jack's predisposition toward worrying was so well known that, in regard to his propensity for getting up at 6:00 A.M., a good friend of his commented: "Jack Benny is the only man in Hollywood who at eight o'clock in the morning has already been worrying two hours more than anybody else.")

After his twenty-minute recess, Groucho came back into the studio, the cast breezed through the script with the laughs landing where they should have, and it eventually turned into an excellent show.

Let me digress at this time to point out that it was on this very same day that I lost some of the adoration that almost every creator of comedy had for Groucho. We broke for lunch after the reading, and Jack asked Groucho if he'd like to sit in with us at the rewrite and cutting session. Groucho accepted the invitation, and he and Jack lunched together while we writers went off by ourselves. As I mentioned, this was 1944, World War II was reaching a catastrophic crescendo, and the local newspapers were publishing extra editions with scare headlines almost every hour.

As we writers were returning to the studio, I bought a paper whose headline screamed, "SIX U.S. SHIPS SUNK BY JAPS." A quick perusal of the story under the headline revealed that these sunken vessels were not cruisers, destroyers, aircraft carriers, or battleships, but small oil tankers. Their loss was not a mortal blow to our Navy, but it was still a tragedy, especially to the families of those who might have been killed or injured in this action.

When we returned to the studio office for the rewrite, Jack and Groucho were already there. As we started to sit in our customary seats, Jack saw that I had a newspaper and he asked me what the headline was. I answered: "Six U.S. Ships Sunk by Japs." Groucho asked: "What kind of ships?" I answered, "Tankers." He said, "You're welcome."

The ensuing silence was the most deafening I had ever heard. Jack, the easy audience, didn't so much as smile. Neither did any of the writers or our secretary. We simply finished rewriting the script without another word about the incident. However, I was greatly disillusioned to find that one of my idols had feet of clay.

32
The Men Jack Disliked, and Vice Versa

It is an accepted fact that everybody in the industry loved Jack Benny and that Jack loved them all. This is not quite true, but it is almost true. I have had writers, producers, directors, and other creative people tell me how much they envied my years with Jack, and they had a right to be envious. For the most part working for Jack was not working in the true sense of the word. It was spending most of your time with your best friend and being paid handsomely for it.

It would be nice to say that I knew absolutely no one who ever even quarreled with Jack, but it wouldn't be true. Over the years I myself had a few disagreements with him—strong disagreements—but show me a man who hasn't had fights with his wife or other loved ones, and I'll show you a man who has neither guts nor emotions. Jack had both, and so do I. Therefore, I don't count those squalls and squabbles that come up like sudden storms and quickly clear away. I'm talking about the long-lasting bitterness that breaks up friends and marriages.

The only man I know who held such hatred for Jack was one of his long-term associates. Moreover, the animosity was all one-sided—and it wasn't on Jack's side. After many years of working for Jack, this man took offense at an imaginary insult. There was no insult, nor was any insult ever intended. And if, even by the strongest stretch of an oversensitive imagination, there was an affront, it was so infinitesimal that only a high-powered mental microscope could magnify it to be visible at all.

I won't mention the man's name. The fact that he worked for Jack for well over twenty years is sufficient identification. To those who know the man, this fact will serve to identify him just as much as naming him would. To those who don't know him, there's no need to name him and subject him to humiliation. I will name others whom Jack didn't like, but Jack *liked* this man. It was he who suddenly nurtured an almost psychotic enmity toward Jack.

The imagined insult took place some time after Jack had quit his regular weekly broadcasts on CBS. He was then signed for a series of one-hour television specials by NBC, the first one to be shown on September 25, 1964.

Jack had his combination press agent/manager/agent/friend, Irving Fein, phone several people to hire them to help him with these specials. When Fein phoned this man, he turned Irving down vehemently, and from that point on, his anger and animosity increased.

Several months later, although I hadn't been on Jack's regular writing staff for over ten years and my only services to him were in the areas of nightclub material, TV specials, and guest shots on Lucille Ball's series, I received a Christmas present from Jack. It was one of those huge baskets of goodies stuffed with rare wines, liquor, liqueurs, boxes of biscuits and candies, canned delicacies, fresh fruit and nuts, and, most of all, tons of varicolored strips of cellophane that made the basket seem to hold three times its considerable consumable contents.

I don't make a practice of going around having gifts evaluated, except in the case of expensive jewelry which I am obliged to do for insurance purposes, but I would estimate that this thoughtful and generous gift cost Jack well over a hundred dollars. The cellophane alone must have cost fifty dollars. You could have gift-wrapped the *Queen Mary* with it.

A few days later I met the man who was mad at Jack. Through mutual friends I had learned that Jack had sent him a similar gift, but twice as large as mine, which was perfectly all right with me because the man had worked for Benny twice as long as I did. This man, whom I'll call "Quentin" because I know of no Quentin who was ever employed by Benny, was furious. He said to me in strident tones: "How do you like that . . . [expletive deleted] Jack? He can take his . . . [double expletive deleted] gift and shove it up his . . . [double expletive deleted]."

I told Quentin that I thought it was a friendly gesture and a thoughtful token of esteem. "Bullshit," he answered. "It was a subtle insult. It was his way of saying to me, 'Since you won't work for me, and are probably broke, I'm sending you a Care Package.' " I tried to tell him that his reasoning was ridiculous, but our conversation became one-sided—his side.

From that moment on I dreaded contact with Quentin, because on every occasion that we met, he launched into a tireless tirade against Jack, and I felt, as did all acquainted with the incident, that Jack had done nothing wrong. In fact he was being senselessly condemned for a friendly act.

A few more months passed and Jack appeared as a guest on a Lucy show I had written. I was having lunch with him at the Paramount commissary one afternoon and I tactfully asked about the argument he had had with Quentin. Jack told me that it did indeed start when he had Irving Fein call several people to work on his TV special, and he mentioned how Quentin had hung up on Fein in anger. Then Jack thought for a moment, and with a trace of sadness he said, "Maybe it was my fault. Maybe he figured that I knew him so long that instead of Irving I should have called him personally."

I told Jack that he shouldn't blame himself. Since he hadn't called any of the others personally but had used Irving, who always acted in these matters, to set their deals, then it was entirely proper that Irving was the one who called Quentin.

This assurance that he was blameless seemed to cheer up Jack a bit. Then, knowing how it hurt him to be on unfriendly terms with anyone, I offered to act as mediator and bring the two together. I asked Jack if he would call Quentin and invite him to lunch to talk things over.

Jack said eagerly, "I'd be happy to, Milt, only I'm afraid if I call him, he'll hang up on me. Then, instead of just him being mad at me, I'll be mad at him." I promised that I would handle the matter tactfully and personally.

That night I called Quentin and told him of my discussion with Jack and how Jack wanted to talk to him and resume their friendship, but wanted some assurance that he wouldn't be rebuffed. Quentin broke down and began to cry. He told me how wonderful I was—an angel, a saint—and how he had suffered and couldn't sleep because of the breach with Benny.

While he was extolling my virtues and telling me that he loved Jack, I said, "Look, Quentin. If you feel that way, why don't you surprise Jack and phone him?"

In the two seconds it took me to say that sentence I was demoted from saint to a heel. He screamed that this was all a plot on Jack's part to humiliate him and get him to phone and apologize. It took me ten minutes to assure him that he was wrong and that I'd have Jack make the first move.

The following day, which was the day we were scheduled to shoot the Lucy show, I told Jack that I had talked to Quentin. I omitted any mention of Quentin's reactions to my suggestion that he make the opening overtures toward resuming their friendship. I simply suggested that Jack contact Quentin who was eagerly awaiting his call. Jack said that he would contact Quentin before he flew to New York the following day for a benefit. And that ended the matter—for five days.

Five days later I got a call from Quentin—an angry Quentin. His voice was vitriolic as he accused me of "getting Jack off the hook." I allegedly had done this by letting Jack know that Quentin was willing to make up, and thus I had eased Jack's conscience. But now five days had passed and he had received no word from him, which proved that Jack had no intention of resuming their friendship.

I defended myself from this asinine accusation by telling him that Jack was in New York, and that perhaps he had tried to phone prior to leaving, but Quentin might have been out, and he didn't have a message service. At this point I was cut off with a resounding "Bullshit," and Quentin slammed the receiver down on me. I was very upset, and I vowed that I would never again act as a peacemaker.

An hour later my phone rang. It was Quentin—a crying Quentin. Sainthood was again bestowed on me. He told me that the minute, no, the second he had said goodbye to me (he didn't say goodbye—he hung up), his phone rang and it was Jack Benny calling from New York. Jack told him that he had been trying to get him every day but he was either out or the line was busy. They had nearly a full-hour heart-to-heart talk, and they were bosom buddies again. He thanked me profusely, and this time he said goodbye.

It would be nice to end this incident by saying "And they lived happily ever after," but they didn't. Several months later Quentin again took umbrage at some imaginary slight to his sensitive feelings and became Jack's mortal enemy once more. Quentin was the only man I knew who disliked Jack. And after forty years of friendship, he didn't even have the decency to pay his final respects at his funeral.

There may have been other men who didn't like Jack, but none to my knowledge. And the list of Jack's dislikes is equally skimpy. Perhaps Jack wasn't too crazy about some people, but he never revealed these feelings by any act or deed.

I know of only three men Jack truly disliked, and on occasion—a rare occasion, to be sure—he would speak of them in an uncomplimentary fashion. The first of these men was a cipher whom he never mentioned by his actual name. To my knowledge Jack had never met him socially or in business, but oddly enough I was introduced to this man when he was trying to break into show business. He was Keefe Brasselle.

Around the early 1940s, Al Schwartz, one of the three well-known writing Schwartz brothers, asked me to do him a minor favor. He knew a young man who was trying to support himself until he got the "big break." At the current time it was in mid-November and he was trying to make a buck by selling Christmas cards. Al was trying to help him by calling all his friends and asking them to buy their cards from him. As a result I ordered my Christmas cards from Keefe Brasselle.

Then he got a shot at pictures and reached the pretty high position of star—not STAR, but star. He played the lead role in *The Eddie Cantor Story*. It was a shot at the big time, but for some reason it didn't hit the target. The picture received a lukewarm reception, and Keefe Brasselle, as far as I know, starred in just a handful of other movies—none as important as *The Eddie Cantor Story*. And, as I have indicated, that epic didn't exactly burn up the box offices.

The next I heard of Keefe was when he became the right-hand man of the famous, or infamous, James Aubrey, the man in charge of television programming for CBS. Mr. Aubrey was as efficient as the most perfect computer, and just as cold and seemingly lacking in human emotions. He was called many things by those in TV, the most complimentary being "The Smiling Cobra." A man in his position has the thankless job of informing a star that his TV show is canceled, and most of his contemporaries, predecessors, and successors felt squeamish about performing this unpleasant chore. Aubrey reputedly took pleasure in it, and sometimes he even went against the wishes of his boss, William Paley, the head man of CBS, to reap some personal revenge. One such event supposedly happened in the case of Garry Moore.

Moore had a successful and entertaining variety hour that we should all remember lovingly if for no other reason than the fact that it gave us the delightful Carol Burnett. At this particular time Moore's option status was in the "iffy" category. If he improved his ratings slightly, he would be renewed; if he slipped, he would be dropped. William Paley was inclined to retain the series. Aubrey was not.

Mr. Paley frequently gave lavish parties that were attended by his friends, and since many of the CBS stars fell into this category, Garry Moore was usually on the invitation list, as was James Aubrey. And during the period when Moore's TV fate hung in the balance he was invited to one of Mr. Paley's parties. One of the first men he ran into there was Aubrey who greeted him cordially and then added: "By the way, we're dropping your show."

Now these are the facts as I heard them. I can't vouch for the complete truth of the incident because I wasn't there—but the story has been repeated so often that there must be some truth in it.

Legend has it that Moore turned right around and left the party without even greeting his host. The host, Mr. Paley, was infuriated when informed of the incident, and he personally apologized to Moore. However, Garry's show went. Aubrey remained.

And now Keefe Brasselle, the former movie star and Christmas card salesman, was on the CBS payroll in an executive capacity assisting James Aubrey. Brasselle tried to model himself after Aubrey, and from all reports he succeeded to some degree—at least in personality if not in business acumen.

My first inkling of Keefe's new character came from Al Schwartz who had an idea for a TV series. All new series ideas had to be okayed by Aubrey, and to get to Aubrey you had to go through Brasselle. Therefore, Al called Keefe, and when he was informed that he was busy, Schwartz left his name and phone number. Nothing happened. A week later Al called again with the same result. For four more weeks Al called, and then he stopped because he realized that he was getting a brush-off.

It should be made clear that the names of the Schwartz brothers carry some weight in the broadcasting business. Al's brother, Sherwood, sold CBS the financially successful although not critically acclaimed series *Gilligan's Island.* He also created and produced *The Brady Bunch* which had a five-year network run. Both shows were subsequently made into animated cartoons as children's programs on television. As for Al himself, he had been a writer of long standing and had impressive credits, such as many years with Bob Hope and Red Skelton, and he had also won an Emmy for comedy writing. Therefore, even if he hadn't helped Brasselle over a rough financial period a couple of decades ago by getting many people to purchase Christmas cards, he deserved the courtesy of having his phone calls answered. They never were.

Eventually the CBS top brass, perhaps Mr. Paley himself, decided to rid the network of James Aubrey—and along with Aubrey went Brasselle. Mr. Aubrey soon became a top executive with MGM where he helped reduce that company from the most powerful motion picture studio in Hollywood to a gambling casino in Las Vegas. He is no longer with MGM.

After their departure from CBS, the relationship between Aubrey and Brasselle cooled off and finally developed into an enmity.

Brasselle showed his gratitude to Aubrey by writing a book called *The Cannibals,* a thinly disguised description of his years under Aubrey at CBS and the machinations in the top echelons of television. The "heavy" in the book was based on James Aubrey's character, and the hero was obviously patterned after the model of goodness, Keefe Brasselle. And in the book there is a third character named "Jackie Benson," described as "a washed up comedian who hasn't got the brains to lie down and die."

There was no doubt that Jackie Benson was supposed to be Jack Benny. In fact, "Jackie Benson" was a name we had occasionally used on radio programs when we wanted someone to embarrass Benny by introducing or identifying him incorrectly. Brasselle's delineation was scandalous sensationalism at its nadir, even though creating fictitious characters based on actual people has always been an acceptable gainful gambit. In Jacqueline Susann's hugely successful best-selling novel *Valley of the Dolls,* the three leading lady characters are cast in the images of composites of several prominent actresses, but in the Hollywood guessing games which always follow publication of such books, they were almost unanimously identified as Judy Garland, Ethel Merman, and Marilyn Monroe. Interestingly enough, another of Jacqueline's best-sellers, *The Love Machine,* featured a duo who were doubtlessly inspired by this oddest of "odd couples," Aubrey and Brasselle. And there have been books in which the lead characters were supposedly based on Jane Fonda, Frank Sinatra, and others. The roman à clef was not invented by Keefe Brasselle.

However, in his novel *The Cannibals,* Brasselle's portrayal of Jackie Benson, a blatantly obvious and cruel caricature of Jack Benny, was offensively vicious and totally baseless. Perhaps the author figured that by attacking broadcasting's best loved star, he could get word-of-mouth publicity which would lead his novel to the top of the best seller list. The ruse didn't work, probably because Brasselle's writing skills were not quite on a par with his talents as an actor, executive, and Christmas card salesman.

In *The Cannibals* he evidently wanted to insure the identification of Jackie Benson as Jack Benny, so Brasselle wrote that Jackie Benson tried to get laughs by driving an ancient Stutz Bearcat, that he used to be a star in radio and was the first really big star to jump from one network to a competing company, and that his program remained on the air only because of his friendship with the head of the network.

It was no secret in 1948-1949—in fact it was very widely publicized—that Jack Benny had left NBC to go to CBS, and it was common knowledge that he was friendly with William Paley, the head of that network. However, Mr. Paley's network had to pay two million dollars to purchase Benny's company and acquire his services. And it is also a well-known fact that Jack was equally friendly with Robert Sarnoff, who was then the president of NBC, and who afterward was promoted to run the parent company, RCA.

In 1963, when Jack terminated his regular weekly CBS appearances, Mr. Paley was anxious to retain his services on some basis. However, Robert Sarnoff was equally anxious for Jack to come back home to NBC, which he did, and he presented successful one-hour special television shows on that network until the very end.

Friendship had nothing to do with Jack Benny's longevity on the airways. Both Robert Sarnoff and William Paley were astute enough to recognize his talents and popularity, and from a business point of view he was a valuable commodity. Yet according to *The Cannibals,* "The guy [Jackie Benson] was one of those no-talent hams supported by characters and pieces of stage business. Benson's format had worked for years but now the public was tired of it, and the ratings were way down. In short, Benson had two chances to stay on the air: slim and none . . . but they [the mythical network in the novel] had a hole in their schedule and could use the tired name for one last season, after which Benson could be led out to pasture playing cards at the Hilldale Country Club." (Jack belonged to Hillcrest Country Club, but went there for golf. Although he sometimes played cards, it was not one of his passionate pastimes, as it is with other members.)

The Cannibals contained other ridiculous falsehoods besmirching Jack Benny in the character of Jackie Benson. In the book Jackie Benson was vain, petulant, and vengeful. Also, I believe, the book stated that Jackie Benson, who was "a washed up comedian who hasn't got the brains to lie down and die," later was powerful enough to prevent programs he didn't approve of from getting on this mythical network.

I read the book because Al Schwartz, who first introduced me to Brasselle, had read it, and since he had had some contact with Jack, he immediately respected him as all writers did. Al resented this unwarranted character assassination and loaned me his copy. I was infuriated as I got deeper into the story because Jackie Benson was so patent an attempt by the author to have the reader immediately identify the character as Jack Benny, and the characteristics attributed to Jackie Benson were so scurrilous as to border on the libelous.

The book was a failure, a fact which made me happy. However, some people in the industry read it, and all of those who knew me queried me about its veracity. I said that there wasn't an iota of truth in any of it. I was hoping that Jack hadn't read it, but unfortunately he had, and eventually I discussed it with him during a rehearsal of some show we were doing.

Jack was more hurt than angry, and he said: "I don't think I ever met the man, Milt. Why should he tell lie after lie about a guy in his book who is definitely meant to be me?" I assured Jack that everyone who knew him realized that the Jackie Benson caricature was a tissue of lies. Jack said, "Oh, I know that. But what about the millions who may read it and not know me personally? They'll think I'm a terrible person." I told him that the chances of millions of people reading the book were remote—probably thousands or hundreds would be nearer the truth. This seemed to cheer Jack up, and he said, "I hope Keith Brazil falls on his ass." It was odd, but he never called him anything else but Keith Brazil. Either Jack subconsciously didn't want to admit the existence of a person named Keefe Brasselle, or he did it intentionally, meaning it contemptuously or humorously. But on the few other occasions that Keefe Brasselle's name cropped up in conversation, Jack would talk about Keith Brazil.

The book came nowhere close to being a best seller. Even its supposedly inside spicy facts about CBS, Jim Aubrey, Jack Benny, and others didn't lead to substantial sales in Hollywood, and in other parts of the country it had the very limited sales it deserved.

The last time I discussed Brasselle with Jack was a couple of years before Jack passed away. Keefe had fallen on hard times and had gotten himself in an unsavory scrape with the law. He was involved in a shooting incident and was given several years of probation as his sentence.

I mentioned this fact to Jack who hadn't heard about it, and his reaction was typical of him. He was genuinely upset. "Gee, that's a shame. I feel sorry for that Keith Brazil." This was no sarcastic gloating over an enemy's ill fortune. Jack was a compassionate man, and he forgot the mental anguish that Keefe Brasselle had caused him. However, he evidently didn't forget completely, because though the sentiments he voiced were sincere, he still called him Keith Brazil.

The second man that Jack disliked shall be nameless, and for a very good reason—I never did know his name. And while Jack knew his name, he again didn't know the man—nor did he want to.

It started in Palm Springs where a group of men had gathered to build a golf course and form a club. Golf courses have proliferated in Palm Springs since World War II, and I believe that on a per capita basis Palm Springs has more of them than any other resort its size.

At the initial meeting the big question came up: Should the club be restricted or open? One of the men made an impassioned plea. He said that to keep the club classy it must be restricted. The admission of Jews would lower its social prestige because Jews were loud, greedy, and grasping. He then added every other baseless, bigoted, stereotyped slander that has been aimed at Jews through the years. The man's harangue made it quite evident that he didn't choose to mingle with the Chosen People, and he ended his diatribe by adding the final clincher: "I know what I'm talking about from experience. I'm Jewish myself."

Palm Springs is a small town, drawing most of its population—permanent, semi-permanent, and temporary—from the entertainment industry. And since gossip is the second most popular pastime of those working in the entertainment field, this story soon got around. It probably was heard by ninety percent of the people in Palm Springs and by fifty percent of those in the movie, radio and TV studios in Hollywood within twenty-four hours of its happening. It was a sensational tidbit for one day, and died away.

Several years passed and then for some unknown reason the sole Jewish member of this club, the man whose arguments had led to its adoption of a restricted policy, quit, or perhaps he was asked to resign. I never knew the facts. I did know, however, that he didn't want to give up golf, so he applied for membership in Tamarisk, another Palm Springs golf club. Tamarisk is not only not restricted, but it is also predominantly Jewish, and its membership included Jack Benny. When Jack heard that the man was applying for admittance, he became, for the only time I know of, vengeful.

Now Jack rarely, if ever, suffered because of anti-Semitism of any type. True, his programs received occasional hate mail, but so did all others. And, oddly enough, his portrayal of a man who loved money, was avaricious, greedy, and miserly, and was unwilling to part with a penny (all inborn vices attributed to Jews by their enemies) never caused any anti-Semitic comment, publicly or privately. Jack never understood this. He made no secret of being Jewish, but even the racists who frequently unite in deluging celebrities with vicious and malicious mail seldom made Jack the target of their hatred. Thus Jack's actions against this man were not caused by deep-seated wounds or a hunger for revenge. However, since he felt that what the man did in making the first club restricted was an unconscionable deed against not only Jews, but all minorities, he went out of his way to see that this man, who was evidently ashamed of his own beginnings, would not be allowed to enjoy the pleasures he so readily denied to others. And even though it took only two dissenting votes to blackball a prospective member, Jack made many phone calls to his friends at the club, and he reveled in the results when the man was not allowed to join Tamarisk.

The third and final man whom Jack didn't like was the famed vaudeville star and actor Frank Fay. Jack was not alone in his feelings about Fay. It was once said: "The friends of Frank Fay could hold a meeting in a telephone booth while it was being used by Kate Smith."

Fay was a tremendously talented man, yet the distaste his fellow performers had for him was not nurtured by jealousy. There were numerous reasons why many famous stars had low opinions of him, and not the least of these was the high opinion he had of himself.

Fay's ego was so great that more than once have I heard, and read, the legend that he once had to appear as a witness in a lawsuit. At the start of his interrogation on the witness stand, he was asked what his occupation was, and he immediately answered, "The world's greatest comedian." Later a lawyer told him that he had probably antagonized the jury with this shameless immodesty, and then the lawyer asked, "Why in the world did you say you were the world's greatest comedian?" Fay answered, "I had to. I was under oath."

If Fay had been jesting, it would have been looked upon as a witty remark, but he was in earnest. Fred Allen despised him for many reasons, including his colossal conceit. Fred once said, "The last time I saw Frank Fay he was slowly strolling down Lovers' Lane holding his own hand." Allen also said, "If Fay's ego had been acid he would have consumed himself." And Fred, like Jack, was never jealous of another man's talents.

Fay earned the dislike, and even the enmity, of his peers in various other ways. In a business known for its lack of bigotry, he was a bigot. This was no secret, but was widely known and well substantiated. In his autobiography Milton Berle tells how Fay referred to him as "a little kike." Berle relates that he was a youngster then, but he was so infuriated that he took a punch at Fay and had the pleasure of bloodying his nose.

Fay referred to other comedians as "Jew bastards," but he never designated Jack Benny as such. "At least," Jack told me, "I never heard about it."

Fay's bigotry had little to do with Jack's distaste for him. It may have been a subconscious factor, but Benny never mentioned it. Jack disliked Fay for several reasons, and among them were Fay's ego and unprofessionalism. Jack once discussed this and said, "When he appeared in vaudeville he rarely changed his act or polished it. He never bothered to remove jokes or lines that were dated. His attitude toward the audience was, 'You people are lucky enough to see the great Frank Fay no matter what I do.'"

Possibly the prime reason for Jack's unfriendly disposition toward Fay was because of the fondness that he and Mary had for actress Barbara Stanwyck. When Barbara was a young chorus girl, known by the name of Ruby Stevens, she was briefly and tumultuously married to Fay. It was no secret that some of the connubial bliss endured by Barbara included frequent beatings by her husband. Rumor had it that he used to slap her around and punch her repeatedly and regularly.

Jack told us of an incident involving Barbara when she became a movie star. She was filming a dramatic scene where her leading man was supposed to get angry, lose his temper, and slap her in the face. Three times they filmed the scene, and three times the actor slapped her, but he didn't want to hurt her and "pulled his punch," and each "take" was unusable because the slap looked artificial, feeble, and gentle. They did a fourth "take" of the scene with the director pleading with the actor to hit her harder, but still his slap lacked sting and zing. As they prepared for a fifth "take," Barbara broke everybody up by telling the director, "Why don't you get Frank Fay as technical advisor for this scene?"

I was in New York with Benny at the time when Frank Fay, after having been in oblivion for years, made a big Broadway comeback as the star of the famed hit *Harvey*. During our stay in New York Jack took a party of people, including his writers, to see the play, and Jack laughed uproariously throughout the show at Fay's perfect performance. A few days later he went again, and then a third time. When I heard that he had bought tickets for a fourth viewing of the show I said to Jack, "I thought you didn't like Frank Fay." Jack answered, "I don't. But I'm not going to the show to see Frank Fay, the man. I'm going there to see Frank Fay, the actor."

33
Jack's Character Takes Over

The intrusion into one's personal life of a long-running role is not unusual in actors and actresses on the screen and in the theater. And when the charade is continued through several movies or shows, it can frequently worm its way into the performers' psyche either consciously or unconsciously. Raymond Burr, who played the role of Perry Mason for many years, is frequently asked for his opinion on legal matters and Robert Young, alias Dr. Marcus Welby, has been asked to aid an ailing woman at a party. The same situation was true in the case of Jack Benny.

To some extent, Jack Benny was "Dr. Jekyll and Mr. Hyde." Offstage he was the kindly, sweet, benevolent "Dr. Jekyll," but before a microphone or camera he became the greedy, grasping "Mr. Hyde." Not that Benny's "Mr. Hyde" was a vicious villain, but the character that Jack portrayed had several somewhat unsavory qualities created for laugh purposes. He was cheap, vain, and unfair, and among his other assets while performing (although they are liabilities in true life), Jack was the all-time *shnook*.

Shnook is a word which Leo Rosten ably defines in his best-selling book *The Joys of Yiddish* (McGraw-Hill, 1968). According to Rosten, the word was first used on coast-to-coast radio on the Jack Benny broadcast of October 9, 1951, when Mary told Jack, "Don't be such an apologetic *shnook*." One of the basic keystones of Jack's character was being a *shnook*—a sad sack, a patsy, an ineffectual type. A *shnook* is also a *shlemiel* and a *shlimazel*. As for the almost infinitesimal difference between *shlemiel* and *shlimazel*, we turn again to Rosten's book: "A *shlemiel* is always tripping and spilling soup. The *shlimazel* is the man the *shlemiel* spills the soup on." As Rosten pointed out, we were the first program to use the word *shnook* on national comedy broadcasts. We also used many other Yiddish words that have become, or are fast becoming, part of the American vocabulary via show business. In fact we got a tremendous laugh in one script, when Roland Colman finally got so mad at Jack that he couldn't restrain himself, and in his inimitable and impeccable British intonations he said: "Why you . . . you *shlemiel*." After a long laugh, because it sounded funny even to those who didn't understand the meaning of the word, Jack repeated in a questioning tone, *"Shlemiel?"* Colman said, "Yes, *Shlemiel* . . . S, H, L, E, M . . ." at which point Jack interrupted angrily, yelling, "I know how to spell it. Heaven knows I've been called it often enough." I don't believe that more than thirty percent of our studio audience that day knew what the word meant, but we got one hundred percent laughter because it's a word that sounds as though it means something funny, and because of this the audience laughed heartily each time it was repeated.

In any analysis of Jack's comedically created character, one must list that Jack was the penultimate in the *shnook-shlemiel-shlimazel* character, and it had nothing to do with religion or racial background. Lucille Ball, during the period her children were going through adolescence, said many times on television talk shows, "I'm a typical Jewish mother, even though I'm of a different faith." Lucy was also fond of quoting the line, "You don't have to be Jewish to be a Jewish mother." For another example, there was Jackie Gleason who portrayed a one hundred percent certified *shnook* every time he played the part of "The Poor Soul" on his programs. Gleason performed "The Poor Soul" in pantomime, and thus there was no dialogue to distract the viewer from his Irish features, but even so the *shnookiness* of the character came through clearly.

However, in all deference to Gleason, Benny was the all-time *shnook* on radio and TV, and his *shnookiness* eventually crept into his private and personal life. In real life he was the man nearest to the curb and thus inevitably destined to get splashed by a passing car speeding through a puddle of muddy water. He was the Good Samaritan who would be punched in the nose for his attempts to help others or for acting as a peacemaker between two arguing people. If a group of six went into a swank restaurant and were being seated by an attentive waiter, Jimmy the Greek would give odds that Jack would sit in the chair on which someone would inadvertently spill water. On a hike through a desert area, if the participants sat down for a few minutes of rest, Jack would sit on the only piece of poison ivy in the arid wasteland, or within a thousand miles for that matter. He was the guy who would go to the theater and get seats behind the pole in the auditorium, or else he'd be seated in front of the popcorn-gorged kid who would throw up. He could be at a football game, hardly visible in the midst of a hundred thousand cheering spectators, yet a passing pigeon would unerringly choose Jack as his target. He was the eternal innocent bystander, positioned directly behind the target who ducked when a pie was hurled at him, so that Jack got it full in the face. On the air our pies were verbal pastries, not the Soupy Sales kind, although on television Jack did, on rare occasions, get a pie in the face. However, in real life he was an eternal target.

During many discussions Jack told me that this had been his fate since childhood. Kismet seemed to have kissed him and said, "I love you, boy, but am I gonna make you a *shnook!*" Thus Jack's radio character, excepting for such characteristics as vanity, greed, and a few others, was patterned after his basic life-experience.

On Jack's radio and television appearances you could rest assured that if the program was interrupted by the lowliest bit player portraying the smallest part, the big laugh would always go to this unknown performer, while the celebrated star, Jack Benny, would end up with the proverbial egg on his face. And this carried over into real life. Jack would get topped by policemen, telephone operators, mailmen, salesgirls, caddies, and errand boys. Other comics bested by non-professionals would immediately have five or six standard lines, or toppers, to put the miscreant in his place, but Jack never did. Needless to say, he knew the standard squelches that all comics have in their arsenal of insults, a repertoire of repartee to be used to halt hecklers on occasions like this. However, he would be so doubled up with laughter that he couldn't utter a single syllable in his defense. And even if he could, he would not humiliate an underling for making him the butt of the joke.

Jack would laughingly and happily tell us of his many experiences of this sort, such as the time that President Truman invited him to an afternoon affair at the White House in honor of a group of reporters and photographers. Jack knew that he would be called upon to entertain, as he always was, so he brought along his violin as a prop, and he also hoped that he could get Harry Truman to join him in a duet of "The Missouri Waltz." (He did.) Jack drove up to the White House, and as he approached the gate, the guard, who not only recognized Jack but had his name listed among those invited, stopped him as a mere formality and asked, smilingly, since he knew the answer in advance, "Your name, please?" Jack answered, "Jack Benny." Then, almost apologetically, the guard pointed to Jack's violin case and asked, "What do you have in there?" Jack figured that he should at least try to live up to his reputation as a comic, and so he answered, "I have a machine gun in there." The guard replied: "Thank heavens! I thought it was your violin." Jack then would tell us that the grass stains on the seat of his pants, from falling in laughter on the White House lawn, were almost impossible to remove, but he always added, "Isn't that just like me—getting topped by a guard!"

On one occasion we were in Chicago preparing the following Sunday's show which would come on Mother's Day. We were having lunch in a restaurant where there was an enterprising Western Union boy going from table to table soliciting business. When he came to our booth, he asked if any of us would like to send a Sunday Mother's Day telegram. Jack politely, and a bit sadly, informed the youngster, who now recognized him, that unfortunately his mother had passed away many years ago. Three of the writers selected messages to send, but one of the group, for some reason or other, didn't even deign to answer. Unabashed, the kid continued and again asked the recalcitrant writer if he'd like to send his mother a telegram on Sunday, at which, in another attempt to prove he was a comedian, Jack said, "Leave him alone, son. He's a mean man. On Mother's Day all he sends his mother is a bone." Without a second's hesitation the boy turned to Jack and said, "Well, maybe he'd like to send it by Western Union." We all screamed, but no one louder than Jack. The Western Union messenger flashed a feeble smile, not really realizing how funny the remark was. Jack then insisted that we all send our mothers boxes of candy by Western Union, and he paid for all the sweets, too.

During the late 1950s or early 1960s Jack went on a benefit concert tour of Israel with Larry Adler, the harmonica genius. On one of their days off they went sightseeing and visited all the typical tourist places and bazaars in the Arab section, purchasing quite a few of those souvenirs that look so desirable in their native lands but are shoved away as junk back home. Although they spent freely, they made their choices carefully at the various booths in the bazaar. One persistent Arab salesman kept following them throughout their expedition, trying to sell them a most useful commodity that no home should be without—a riding crop. No matter where they went, or what they examined, he was at their heels, doggedly offering his single item of stock, and he kept repeating the few English words that seemed to comprise his complete English vocabulary: "Riding crop. Very good. Two dollars. Riding crop. Very good. Two dollars." For the better part of an hour he was their constant shadow, and all he kept saying were the now irritating words: "Riding crop. Very good. Two dollars."

Finally, annoyed by this haggling harassment, Jack turned to the man and said in mock anger, "Oh, take your riding crop and shove it."

The man immediately asked, "Up ass?"

So now Jack had to brush the sands of the Sahara off his suit, for naturally he fell down, and just as naturally he wound up buying two riding crops.

In the early 1970s, while appearing in person at a lush Las Vegas casino, Jack launched into one of his casual chatty monologues as a prelude to playing a solo on his fiddle. He was extolling his violin's virtues, telling the audience that it was a genuine Stradivarius made in 1699, when a man in the audience loudly inquired, "Did you buy it new?" Jack appreciated the gag as much as the audience did and told the waiter to bring the heckler a complimentary bottle of champagne because he intended making the line a permanent part of his act.

Because Jack's character was filled with human frailties, it was easy for anyone to top him, and he told me once how a nurse did it as well as any professional comedian. He had gone to the hospital for his annual checkup and, as he put it, to relax a bit. It was the famed Cedars of Lebanon, and most of the staff knew him quite well. On this occasion, however, he had hardly settled back in bed when a new nurse entered, handed him an empty bottle, and said, "Fill this with a specimen." Jack told her that it wasn't necessary because he was actually only there for a little rest and there was nothing physically wrong with him. When she continued to insist that he fill the bottle, Jack stubbornly refused, pointing out that he had just gone to the bathroom a few moments ago. But despite his protests, the nurse was adamant. She forced the bottle on him and said, "Just do the best you can."

Well, no matter what he attempted, Jack always did the best he could, and this time he managed to squeeze a miniscule specimen into the bottle. When the nurse came back she took the bottle, looked critically at the tiny amount it contained, and then said to him: "Gee, you never give *anything* away, do you?"

When my older son, Alan Roy, reached the age of thirteen, we celebrated with the customary bar mitzvah party. Jack attended this lavish affair and sat at a table with several non-Jewish guests, including Dolores and Bob Hope and actress Dorothy Malone. Dolores Hope, a devout Catholic, expressed interest in the tradition of the bar mitzvah, and Jack explained as best he could, pointing out that it's a ceremony during which a boy is accepted officially as a man, and that it takes place when he is thirteen years old. Then

Jack added thoughtfully, "But I never remember anything like this happening to me." Dorothy Malone replied: "Of course not, Jack. When you were thirteen, you kept insisting that you were only twelve."

When we first moved over to television, our shows were broadcast from the CBS studio on Fairfax Avenue. Fairfax Avenue was, and still is, a street largely populated by Jewish people. It had kosher butchers, grocers, fish stores, and, best of all, some of the greatest delicatessens in the city.

We liked to eat at these pastrami palaces once or twice a week, but time was short, and during the lunch hour there were always long lines of customers waiting for tables. Finally we got the bright idea of postponing our lunch hour and going out at 1:00 P.M. instead of noon. This worked fine the first few weeks we tried it, but soon we'd find that the sparsely filled deli was getting rapidly crowded within a few minutes of our arrival.

It took us a few weeks to discover the secret. As soon as we entered, the enterprising store owner would put a hand-lettered sign in his window reading: "Now Having Lunch Here, Jack Benny—In Person." Far from being offended, Jack took it in good spirits, but he made the owner promise not to put out the sign until we had given the waitress our order.

Jack Benny was among the first, if not the first, radio comedian to kid his sponsor's commercials by making them humorous and integrating them into the body of the script. Some claim that Ed Wynn did this first back in the very early 1930s when he was radio's hottest attraction. However, records show that Jack was kidding commercials from the very start of his broadcasting career in 1932, a fact that almost led to his early undoing.

Jack's very first sponsor in 1932 was the famed soft drink manufacturer, Canada Dry. Rumor had it that the company was anxious to get on the air because all through the era of Prohibition, when alcoholic beverages were verboten in the United States but still legal in our neighbor to the north, almost all vaudeville comics used a joke that went, "Last week I drove up to Montreal and tried to drink Canada Dry." Perhaps the strong sales of their competition, "Clicquot Club," a soft drink company which saw its sales soar by becoming a pioneer air advertiser, also influenced Canada Dry to try the new entertainment medium. Whatever the reason, the program they sponsored was headed by a new sophisticated young comic named Jack Benny.

After considerable effort, Jack eventually succeeded in breaking the mold of just "joke" comics. He conceived his comedy offerings with continuity as a dominating factor, hoping to get his laughs out of characters and situations rather than individual one-line jokes.

And one of the innovations that he invented, or at least popularized, was the comedy commercial.

Jack told me that one of his first attempts at comedy commercials was for Canada Dry. And as near as he could remember, it went like this: "While walking through the desert I came across a caravan of explorers who had been lost in the Sahara for six weeks. Their water supply had been exhausted a long time ago and they were all dying of thirst. Quickly I rushed to them and gave each one a bottle of Canada Dry, *and not one of them said it was a* BAD *drink!*"

This irreverence toward his sponsor's product got an appreciative audience reaction, but it also got Jack into a jam via sharp notes from the sponsor, the network, and the advertising agency. They all advised him that he should stick to jokes during the comic part of the program, since the commercial was sacrosanct and was not to be touched or tampered with by him or his writers. As a result, Jack soon sought a new sponsor.

As the years went on, Jack's kidding of the commercial became a high plateau of humor on his programs, and the public looked for it as eagerly as the rest of the show. Instead of considering the commercial to be a bore or a chance to leave the room, his listeners waited in anticipation to see how he would rib his sponsor.

Getting these comic sales messages across was very important, and difficult, for Jack and his writers, but they were definite sales boosters. We tried every device. We had opera singers extol the product's value in parodied arias, we paraphrased Shakespeare and had the greatest dramatic actors read these with all the fervor of Hamlet's "To be or not to be," and we even midwived an expensive group of singers, "The Sportsmen Quartet," which sang about the virtues of our various offerings via appropriate lyrics to popular songs.

During this period, around the time that the 1940s were becoming the 1950s, a childhood friend of mine, Paul Mosher, was working as a press agent, and a temporary task he had on the West Coast was to publicize "The Ink Spots," a singing group of black balladeers who were immensely popular and were now riding the crest of the wave of success through a sensationally successful recording of a hit number, "If I Didn't Care." In this song, while the rest of the group handled the background with deep voices, the lead singer handled the melody in a voice two octaves higher than a eunuch's. When Mosher asked me if there was any way I could plug this group on our program, I replied that it might be possible not only to mention them, but also to get them a guest shot on the show. My idea was that they could be introduced as friends by Rochester, and then do a commercial parody of their hit tune.

When I suggested their appearance at a meeting, simultaneously

Jack, the other three writers, our script secretary, Jeanette Eyman, and Jack's personal secretary, Bert Scott, all immediately suggested that The Ink Spots do a parody of their hit tune as our commercial. This proves that I have an uncanny grasp of the obvious. We hired The Ink Spots, and they vocalized their version of our commercial the following week.

I don't remember the words of the song, nor how we revised them. I do know that while the other members of The Ink Spots were harmonizing in their deeper than baritone voices, the lead vocalist sang out, in amazingly high and crystal-clear silvery tones, the first chorus of "If I Didn't Care." Then he went into the commercial which was written along these lines:

If I didn't care,
I'd smoke any cigarette,
But I do care,
So it's LS/MFT for me.

He sang an entire chorus, fitting our essential selling points into the lyrics—slogans like "They're so round, so firm, so fully packed," "With men who know tobacco best it's Luckies two to one," and "Be Happy, Go Lucky."

The Ink Spots finished to the loudest applause I ever heard a commercial get. Later the sponsor called Jack person-to-person to congratulate him, and when he found out how much this singing group had cost Jack out of his own pocket, he insisted that the advertising agency reimburse him. The kudos that commercial got from the press and the public were most gratifying.

Several years later, Jack was booked at one of those benefits that had, as the ancient slogan of MGM modestly advertised, "More Stars Than There Are in Heaven." While wandering backstage, Jack was fraternizing with various performers when over in one corner, rehearsing a song, he spied a group of black singers. He approached them and smiled, and they returned his smile. Then, to show that he remembered them, he sang, "If I Didn't Care"—not just a line or two, but the several choruses of the song. The singers listened appreciatively until he was through, and then one of them said politely, "Mr. Benny, we're The Mills Brothers, not The Ink Spots." Jack told us that he tried to ad-lib his way out of the situation with some corny gag about knowing who they were, and that singing a rival group's hit song was his idea of a joke. They all laughed politely, but as Jack finished telling us the story he said, "Fellows, they knew, they knew."

Sure, it could happen to anybody—but it happened to Jack Benny. It would have been a perfect routine on the program, with

Jack singing, "If I Didn't Care" to them, and Mary putting him down by interrupting and saying, "Jack, don't be a jerk—they're The Mills Brothers, not The Ink Spots." Come to think of it, it couldn't have happened on the program, because if one of the writers had suggested such a situation, Jack would have objected by saying, "No, it's too unbelievable. People will accept me as a *shnook* but not as an idiot."

Although his millions of listeners believed that Mr. and Mrs. Ronald Colman lived next door to Jack Benny, their residence was a few blocks away. However, for several years, Jack's actual next door neighbor was Lucille Ball, her children Lucie and Desi Arnaz, Jr., and her husband, Gary Morton. This proximity led to another "it could only happen to Jack" incident.

Gary related the story to me, which started when he and Jack were sunning themselves around the Benny swimming pool late one summer afternoon and Morton casually mentioned that he, Lucy, and the children were dining at home that evening.

Jack, always one for a practical prank, conceived the following gag with Gary. The Mortons' dinner was scheduled to start promptly at six. At 6:15 Jack entered via the rear door which had been left open by Gary. He had his violin with him, wore a phony moustache and bandanna over his head, and silently slipped into the dining room and began serenading the group like a wandering gypsy.

Now Lucy is a laugher too—not in the class of Jack Benny, but she is probably the feminine champ of lusty laughers. Lucy got hysterical and so did Lucie and Desi Jr. as Jack circled their dinner table and played two numbers while never cracking a smile (an accomplishment in itself). Then, still playing, he started to exit via the front door. Gary opened it for him. He and Jack were visible from the dining room, and Gary completed the gag by giving him a dollar bill as a tip.

Now all this was a fairly normal, even if somewhat corny gag, and for anyone else it would have ended then and there. However, this wasn't anyone else; it was Jack. Just as he was accepting the dollar tip from Morton, a sightseeing bus that was filled to capacity rounded the corner, and the gaping tourists were not only treated to the sight of the homes of Lucille Ball and Jack Benny, but they also saw Jack living the role of his radio character—a man who'd do anything for a buck.

The minute he saw the bus, Jack broke up. The bus then came to a stop, and Eastman Kodak stock must have jumped three points that day because every passenger on that bus kept shooting pictures, stills, and movies.

The commotion made Lucy and her children rush to the door.

When she saw what was happening, Lucy added to the situation by yelling after Jack, "Next Saturday we'll pay you time and a half for overtime." Then they closed the door, leaving Jack standing alone like the perpetual patsy he always was.

Some time later Jack told me about this incident and how it all ended. He said: "I made the most of the situation. I approached the bus and started playing a violin solo, strolling from one end of the bus to the other. The tourists got into the spirit of things and threw coins at my feet. One man even threw a dollar bill. When I finished the number, I calmly picked up the money and told them as I was leaving the bus: 'If you think I'm going to return this, then you don't really know me.' At that the bus driver stuck his head out of the window and called out to me: 'Okay, Mr. Benny, I'll be back the same time next week, and don't forget to give me my cut.' Even bus drivers top me. But, what the hell, I made nearly seven dollars that day, which is practically the most money I ever made with my violin." He paused for a moment and then added, "Gee, I wonder if I have to tell my agent about this—or report it on my income tax."

Two of Jack's other nearby neighbors and good friends were actor Jimmy Stewart and his wife Gloria. One day Jack was taking his usual afternoon walk, and he found himself near the Stewarts' house. Knowing that Jimmy was between pictures and probably at home, Jack decided to pay him a surprise visit.

In order not to be seen coming up the walkway and thus spoil the surprise, Jack took a shortcut and walked diagonally across the Stewarts' spacious front lawn. He was almost exactly in the center of it when every sprinkler in that lawn went on full force. However, Jack couldn't run because the whole thing struck him as so funny that he was convulsed with laughter. He sloshed to the entrance, rang the bell, and the door was opened by Stewart's beautiful wife, Gloria, who was amazed and appalled to see a dripping Benny standing there.

Jack, soaking wet but still laughing, said, "That was the most fantastic, funniest trick anyone ever played on me, and I want to tell Jimmy that even though he ruined my suit, the laugh he gave me was worth it."

Gloria said, "Jack, Jimmy's not home."

Jack hesitated a second. Then he pointed to the still gushing sprinklers and said: "Gloria, you mean you were the one who turned. . . ." But she interrupted him by explaining: "No, Jack. We have an electronic system which starts the sprinklers automatically."

Now Jack fell to the floor. When he stopped laughing long enough to speak coherently, he said, "If Jimmy had turned the sprinklers on intentionally, that would have been the funniest thing that ever happened to me. If you had done it, Gloria, it would have been even funnier. But the fact that automatic electronic gadgets hate me and play tricks on me, that's really the *funniest*."

One other brief incident illustrating how Jack was victimized by his created character bears telling here. He once had occasion to use the bathroom while in the lobby of an out-of-town hotel. As he left the lavatory, he instinctively reached for the pocket in his pants where he kept his wallet. The wallet wasn't there. He rushed back to the bathroom, knelt down in front of the booth he had occupied, and spotted the wallet at the rear wall, quite a bit out of his reach. It was one of those pay toilets and Jack didn't have another dime in his pocket. In fact, he didn't have any change. All his money was in the wallet.

Since he was the only occupant of the room, he figured that he'd crawl under the door to reach his wallet. He bent down and started squeezing through the opening when he heard a door open and footsteps approaching. He pulled his head out and looked up to see a man staring at him in both amusement and surprise.

The surprise turned to shock as the stranger instantly recognized the well-known face, and Jack began to laugh at his ridiculous predicament. He imagined the man thinking, "Gee, it's true. He's a millionaire and yet he tries to sneak into pay toilets." Shaking with laughter, he tried to explain his situation to the man, asked for the loan of a dime, and said he would repay it as soon as he retrieved his wallet.

The man said, "Hell no, Mr. Benny. I won't lend you a dime—I'll *give* you one. It's worth it." The man gave Jack the dime and refused payment.

When Jack would tell this story, he would add, "Somewhere in America there's a man who probably keeps telling people that he saw Jack trying to sneak a free crap. I really don't mind because he did give me the money, and after all, a dime's a dime."

Jack loved Palm Springs and we did several radio shows from there each season. He was well known by everyone there, and this eventually proved to be a lucky break for him.

Jack's favorite night spot was Charles Farrell's Racquet Club. One night he drove there alone to have some coffee and talk with a few friends. After a couple of hours he left and started to drive back to his hotel at a leisurely pace. Jack was an extremely careful driver, so as he drove down Indian Avenue and heard a police car's siren and saw the flashing red lights behind him, he was sure that the law was after someone else, not him.

He was wrong. The police car pulled alongside and Jack realized that he was their quarry, so he drove his car into an open parking space, wondering what law he had violated. His wonder turned to fear as one of the two policemen in the black-and-white car jumped out, drew his gun, and sharply ordered him out of his car with his hands up.

When Jack opened his door to exit, the cop got his first clear look at Jack and he gasped in recognition and amazement, "Mr. Benny!"

Jack said, "Y-y-yes. What did I do?"

The policeman carefully put his gun away and said, half-amazed and half-apologetic, "You stole this car."

Jack smiled at this and thought it might be some sort of practical joke. He told the policeman, "Look, it's mine. I drive a black Cadillac Coupe De Ville." Then he told him the license number. The policeman motioned Jack to the front of the car and pointed to the license plate. It was an entirely different number.

What had happened could only have happened to Jack. Another man driving a car that was identical in make, year, model, and color had parked alongside of Jack at The Racquet Club. Jack came out, walked to where his car was parked, got in, put the key in the ignition, and it fit perfectly. However, when the other man came out, he got into Jack's car, which was an exact duplicate of his, but for some reason his key didn't fit Jack's ignition. He phoned the police, and they spotted Jack a few seconds later.

Jack then drove back to The Racquet Club with the police, and they told the worried victim that they had apprehended the car thief. Then Jack came in and the man's eyes nearly popped out of his head. He kept saying, "They'll never believe this, they'll never believe this."

Jack laughed and said, "They will because I'll give you an autographed picture which says 'To the man whose car I stole.' You won't even have to pay me for the picture if you'll drop the charges."

There is a legendary law called "Murphy's Law" which is almost as well known as Newton's law of gravity. Murphy was supposedly the man who first said, "Anything that can happen will happen to me." It could just as accurately have been called "Benny's Law."

On *The Jack Benny Show* we had a running gag which we used, with ever-changing variations, whenever the telephone rang in Jack Benny's house. Rochester would answer it with his rasping tones and say, "Hello, this is the residence of Jack Benny, star of stage, screen, and radio, and curtains cleaned remarkably cheap." Or, "This is the residence of Jack Benny, star of stage, screen, and radio, and will entertain at bar mitzvahs remarkably cheap." This device was a sure and easy laugh-getter which served a double purpose: Rochester would get at least a chuckle, and he would also be able to announce to Jack, and his viewers simultaneously, who the caller was.

One Saturday, after the cast reading and rehearsal, Jack told the writers that instead of lunching with us, he had a date with an important business associate, but he would meet us immediately afterward for our rewrite session. Those were the days when the Brown Derby restaurant on Vine Street, within walking distance of the NBC studios, was *the* place to eat. We writers walked over and were given our usual booth. Suddenly one of us noticed that our boss was also dining there. He was seated in a corner, at the other end of the vast restaurant, with his back toward us, so that we were not visible to him.

I must explain that in those days the number of times you were paged by the Brown Derby telephone operator on the public address system was a direct reflection on your status in the business, and it was widely believed that several talent agents had their secretaries phone them frequently during lunch so that their names would constantly be called out.

This day we had what we thought was a humorous idea. We asked our waiter to bring us a telephone and plug it in, and then we gave the operator a message. Five seconds later, in the operator's loud, crystal-clear tones, the dozens of diners in the Brown Derby heard the P.A. system boom out the announcement: "Telephone call for Jack Benny, star of stage, screen, and radio, and cars washed while you wait." We were rewarded by a large laugh from the "in" group eating there.

However, we didn't hear the end of the story until we returned to meet Jack at our script-polishing session. Jack came into the office and he was so overcome with laughter that he could hardly talk. He told us, "Fellows, with any normal human being, experiencing an embarrassing call like the one you guys paged me with would have been bad enough—but not me. I had a mouthful of chicken soup when I heard it, and I laughed so hard, I sprayed it all over my guest. And I feel you ought to know, I made a mess out of him—and he wasn't just anybody. He was our sponsor!" There was no chastisement or recrimination from Jack because we had embarrassed him and made him look like a slob in his sponsor's eyes. To Jack it was just something that could happen to him and him alone.

In each man's life there comes a time when a series of uncontrollable events forces him into untenable situations. This happened one weekend to Rochester, but we never knew what was happening until it was all over. Rochester, like everyone else, knew Jack's fetish for promptness. Jack was always punctual, and one of the few things that irritated him was tardiness. Cast readings and rehearsals may not have always started promptly at noon Saturday, but you can safely wager that every member of the cast and crew was there at least several minutes earlier—except on one occasion.

This incident happened in the late 1940s when Mr. and Mrs. Ronald Colman were frequent and welcome guests on the Benny program. Not only because of Jack's wishes, but also out of deference to our busy guests, we made every effort to begin the cast reading promptly at the stroke of noon. However, this Saturday Rochester was late—very late.

Jack began to bite his narrowing lips, an indication as definite as a rattler's rattle that he was to be taken seriously. Finally our producer, who at that time was either Bob Ballin or Benny's brother-in-law Hilliard Marks, suggested that we begin the reading. After all, Rochester wasn't due to make his entrance until late in the script, and probably by the time we reached Roch's routine, he would be there.

We read through the script not once but twice, and everyone was affected by Jack's futile attempt to conceal his anger. What we considered to be a fairly funny writing effort turned into a wake. After we finished the second reading, Jack grimly announced to the writers that if it was all right with us, we would skip lunch and send out for sandwiches instead. And even if any of us had had important plans or a date, it wouldn't have made any difference, for we knew enough not to disagree with Jack during one of his extremely rare angry moods.

When we reached the office, Jack picked up a telephone, dialed his manager, and said that he wanted to know his legal rights in a precedent-shattering move on his part—cutting Rochester from the script without compensation. He was assured that contractually he was completely within his rights, and he announced to us that this was exactly what we were going to do—eliminate the Rochester sequence and replace him with another routine.

As I mentioned, Rochester's sequence in the script was at the very end, so we didn't reach it until after three P.M., a full three hours after Rochester was supposed to be at the rehearsal. At this point an NBC page boy timidly knocked on our office door, entered, and informed Jack that Rochester was here and would like to see him. His blue eyes ablaze, Jack told the page to inform Rochester that he did not want to see him, and that he needn't bother showing up the following day since his part was being deleted from the script.

The page boy nervously left, but ten minutes later he was back with a brief conciliatory message from Rochester saying that he could explain everything if only he were given an opportunity. However, Jack was adamant, and his answer was "No!" The page boy then showed a bit of initiative, which I believe was a part of this kid's make-up and marked him for subsequent success, which he must have achieved because, as far as I can recall, he had the good fortune to never become one of NBC's temporary presidents. The boy told Mr. Benny that Rochester seemed truly shaken and on the verge of tears.

Although Jack was unmoved, the boy's observation did make an impression on the writers, and we urged leniency. We pleaded Rochester's case by saying that he was always prompt, always knew his lines, and was an exemplary member of the cast in every other way. This magnanimity on our parts was not completely unselfish. We knew we had a funny Rochester routine in the script, and excising it would probably hurt the show—not to mention giving us an extra couple of hours' work replacing it.

The four of us finally prevailed on our reluctant boss. He sent a script out to Rochester via the page boy with the message that a face-to-face confrontation at this moment might result in his losing his temper. Therefore Rochester should take the script home, study it diligently, and be completely prepared for the following day's broadcast.

And then the following day came—but Rochester didn't. Again there was no sign of him. And once more the cast rehearsed the script without Roch, hoping that he would arrive before the time for his entrance was reached, but no such luck. Jack was annoyed and angry, and his aggravation was increased because both of these breaches of business etiquette and common decency had occurred in the presence of two people he respected and admired very much, Benita and Ronald Colman.

All this time, as was usually the case on Sundays, we writers were sitting in the control booth, a sound-proof glass-encased room where we could see everything and hear the voices and sound effects exactly as they would go out on the air. We were quite upset and more than a little in a state of panic, especially when phone calls to Rochester's home were not answered.

The producer suggested running through the lines again from the top, and the cast and a boiling Benny did just that until they reached the spot where Rochester was supposed to make his entrance. Then Jack, in a rare flare-up of temper, threw his script to the floor and angrily strode out of the studio. When he reached the control booth he yanked the door open and screamed at the writers, "I have you four fellows to thank for this!" and then he angrily slammed the door shut. And that's when Benny's radio character supplanted his real-life role. For anyone else the door would have slammed shut with a wall-shaking, ear-shattering smash. But not for Jack.

This was one of those doors with an air control gimmick at the top to ensure that the door will have an easy and noiseless closing. But for some perverse reason, perhaps inaugurated or aided by the extreme force with which Jack slammed the door, the air control device at the top didn't work. Maybe the sharp slamming caused some freak of air compression. But whatever it was, the door gave Jack a loud and raucous raspberry—a Bronx cheer. It was loud and room-rattling. And despite the rare but genuine fear on the part of the writers, we simultaneously broke out in a loud laugh which sent Jack rushing out of the studio looking like a demented demon. After all, it's okay if Fate deals you bottom cards from a cold deck, but when a man is righteously angry, he shouldn't get a raspberry from a door.

Afterward, when things had calmed down, Jack told us that he rushed into his dressing room where he was shaken by alternate fits of tears and laughter—angrily crying at the untenable position he was placed in, with an irreplaceable three-minute hole in his broadcast that was just an hour away, and then laughing hysterically at the fact that even an inanimate object like a door would get the better of him and give him a Bronx cheer. When peace was finally restored, he told us, "Fellows, between my laughing and crying I thought that I would wind up on a funny farm, or at least on a psychiatrist's couch." And then, when he eventually heard the reasons for Rochester's flagrant infraction of show business' prime protocol that demands punctuality for rehearsals, he was genuinely upset. Here is what happened to the hapless Rochester that well-remembered weekend.

On Saturday, Rochester's mother-in-law, whom he adored, passed away. His wife was too upset to make the funeral arrangements, so Roch said that he would handle them. At the mortuary they asked him if he would like to select the gravesite, and he agreed to this thinking that the cemetery would be only a few minutes away, but it was an hour-and-a-half drive. The minute they arrived, Rochester knew that he was going to miss the rehearsal. He called NBC, but they were under strict orders, as they always are, not to interrupt rehearsals or broadcasts for anybody, no matter how important the message. He then left word with the operator (which we found out to be a true statement), but something went wrong and no one connected with the program ever got his message. So much for Saturday.

On Sunday, broadcast day, Rochester started to drive to the studio early enough for him to arrive a full hour before we began—but once again Fate stepped in. As he was driving along, a station wagon several cars ahead of him jammed on its brakes, causing one of those chain reactions that make driving on the Los Angeles freeways an adventure comparable to "automobile roulette." Three cars slammed into each other, but he stopped in time. So did the car behind him, but the following one didn't, and another three- or four-vehicle fender-coupling car crash took place. Not only that, but the groups of gapers who feel no accident is official unless they witness it turned to view the freeway Destruction Derby, and since several of these people were not pedestrians but drivers, they too crashed into each other. As a result, Rochester's car was trapped in a maze-like motor mixup that would take hours to unscramble. The first policeman to arrive refused to let Rochester leave the scene of the accident even though he was neither hitter nor hittee, just trapped. In the course of time other officers arrived via motorcycles and police cars. One of them, either a compassionate cop or a Jack Benny/Rochester fan, realized that the comic would be late for Jack's broadcast, so when the accident had more than sufficient men in blue on the scene to unscramble the metallic mixup, he offered to drive Rochester to the studio. Not only did he do that, but he went inside and explained to Jack that the accident was in no way Roch's fault, and that if it had not happened, Rochester would have been an hour early. A mollified Jack Benny accepted this explanation, and then when he heard the tragic tale of why Rochester had been so late the previous day, genuine tears filled his famed blue eyes, a combination of empathy for his co-worker and friend, and shame over the fact that he had been so incensed.

We did the program, and I don't remember how good it was, but with the Colmans we rarely did anything but an excellent or, at worst, a very good show. What I do remember was that Rochester was letter-perfect in his delivery of every line, he took every proper pause, his delivery was flawless, and he got more laughter out of his material than we could possibly have hoped for.

Jack asked the cast and crew to remain after the audience had left at the conclusion of the show. Then he made a very contrite and sincere apology, not only to Rochester and the writers (whom he now thanked for forcing him to let Rochester stay on that episode), but also to everyone there who had heard him lose his temper.

It was one of the very few times that I had ever seen Jack really lose his temper, and it was the last time that Rochester, or anyone else, ever came late to a rehearsal or program.

Trite as it sounds, this combination of events to cause Jack's frustrations couldn't possibly have happened to any other public figure except him. Somebody up there liked him and wrote special situations for him.

Another indication of how Jack's *shnookiness* superimposed itself over his genuine character took place several years later. No one would ever have known about it if Jack didn't take a definite delight in telling about all incidents where he was low man on the totem pole.

Jack was driving along Canon Drive, one of the most fashionable and consequently busiest shopping sections in Beverly Hills. Street parking is done diagonally there, and has always been at a premium. The parking meters only charged ten cents for an hour in those days, while parking in lots started at a dollar an hour plus thirty-five cents for each additional thirty minutes. Thus finding an open and available parking space on the street was just a little less likely than finding a pearl in an oyster stew.

On this day as he cruised leisurely down the street, Jack suddenly spotted an open space. And not only was it open, but it still had forty minutes of free parking time on its meter. Jack quickly and triumphantly turned his car into the vacant space. As he got out, he was recognized by several passers-by, one of whom yelled, "It's just like you to find the only parking in town with free time left on it." Jack acknowledged this in complete character with a smile and a hand wave to others who greeted him and proceeded to walk briskly for several steps. Then suddenly he stopped, for it had dawned on him that he didn't want to buy anything. In fact he wasn't going shopping, but was on his way to play nine holes of golf at Hillcrest Country Club.

As Jack tells it, "I turned back to my car, but there were still several people around who had seen me park, including the woman who had made the joke about my finding a parking meter with free time. I didn't want them to think I was such a *shnook* or leave myself open for any other insulting ad-libs, so I proceeded to get something I could always use. I went into the tobacconist's and bought a box of cigars. Then, very self-satisfied, with my package prominently displayed, I went back to my car and proceeded to drive to my club. I was halfway to Hillcrest when I suddenly remembered that six months ago I had given up smoking." Jack would wind this story up with a little laugh as he added, "To this day George Burns doesn't know why I gave him a box of cigars as a present. I told him that if he could guess the reason for the gift, I'd tell him the whole story, and he hasn't guessed it yet."

Another incident in the "It-could-only-happen-to-Jack" category occurred several years ago when he had reason to visit San Francisco. I believe he was accompanied by Bert Scott, his personal secretary for over a quarter of a century, or Irving Fein, his able press agent and business manager. They had been there a few days, and during one noontime break they took a walk and looked for an interesting place in which to lunch. They found one—a restaurant featuring topless waitresses.

Neither of them had ever tried such a spot before, so on the spur of the moment they decided to eat there—but they didn't get in.

Jack is the only one in the world it could possibly have happened to, but he was denied admittance for an unbelievable reason. He didn't have on the proper attire. He wasn't wearing a tie!

Now all of the foregoing should give you a strong indication of the truth in the fact that in real life Jack did things as silly and improbable as those that his writers made him do on the air. However, I have saved the best for last. At least I think it's the best.

There is no doubt that, starting with his debut in radio and continuing for well over forty years, Jack was one of the few stars truly deserving of the title "Star." Yet despite his world fame and long list of achievements, Jack once developed a bashful and boyish crush on an actress. The object of Jack's secret admiration was typically not a sex symbol or a starlet. She was a mature, beautiful, and amazingly able actress who had given many excellent performances and once won an Academy Award. The object of Jack's undeclared devotion and affection was Greer Garson.

Nothing ever happened in even the most remote romantic sense, and I don't know whether Miss Garson ever knew of her conquest. Mary and the rest of us knew about it, because when Jack liked anything, he kept no secrets. Mary actually got a kick out of Jack's crush, and she voiced no jealousy, nor was there the slightest reason for any. Jack's crush on Miss Garson fit into the category of the lady who was told that her husband was a woman chaser, and she was unperturbed. "Listen," she said, "I've seen dogs chasing cars, but I've never seen a dog driving one."

Jack's mental affection grew into ardent admiration when Miss Garson and her husband moved into a house within a mile or so of Jack's, and he would occasionally see her driving by. At that time Jack was an early morning walker—in fact one of the greatest walkers in the history of walking. Every morning he'd get up prior to six A.M. and take a two-mile hike through the deserted streets of Beverly Hills. Most of the movie colony are early risers because they have to get to the studio for make-up, costume, lighting, and a dozen other reasons, and so they'd frequently drive to the film factories in the pre-dawn hours when most of the so-called hard-working people were enjoying a couple of extra hours of sleep. But Jack was a walker, not a rider, and during those early hours he became a familiar and suspicious figure to the Beverly Hills police force who used to stop him daily, since any pedestrian in Beverly Hills is considered a vagrant. Eventually all the police got to know Jack, and he was always given a friendly wave and never stopped.

On this particular day he was winding up his walk when he stopped at a corner. Suddenly, on the other corner, diagonally across the street, stopped by a red light, sat the gorgeous Greer Garson in a spotless white convertible, her crimson gold hair gleam-

Jack breaking up Milt Josefsberg, 1953. In background director Ralph Levy and musical conductor Mahlon Merrick.

Mel Blanc breaking up Jack during the annual Christmas shopping show.

Gregory Peck breaking up Jack, early 1970s.

Simian violinist breaking up Jack at an NBC Press Reception Dinner, January 12, 1973.

George Burns breaking up Jack, 1971.

Milton Berle breaking up Jack, 1973.

ing in the sparkling sunrise. She spotted Jack and called out to him: "Why, Jack, what a coincidence. My husband and I are having a housewarming next Saturday and we'd love to have you and Mary join us." An elated Jack, on the furthest corner from her, immediately answered, "We'd love to come." Miss Garson began to call out the date, time, and address, when Jack, trying to be the suave gentleman, said, "One moment, Miss Garson, I'll come over."

Benny started to cross the street, reached into his pocket for a note pad and pencil to write down the address, didn't watch where he was walking, tripped, and fell flat on his face. And to make matters worse, what he tripped over and fell into was the only pile of horse manure he had ever seen on a Beverly Hills street. As Jack said when he told us the story, "I guess she thought I was kind of odd, lying in the street, laughing hysterically as I kept rolling in a pile of horse shit!"

Believe me, no writer could dream up these outlandish, outrageous things that happened to Jack. His character, and fate, took over.

34
Jack Benny—Smuggler?

In 1951 Maurice Zolotow, one of the best biographers of Broadway's and Hollywood's famous folks, was commissioned by *Cosmopolitan* magazine to write an "in depth" article on Jack Benny and his radio show. In addition to his excellent literary skills, Zolotow is one of the most zealous and tenacious researchers in the business. In trying to get a complete picture of his subject, he spends endless hours interviewing friends, co-workers, employers, owners of stores where the subject shops, doormen at theaters or studios, shoeshine boys, and sundry others so that he gets views from every angle imaginable, both biased and unbiased.

To give you an idea of his thoroughness, Zolotow wrote a biography of Marilyn Monroe in 1960 that eventually served as one of the major sources of Norman Mailer's book on Miss Monroe a dozen years later. Mailer used so much material from Zolotow's earlier volume that a literary lawsuit was avoided only by a rather large sum of money paid by Mailer to Zolotow.

To most writers, research can be tiresome, yet through this tedious task Zolotow has written eminently readable, best-selling biographies of Miss Monroe, John Wayne, Lunt and Fontanne, and many others. With the same painstaking, infinite patience he has investigated the highs and lows in the lives of hundreds of celebrities for articles that have appeared in all the best magazines.

When he started compiling facts for this essay on Jack, Zolotow spoke to everyone and anyone who was connected with him, no matter how remote that connection was. He saved me for the last on his list because we have known, liked, and admired each other since we first met in the late 1920s while cutting classes at New Utrecht High School to attend a vaudeville show at the Loew's Metropolitan on Fulton Street in Brooklyn. I may be wrong, but I think that the star of the bill that week was Jack Benny.

Zolotow and I have always been completely honest with each other, or as completely honest as two men can be. He felt that if anyone could give him the bottom line on Jack Benny, I was that person. He had queried numerous other associates of Jack and had saved me for last to corroborate their facts. As he started his interview, he turned on his tape recorder and began to ask me questions about Jack. After ten minutes or so he flicked off his recorder and in a slightly irritated voice he said, "Damn it, Milt, you're giving me the same crap that everyone else gave me." He then went on to explain that he had talked to nearly two dozen people and they had all given him almost identical answers: Jack was a gentleman, thoughtful and kind. Jack was a wonderful boss to work for. Jack was an easy audience who laughed frequently and heartily. Maurice continued, "With all the answers I've gotten, this piece will read like something written by his press agent. Nothing but compliments. Isn't there anything you can tell me bad about the man?" I thought for a moment and said, "Well, once Jack and I went into a public restroom together, and after washing our hands we each took one of those paper towels that say 'Rub, Don't Blot!' And Jack blotted, he didn't rub."

Zolly kept trying to probe my memory for any bit of gossip that might lend spice to his efforts. Then he said, "The only slight scandal I could dig up was the diamond smuggling business, and that's not the type of thing I want in this article." That single sentence lit the fuse and my memory exploded. I immediately remembered most of the details of the famed diamond smuggling incident, and I apologized to Maurice for seeming to hold out on him. Yet the affair was so ridiculous that I didn't even think of it until he jogged my memory. If I had thought of it, I would have told it to Zolotow, after first extracting a promise from him not to print it. Zolotow has made many such promises to his sources and has always kept them all. However, he was the one who reminded me, and while it didn't fit in the short magazine piece Maurice was doing, it certainly fits in here and should be told.

Let me say that if I felt that revealing this episode could in even the most remote manner be a reflection on Jack's reputation, you wouldn't be reading it in this book. The whole occurrence was truly stupid, and Jack's "guilt" was only further proof of his real-life character taking on the *shnook* facets of his writer-created comedic character. As on so many programs that he did, he tried to be a nice guy and wound up with the proverbial pie in the puss.

In the summer of 1939 Jack and Mary went to Europe for a vacation with their best friends, George Burns and Gracie Allen, and while there they met a most charming gentleman who couldn't do enough for them. Unfortunately that was his true aim—to do them. To put it charitably, he was a "con" man.

This happened four years prior to my joining Jack, and it wasn't until several years after it happened that I heard his version of the incident. It wasn't a topic he discussed openly or often. The memory of it always pained him, because when it occurred, the daily press and broadcasting commentators had a Roman holiday flinging mud at four of the entertainment industry's biggest idols. Jack was the star of the highest rated radio show, and Mary was an important part of it. Furthermore, George and Gracie were near the top of the popularity polls too.

Jack recalled the unsavory story haltingly, since he sometimes had a tendency to be forgetful—not in all matters, but when it concerned a distasteful subject he would become slightly hazy as to the exact details. He told us that he had met the man in France, and in this respect the newspapers corroborate him. He said that the man's name was Arthur Chapereau. Research proved it to be Albert N. Chapereau. However, Jack was truly confused as to whether Mr. Chapereau was going to gain any personal benefits from the gracious favor he would do for the Bennys and Burnses.

While in Europe, Jack and George had each bought some jewelry for their wives—no big diamonds, just baubles. Jack said that he thought the total cost was under two thousand dollars for Mary's, and he couldn't recall what George had spent on Gracie.

Mr. Chapereau claimed that he had some sort of diplomatic immunity, and over Jack's and George's protests he volunteered to bring the jewels into the United States duty-free. In this first telling of the tale there was no financial reward for Mr. Chapereau, but when Jack repeated the story some years later for the second and last time I heard it, the version was slightly different. Now the jewels were purchased for them by Mr. Chapereau who claimed that he would not only get them a bargain, but that they would save quite an additional sum because he would personally see to it that the United States would levy no tariff or tax at the port of entry.

However, each time he told the tale, Jack was adamant on one point—namely that both he and George thought the matter too trifling to bother with, and that they wanted to bring the jewels through customs, but that Chapereau convinced them by saying: "Everyone does it. You would probably be soaked a much higher duty on them because you're celebrities. And I insist. It will be my pleasure."

Chapereau's pleasure almost cost the Bennys and Burnses their careers. The charming con man was eventually exposed as a phony and arrested, and soon all America was reading that two of their favorite funny men were indicted and to be tried for smuggling.

Although morally innocent in their own minds, Jack and George were told to plead guilty, and because of their fame, the affair naturally received wide publicity. The judge, possibly because he wanted to show the world that he could be tougher on celebrities than on ordinary guys, handled them with barbed wire gloves.

"He treated us like criminals with long records," Jack recalled angrily. "We admitted that we had made a mistake, but he screamed and yelled at us. Once when I was sort of slumped in my chair, he yelled at me to 'sit up straight,' or 'stand up.' I don't remember which, but I stood up, at attention, while some of the charges were read."

Jack was equally bitter against John Cahill, the United States Attorney who prosecuted Benny and Burns on the smuggling charge. According to Jack, "Cahill didn't prosecute us—I thought he persecuted us." Considering the fact that Adolf Hitler was near the zenith of his infamy in 1939, many others thought as Jack did. And also because of the times, this incident led to an unusual rise in the normally minuscule amount of anti-Semitic mail Jack usually got. This hurt Jack more than anything else. He said, "I got letters saying, 'Dear Jew, Hitler is right,' and others not quite so polite. And much to my sorrow, I got scolding letters from fellow Jews telling me what a thoughtless louse I was trying to chisel a few bucks in those times."

I believe these were the only times I ever heard Jack indulge in self-flagellation, and his eyes seemed brimming with tears as he recalled the sad events. One had to hear the sorrowful quiver in his voice the two times he talked about the episode to fully understand the mental anguish he had suffered.

In addition to their reprimands, the comics each received fines and suspended sentences, and they had to pay extra duty on the jewels. However, once the trial was over, the publicity about it didn't cease for quite a while. Some columnists called them naive or stupid or both. To an outsider these seem fair appraisals, yet neither was wholly true. They were simply victims of their own popularity.

Superstars are used to having total strangers go out of their way and actually burden themselves to do favors for the "big names." Dealers and manufacturers of every commodity give better deals to those who can afford to pay more if the buyer has "big name" value. Auto dealers frequently grant lower prices to celebrities just to brag that "so-and-so bought his car at my place." Moreover, it obviously doesn't hurt to have a star drive a car with the dealer's name discreetly displayed on the frame covering the license plate. And even if there is no attendant beneficial publicity for the dealer, there is a sop to his ego, a reflected charisma that brightens his own personality.

Both Benny and Burns had been recipients of dozens of similar favors, and they had no reason to doubt their new-found friend's honesty. To them he was just an autograph hound with a pedigree. To them it was the norm, for it was not unusual that a celebrity buff should go out of his way to curry favor with them.

While the trial was going on the entire Hollywood film and radio industry seemed to talk of nothing else. Neither Jack nor George had any enemies, and both were known for their generosity and charitable work. Everyone, from the top movie moguls running the studios and networks, down to the extras, doormen, parking lot attendants, and waitresses in the commissaries, knew, respected, and actually loved Jack and George. Further, as one reporter said, "Even if they were stupid enough to attempt a pointless stunt like that, both Mary and Gracie would throw them out of their respective houses rather than wear hot ice."

Jack's radio program was on the air at the time of the trial, and both his network and his sponsor stood one hundred percent behind him, as did most of the public. Nevertheless, everyone wondered whether Jack would make some formal serious announcement as to his innocence on the program, or treat the situation with humor or ignore it totally. What he did was typical of Jack Benny.

The papers had carried the story of the "smuggling" for weeks. It was news from the time the charges were first made and continued to be so right through the period of the trial. And at the height of all this, Jack was doing his usual radio show. In one Sunday's script he was supposed to be walking in the desert in Palm Springs with Rochester, discussing the climate and the beauty of the desert. Suddenly on the air the audience heard the loud, angry, unmistakable sound of a rattlesnake. Rochester called out in fear, "Boss, Boss, look out! Right in front of you, there's a rattlesnake." Again we heard the angry sound of the snake's rattlers, and then Jack said in a plaintive voice, "Please, Mr. Snake, leave me alone—don't I have enough trouble?"

The audience laughed, screamed, and applauded, showing not only their appreciation of the joke, but their complete belief in Jack Benny's honesty. Not another reference was ever made by Jack on any of his programs to the so-called smuggling affair.

35
Some Sugar, A Little Spice

In Milton Berle's autobiography he talks freely and frequently about his sexual conquests. Most men do this, but their reminiscences about their exploits are, for the most part, exaggerated. In Berle's case I believe these encounters to be true because during the two years I wrote for him I heard the stories personally. The only fact that surprised me was his claim that he had fathered an illegitimate son with a Hollywood glamor girl whom he wished to marry, but she turned him down. However, I also believe this to be true, because in humiliating himself by admitting that someone rejected him, Milton was going not only against his own background, but the tradition of every actor I've ever met.

Benny, like Berle, had affairs, but all of them—let me repeat, *all of them*—before he met and married Mary. Throughout their entire marriage Jack was so madly in love with "Doll," as he called Mary, that he never chased other women. The fact of the matter is that they chased him. Jack was a handsome man, gentle, and great fun to be with. At times he was so much like a helpless babe that he was given more than adequate opportunity for sex and swinging by gals who were attracted to his childlike charm and charisma. However nothing happened, because to Jack not even the most gorgeous glamor girls could compare to Mary.

Jack told us about a couple of his early adventures—and when I say us, I mean either the four writers, or Tackaberry and me, or just me. At this late date the many hundreds of meetings between Jack and his writers merge and blur, and a particular one will stand out only when there was a definite reason or incident for it to have been indelibly imprinted in my memory. And when Jack would tell us of these long-forgotten liaisons, he was neither boasting nor bragging, but just illustrating to us how Fate had cast him in the role of the super *shnook*.

The first liaison took place, according to Jack, when he was playing a circuit of theaters that took him to Brooklyn where he would appear either at the Loew's Metropolitan or the RKO Albee once or twice a year. On these trips he would always see a girl whose name we never knew because Jack was too much of a gentleman to reveal it to us. For the purposes of this story I'll call her Helen.

Helen was also in vaudeville, but not a star. They originally met while playing the same theater, and like all vaudeville performers, their paths crossed frequently. Jack enjoyed a romantic relationship with Helen that neither of them took seriously, but both enjoyed. And when Helen wasn't working, she lived with her family in Brooklyn.

Jack looked forward to the weeks his tour took him to Brooklyn because he not only saw Helen, but also enjoyed home-cooked meals with her family. Even though her folks were Irish and Jack was Jewish, and despite the fact that they knew, as Jack said, a little hanky-panky was going on with not the slightest thought of marriage, they all adored Jack. When he would arrive in Brooklyn he'd get settled in his hotel room and rush to the theater to give the orchestra leader, electrician in charge of spotlights, and any other involved workmen his cues, music, and so forth. Then he would phone Helen. If any other member of the family answered, Jack would simply say that he was in town and would see Helen after his last show.

As Jack told us, this had been going on for a couple of years when once again he was booked in Brooklyn. On this occasion, taking care of all necessary arrangements for his act took longer than usual, and he found that he only had a few minutes before it was time for his first show. He rushed to a telephone and called Helen's number. Her mother answered, and before she could say anything Jack heard the backstage cue telling him that he would be "on" in one minute. Therefore he very quickly told Helen's mother, "This is Jack Benny. I'll be over to see Helen tonight." Then he hung up without giving the lady a chance to say a single syllable, because the orchestra had already started to play the opening strains of his entrance music.

Jack did his first show as well as the two or three others for which he was scheduled that day. After his final evening appearance he removed his stage make-up, dressed in his best suit, went out, took a taxi, and gave the driver the address. When he arrived there he rang the bell, and the door was opened by someone whom he had never seen before. Without a word this man ushered Jack from the tiny entrance hallway into the living room where he saw Helen. She was lying in her coffin!

Jack said that he almost fainted at the sight of her body. Helen's mother came over to him, tearfully took his arm, and said, "Jack, I *knew* that if you were in town nothing could stop you from attending Helen's wake." Other members of the family came over to him and murmured some words of sympathy that caused Jack to cry— not pretend to cry, but actually cry. Jack said that his grief was genuine and he couldn't control his tears. He was more than fond of Helen, and he hadn't had the slightest idea that she had even been ill. Her friends and family had taken it for granted that Jack, upon arriving in town, had seen her obituary notice in the now defunct *Brooklyn Eagle* and had come to pay his respects. Jack sadly told us, "Believe me, fellows, I would have done so had I known of her death. And fellows, let me tell you," Jack added sadly as he concluded this tale, "there is nothing in the world that can make a man feel more like a louse than when he visits a girl with hanky-panky on his mind and finds himself at her wake."

Jack couldn't attend the funeral because one of his theatrical performances was scheduled at the same time as the services, but he did send a huge, expensive wreath, and he visited the family after his final performance every night during his run at the theater.

Let me again repeat that this happened before Jack met Mary. It occurred more than fifty years ago, and Helen's parents are long gone (if not, both of them are well over a hundred years old, which is an unlikely prospect). I fail to see how revealing this bizarre episode will hurt anyone, and so I am including it in this book.

The other incident about which Jack told us took place much later, and while it is just as incredible as the story of Helen, you can believe that with Jack's penchant for being fate's football, it would and did happen to him.

As I've stated before, and as was well known, Jack didn't play around or cheat. And again, I repeat, there were many women who would have liked an opportunity to dally with him, but Jack was blind to the charms of the opposite sex, except for Mary. However, once something almost did happen, and as accurately as I can, I'll describe the incident the way Jack revealed it to us.

Once again Jack wouldn't reveal the lady's name, or even the year, but I have a hunch that it happened in the late 1940s or early 1950s. The lady in question (and I don't mean that she was a questionable lady because Jack made it quite clear that she was exactly that: a lady) first met Jack at a Beverly Hills party. At social gatherings in the entertainment industry everybody kisses everybody else—and, in recent years, even those of the same sex. These kisses are as meaningless as a handshake at social gatherings in any other city. Sometimes these kisses are accompanied with whispered words of endearment. Usually they are just empty phrases, but occasionally they serve as an opening gambit to see if the fish will rise to the hook.

Since Jack and Mary were popular at parties, they were invited to far more than they could attend, and this actress (that was an unintentional clue to her identity that Jack gave us) attended many of the same functions that the Bennys did. Jack said that they always greeted each other with a casual kiss on the cheek, and each would kiddingly whisper phrases like "I could go for you" on Jack's part, and "Jack, darling, if only I weren't so fond of Mary" on her part. Jack thought nothing of these seemingly tender terms of endearment. They are simply Hollywood's way of saying "Howdy."

One night while Mary was out of town for a few days, possibly in Palm Springs, Jack attended some soiree where this lady was also present and also unescorted. They greeted each other in the usual affectionate way, but, as Jack said, they paid no more attention to each other than at prior parties. A sumptuous sit-down dinner was served, and Jack was seated at a different table than she was. After dinner Jack said that he felt slightly uncomfortable because he had eaten too much of the rich repast, and also he was a bit bored because Mary wasn't there, so he left early.

At home he got into bed and started to read himself to sleep, but after an hour he was still wide-awake. He took a couple of mild sleeping pills and a shot of Scotch, hoping that this combination would send him off to slumberland.

Just as he began to doze, his phone rang. It was the lady. She told Jack that she had also left the party early. She was blue, depressed, and down in the dumps, and was having trouble falling asleep. Jack confessed that he was in the same predicament. "Perhaps," she suggested, "if you come over and we just gab for a little while, we could cheer each other up."

Jack told us that he really didn't feel like it, and there was absolutely no thought of sex in his mind, but the gal seemed so terribly despondent (she had recently been divorced, another clue that Jack let slip) that he decided to be a Good Samaritan. He dressed, got into his car, and drove to her house.

When he arrived he found her fully clothed, confirming his feelings that she had called him for conversation and not a quick roll in the hay. She had prepared some hors d'oeuvres and had a bottle of vintage brandy and two snifters. Then for nearly an hour they nibbled on the hors d'oeuvres, inhaled and sipped from their snifters, and talked—just talked.

Finally Jack felt that their conversation was beginning to turn to more intimate topics, and he figured that he had better leave before the situation slipped out of control. However, he made it perfectly clear to us that it may have been just his imagination, because the lady was extending neither an overt nor covert sexual invitation. He told her that he thought he had better leave, and she said nothing to detain him. She did say, "Jack, you've been so wonderful. I'd like you to kiss me goodnight."

As near as I can recall Jack's words after these many years, this is what he told us next: "I leaned over to kiss her. I don't know whether it was the heavy meal I had eaten at the party, or the sleeping pills and Scotch I had taken at home, or the hors d'oeuvres and brandy I had at her house, but just as I was about to kiss her, I threw up all over both of us and passed out cold."

Now, with any normal man that would be the end of the story, but as Jack would often say on radio programs when doing parodies of famed books or movies, the fickle finger of Fate had pointed him out to be a victim of circumstances beyond his control.

When Jack regained consciousness the lady was mopping his brow with a cool, damp cloth. He had been in a deep sleep for nearly three hours. The lady had cleaned him off and everything else. However, it was now past four A.M., and she didn't think it would look nice for either of them if he were to be seen leaving her home in daylight or if his car were left standing in front of her house overnight. She offered him black coffee to make sure that he was completely capable of driving himself home, but Jack assured her that he was not inebriated, and that what had caused his upchucking accident was to be blamed more on food than liquor.

He chastely kissed her on the cheek and left. However, when he got into his car, inserted the key, and turned on the ignition, nothing happened. He tried again and again, but got nowhere. Then, since he lived only a mile or so away and was one of the world's happiest walkers, he decided to walk to his home. Upon getting there he awakened his handyman (or butler, or someone—we'll just say he was a handyman) and told him to take the battery out of one of his other cars, put it in a third car, drive to where the first car was, remove said dead battery from the first car, install the extra battery, drive home the second car taking along the dead battery, and then walk back to the original car and drive it back with the new battery. Having given his handyman these complicated instructions, Jack went to bed and fell into a deep sleep.

But not for long. An hour or so later the insistent ringing of his front doorbell awakened him. He jumped out of bed, threw a robe over his pajamas, rushed down to the door, opened it, and was amazed to see two policemen standing there, with his handyman, now wearing handcuffs, between them. They informed Jack that they had caught this "crook" trying to steal the battery out of his car, which he also probably stole because it was stalled on a street a mile away. And since the man (who was staring shamefacedly at the floor because he felt he had let his boss down) had told them that he worked for Mr. Benny, they thought that they had better check it out with Jack.

Now only Jack Benny could get into a situation that had this type of culmination. He was aware that the two cops knew in front of whose residence his car was parked, and he *knew* that they knew he knew they knew. But, despite all the television, radio, and movie comedies depicting our officers of the law as having flat feet and low I.Q.'s, this is not true in real life. Furthermore, the Beverly Hills police are as intelligent as any law enforcers in the country, and these two asked no embarrassing personal questions.

Jack told the cops that the man did indeed work for him, that his car had gone dead earlier that evening, and that this employee had only just gotten around to changing the batteries. Then he told us: "As I explained this to them, they listened attentively as though every word I had uttered was the gospel truth. They never even mentioned that they knew who lived in the house where my car was stalled. They drove my employee back and helped him get the original car and the second one back. All this was done before the dawn's early light, and as far as I know, no one ever learned of the incident. The two officers turned down a generous amount of money I offered them. They didn't even ask for an autographed picture. And to my knowledge no one ever heard of the incident, and that was the end of it. But to this day I have never turned down a request to entertain at any police show or benefit."

36
Jack's Walk

Jack Benny's mincing walk occasionally caused people to question his basic fundamentals. In a town that spawns scandal via hundreds of press agents, and that at one time supported more gossip columnists than any other city in the world, anything that deviates from the accepted, supposedly normal pattern is suspect. And because of his walk, I've been asked occasional questions about Jack's virility. Before getting to the answers to some of these questions, let me state definitely and unequivocally that of all the wild rumors I've ever heard in my life, this one is the most ridiculous.

The rumors about the possibility of Jack being gay—and they were just that, rumors—were initially induced by his walk, and they were spread widely by Jack himself who always joked about his seemingly feminine gait. On a Johnny Carson show in the late 1960s or early 1970s, Jack kidded about it and told one of his favorite and oft-repeated stories.

After Jack was introduced by Carson and got his usual standing ovation, he said, "You know, Johnny, this is the first time you've ever introduced me and didn't walk with me to show how I walk."

Carson replied: "You've been kidded a lot about that walk, haven't you? What was it Phil Harris said about your walk? He made the classic remark about your walk."

Jack answered: "Yes, but first I want to tell you about Bob Hope. Hope kids me about my walk all the time. He thinks I walk ... well, you know ... Now Bob Hope walks *exactly* like I do, but here's what he does with his hands."

Jack then rose and illustrated his effeminate walk to much laughter, after which he repeated, "Now, Bob Hope walks exactly the same way, but he cups his hands." Thereupon he illustrated Hope's walk, and after receiving long laughter and enthusiastic applause for his imitation, he said: "Bob Hope walks like a headwaiter who is leading a guy to a good table. Now for the Phil Harris story. We arrived in Chicago for a show. We left the airport and I was wearing a trench coat and no hat and was walking about twelve feet in front of Phil. Phil Harris was walking behind me with Frank Remley. Phil turned to Remley, pointed to me, and said, 'You know what, Frankie, you could put a dress on that guy and take him anywhere.'"

Jack did countless gags about his walk, and the only time he turned thumbs down on them was when he thought they weren't funny. I wrote one joke for him on a Lucille Ball program in the early 1970s which he read, laughed at, and then predicted, "They're going to beat us to this one, Milt." (Jack meant by that expression that the audience would anticipate the joke and laugh before we got to the punch line.)

It was a very simple bit and frequently done in many forms. Lucy was supposed to show Jack something that was in another room. She was to start to exit and say "Walk this way," and as she walked away from him in a ladylike way, Jack was supposed to reply, "I always do."

Jack was one hundred percent correct—his usual batting average on intuitive instinctual comedy. Lucy said, "Walk this way," and started to precede Jack out of the room, in her ultra-feminine walk. A split second after she said her line, the audience screamed ... and screamed ... and screamed ... and Jack waited ... and waited ... and waited ... until finally he ad-libbed an apologetic shrug to the audience and said, "I always do," which got a bigger laugh from the audience, and then he started to walk, mincing a mite more than usual, and this got the biggest laugh and even applause at his exit.

Perhaps another contributory fact to the occasional snide and secretive inquiries as to Jack's masculinity was the fact that several times he appeared on TV and in movies "in drag." In these enlightened times we all know that when a man appears in drag, it means that he dresses as a woman. In most of the entertainment media this is done for comedic purposes, but in recent years there have been dramas, even on television, dealing with the subject of transvestism.

Milton Berle appeared in drag more than any other performer, especially at the height of his career as "Mr. Television." He appeared so often that one wag said he wouldn't be surprised to see Berle named on the annual list of the "Ten Best Dressed Women." In nightclubs Milton also occasionally lisps his lines in the manner that men of dubious gender reputedly do. However, if you know him as I do, and read his book as I have, you know that Milton is a man.

Jack appeared in drag several times. The first occasion was thirty years ago when he played the title role in *Charley's Aunt.* In the years since it was written, countless famous actors have dressed as the grande dame heroine in this immortal comedy which has been made and remade as a movie and a play under various titles. In this role Jack played the part of a man who on occasion had to disguise himself as Charley's aunt. The period of the play was at the turn of the century, and Charley's aunt was a middle-aged maiden with graying hair. The fact that Jack played the leading man (or lady) in this classic was the basis for the first rumors I heard of Jack having a streak of lavender in his make-up. This was before I joined Jack, and I didn't believe it then. Further association—and a very close and long association it was—gave me no reason to doubt my early disbelief. Moreover, in a previous chapter I have dwelled briefly on his romances, based on stories that he told me and that I heard elsewhere. I am quite sure that Jack had many more pre-Mary affairs than I have recounted, but he was the modest type and rarely spoke about his achievements, sexual or otherwise.

During my years of writing for Jack, he did a television show in January 1952, where he was supposed to have George Burns and Gracie Allen as guest stars, but, according to the script Gracie didn't show up. George explained Gracie's absence via her typical type of logic. He mentioned that on one occasion he had said he'd like to have a Denver sandwich, and the next day she phoned him from Denver to ask whether he wanted it on white or rye. Then he further explained to Jack that he had a hunch she wouldn't be in town for Jack's show that night because unfortunately that morning he had expressed a desire for Philadelphia Cream Cheese.

In the script Jack griped to George that they would have no show because his guest stars were supposed to be Burns and Allen, and the whole script was written for them. George then got the bright idea of Jack dressing in Gracie's costume, which we'd have let out at certain places and taken in at others. Benny would play Gracie and Burns would be himself.

In our program George forced an angry Jack into doing it, and then Jack became the most charming Gracie possible, outside of Gracie herself. The skit got laughs, and when Jack was dressed for the part, the script had him ask "How do I look?" with George answering "You never looked lovelier."

In a sense this was true, for Jack did not try to make himself look like a caricature, as Berle would do when he dressed as Carmen Miranda. Instead he tried to look and act as much like the dainty Gracie as he could. He wore high heels, and in addition he had very shapely legs that looked almost feminine in silk stockings. The critics were kind to the program, and quite a few commented on the fact that Jack made a lovely "Gracie."

Within the next few weeks I heard two rumors that Jack had insisted on doing this show and had ordered the writers to fashion a script where he could dress as a woman. That was sheer nonsense. The idea for the show was conceived at a meeting of his writers (six now, with the addition of Al Gordon and Hal Goldman), and when we settled on the idea as a funny one, we presented it to Jack. Yes, I'll admit that he loved the idea—not because he could appear in drag, but because it was basically a funny and typical Benny broadcast.

In 1971 we filmed a show in which Lucy was fired from her job as Gale Gordon's secretary and went to the unemployment office where, as she told Gale, she'd get her first raise in five years. There she met another unemployed secretary, played by Carol Burnett. The girls then got the idea of trying to earn money by putting on a show starring all the unemployed talent they found waiting in line to collect unemployment insurance. They asked the others "Would you like to join our show?" until they came to the first man on the line waiting to collect his unemployment money. His back was to the audience. When they asked him the question, he turned around and it was Jack Benny.

The sight of Jack waiting on line for unemployment insurance was almost a guaranteed laugh, and when we asked Jack if he would do this tiny cameo part, he willingly agreed, as he did on the many occasions we asked him to do "walk-on" bits. However, while the bit was funny, it didn't quite seem to end or black out the scene, so Jack himself thought up the blackout. After getting his laugh, he exited from the office with his usual walk as Lucy and Carol both watched him. And just as he reached the door, Carol Burnett said ever so wistfully, "Gee, I wish I could walk like that." It gave us a very big blackout, and once again it showed that Jack had no inhibitions when it came to kidding his walk. But again it must have given rise to a few rumors, because in order to make the bit play funnier, Jack again walked much more mincingly than he usually did.

However, rumors are notoriously hydra-headed. Snip off one head and two or more grow to replace it. Moreover, certain rumors and accusations present strange situations. The negative is difficult to deny, while the positive is easily provable. It's very simple for a man to admit and prove that he is, or was, a Communist. Let him show a membership card in any organization remotely connected to Communists and simply state, "Yes, I belong," and people will accept this as a complete confession. On the other hand, let him deny membership, let him say that he abhors their ideology, loathes their philosophy, has contributed to anti-Communist causes, and, in fact, is a full-fledged dues-paying member of The John Birch Society, and people will regard this as insufficient proof that he is not a Communist. His accusers will smile knowingly and say, "Naturally all of these are perfect covers for a clever Communist." Many people, especially celebrities, have been falsely accused of being fags or Communists or of having other alleged flaws in their character, and no amount of proof to the contrary can scotch these libels permanently.

Probably another tiny factor in the baseless rumors that Jack was a bit gay lay in the conversion of our radio shows to the TV tube. When television began to gain strength, so did the gay guys associated with the theater. They flew in from New York like a flock of geese heading South for the winter. Every TV show had at least one homosexual on its staff, and there was a then-current quip going the rounds: "Every television show should have two fags—in case one gets sick." In these days it's considered good citizenship to have at least a token black on a series. In those days it was fashionable to have a token homo.

Jack paid little, if any, attention to any person's private peccadilloes other than his ability and his qualifications as a talent and person. In the early days of Hollywood, any performer of doubtful gender would be a social pariah. In the early days of TV this stigma wore off. Today I think that the general attitude toward homosexuality in the entertainment business is very much like the old Jewish joke about poverty: "It's no shame being poor. On the other hand, it's nothing to brag about either."

During the late 1930s or early 1940s actor Laird Cregar, who had a brilliant career cut short by death, once was signed for a picture by Twentieth Century-Fox. As the first day of shooting was about to begin, Cregar mounted a small podium, rapped for attention, and made the following announcement: "Ladies and gentlemen," he supposedly said, "on every picture I work there is usually a good deal of valuable time wasted by gossip and conjecture as to my sexual habits. To save time, let me answer the question of whether or not I am a homosexual. The answer is: Yes, devoutly so."

Other actors, and an occasional actress, didn't go so far as to publicly admit the innuendos, but eventually they stopped denying them so vehemently. In Jack's case he never denied it because, as far as I know, no one ever confronted him with the accusation.

I remember only one incident involving Jack and a homo. It took place during the filming of our opening TV show for the 1953-54 season when our guest was a rising young actress named Marilyn Monroe—and regardless of the stories about her laxness and lateness later in her career, she was punctual and a pleasure to work with in those days.

One of the great pleasures that all the men on the set enjoyed was watching Miss Monroe walk, either toward them or away from them. She was rehearsing a scene where she was on the stage solo and had to walk away from the camera. All of us, including Jack, sat in the front seats of the studio watching her. Our director, one of TV's best, a young man named Ralph Levy, made her repeat the walk several times. Each time she did so, there would be some whispered, off-color comments by those of us seated in the studio. Finally Jack, in an attempt at humor, whispered, "I don't know why everyone raves about Marilyn. I've got a pretty attractive ass myself." This caused a light giggle, which erupted into a volcanic laugh when the "company fag" lisped, "You can thay that again!" No one laughed louder than Jack. And no one felt offended by the gay guy's line which we all took for the joke he intended it to be.

The climax of this chapter took place several years ago when I attended one of those typical parties where we would gather and gossip in little groups. One of the men in my circle told me that he had heard that Jack was having a torrid affair with a then prominent lady entertainer. I had absolutely no knowledge of this, and I said so. I then wandered on to the next tight little circle, and immediately someone said, "Milt, did you know that Jack is having an affair with . . .?" and he named a *man* prominent in the profession. The proximity and contradictory contents of these two gobs of gossip astounded me so much that I grabbed informant number two and dragged him over to scandal monger number one. After requesting both of them to impart their information to each other and telling them to fight it out, I walked away from both of them.

During the ensuing years the rumors persisted, but to a lesser degree. All I can add to this foolish, thankfully seldom-heard story is the following: If Jack Benny was a homosexual, then Golda Meir was an Egyptian spy.

37
Jack Switches Sponsors— Then Networks

There is only a remote and somewhat tenuous reason for includ- ing this chapter among those relating the alleged scandals in Jack's life. True, his change of allegiance to both sponsor and network spawned some rumors and gossip, but none in the category that is usually whispered about with leers or knowing smiles. However, because of a connection with an unsavory incident a decade earlier, I have decided to incorporate it here.

Comparing our current crop of celebrities and idols to goldfish, and the general public to their creators, is not the newest gambit in literary circles. Yet, old statements, like old jokes, sometimes illus- trate the truth best.

When an individual achieves star status in show business, he can rightly expect rich rewards, but there are also some liabilities, not the least of which is a loss of privacy. If an important business executive with a major automobile manufacturer in Detroit were to threaten to quit his job because his office was poorly ventilated, it might cause some talk in his company, and at most it might rate a brief mention in *The Wall Street Journal.* Yet when Redd Foxx ab- sented himself from his successful series *Sanford and Son* for a few programs because his dressing room didn't have a window in it, it was front-page news from coast to coast, and Carroll O'Connor's threatened withdrawal from his role as Archie Bunker on *All in the Family* rated the same headlines as the threat of a new outbreak of war in the Middle East. Also, it's mostly forgotten now, but when Arthur Godfrey casually announced that Julius LaRosa would no longer be singing on Mr. G's weekly shows, the furor it caused in the press rivaled the publicity given to the discovery of the Salk vaccine. When it comes to the outstanding personalities in the fields of the movies, sports, television, and radio, their every move is magnified by a multitude of eager journalists who seem to have majored in some special course called "Making Mountains out of Molehills."

Several times in Jack Benny's career he had certain private minor matters that were publicized and transformed into earth-shaking events; however, after being discussed in the public prints for a brief time, they were then quickly forgotten—and rightly so. The first of these had its inception in the spring of 1944. The public had read and heard about it during that summer, but the big event didn't actually take place until Jack made his annual autumnal return to radio for a new series of broadcasts on October 1, 1944. On that date Jack didn't open his show with his well-known greeting, "Jello Again." He had changed sponsors, going from Jell-O's manufacturer, General Foods, to the American Tobacco Company, makers of Lucky Strike cigarettes. Instead of plugging Jell-O's famous flavors—strawberry, raspberry, cherry, orange, lemon, and lime—Jack's show would now be shouting, "LS/MFT, LS/MFT."

As a matter of long-forgotten fact, when Jack switched from General Foods he was not originally supposed to broadcast for Lucky Strike cigarettes but for one of the American Tobacco Company's other brands, Pall Mall. I remember many meetings that Jack, his writers, and some advertising executives had in the summer of 1944, and while the Allied troops were locked in bloody battle with Hitler's Axis army, we discussed even more important matters, such as how to convince the public that Pall Mall was not pronounced Paul Maul, but Pell Mell. I remember somebody suggesting the slogan, "Ring the Bell with Pell Mell." And I also remember that because the president of the American Tobacco Company was the dictatorial George Washington Hill, characterized so well by actor Sidney Greenstreet in the movie version of Frederic Wakeman's novel *The Hucksters*, Jack had a special clause included in his multi-million dollar contract. George Washington Hill demanded, and got, complete loyalty from every employee. They all dressed according to his demands, yessed his every order, and used his products and no rival ones. Mary Livingstone, however, was partial to Parliament cigarettes, which were not manufactured by any of Mr. Hill's companies. As a result, the group of high-priced lawyers negotiating for both sides arranged a clause in the contract that Mary could smoke any cigarette she pleased, or that pleased her.

Another sidelight of the sponsor switch was the complete secrecy with which the negotiations were conducted. Perhaps these proceedings were of little interest to the general public, but such a sponsor switch was almost akin to the Second Coming to the broadcasting industry, and news of Benny's change could possibly have had some effect on Wall Street because of the two major manufacturers involved.

Now in the days of radio when comedians and their writers worked, ate, played, and sometimes slept together (separate beds, of course), it was difficult for a comic to keep secrets from his writing staff, but Jack succeeded fairly well, although we did notice that he was having numerous private meetings with people who were unfamiliar to us. Finally, after a broadcast on a Sunday late in the spring of 1944, Jack told us that he was going to Palm Springs on some private business but would return for our usual Friday rewrite session, at which time he might have some exciting news to give us.

The following Friday morning we met with Jack, and his face, slightly tanned from the Palm Springs sun, was lit up by that little-boy smile that always informed us that he had a secret—some good news to impart. In situations involving secrecy the happy-kid quality always evidenced itself in Jack. He closed the windows of the office as though he was preparing to reveal atomic secrets to us and Camden Drive in Beverly Hills was a hotbed of Nazi spies. Then he whispered, "Fellows, I'm taking you into my confidence, but you must promise not to breathe a word of this to anyone, not even to your wives. We don't want the news to break for another week, but here it is. Next season we won't be on for Jell-O. Our sponsor will be Pall Mall cigarettes." However, Jack's big bomb fizzled because George Balzer whipped out a copy of that morning's *Daily Variety*, which we had all read prior to Jack's arrival. The front page headline in *Variety* said, "Benny Ankles General Foods To Puff American Tobacco."

Jack was amazed and aggravated that the news had broken. He pointed out that only he and his trusted business agent and two representatives of the tobacco company knew the news, and they were all pledged to secrecy. Probably they had forgotten to sign the pledge in blood, because one of them had become the Benedict Arnold of the broadcasting industry, and the news was all over town.

We did our next season's opening show for American Tobacco, but instead of Pall Mall, our sponsor was Lucky Strike cigarettes. None of us knew the exact reasons behind this switch. One executive informed us that it was because "Lucky Strike's Green Has Gone to

War." Today this phrase means very little, but in those war years it almost seemed more vital to our war effort than the slogan, "A Slip of the Lip May Sink a Ship."

Prior to World War II, Lucky Strike cigarettes were wrapped in packages that were entirely green, except for the center circle which carried the name "Lucky Strike," and any other printing. Then suddenly, in an unselfish, generous gesture to help us win the war, the manufacturers announced, "Lucky Strike's Green Has Gone to War," and their contributions to lung cancer were now packaged in antiseptic white. There was some reason why it was necessary to convert from green paper to white to whip Hitler and Hirohito. Maybe the green dye contained some chemical that sunk enemy submarines. Maybe the green contained a pigment useful in camouflaging tanks. Or maybe Lucky Strike's green had that secret ingredient that the Army, Navy, and Marine Corps allegedly put in their men's coffee to make them forget about the opposite sex—or even to forget that there was an opposite sex. Whatever the reason was, Lucky Strike's green had definitely gone to war, and Jack Benny's radio program was to be used to boost that butt's sagging sales instead of teaching people to say Pell Mell instead of Paul Maul.

Eventually the furor caused by the program's sponsor switch died down and was forgotten—although never really forgotten, because in a poll taken in 1973 of middle-aged Americans who were asked to name Jack Benny's radio sponsor, forty percent of them immediately answered "Jell-O," even though Jack was on for Lucky Strike almost twice as long as he was for Jell-O. This was probably due more than anything else to Jack's familiar salutation "Jello again" and certainly is no reflection on his ability to get sponsor identification, because when the same poll inquired as to what program was sponsored by Pepsodent toothpaste, far more people answered "Amos 'n' Andy" than Bob Hope. Amos 'n' Andy were on for Pepsodent for a few years until Bob Hope took over in 1938, and Bob remained with them for so many years that he once quipped, "I was with them for so long that I went from Pepsodent to Polident."

For several years *The Jack Benny Show* made no unusual headlines but received the customary publicity that might be expected for a program with a star of his magnitude. Then came the second switch, and an even bigger and more earthshaking one (to the industry) than his change of sponsors. Jack switched networks. And not only did he switch networks, which was occasionally done by other programs, but he did it in an unusual way—in mid-season, with his sponsor going along with him too.

When a show, for whatever reason, went from one network to another, it was customary to finish the current season in June on the original network and then start the new series of shows on the new network at the start of the new season in September. This had happened several times before, resulting in little more than a casual line or two in the radio columns or trade papers.

However, Jack was different. On December 26, 1948, after having broadcast almost exclusively for NBC during his entire career, he did his last broadcast for that network, and on the following Sunday he began broadcasting for their biggest rival, CBS, in the same time slot, and thus opposite the one he had previously occupied.

The reason for Jack's change was simple and easy to understand. Several years before Jack Benny had formed a company called "Amusement Enterprises" which had produced radio shows and at least one motion picture, *The Lucky Stiff,* starring Dorothy Lamour and Brian Donlevy. CBS was willing to give Jack a more than munificent price for his weekly radio series, as well as purchase his company for over two million dollars—which would be a capital gain for Jack and several other smaller stockholders. The United States Government foolishly—and unsuccessfully—fought against Jack getting a capital gain, but it was a legitimate transaction because his company had been founded many years prior to any indication of a potential offer from CBS.

Prior to the switch there was headline publicity again, and of course a great deal of conjecture as to why Jack was changing networks. All of the Broadway and Hollywood gossip columnists gave their own ideas—always wrong, and usually wild—as to the real reasons behind the move. They all knew about and revealed the details of the two million dollar deal, but they all also hinted at mysterious motivations and behind-the-scene happenings that instigated the move.

As I mentioned, the Sunday after we left NBC we did our very first program on CBS—same time slot, same sponsor, same cast, different network. And, needless to say, we gave this initial broadcast much thought. Jack's intuition—and in these matters he had a high batting average—was not to do any kind of special important show with big guest stars. Instead we were to write what we called a "bread and butter" program—an average weekly show. The only difference was that we would acknowledge our new home on the airwaves.

We wrote a simple show, and the theme was natural—how Jack and the cast liked their new quarters at CBS. In the script Jack wandered around the building, running into various cast members, and also a couple of CBS stars who made brief "cameo" appearances. He ended each of these encounters by saying that he had to leave because it was important for him to see Mr. Thornberg who was the CBS vice president in charge of the West Coast. (Thornberg was the actual name of the head of CBS in Hollywood.) At the end of the program, after having said several times that he had to see Mr. Thornberg on an urgently important matter, he entered this gentleman's office. Thornberg said, "Jack, I understand that you want to discuss something quite important with me." Jack said, "Yes." Thornberg asked, "What is it?" And Jack said, "Do you have the authority to validate my parking ticket?"

It was a typical ending to a typical Benny broadcast, but the newspaper columnists and trade papers read more into it than just the joke we created for the blackout. It was widely reported that this small indignity—the fact that NBC had made him pay for parking—had infuriated Jack enough to gamble on switching the nation's listening habits by changing networks. The facts were that Jack, and all other stars, had free parking at the NBC lot. At CBS at the time there was no free parking, although some executives with the network must have believed the rumor because Jack was immediately given an easily accessible free parking space. On the other hand, we writers who invented the gag about "validating the parking ticket" always had free parking space at NBC, whereas at CBS we had to pay.

However, this is not the end of the story. There was a very deep underlying psychological reason why Jack eventually went to CBS, and as far as I know, the true facts are known to very few people. When CBS first made overtures to Jack to join them, the news got to NBC. Needless to say, NBC was more than a little upset at the thought of losing one of its biggest, if not its biggest, star. Jack, or perhaps his representative, was quickly contacted and asked if NBC might not be given the privilege of bidding to keep him. He agreed to this quickly, and it was believed among those of us who knew him that NBC only needed to meet, not beat, CBS's offer, and Jack would remain with them quite contentedly.

NBC sent out a contingent of, I believe, three legal experts to negotiate. John Tackaberry and I were working in his office when Jack left for this meeting and we wished him well. In a little over an hour—a rather limited amount of time for a complicated and large financial deal—Jack returned. His grim face told us that something had gone wrong, and we knew him well enough to realize that if we would wait for a few minutes, he would volunteer the details of the meeting. His opening remark was, "Well, fellows, we're going to CBS." Both Tackaberry and I began to ply him with questions: Wouldn't NBC meet the CBS offer? Wouldn't they buy his company? Wouldn't they give him a capital gain? Jack cut us short by saying, "Fellows, I don't know what they would or wouldn't do, but even if they gave me a better offer, I'd still turn them down." He said this in bitter, angry tones, and that was most unusual for him. Al-

Kenny Baker was vocalist on the show, late 1930s. *Photo courtesy of Gene Lester.*

Jack and Phil Harris clowning, 1939. *Photo courtesy of Gene Lester.*

Jack going over script with Hilliard Marks, Andy Devine, and writer Bill Morrow, 1939. *Photo courtesy of Gene Lester.*

Don Wilson laughing, 1939. *Photo courtesy of Gene Lester.*

With Mary, Molly, and Fibber McGee, July 1937.

The Jell-O cast: Mary Livingstone, Don Wilson, Andy Devine, and Sam Hearn (Shlep-perman), January 1938.

Portland Hoffa holding back Jack, Mary Livingstone holding back Fred Allen, March 1937.

The Sportsmen Quartet, March 1947.

With writers Bill Morrow and Ed Beloin, March 1938.

With his tout, Sheldon Leonard.

Jack, Mel Blanc, and Al Jolson, 1947.

Mel Blanc and Artie Auerbach ("Mr. Kitzle"). *Photo by Bud Berman.*

Jack, George Burns, and Bing Crosby portraying a vaudeville trio, "Goldie, Fields, Glide" in 1954.

Jack and a Marquis Chimp, December 1964.

Jack and Johnny Carson, March 20, 1968.

Jack and "date" Joan Marshall, with Gloria and Jimmy Stewart. Waiter played by Scott Elliott, October 1964.

Jack on a TV special with Lawrence Welk, Lucille Ball, Jerry Lewis, Ann-Margret, and Dennis Day. *Photo by Yani Begakis.*

371

George Burns, Gregory Peck, and Jack on a TV special, early 1970s.

Jack and Frank "Yesssssss" Nelson, 1970.

Jack and Frank Sinatra, 1970.

Jack and Rochester, 1970.

Gary Cooper ad-libbing a "yup" into Jack's script.

Jack with fellow comedians Edgar Bergen and Red Skelton.

Jack and Dinah Shore on NBC-TV's *Dinah's Place*, January 23, 1974.

Jack and John Wayne.

though bursting with curiosity, Tackaberry and I kept quiet, knowing that he would tell us everything in his own time. After a few minutes, during which he went to the refrigerator and poured himself a soft drink, he sat down, sipped the soda, and continued more calmly.

"I went to the meeting with an open mind," Jack said, "but the moment I walked into the office I knew that even if they doubled the other offer I'd turn them down. They had the colossal gall, the nerve, the *chutzpah*, to send three lawyers to talk me into staying with them, and one of these lawyers was the man who once caused me more mental anguish than anyone else. He was the United States District (*sic*) Attorney who gave me such a hard time about ten years ago in that so-called smuggling case."

Once again Jack's memory refused to recall—or he couldn't bring himself to utter—the name of a man who caused him pain. He was referring to John Cahill, the United States Attorney who, as Jack twice told me, "persecuted rather than prosecuted me." Cahill, no longer employed by the Federal Government, was now associated with NBC. And he was the final reason that Jack disassociated himself from his long-time broadcasting base.

Jack was truly upset at either the stupidity of NBC in sending this man as a good-will ambassador, or, as Jack later believed, the thoughtlessness of Cahill in not informing NBC that he was hardly the most likely to succeed as an emissary because of his previous legal harassment of Jack. Although we were never able to pin it down, it seemed more and more obvious that NBC was blameless, and in later years, when Jack gave up his weekly TV series on CBS, he did almost all of his one-hour "specials" on NBC.

Thus the reporters who insisted that there was some mysterious reason for Jack changing networks were right—but none of them knew the truth. Rumors and stories were printed about "mysterious reasons" many months before Jack and his encounter with this man from NBC, and the only concrete "fact" that the reporters could point to was based on our joke that we used to black out the first program—namely that Jack took a multi-million dollar gamble and switched networks to save fifty cents a week in parking charges.

One added note: It's difficult to scotch a legend, no matter how ridiculous, if it is interesting, humorous, and concerns a well-known personality. In the summer of 1975, Playboy Press published a fact-filled book called *CBS* written by Robert Metz and dealing with William Paley and his broadcasting empire. There are numerous references to Jack Benny in this tome, and Mr. Metz has done his research homework quite thoroughly. I can quarrel with few of his findings. His facts concerning Jack's switch from NBC to CBS coincide with mine, and he, too, reveals that the deciding factor in Jack's changeover was NBC's gaffe at sending former United States Attorney Cahill to sweet-talk Benny into remaining with them (although perhaps this pejorative decision was exclusively Cahill's). However, Metz also writes, "During the negotiating period, Jack cracked, 'I wonder if they have free parking at CBS.' "

Jack made no such remark while the bargaining sessions were continuing. This line was created after the deal was a *fait accompli* and Jack was firmly bound to his new network, and only then, after the contract was consummated, did Jack himself hear the line. It was on Friday, December 31, 1948, that the line was born as the blackout of the first broadcast Benny was to do for CBS on Sunday, January 2, 1949. And when the line was ad-libbed during the writing session, Jack greeted it with his usual fall to the floor and said, "Fellows, CBS could have saved a million bucks on the deal if they had given me that line."

38
Television

Jack Benny went into television like a man taking the season's first dip into the ocean—very slowly, a little at a time, toes first, testing the temperature.

Television first began to give radio serious competition in 1948, and the pressure continued to increase, with television quickly moving to the forefront mainly through the efforts of comedy favorites like Milton Berle, Sid Caesar and Imogene Coca, Lucille Ball, and Jackie Gleason, and also because of well-remembered weekly dramas like *Playhouse 90, Studio One,* and many others.

Jack did his first commercial network television program from New York on October 21, 1950 via CBS, and his time slot was from 8:00 to 8:45 P.M. That's right, it was a forty-five minute program. This was a new medium, and Jack figured that a half-hour program was too short and that one lasting an hour would be too long, so he asked for forty-five minutes, and they gave it to him. To my knowledge it's the only occasion that a prime-time network comedy program split the difference between a half-hour and an hour show, but television was in its infancy, no traditional or binding precedents had been set yet, and name stars like Jack Benny could and would try anything. Moreover, everyone who got involved in this new medium considered himself to be an expert.

When Ed Wynn did his very first show a season or so earlier, he started that first program by telling a few jokes. Then a stooge, playing the part of a network executive, walked onstage and told him that he must face the camera, stand on his mark, and project more. As he continued giving Ed advice on how to perform in this infant of the entertainment industry, Wynn interrupted him and in his slightly lisping tones said, "Listen, young man, you don't have to tell me. I know everything there is to know about this. I'm a veteran. I've been in television for five minutes already."

Although Jack didn't do his first network show until the fall of 1950, he had made a brief local appearance in March 1949 at the dedication of Station KTTV in Hollywood. Furthermore, even prior to this date we had begun to discuss the eventual change-over from sound to sight.

Jack's radio programs were still outdrawing the most popular television shows in the early 1950s, but we knew that we would have to switch sometime soon, and we tried to prepare for that inevitable day. As we did so, the debates and discussions between Jack and his writers were simultaneously serious and ridiculous— but with good reason. We had all written his radio show for years, and we had heard his programs for many more years prior to joining his staff. I frequently quote a famous Fred Allen line comparing radio and television because it ably described our dilemma. Allen felt that radio was a far better medium than TV because it left more to the imagination. Fred said, "Television is much too blunt. Radio is more subtle and lets each listener enjoy it on his own intellectual level."

That was part of our problem. We all had different mental pictures of Benny's home, his den, his living room, Rochester's quarters, the vault, and other familiar locales for which sets would have to be built in television. In radio, if we heard a doorbell ring Jack would say "I'll answer it" or "Rochester, please get the door." Then we'd have the sound effects of footsteps and a door opening. It was that simple. But for television each of us had a different concept of how an unimportant brief scene like this should be done. One thought that there should be an entrance hall. Another said, "No, the door should open right into Jack's den." The third writer thought that there should be six locks and bolts on the door, while the fourth wanted to know if we were discussing the front, side, or rear door.

Jack himself visualized his television home as almost an exact replica of his actual one. We all fought Jack on this point, saying that a character as parsimonious as he was would not live in so luxurious a mansion. Jack defended himself by emphatically stating, "Fellows, I've lived in that house on my radio program for twenty years." It then turned out that Jack and each of the writers subconsciously had integrated characteristics of his own home into Jack's imaginary radio residence, and then each had drawn his own individual conception in his mind of what the rest of the house would look like.

In radio we would use a simple line, such as Jack saying, "I'm going upstairs to bed," and we'd hear the sound of footsteps ascending the stairs. No member of the writing staff ever questioned a line like this on radio. However, on television just the question of where to locate the staircase took hours to decide. Some people pictured it in the entrance hall, while others, including the writer who visualized the house as having no hall, said that it would be next to the den or the living room. There were more days of debate about the kitchen. Did he have a large or small refrigerator? Was there a lock on it? On some radio programs, when Jack or Rochester would say he wanted orange juice or milk, we'd hear the refrigerator door open and close. However, on one show, we had Mary, during a visit to Jack's house, say that she was thirsty and was going to the refrigerator for a cold drink. A few seconds later she returned and Jack asked, "Did you get your drink?" Mary answered, "No, I couldn't open the refrigerator; you changed the combination on the lock again."

This sounds like a hair-splitting triviality, but in radio we knew that one week we could say the refrigerator had a lock on it and forget about it the next week. On television we felt that once the audience *saw* a lock on the refrigerator, the impact would be so strong that the audience would remember it, and we would have to keep the lock on permanently.

These discussions weren't daily affairs, but once a week or so, during free time or rehearsal breaks, we would sit down and dissect, analyze, and verbally reconstruct the sets we knew would have to be permanent once we had established them on television. We had to consider every angle, and not the least of these was finances.

Building sets for movies and television is very expensive. Every comedy show you see on the air has two or three permanent sets. *All in the Family* has the kitchen and living room of the Bunker house, and almost every episode of that series has at least one or two scenes of the show taking place in these two sets. Sometimes they show Archie and Edith's bedroom, and occasionally Gloria and Mike's. However, they don't often do an outside scene, and for a very good reason—money. For example, on the show where Archie and Edith went out to vote on Election Day, this entailed building a new set with voting booths and other appropriate furnishings that were likely to be used only once, and the cost of that set was several thousand dollars.

Similarly, on *The Mary Tyler Moore Show* you frequently see Mary's apartment, the newsroom where she works, and Lou Grant's office. Most scenes in *Maude* take place in her living room, kitchen, and bedroom. *Sanford and Son* usually just has a living room and a kitchen, while *Chico and the Man* has the garage and the office where Jack Albertson keeps his booze in the cash register. People are almost as familiar with these living and working quarters of their favorite programs as they are with their own.

During my years with Lucy, we had her home and office as our permanent sets, always on the stage, never to be dismantled. Like the other programs we occasionally had our action take place on different sets that were used just once for that particular show, but we built these sparingly because they were big burdens on the budgets.

As we prepared for television, we were aware of all these aspects of the new medium, and we tried to keep abreast of changes and innovations in TV which were occurring with remarkable frequency. Words like "coaxial cable," "kinescope," and "chroma-key" were used daily then, but are almost forgotten now. We had to change our thinking. We had to write for the eye as well as the ear.

On radio a member of the cast could come into Jack's house and say, "Oh, I see that you've had your whole house repainted." And Jack could answer, "Yes, I did it all in blue to match my eyes." Our listeners would take our word for it, and the moment they heard it said that the house was painted blue, they accepted it. In television, and particularly later on with the advent of color television, to change the color of a room took lots of labor, material, and money. In fact, even the color of the rooms in Jack's home caused controversy. We initially wanted the walls of his den done in blue to match his eyes. Then someone said that the room should be painted in Jack's favorite color, "Dollar Bill Green." However, all our talk on this point went for naught, because the set designer and cameraman eventually decided what color would photograph best. I don't know their name for it, but we called it "Kinescope Gray."

We discussed the sad fact that our expensive cast of characters couldn't be kept intact because finances would finally break up Jack's famous radio family. We knew the value of each member of the cast, the chemistry between them, and the deluge of complaining mail we would get if for some reason we left a regular off even a single show.

To avoid this, we talked of doing the show as an animated cartoon, or making a full set of puppets resembling Jack, Mary, Don,

Dennis, Phil, Rochester, and the supporting players, and then have these people dub in their well-known voices. These ideas were dismissed eventually because we were convinced they were foolish. However, nowadays shows like *The Brady Bunch* and *Gilligan's Island,* having had their network flings, have been converted to animated cartoons, and there are also puppet shows on the air today.

Any idea or suggestion was given consideration in those trial-and-error days, and was discarded only when the majority of us thought that it was silly or impractical. One that interested us, if only temporarily, was the possibility of broadcasting our radio shows as television shows. The millions of outside listeners and the few hundred people seated in our studio audience each week had loved and remained loyal to the program through the entire history of radio. Maybe, we thought, if we just televised the cast reading their scripts into a microphone and showed the sound effects men making their necessary noises, we could still retain our huge army of fans.

With the tremendous technical improvements that have come along in a short quarter of a century, these ideas seem idiotic now, but it is possible that in those early days they may have worked for several seasons. After all, during those first years when the roofs of the nation's houses seemed to be sprouting an ever-increasing forest of TV antennas, Jack's radio programs continued to be fully sponsored for over seven more years. It was only when we felt that we couldn't postpone the day any longer that we took the big jump.

Jack's first television appearance on his own show, the forty-five minute one, saw him supported by several regular cast members— Don Wilson, Rochester, The Sportsmen Quartet, "Mr. Kitzle," and Mel Blanc. Dennis Day didn't appear on the program because he had a prior commitment and had to stay in Los Angeles. Phil Harris was no longer with us at the time, and Mary Livingstone had asked not to be written into the show. She had never been too crazy about appearing on radio, and she liked television even less. Her appearances on the small screen were quite limited. The guests on that premiere program were Dinah Shore and comedian Ken Murray.

The critics were kind, but not overly so, to Jack's debut. For the most part the show got good reviews, but few real raves. On the other hand, while some of the reviews were not too favorable, there were no real slams either.

One columnist made a valid point when he accused the program of using too many "radio lines," and those two words became anathema to all of us. For example, on radio, if Jack were going out, he'd say, "I'll get my coat and go out." On TV there was no need to do this. The audience didn't have to hear Jack say "I think I'll put on my tie." They would see him do it, and hence there would be no need for the "radio line."

Jack didn't do his second show until nearly eight months later, on May 20, 1951. Rochester and Don Wilson again appeared on the program, Mary Livingstone made her debut, and we had Mel Blanc as "Professor LeBlanc," the French violin teacher, as well as a special guest star, Ben Hogan.

We writers were determined to avoid "radio lines" like the plague in this show. In one scene in Jack's home, we had the telephone ring, and we didn't put in a line like, "Oh, there's the telephone; I'll answer it." Jack, from force of habit I think, wanted to say this, but we, like Ed Wynn, were veterans of the medium—we had already done one show—and we told him that the audience would see him walk toward the phone and pick it up and answer it. Hence there would be no need for the "radio line."

Then we discovered that in the scene it would take several seconds for Jack to "cross" from where he was to where the phone was, and we would have dead air. The audience would have nothing more entertaining to watch than Benny's walk, which we knew would at least get giggles. They would hear nothing but the ringing of the phone.

One writer suggested that we place a small hassock in the middle of the room between Jack and the phone, and when Jack reached it he should do the funny little hop, skip, and heel-clicking jump that he sometimes did, and go over the hassock. At this point Jack said, "Fellows, let's have a serious discussion before we continue writing."

It really wasn't a discussion. It was more of a lecture from Jack. He wasn't angry but he talked firmly and decisively. He said, "I'm sick of this shit about 'radio lines.' And I'm not going to make a fool of myself by doing idiotic things. First of all, why in the world would a hassock be in the middle of my room? In the second place, if the hassock were there, I'd walk around it. In the third place, I must have answered the telephone a million times in my life, and not once did I ever jump over a hassock to do it."

The above is not an exact quote but it contains the gist of his speech. He went on and said (again this is not an exact quote, but the meaning is the same): "I agree that there are certain bits of dialogue which can be classified as 'radio lines.' However, good, crisp, funny dialogue is worth watching and hearing, and I don't intend to do a jig or a cartwheel everytime I deliver a line or answer the phone or door."

Maybe we didn't all agree with him completely at first, but, as usually proved to be the case, in retrospect Jack was instinctively right. In those early days the comedy shows were quite funny, but frenetically physical. I recently viewed some grainy kinescopes of the first big comedy hits, and while they still retain much of their humor, they seem like museum pieces even though only twenty-five years have passed. It was like watching the speeded-up actions of the silent screen's great comics, Chaplin, Lloyd, Keaton, and others. Then came the era of "family" situation comedies—*Father Knows Best, Ozzie and Harriet,* and programs of this type which went for chuckles and smiles instead of belly laughs. Also at that time a show came along called *I Love Lucy,* but nobody paid any attention to this beautiful but obviously dumb redhead who was stupid enough to insist that her Cuban-accented husband should play the part of her Cuban-accented husband. And if this wasn't proof enough of Lucy's lack of show-biz savvy, she also wanted to spend extra money to *film* her shows—and in front of a live studio audience yet—so that they could be shown over and over again.

We didn't know any of this at the time Jack gave us his lecture. As the old Pennsylvania Dutch proverb puts it: "We grow too soon old, and too late smart." We continued writing program number two, trying to combine our own thinking with Jack's and that of the many people who constantly gave us advice—usually bad advice.

The second show, the usual thirty minutes in length this time, turned out a bit better than the first. One of the high spots was the purely physical, visual humor involving Jack and guest star Ben Hogan. We had their scene start with Hogan coming into the locker room of Jack's golf club where he was going to play a practice round. He was immediately greeted by one or two extras who said something along the lines of "Nice to have you here, Mr. Hogan" or "Hope you like our course, Ben." Then Hogan was informed that if he wished to take a few practice swings, they had an area inside the locker room where he could do so. Hogan walked over to this spot and, using a driver, demonstrated his perfect swing twice. At this point Jack entered the locker room and saw this stranger with his back to him practicing. Every time Hogan swung, Jack would shake his head pityingly like the greatest professional in the world watching the ineffectual efforts of the worst hacker in golfdom.

Finally, like a Good Samaritan helping a hopeless case, Jack said, "Excuse me, Mister, but you're doing it all wrong," and he then proceeded to give Ben Hogan a golf lesson, not knowing who his pupil was. He changed Hogan's stance, bent his knees way in, bent his elbows way out, pushed his head down until he had his chin on his chest, and then made him crouch as though he were sitting in an invisible chair.

All of these moves got excellent laughs from the audience, and the biggest one came when Jack made Hogan swing from the contorted position in which he had placed him. Hogan swung, got his arms and legs twisted around each other, and looked like a human pretzel, getting another big laugh. Then Jack looked at Hogan, who was now acting as though he couldn't straighten himself out, patted him on the shoulder, and said, "Now you've got it."

This show opened with Jack getting a violin lesson from his teacher, Professor LeBlanc. On the wall of the room where the lesson was taking place were pictures of Mischa Elman and Jascha Heifetz whom, via dialogue, we identified as two of the world's greatest violinists. When Jack played his first note, both pictures fell off the wall and smashed on the floor.

Later in the program, at the start of the locker room scene, before Jack entered, we had Hogan look at some pictures on the wall there. These were pictures of Gene Sarazen and Bobby Jones, and through dialogue we identified them as two of golf's greatest immortals. After Jack showed Hogan how to swing, we did one of the show's trademarks—the running gag or the playback. Jack told Hogan that he could learn more by watching how *he* swung. Then he took a practice swing with a golf club, and the pictures of Jones and Sarazen fell off the wall and smashed on the floor.

Hogan gave an excellent performance, proving that he was as good an actor as he was a golfer, while Jack proved that he was as good a golfer as he was a violinist. Of course, in the script Jack didn't find out whom he was instructing until several minutes later, and then his embarrassment received the expected excellent audience reaction.

We got Hogan as a guest through a series of lucky coincidences. Jack belonged to the Tamarisk Country Club in Palm Springs which had two golf professionals. One was a young pro who gave lessons to members. The other was Ben Hogan who was hired for prestige purposes and who also occasionally gave playing lessons to members.

Jack wanted to play a few holes with Hogan and get some pointers, but he was still under the young pro's tutelage, and he felt that if he took a lesson from Hogan, he might hurt the youth's feelings. He told another member of his predicament, and this man suggested that Jack ask Hogan to be his opponent for a nine-hole match, and they'd play for five dollars a hole. He was sure that this would tickle the great golfer's sense of humor and that he'd be pleased to play with Jack. Also, Hogan would certainly win every hole, he would collect forty-five dollars, and there was no doubt that during the match Hogan would give him some tips on improving his game. This was a happy solution to the problem, since Hogan would earn a little expense money, Jack wouldn't actually be taking a lesson, and the young pro's feelings would be spared.

The match was set up. However, golf is a game where a rank amateur can play for money on even terms with the most polished pro because of the handicap system. Without getting too technical, it should be pointed out that Hogan had to give Jack at least one stroke on every hole, and two strokes on several of them. Not only that, but as they proceeded around the course, Hogan gave Jack some tips and advice that were the equivalent of a playing lesson. In fact, he helped him so much that Jack played an excellent nine holes and wound up winning fifteen dollars from Hogan.

Embarrassed at not only getting a free playing lesson but also taking fifteen dollars from Ben, Jack arranged another match for the following day—this time at ten dollars a hole. He figured that Hogan would get his money back plus a little extra.

This time the news got around and a gallery of about a hundred people watched the match. I was fortunate enough to be among them. Jack teed off and hit the ball quite well. Then Hogan, who was rather small for so formidable a player, stepped up to the tee and connected with the ball perfectly. The audience applauded, and Ben modestly said, "That's the best ball I've hit in months." I said to Hogan, "See, kid, I told you—swing slow and you'll hit it better."

Hogan stared up at me (I'm a couple of inches over six feet) as though he had just met a maniac. Then he stared down at the grass where Jack was lying laughing, and naturally this too puzzled Hogan. Not until Jack introduced me to him as one of his writers did Ben stop eyeing me suspiciously.

The match was an interesting one. Hogan gave Jack some excellent advice, and as a result Jack shot the best nine holes he ever did, and this time he beat Ben out of thirty dollars. Jack was so embarrassed at taking money from Hogan for a second time that he signed him then and there for a guest shot on his TV program.

We all kidded Jack because we said that Hogan purposely played a "customer's game," losing a few bucks intentionally to get on the show and pick up the fat guest shot fee of five thousand or seventy-five hundred dollars. Jack said that he didn't care because during the games he played with Hogan he shot the best two scores he ever had. Then he told me, "Milt, that gag you pulled on Hogan on the first tee will serve as a springboard for the story line—having Hogan get a golf lesson from a *schmuck* like me." I think Jack was hinting that I was the *schmuck* because I didn't recognize my own idea first.

After we did the show, Jack congratulated Hogan on his performance and said, "Ben, you not only helped me with the two best golf games I ever played, but you gave me the best television show I ever had."

If Hogan realized that it was only the second TV show that Jack had ever done, he didn't let on. He apparently took it for a compliment, and I'm sure Jack meant it that way.

Thus in his first full season on the tube, Jack Benny did only two programs.

39
Was Jack Better on Radio Than TV?

Although Jack Benny was on television for almost as many years as he was on radio, he did far fewer programs. On radio he started his career in 1932 by doing two half-hour programs each week that season. During his remaining years in radio he did a show each week every year, never doing less than thirty-five, and more frequently thirty-eight or thirty-nine.

In his first year on television Jack did two shows. In his second year he doubled that to four programs. The next few years saw him doing six or eight live television shows per season, but at the same time we were transcribing thirty-nine new radio shows. In the 1953-1954 season Jack did thirteen television programs and was on the air every third week, with the other two weeks out of the three in that time slot used for telecasts of Ann Sothern's *Private Secretary* series. This was also the last year of his radio series, and we again transcribed thirty-nine new programs. After the final radio show, heard on June 6, 1954, the network continued to play the tapes or transcriptions of Jack Benny programs that had been broadcast in previous years. This was done for two additional seasons.

In the 1956-1957 season, Jack began broadcasting every other week. He alternated one season with John Forsythe's *Bachelor Father* and another season with George Gobel.

In 1960, after sixteen years of being sponsored by Lucky Strike cigarettes, Jack began broadcasting for Lever Brothers, but he didn't begin doing a regular weekly TV series until October 1960. Even then it was still a truncated season because Jack's contract permitted him to repeat a certain number of shows he had filmed in previous years. Therefore Jack was actually in television for nine years before he started being seen on a regular weekly basis, as was customary for all other half-hour comedy shows. (Bob Hope has never done a weekly half-hour TV series, but restricts himself to six or eight hour-long special shows a season.)

Jack maintained this grueling schedule of weekly shows for only three or four seasons. Then for the first time since his debut in radio in 1932, when his sponsor canceled him after one season, Jack was canceled again. Also, he again changed networks. He went back home to NBC.

Jack was philosophical about being dropped. His competition at that time was *Bonanza,* just starting its climb in the ratings which kept it on the air for so many years. *Bonanza* was on NBC from 8:00 to 9:00 P.M. while Jack was on CBS from 8:30 to 9:00 P.M. It's an accepted belief, if not a known fact, among network programming executives that an hour-long show starting on the hour has an advantage over any program slotted opposite it starting on the half-hour.

Jack told me that he had a premonition that his ratings were slipping when he heard more and more people talking about *Bonanza* and less and less about his program. "Because of this," he told me, "I decided to watch the first half-hour of *Bonanza,* which I'd never seen, to find out what was so special about this series. I figured that I'd watch it until 8:30 and then tune in on my own filmed show. So I watched it, and it was good—darned good. I became absorbed in the program, but subconsciously I knew that I wanted to switch channels to see my own show. When I figured it was time and I looked at my watch, it wasn't 8:30, it was 8:50. My program was two-thirds over and I thought, 'Hell, if I myself get so absorbed in *Bonanza* that I forget my own program, what chance have I got with the millions of other viewers!' I knew I was through."

But Jack wasn't through. He went back to NBC in September 1964. Then he began presenting a series of hour-long specials once or twice each season, and he soared right back to the top of the ratings. At the time of his death he was preparing a special to be broadcast in January 1975, but he never finished it.

There are those who say that Benny wasn't as popular on TV as he was on radio. That may be true, but he still was on television for twenty-three consecutive years with either specials, bi-weekly programs, weekly programs, or occasional shows which he did at the very start of his TV career. Others feel that he came into TV too late because the new medium had given birth to new stars like Milton Berle, Sid Caesar and Imogene Coca, Lucille Ball, and others who had a head start with the fans. This also may be true, but when Jack first started broadcasting back in 1932 he had to compete with such established radio comedians as Ed Wynn, Jack Pearl, Eddie Cantor, Phil Baker, and many others who had a head start on him in that then new medium. However, just as Jack outlasted all of these giants of radio, so did he outlast all the television biggies who had regular weekly programs—all, that is, except for Lucille Ball.

There is no doubt in my mind, and in the minds of most others, that Jack Benny was bigger in radio than on television, and there are many theories about why this was so. One reason is that he never established the regular family cast on television that he was so identified with on radio. True, he had Rochester and Don Wilson on almost every TV show he did, but Mary, Dennis Day, and Phil Harris made only occasional appearances.

A second important factor could be the loss of closeness with his writers. In the days of radio, performers had the greatest and easiest jobs in the world. All they had to do was show up for one hour of rehearsal the day before the broadcast, read the script, make a few mental notes, and leave. The following day they could show up three or four hours before the broadcast, read the revised script, and then sit around for an hour or so while the material was being cut for time and any last-minute changes necessary. Their total work week consisted of five or six hours, and their salaries put them at the top of the upper brackets for the least amount of labor.

This held true for Jack Benny too. With all the free time he had in radio he was able to spend many hours with his writers polishing, rewriting, and refining the script. He was practically a fifth writer on our team, and an editor who could invariably be more objective than any of us.

This changed in television. The performers' lot was no longer an easy one. They had to rehearse long hours, memorize lines and moves, go in for costume fittings, and spend time with the make-up people. In short, they had to put in at least ten times the number of hours that they formerly spent rehearsing radio shows.

While Jack still conferred with the writers, now his director became all-important. In our radio years we never had an official director. Jack did what little directing there was, and all we had to worry about were the lines the performers read off the script. If we felt that a performer was giving a wrong reading, inflection, or intonation to a speech, we mentioned it to Jack, and if he agreed with us—which he usually did—the performer was informed and the correction made.

Another factor to be considered is that there are certain types of humor that, contrary to the proverb about children, should be heard and not seen. For example, Dennis Day didn't really look so much like a silly kid when seen on the tube, and the Maxwell, one of our strongest standard laugh-getters, was a disappointment on TV. On radio, no one, not even the studio audience, saw any car at all. They heard the sound effects of an ancient motor, plus Mel Blanc's classic wheezing, snorting vocal accompaniment, and this was much funnier than seeing the physical presence of the Maxwell. On radio it sounded funny. On television it merely looked like a collector's item. A car buff friend told me that it looked like a classic model for which a true collector would willingly pay ten thousand dollars.

The vault, which we imagined would be far better received visually, also disappointed the viewers. No matter what gimmicks we thought up as Jack's burglar-proof protection for his vault, it couldn't equal the imagination of the viewers. We had man-eating plants, a moat with crocodiles, a guillotine, and other gimmicks, all of which our "prop" men prepared perfectly, but the overall effect still missed its mark slightly. These were all funny, but not as funny as on radio.

I have mentioned elsewhere that I received a 1968 Emmy nomination (with collaborator Ray Singer) for writing a Lucille Ball show called "Lucy Gets Jack Benny's Bank Account." In it we wrote our version of the vault, and it was climaxed with a single special effect of Lucy and Jack sinking up to their chins in quicksand. Jack told me that this was the best vault scene he had ever done on TV, but all of our special effects—including the quicksand—cost in the neighborhood of twenty-five thousand dollars—and that is a neighborhood you can't afford every single week.

We lost more than we gained in the transition from radio to television. Certainly some of Jack's shows had humorous high spots that were strictly visual. His program with the Marquis Chimps is a classic comparable to any other series' outstanding shows. Here Jack performed with a group of remarkable monkeys whose mimicry of his every move and gesture, and even his stare, was side-splitting. (And I can say this without being accused of having an inflated ego because I was not one of the writers of this show.)

Yet while Jack gained certain advantages in television, he lost others—mainly the listeners' mental picture of what they only heard. One such example of pure radio humor took place when Rochester was baking a cake and discovered that he was out of sugar. Jack volunteered to go next door and borrow some from the Colmans. As he was leaving, Rochester called after him, "Boss, here, take this measuring cup." Rochester threw it to Jack who dropped it, and so we heard a tinny sound of the cup hitting the floor. We had a joke or two about this, but our main purpose was to establish that Jack was carrying a tin cup.

Next we heard Jack open the door and his footsteps on the sidewalk as he walked to the Colmans' house. Then, in addition to Jack's footsteps, we heard the sound of a woman's footsteps approaching Jack. Suddenly we heard the clink of a coin in the tin cup, and Jack said, "Oh, thank you, madam." Now this was one of the biggest bits we ever had, but it could only be done on radio, not television.

On television this routine would have been very artificial and contrived. Jack would have had to be walking not with the cup in his hand hanging down by his side, which is the natural way it would be carried. He would have had to be holding it in his hand with his arm outstretched, which would immediately tip the viewers off that something unusual was planned. Then we would have had to show a woman approaching him. She would have to have an expression of pity on her face. Also, she would have to open her purse and remove a coin and drop it into the cup. All of these moves would have made the joke so forced and obvious that it would never have been done.

However, on radio Jack carried no cup. Because of the previous bit with Rochester when he dropped it and the audience heard the sound of a tin cup hitting the floor, the listeners, in their mind's eye, saw Jack carrying a tin cup. When they heard the sound effects of the woman's approaching footsteps, again they visualized a woman where there actually was none. And when they heard the sound of the coin hitting the tin cup, again done by the sound effects men whom even those in the studio audience were not watching, they immediately conjured up the picture of Jack holding a tin cup like a panhandler and mooching a dime or quarter from this passing stranger.

This was pure radio humor. That type of humor, when it was good, was very very good. It was subtle, it was funny, and it was kind to the budget because we didn't have to hire an actress to play the imaginary lady.

The radio listeners formed strong mental pictures that the viewers of television seldom get. I don't think Fibber McGee's crowded closet has been on the air for more than two decades, yet I frequently hear people over forty say, "He's got a regular Fibber McGee closet." I also read references to it occasionally, and I have heard the mere mention of it on TV get reminiscent laughs from the audience.

One of the things that bothered Jack about television was the Jolly Box—in other words, the Laugh Machine. In radio all his shows were done live before studio audiences, and their laughter

As the master of ceremonies in MGM's *Hollywood Review of 1929. Photo by Clarence Sinclair Bull.*

With Marie Dressler in MGM's *Chasing Rainbows* (1930). *Photo by Robert Castrey.*

In *It's in the Air* (1935). Una Merkel is on the right.

In MGM's *Broadway Melody of 1936* with Movita and Mamo. *Photo by Tom Evans.*

With Sid Silvers in *Broadway Melody of 1936.*

With Burns and Allen in *College Holiday (1936).*

With Mary Boland in Paramount's *College Holiday*. *Photo courtesy of the Paul Ballard Collection.*

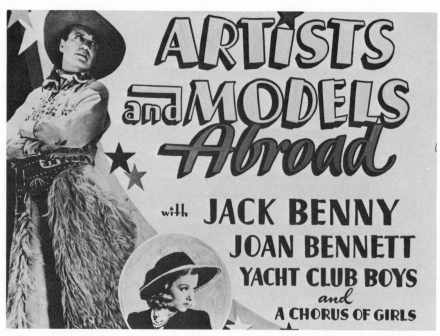

Billboard advertisement for *Artists and Models Abroad* **(1938).**

Rochester plugging *Buck Benny Rides Again* **(1940).**

Fred Allen, Mary Martin, and Jack in Paramount's *Love Thy Neighbor* (1941).

In *Charley's Aunt* (1941), playing the title role. *Photo Courtesy of the Paul Ballard Collection.*

With Carole Lombard and Ernst Lubitsch, at a story conference for *To Be Or Not To Be* (1941). *Photo courtesy of the Hedda Hopper Collection.*

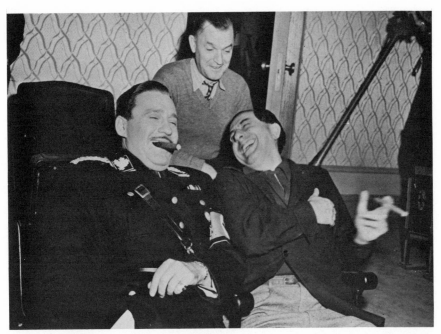

Jack in Nazi uniform, with Ernst Lubitsch, on the set of *To Be Or Not To Be*. *Photo courtesy of the Hedda Hopper Collection.*

Jack and Rochester in Twentieth Century-Fox's *The Meanest Man in the World* (1942).

As Joseph Tura, the great Polish actor, playing Hamlet in *To Be Or Not To Be*. Photo by *Coborn*.

Jack in Warner Brothers *The Horn Blows at Midnight* (1945).

With Alexis Smith in *The Horn Blows at Midnight.*

With Efrem Zimbalist, Sr. and Bette Davis in Warner Brothers' *Hollywood Canteen* (1944).

With Chanin Hale in *Guide for the Married Man* (1967).

was the only reaction the outside listeners heard. With the exception of the dropped-pants gag he once pulled on Fred Allen, Jack never resorted to tricks to induce extra laughter from his audiences. Of course he did his stare which broke up the studio audience, but the outside listeners knew what he was doing and mentally saw him do it.

Many lesser comedians resorted to visual devices in radio to goose the laughs up. One comic did just that—he goosed his stooges on punch lines. Another comic would pretend that he was going to hit his stooge in the crotch, while in the case of women he made a gesture as though to grab their breasts. Sometimes the feeblest jokes got the biggest laughs because of this, and the outside listeners never knew why.

Television was tough on comedy shows performing before live audiences. In radio the performers stood alongside the microphones, and the studio audiences had an unobstructed view of their faces. In television the cameras and equipment would get in the way of the viewers sitting in the audience while the show was being done.

Live TV comedy shows were soon abandoned for the convenience of film which also had the added attraction of being valuable for reruns. Film was clear and sharp and could be shown repeatedly. However, although residuals have brought me a sizable amount of money, I feel that reruns are the living proof of Shakespeare's maxim, "The evil that men do lives after them."

Most comedy shows today have gone back to filming in front of live audiences, and the laughs you hear are earned and generally genuine, although sometimes they are "sweetened" a bit by sound technicians who can increase their volume. With the passing years, techniques have improved so that most comics prefer to film or tape their shows in front of audiences. In fact, all of the one-hour specials that Jack Benny did on NBC from 1964 on used this technique, filming live on tape, or film, in front of live audiences. His very first shows were actually broadcast live. So were Berle's, Caesar-Coca's, and many others. You saw it on your set as it was happening on the stage—unless you lived on the West Coast where you got a poor-quality kinescope a week later.

There was a period when most of the comedy shows were filmed like motion pictures—a short scene at a time, some of them shot out of sequence, and then all patched together in continuity and turned over to the man with the machine who put the laughs in.

I'll never forget our first experience with this device. We had completed our first filmed, audience-less show. We had cut it down to size and we viewed it without a laugh track. We discussed the size, length, and volume of each laugh we wanted after each particular joke, and then we waited for the technicians with the Jolly Box.

When they came, Jack started to explain to them what he wanted. They smiled knowingly at him and assured him that they were seasoned veterans at this specialized work. And they were—they had been in television for over a whole year. They asked us to let them take care of it and stop worrying. We were to return two days later at noon, and when we viewed the results, they promised that we'd jump for joy.

We returned at the appointed time and sat in the small darkened projection room as they started the film, now complete with sound track and laughs. Their prediction was correct. We jumped—but not for joy. After a couple of minutes of viewing it, Jack started screaming, "Stop it. Turn the damned thing off." They did, and the man in charge of the machine asked, "What's the matter? Aren't the laughs big enough or loud enough for you?" Jack's lips narrowed and his blue eyes blazed as he fought to control himself, and he succeeded fairly well.

"Look," he said to the man. "I've been in broadcasting for thirty years and done maybe a thousand shows and opened almost each one by saying, 'Hello again!' and usually I get a chuckle or giggle from the audience. On this film I open the program and say 'Hello again' and I get the biggest friggin' laugh I have ever gotten on any show. Now tell me, what the hell's so friggin' funny about my saying 'Hello again'?" Jack rarely resorted to rough language, but two "friggin's" and one "hell" in a single speech let us know how upset he was.

The meeting ended with Jack refusing to watch the rest of his program. He left, telling the writers that he wanted the amount of laughs cut in half, and the volume of each laugh diminished by at least fifty percent. When he saw our revised version he was happier, but still not completely satisfied. He said, "Okay, it'll do, but I'm not that funny."

From that time on, the technicians who inserted the laughs into the show did good jobs, but they must have had peculiar opinions of Jack. He kept telling them to make the laughs lower, while every other comedian wanted them made louder.

40

Jack and the Movies

Despite his modesty, and frequent self-denigration, Jack had enough latent egotism to have it surface at times and make him sound unduly immodest. This held true in all his endeavors except one. He was not particularly proud of his motion picture career. He made a score of films and loathed most of them. He liked three—*Charley's Aunt, George Washington Slept Here,* and *The Meanest Man in the World*—and loved one, *To Be Or Not To Be,* directed by the justly famed Ernst Lubitsch, and co-starring Carole Lombard in what was destined to be her last appearance.

Jack got his start on the screen not so much through some sought-after inherent talent or extreme handsomeness, but because the movies learned to speak. As the 1920s ended and the silent screen became more and more audible, Hollywood producers rushed to sign stars of the legitimate theater whose facial features were only fair but who were sufficiently versed in elocution to be able to utter simple sentences with some degree of clarity. During the early days of the movies, a perfect profile was a passport to pictures. It mattered not that a leading man spoke as though he were having difficulty swallowing a mouthful of oatmeal or with accents ranging from foreign to the unmistakable "dese," "doze," and "dem" of the streets of New York. An Arrow Collar profile was a bankable asset, whereas a pleasingly pitched vocal tone was nice to have at parties, but served no other useful function.

Then Al Jolson made *The Jazz Singer,* and silence was no longer golden. Suddenly the voice had to match the physical appearance. John Gilbert was the greatest female pulse-quickener since Valentino, but when talkies came his career went. Though there was nothing swishy about him, his high-pitched, effeminate-sounding voice didn't match his virile macho appearance. And other actors and actresses saw their careers terminated because of their inability to project their images vocally as well as visually. Diction teachers became highly paid professionals throughout the industry, and silent stars could be heard intoning "How now, brown cow?" from the Hollywood hills to the Malibu beaches. Broadway stars like Walter Huston and Ruth Chatterton, whose faces matched the image of middle Americans more than they resembled the classic pristine perfection of Greek gods and goddesses, began to star in the new all-talkie movies. And when the moguls running the studios couldn't sign stars of the legitimate theater, they turned to vaudeville for their new faces and voices.

In the late 1920s and early 1930s the silver screen was filled with a plethora of musical comedies peopled with singing, dancing, and wise-cracking performers. Every major movie studio launched a series of these divertissements and offered them annually with no title changes except for the date of the current year. We were treated to MGM's *Broadway Melody of 19—* almost annually, while Paramount Pictures fired a double-barreled batch designated as the "Big Broadcasts" plus their "Artists and Models" of various years. Jack appeared in *The Big Broadcast of 1937* plus *Artists and Models* (1937) and *Artists and Models Abroad* (1938). These movies were all made from the same mold, but instead of breaking the mold they kept remaking the same stories in different locales with new names. The plots would easily be switched from one movie to another, and frequently were. The stars, as well as the scripts, were interchangeable.

Fortunately most of Jack's earliest efforts lie slowly disintegrating in the vaults of movie studios that now have been converted to turning out television series or running lavish Las Vegas hostelries. These films are forgotten, as they should be, only occasionally turning up on TV's late movies. If any of the pictures Jack made prior to 1940 are resurrected, even in cinema seminars, do yourself, and his memory, a favor by missing them.

Because Jack had appeared in several Broadway musicals and was a vaudeville star of almost prime magnitude, he made his movie debut in an MGM musical, *Hollywood Review of 1929.* With great astuteness the producers cast Jack Benny, the suave master of ceremonies of Broadway musicals and vaudeville, in the role of "Jack Benny, M.C." Except for a couple of comedy scenes and exchanging a few lines of dialogue with some of the many MGM luminaries appearing in the movie, that was the sum total of his role.

Jack had hoped to fashion a career as a leading man in a light comedy vein, much as Cary Grant, Jack Lemmon, and others eventually succeeded in doing. He often complained about these early epics, saying: "They always cast me as the Jack Benny character I portrayed in vaudeville and radio, and that isn't me. Hell, if only once they had cast me as Benny Kubelsky, I might at least have had a character part to play which would have let me act."

Jack's complaint was not groundless. From 1929 through 1940 he made an even dozen pictures in which he played Jack Benny no matter what name the character he portrayed was called. This was because the producers figured the public loved Jack Benny as Jack Benny, so why change him? Why take chances? It was almost mandatory that when a radio star began to zoom to the top of the popularity polls, the movies would immediately try to capitalize on their then deadly enemy, free radio entertainment, by taking broadcasting's biggest attractions and featuring them in films.

During one of his one thousand eight hundred and thirty-eight radio shows Jack played the part of a cowboy, and on the program portly, raspy-voiced Andy Devine called him "Buck Benny." Andy's greeting to Jack on subsequent shows was "Hiya, Buck," and in that less sophisticated era those two words became a national catch phrase. Paramount Pictures immediately produced a contrived comedy called *Buck Benny Rides Again,* starring Jack and his entire cast, with the exception of Mary, who was never too anxious to work and who kept appearing on the radio series mainly as a favor to Jack.

Jack was probably less fond of *Buck Benny Rides Again* than most of his other cinema works. He once complained, "After over ten years of making movies I was back to playing Jack Benny again in name as well as character." He admitted that it was his own fault, since he was doing sufficiently well to have turned down the picture. "However," he added, "I always felt that, given the right vehicle, I could make it in movies. I wanted to be cast as an interesting character and not a stereotyped caricature of my radio personality, but this was better than nothing." Then he smilingly added, "Besides, I'm a ham and the money was great."

Oddly enough, Jack fell into the same velvet trap in his very next picture a year later, in 1940. At that time the Jack Benny-Fred Allen feud was zooming to its zenith, and the movies tried to dredge gold out of this widely publicized battle of wits by quickly concocting an opus called *Love Thy Neighbor.* The title was self-explanatory, and Hollywood felt that the presence of the two so-called mortal enemies, plus a young singing ingenue named Mary Martin, would be a box office bonanza. They were wrong. *Love Thy Neighbor* reaped no great harvest, but like its predecessors of the same ilk, it didn't lose money either. In those pre-World War II days, very few pictures did. So Hollywood kept grinding them out to fill the bottom halves of double-feature attractions. Once again Paramount was the guilty studio.

In 1941 Jack was cast in what he considered his first real acting challenge. He played the title role in *Charley's Aunt,* following Charlie Chaplin's brother, Syd, who had made the silent version in 1925. Since Jack masqueraded as Charley's aunt, he appeared in feminine attire throughout most of the picture and was able to avoid the Bennyisms that clung to him in almost all prior movies.

In later years, Jack often modestly admitted that *Charley's Aunt* was a fairly good movie, the first that he felt used him as an actor and not a carbon copy of his radio personality. "But even then," he added ruefully, "one critic claimed that so much of my own personality came through that I should have been billed as Jacqueline Benny."

The only movie that Jack made that he considered truly outstanding—and the critics agreed with him—was *To Be Or Not To Be.* Jack was fond of reminiscing about this movie often and enthusiastically. With justifiable pride, he would point out that, much to his surprise and pleasure, he had been personally hand-picked for the part by the director, Ernst Lubitsch. "Ernst thought I would be an actor, instead of a comic," Jack would say, "and through him I realized the dream of every comedian—I played Hamlet." In the movie Jack portrayed a Polish ham actor, famed for his portrayal of Hamlet. In his role of a thespian, and with the able assistance of comedienne Carole Lombard, he helped sabotage the plans of the Nazi invaders who were occupying Warsaw.

Jack used to say: "Lubitsch was about the only director who ever really directed me. In practically all of my earlier pictures the directors would say, 'Jack, you know so much more about comedy than I do, play the scene the way you feel it.' The only trouble was that I knew lots about radio comedy, a little about stage comedy, and nothing about movies." Then he would continue (and while the quotes are not exact, the thoughts are): "Lubitsch told me at the start of the picture that I was to forget everything I ever knew about screen acting—which wasn't too difficult. Then, prior to every single scene, for every move, gesture, and speech, he acted out exactly what he wanted me to do. He was a lousy actor, but a great director."

Jack's assessment of Lubitsch coincided with the unanimous

opinion of the entire film colony. He was one of the few directors who received, as the title of director Frank Capra's biography refers to it, the rare honor of having *The Name Above the Title*. This means exactly what it says. The director's credit—his name—appeared on the screen prior to the picture's title. At that time only a handful of stars, and even fewer directors, were important enough to receive this celluloid accolade.

In addition to Lubitsch and Capra, Cecil B. DeMille was one of the few others to also be honored with the coveted distinction of having his name above the title. Like DeMille, Lubitsch had his imprimatur on all of his pictures. DeMille was recognized for his grandiose awesome spectacles, usually Biblical in nature. He successfully mixed sex and the holy writ. Lubitsch, on the other hand, was the master of the subtle sophisticated blending of sex and comedy. To this day, any director who successfully combines these elements is said to have "the Lubitsch touch."

To Be Or Not To Be definitely had the Lubitsch touch, and the critics acclaimed it. In its March 16, 1942 review of the picture, *Time* magazine said:

"To Be Or Not To Be" is the late Carole Lombard's last picture. . . . It was posthumously released. Fortunately, for all concerned, "To Be" is a very funny comedy, salted to taste with melodrama and satire.

In "Ninotchka" director Ernst Lubitsch deliciously kidded the vagaries of the Soviets; in "To Be" he succeeds . . . in deftly ridiculing Hitler and his Nazis. His story is an actor's-eye-view of the Nazi occupation of Poland. As the Alfred Lunt and Lynn Fontanne of Warsaw's Polski troupe, the Turas (Jack Benny and Carole Lombard) are a brittle couple. The temperamental Turas fit perfectly into the stock company's plot to keep information from the Gestapo that would wreck the Polish underground movement. . . .

He [Benny] is doing well when his vanity pricks him to ask the Gestapo head his opinion of Tura, the pre-war actor. Growls the Gestapo man, "What he did to Shakespeare we are now doing to Poland."

What the Polski company does to the Gestapo is first-rate entertainment—thanks to a score of good performances by the cast, fresh dialogue and plot (authored by Lubitsch and Melchior Lengyel), and the sure and saucy, suspenseful Lubitsch direction. Miss Lombard's natural, likeable, vibrant performance is up to her standard. Mr. Benny, who plays his role straight, doesn't need his prop stogies to be funny.

While the picture was being filmed, Jack joyously felt that he finally had the hit he wanted in pictures, but unfortunately, just as the movie was about to be released, co-star Carole Lombard's career ended in a fiery plane crash while she was on a World War II bond-selling tour.

That tragedy cast a pall on the picture. It was hard for theater audiences to laugh at scenes showing this beautiful vivacious actress when they knew of the tragic and untimely death she had suffered such a short time before. As a result, what should have been one of the most successful comedies of the decade achieved only mediocre success. The fact that it did as well as it did was a tribute to the fine performances Lubitsch had gotten out of Jack and Miss Lombard.

Jack was desolate, but not because of the indirect effect that Carole's passing might have on his career. That, to him, was of relatively minuscule importance. What depressed him was that he had grown tremendously fond of Carole during the period when the picture was being made. He said: "She was one of the few gals you could love as a woman, and treasure as a friend—and I guess my affection for her covered both areas."

Jack would talk fondly of some of the practical jokes attributed to Carole. Once at a party at her home, she had planted an intercom system in the bathroom and then waited until Walter Winchell visited the can. Just as Walter was about to relieve himself in what he thought was complete privacy, Miss Lombard's voice rang out loud and clear with several disparaging remarks, much to the famed columnist's discomfort.

Another prank supposedly perpetrated by Carole occurred when she was due to sign a new contract with her agent. She took the weighty legal document home and then had a lawyer friend retype one page, so that when the contracts were executed they legally compelled the agent to give her ten percent of all his earnings instead of vice versa.

Through Carole, Jack became friendly with her husband, Clark Gable, and though Jack was brokenhearted himself after her death, he tried to cheer up the inconsolable Gable.

Before we conclude our discussion of *To Be Or Not To Be,* an amusing sidelight about that picture and Jack's father comes to mind. When Jack made the movie, he was always ranked as the first or second most popular performer on radio. His father still went under the name of Mayer Kubelsky, but with pardonable pride he always identified himself to everyone and anyone as "Jack Benny's father." True, he didn't go as far as Milton Berle's mother allegedly did. She supposedly had herself paged for a phone call in the lobby of a large hotel, and then answered the phone in a penetrating voice, saying, "This is Sandra Berle, mother of Milton Berle, the television star." Nevertheless, Mayer Kubelsky was proud of his son, Jack Benny—that is, until he went to see Jack's newest movie, *To Be Or Not To Be.*

Mayer Kubelsky had no inkling of the plot ramifications of the picture, which called for Jack to play the part of a double agent, using his cover, as a successful Shakespearean actor, to foil the Nazis while seemingly cooperating with them. In one of the opening scenes, when a very high-ranking German official comes to see him, Jack gives the Nazi salute and says, "Heil Hitler." When he heard that line, Mayer Kubelsky walked right out of the theater.

When Jack didn't hear from his father for a few weeks, he became worried and phoned, but Mayer Kubelsky hung up on him. Jack made another phone call and said, "Pop, it's me, Jack, your son." His father replied, "You're no son of mine," and hung up again. Jack then made another call, and as was true in the case of getting his release from MGM, and also in noticing Sayde Marks, the third time worked. His father angrily berated Jack for appearing in a picture where he saluted and "heiled" Hitler who was the cause of the biggest, most catastrophic pogrom in history. Jack finally calmed his father down. He explained that he wasn't actually a bad guy in the picture, but was really a good guy pretending to be a bad guy to help the other good guys beat the bad guys. He pleaded with his father to go again to see *To Be Or Not To Be* and sit through the entire picture.

Reluctantly Mayer Kubelsky went back and saw the picture in a movie house far from his neighborhood, where he hoped no one would recognize him. Then he saw it again at his local movie house ... and again ... and again. Jack told me that his father saw *To Be Or Not To Be* thirty-one times, and then he lost count. But Jack Benny was back to being Mayer Kubelsky's son again.

After *To Be Or Not To Be*, Jack made two fair pictures, *George Washington Slept Here* (Warner Brothers, 1942) and *The Meanest Man in the World* (Twentieth Century-Fox, 1943). Lubitsch had proved that Jack was indeed an actor, and these two movies tried to capitalize on this talent, but either through uncertainty or a desire to get easy laughs, the producers had him slipping back into the well-known airwaves image of Jack Benny.

In 1944 Jack appeared as himself, as did all Warner Brothers stars, in their celluloid contribution to the war effort, *Hollywood Canteen*. This was a musical review, and a regression back to his very first pictures, but as Jack said, "I would have been an unpatriotic louse to turn it down."

Then again in 1945, as a favor to his friend Fred Allen, Jack once more reverted to the roles he tried to avoid when he appeared in a vignette in Fred's picture *It's in the Bag*. He played the part of Jack Benny, and the makers of the movie tried to capitalize on every Bennyism they could. Mercifully the role was brief, but in one two-minute sequence, during which Fred visited Jack's home, Allen had to put his hat away in a closet which, when opened, revealed a hatcheck girl who charged him a quarter, and when Fred wanted a cigarette, Jack pointed to a vending machine which gobbled up Allen's change. The scene ended with Fred requesting a souvenir of his visit to Jack's home, and Jack took off his tie, sold it to Allen for two and a half dollars, wrapped it, using one of those large wrapping paper dispensers, and finally rang up the sale on a cash register.

Jack was unhappy about this heavy handed belaboring of an overworked facet of his alter ego, but he couldn't possibly refuse to help Allen in his efforts to make a box office hit out of a trite tale. Fortunately for the memories of both of them, if not their pocketbooks, the picture was seen by relatively few fans, although it still pops up now and then on the late movies.

Jack's much berated and uncelebrated *The Horn Blows at Midnight* came in 1945. It was a Warner Brothers effort, produced by former Broadway columnist Mark Hellinger. Once again Jack's fondness for people was his undoing. He said, "How the hell can you turn down a sweet guy like Hellinger? Besides it had an excellent director (Raoul Walsh), a talented leading lady (Alexis Smith), and some wonderful supporting players (Allyn Joslyn, Reginald Gardiner, Dolores Moran, Guy Kibbee, Franklin Pangborn, and Groucho Marx's statuesque perennial foil, Margaret Dumont)."

The plot of *The Horn Blows at Midnight* had Jack portraying the part of a trumpet player in an orchestra who falls asleep and dreams that he is an angel in heaven. His heavenly name is "Athanael" and he is in the lowest echelon of cherubim. Because of this he is assigned the menial task of obliterating a minor sore spot in the solar system—the earth. On midnight of the day of destiny he is supposed to stand atop a tall building and, like Gabriel, blow his horn. The shattering blast would end the world. Of course, prior to this cataclysmic trumpet note, Jack wakes up, and all is well.

The picture had two strikes against it from the start. First, it was a fantasy, and fantasies were seldom money-making movies. Critics might acclaim them, as they did *Here Comes Mr. Jordan,* but such films rarely filled theaters. Second, Warner Brothers guessed wrong in assuming that his strong success in radio would be a box office boon, and instead of giving Jack one of their established box office names as a leading lady to augment his pulling power, they used the beauteous, talented, but then somewhat unknown actress, Alexis Smith, to play opposite him. Jack gallantly absolved Miss Smith of any blame for the film's financial failure. He once said: "Even if they had Olivia de Havilland, Ann Sheridan, Jane Wyman, and Bette Davis collectively [all under contract to Warner Brothers] as my love interest, the picture would still have been a flop. It might have been fun for me, but a flop."

The picture wasn't as bad as Jack and his radio writers painted it.

It wasn't very good, but then again it wasn't the worst piece of celluloid that ever came out of the cameras. Warner Brothers realized long before completion that it wasn't going to be another *Gone with the Wind,* but in fairness to the studio it should be stated that they did everything to shore up the flaccid film. They reshot the ending at a reputed cost of a quarter of a million dollars, they recut the picture, and they added several new scenes while eliminating others that they felt weren't funny. The final version received mostly mixed reviews—mediocre and bad. However, some critics, especially in the smaller towns, liked what they saw and praised the picture, also commenting that its shortcomings were not attributable to Jack Benny.

A few metropolitan reviewers were also quite complimentary. The *Los Angeles Times* movie review by Edwin Schallert on April 21, 1945, bore the headline: "Benny Angels Way Through Outlandish Comedy Show." His review said that the picture was "both novel and highly amusing" and that it would "please those who find Jack Benny a droll personality, for in it he ranges about considerably with his own style of monkey-shining." He also remarked that the movie "has been pretty well tailored to his needs," and he called the ending of the picture "a wild tournament of slapstick." In addition, the *Motion Picture Herald* of July 7, 1945 said: "You'll have grounds for expecting a lot from this attraction, to which may be added the evidence of a Hollywood preview audience which laughed aplenty at the proceedings. . . . The humor ranges from the comedy of manners, which is Benny's specialty, to the most outright variety of slapstick with a couple of long skyscraper-ledge sequences furnishing the high points." Both reviews made mention of *Here Comes Mr. Jordan,* produced several years earlier, as a basis of comparison. That movie, starring Robert Montgomery, though a comedy classic, did not score big at the box office.

The Horn Blows at Midnight had limited engagements at the first-run picture palaces controlled by Warner Brothers and soon finished its brief career at the neighborhood houses. It was well on its way to the cinematic cemetery and oblivion when in one radio script we injected what we thought was a mild joke about that movie's lack of quality. The audience roared with laughter far out of proportion to what the line warranted. As a result, the following week we wrote another gag or two at the expense of Jack and the picture, and the reaction was again gratifying. There was no preplanning in this panning. Like the famed Allen-Benny feud, it mushroomed. People seemed to love Jack's self-castigation, and soon we had a subject that was almost as sure-fire as Jack's stinginess, violin-playing, blue eyes, and all his other laugh-provoking characteristics.

Oddly enough this panning pushed the picture into the semi-successful category. After it had completed its original release, it was reissued and did more business than it had the first time around—which really wasn't a very difficult accomplishment. Jack then had Jack Warner as a guest on his radio show with Warner defending the picture. Warner was a frustrated comedian, and Jack once said: "Jack Warner would rather tell a bad joke than make a good movie."

The great publicity given to *The Horn Blows at Midnight* in the 1950s led to Jack starring in a radio dramatization of the movie, and he also did it on television on *Omnibus,* getting this prestigious program the highest rating in its history.

Soon other comedians began using the picture as a target for their jokes but by then Jack felt that it had worn too thin and we abandoned it. However, several years later we did a program where Jack and Don Wilson were walking down the street and a teenager asked for his autograph. As Jack signed his signature the adolescent said, "You know, Mr. Benny, you're so great, why didn't you make any movies?" Wilson said, "Oh but he did. He made movies like *The Horn Blows . . .*" Jack quickly interrupted Don and sent the youngster away with his autograph. Don said, "Jack, why didn't you let me tell him about *The Horn Blows at Midnight?*" And Jack answered happily, "Just think, Don, isn't it wonderful—a whole new generation that doesn't know."

Subsequently Jack made brief "cameo" appearances in *It's a Mad, Mad, Mad, Mad World* and *Guide for the Married Man,* but from a realistic standpoint he summed it all up by observing, "When the horn blew at midnight, it blew taps for my cinema career."

41

A Parting of the Ways

In Hollywood, according to the not-always-to-be-believed gossip columnists, all divorces and dissolutions of business partnerships are amiable, and frequently the people separated then enjoy a far friendlier relationship than before.

Fortunately an instance where this held true occurred when, after twelve years, I ceased being a regular member of Jack's staff. The two decades that followed our split saw me become closer to him as a friend. We played golf together occasionally and had several lunches or other meetings annually. In addition, I worked on special script assignments for him at least two or three times a year.

I had wanted to quit the series several times prior to our eventual disassociation on a weekly basis, but Jack talked me out of it. Not one of these instances was a result of a direct argument with him personally. They were caused, rather, by conflicts in concepts among the writers, and much to his discomfort and dismay, Jack was always caught in the middle.

I asked for my release once during the first year and twice during the second. At the end of the second season I was adamant about leaving, but Jack made an arrangement that, to my knowledge, never existed before or afterward. He would permit me to work part-time while paying me the same salary I had been getting for full-time work. My duties were to turn in an eight-page spot for each show. I was excused from attending all story and rewrite conferences, except for the Saturday and Sunday cast readings and rehearsals and work on the polishing, cutting, and rewriting of the scripts at that time. Furthermore, I was allowed to double—that is, take on outside writing assignments.

I did this for two years—two highly lucrative but less than satisfying years. In addition to my Benny duties I also wrote for such programs as *Amos 'n' Andy, The Alan Young Show,* and Cass Daley's *Fitch Bandwagon.* Oddly enough, because of the prestige of having a "Benny writer" on the program, these shows paid me more, far more, than I was getting from Jack.

After two years of this setup, Jack suggested that we have a meeting. When we got together, he expressed his feeling that allowing me to work just part-time had been detrimental to the good of the show, and he wanted me back on a full-time basis. Once again he made a non-refusable offer. He promised to increase my wages generously, not only making up for the annual raises I had lost during the past two years, but even exceeding that figure. What is more, he further promised that he would act as arbitrator on any arguments that might take place among his writers, but he assured me that he felt these would be minimal. He had had a long talk with the rest of the staff before conferring with me, and they wanted me back. Thus I returned to the show as a full-fledged member of the staff and began to work regularly in collaboration with John Tackaberry.

Jack was true to his word, and although there were minor skirmishes among the writers, these were a normal occupational hazard, and he never had to assume the role of a Henry Kissinger to establish peace. We settled our squabbles ourselves, and we all reassumed our former "pecking order" positions.

Possibly in no other craft could the situation described in the previous paragraphs exist or be tolerated by "The Boss." Therefore, at this point it would be fitting to explore in some detail the unique relationship between comedy writers and comics.

Probably no other profession had fewer practitioners than that of the radio comedy writer. There were rarely more than a dozen comics on the air at one time, and they usually employed from two to six writers. Thus there were fewer than one hundred people performing in this capacity.

While there were several hundred working comedy writers in Hollywood, many were employed by movie studios. Others devoted their talents to situation comedies like *My Friend Irma, Henry Aldrich, Father Knows Best,* and *A Date with Judy,* or they supplied quiz show M.C.'s with quips. The ones in charge of these writers were the producers of the programs. The star or stars had little, if any, contact with the writers, and not too much to say about the scripts. There was little personal communication here.

The same held true with the motion picture studios. Both musical comedies and straight comedies were staple offerings of the movie-makers, but a writer could finish one script and then work on two or three others before the first script started being filmed. In addition, the actor or actress for whom the project was originally intended could have been replaced numerous times before the cameras started grinding. Again, there was no personal relationship with the performer.

Writing for a star whose name was the actual title of the series (*The Jack Benny Show, The Bob Hope Show, The Eddie Cantor Show,* etc.) meant constant close contact with the comic, although there were some exceptions to this, the most notable being Red Skelton.

Skelton's writing staff rarely saw or conferred with him, except at rehearsals. When the script was finished it was delivered to him by messenger. Moreover, there were no discussions or conferences on the telephone, since Red had a phone phobia and refused to talk to his writers, or practically anybody else, on that instrument. And most of the time, he never communicated with them in any other way.

Red's relations with his writers were unusual, to say the least. When everybody in town was congratulating his head writers, Bob Schiller and Bob Weiskopf, because Skelton's TV show had shot up to the top spot in the Neilsen ratings, Red rewarded this talented and deservedly happy duo by firing them.

Some years earlier, Sherwood Schwartz, a prior head writer, had resigned from the show. Skelton took this news philosophically by saying, "Let him go. At least I've still got my head writer, Al Schwartz." When informed that it was Sherwood, not his brother Al, who was the head writer, Red got angry and said, "Then fire Al, and from now on I don't want any more Schwartzes working on my show."

Skelton's dealings with his stable of writers were probably the oddest in an industry noted for frequent heated hair-splitting differences between employer and employees. There are few, if any, comedy writers who have remained with the same boss for more than a couple of years who haven't quit or been canned on more than one occasion.

Mort Lachman, Bob Hope's head writer and producer for over twenty years, once briefly upset Bob by being quoted as follows in a magazine interview: "Hope and I have the perfect comic-writer relationship," said Lachman. "So far he's fired me ten times and I've quit twelve."

Bob wasn't irritated because Mort's words implied a less-than-beautiful association. He half-seriously said, "Mort, I don't like that kind of publicity, but if you give out these interviews, the facts are that I fired you *twelve* times and you've quit *ten*. And as of today you can make it your thirteenth canning." That happened a couple of years ago. They're still together and I don't know the latest score.

The preceding true stories should give you an idea of the unusual conditions, plus the love-hate atmosphere, that frequently existed and still exists between comedians and their writers.

My record was a good one. During my five years with Bob Hope, I was fired once and quit twice, plus the final time. During my eight years with Lucille Ball, I was demoted once and quit three times. During my year and a half with Joey Bishop, I quit thirty-seven times, and that was just in my last week. The computer hasn't been perfected yet that could estimate all the other occasions on which I asked for my release from Joey's situation comedy.

However, outside of the first couple of times during my initial two years with the Benny series, I never quit again, until the final parting, and this is how it happened.

Toward the end of my employment by Jack, he was appearing on occasional television shows—two, four, or six a season. He was also doing thirty-nine regular radio broadcasts. To aid in this extra work, he hired a team of writers, Al Gordon and Hal Goldman, who, as previously mentioned, were called "The Kids."

I wanted to get into television because, like everyone else, I realized that radio would soon be supplanted by the visual medium. The entire industry was talking about the unbelievably fantastic rewards for those who got into TV on the ground floor. There were tales circulating about Jess Oppenheimer who had helped create the *I Love Lucy* series and functioned as its head writer and producer. For this he received a "top bracket" salary, certain residuals on reruns, and a percentage of ownership in the show. This was estimated to be about eight percent, but at the rate the series was going, in just another year or so his tiny piece of the pie would be worth at least one million dollars.

Since the early 1960s I had been receiving "feelers" from producers and networks to join them in an executive capacity, devoting my time to creating new programs. I was offered a handsome salary plus a hefty percentage of each show I created. However, because I still had a tremendous loyalty and love for Jack, I discussed the matter with him.

Jack said that he didn't want to hold me back, and while he agreed that radio was a dying medium, he said that he'd like me to stay with him until his radio shows were dropped for lack of listeners. At that time he would probably have to cut down his staff, so I was, in effect, helping him make a hard decision.

Early in 1955 we had lunch together, and Jack told me that he would not be doing any more radio shows during the following season. He would confine his activities to television—appearing on the tube every other week for a total of twenty shows.

I informed Jimmy Saphier, my agent, of this, and he concluded negotiations with NBC, according to which I was to join the network whenever I left Jack Benny. I informed Jack of this situation, and he was quite pleased at my new affiliation, but he wanted to know if we could once again work out a deal for my services on a part-time basis.

Jack was very flattering and told me that I was as good as anyone in the business at "coming in cold," reading a completely strange script, and making valuable suggestions for improving it. Therefore, he wanted to know if I would be interested in working out an arrangement where my sole obligation would be in this capacity, just showing up at his first reading or rehearsal and limiting my contributions to no more than a single day.

Saphier and I had meetings with the West Coast heads of NBC, Tom Sarnoff and Fred Wile. They, in turn, talked to NBC's top executives in New York, Sylvester "Pat" Weaver and Tom MacAvity. The consensus of opinion was that while it wouldn't be right for an NBC "Program Executive" (my new title) to aid a rival network's star, something might be worked out because of my personal relationship with Jack. However, under the circumstances there would probably have to be a downward adjustment in my annual NBC salary.

Saphier and I then discussed this privately. We had figured out that the least I would take for the one-day assignment every other week with Jack was five hundred dollars, and that the most we could ask for was one thousand dollars. Taking an average, we decided that I'd probably get seven hundred and fifty dollars a day, or fifteen thousand dollars for twenty days of work. Not bad—except that Jimmy pointed out to me that NBC would probably insist that I start with ten thousand dollars less annually if I continued to work for Jack. This would leave me with a profit of only five thousand dollars from the fifteen thousand dollars I'd earn via my second job. After commissions and various taxes had been deducted, I would be "doubling"—probably under a physical and mental strain—for very little financial reward. Therefore, we decided that I had to arrange another meeting with Jack and tactfully turn down his offer.

When we met for lunch at Jack's club, the Hillcrest Country Club, I tried to tackle the problem tangentially instead of head-on. I said that his suggested arrangement could be very unfair to him and his regular writers, because while I felt that I might be able to offer valuable improvements on certain weak scripts, what would I do if

I came in and heard a script read that was so perfect it needed no help? Wasn't it logical that I might start to suggest several changes just to justify earning my fee?

Jack laughed hysterically at this, although I failed to see any humor in my logic. Then he explained that when he had first had the idea of making this deal, he had discussed it with one of the head men of the giant talent agency handling him, Taft Schreiber of MCA. Jack said that Taft had immediately brought up the same point I did—what's to prevent me from trying to make many changes in a perfect script so that it would seem I had made a major contribution and thus had earned my salary?

I listened to this and said, "Jack, the mere fact that Taft and I both thought of it shows that it's a valid point." He replied: "Milt, I told Taft that you weren't that kind of guy, and the mere fact that you yourself just brought it up proves I was right."

Since subterfuge hadn't worked, I then took the direct approach. I told Jack that NBC would possibly permit me to work for him, but I'd have to start with them at a lower annual figure. Then if my part-time job with him didn't last, I'd have a tough time re-establishing my higher income with the network. However, I added that if he ever had any doubts about a script, all he had to do was call me and I'd give him a day free—and I wouldn't mind if it happened several times a season. Jack nodded. He understood. It was goodbye.

We prolonged that luncheon for nearly three hours as we took turns saying how much we loved and respected each other. In fact, Jack remembered, and used, a line from one of our old scripts to lighten our sentimental speeches. He said, "You know, Milt, I always look upon you as one of my peers, and yet I'm old enough to be your fath—brother."

When we parted late that afternoon, after one of the longest lunches I had ever sat through, Jack wished me one hundred percent luck in every endeavor. I answered by saying, "Jack, I want you to stay one hundred percent healthy and happy, and I hope that all of your programs from now on are ninety-nine percent perfect."

Jack stared at me with a puzzled expression and then asked, "Why would you want my programs to be only ninety-nine percent perfect instead of one hundred percent?" I told him to think about it and to call me if he couldn't figure my reason by the following day. Then his face lit up with a smile as he correctly guessed, "You want me to miss you that one little percent, Milt?" When I nodded, he hugged me and said, "Even if my shows are all one hundred percent perfect, I'll still miss you." That was as nice a compliment as anyone ever paid me.

In retrospect, I feel that leaving Jack may be the reason that I maintained such an excellent relationship with him through the following two decades. I had never had a personal argument with Jack while I worked on his staff or during the many years after. This didn't hold true for the writers who started with me but still remained.

As the years rushed onward, I worked on several annual assignments for Jack and with Jack. I always looked forward to these brief re-establishments of our relationship, and was never disappointed. He was still easy-going, easy-laughing, and easy to satisfy with scripts or special material.

However, I heard rumors about his other writers. They supposedly were complaining that Jack was becoming crotchety and cranky. He was supposed to be more irritable and less patient than he had been, and instead of mildly dismissing a script or routine that didn't meet his approval, he would become overwrought and upset. I was told that time was having an adverse effect on his personality.

The long, tiring hours that television demanded for rehearsal, costume fittings, make-up, lighting, memorizing of lines, moves, and physical action were time-consuming and debilitating. Eventually this led to some bitter arguments that became more the rule than the exception. Both Perrin and Balzer had increasingly frequent flare-ups with Jack that led to periods of open hostility where they didn't talk to each other. I also heard that the same thing was happening between Sam and George themselves.

Although this gossip came to me from very reliable sources, I still couldn't believe this upsetting news. I was writing at least one script with Jack Benny as a guest star on Lucille Ball's programs every year, and this meant meetings with Jack in advance to set up the story and plot, after having it okayed by Lucy, plus a full week of working with him and almost constant companionship while the show was being filmed. In addition to this, I'd sometimes supply him with lines for benefits or personal appearances. Also, I'd work on an occasional one-hour special for Jack or prepare some material for him when he was a guest on some other star's show. On these assignments I'd be in almost constant contact with him on a daily basis for a period of three or four weeks, and it was invariably pleasant.

Yet there was increasing evidence that either the rigors of a weekly television season, or advancing age, or a combination of both was causing Jack to occasionally be testy with those of his co-workers with whom he had his closest contacts.

Ralph Levy, one of Jack's first (and longest-lasting) TV directors, told me the following incident. "Jack loved television," said Levy, "but he frequently complained about how much more arduous it was than radio. He resented the fact that he couldn't devote as much time to the creation of the script as he formerly did, and this led to occasional tiffs with his writers. As long days of rehearsal wore on, he tended to get tired, and the later the hour the more crotchety he became. During a late afternoon rehearsal of one show we got into a discussion as to how a scene should be played, and we were both fairly adamant in our conception of it."

Then, according to Levy, the discussion blossomed into a heated debate and soon flared into an open argument which ended when Jack stalked off the stage to his dressing room. After waiting several minutes to give him a chance to cool off, Levy dispatched script secretary Jeanette Eyman to inform him that they were ready to resume rehearsal.

Jack sent back word via Jenny that he would return when he was "damn well ready," and Levy proceeded to rehearse those parts of the program which didn't depend on Jack's presence. About five minutes later, he sauntered onto the set and told Jenny in a tone of voice that, although not a shout, was much louder than usual, "Tell Mr. Levy I'm damn well ready." Ralph treated this lightly and he said, "Jenny, tell Mr. Benny we will start the blocking from the top."

Ralph told me recently that he was surprised and slightly upset that Jack seemed genuinely angry. For the rest of that day Jack continued to convey all messages to him via Jenny, and Ralph did the same. This childlike charade continued into the following week which, because of the nature of the show, happened to be far less strenuous than usual. In fact one morning they found themselves running so far ahead of schedule that, before breaking for lunch, Levy announced that there would be no need for any further work that day, and therefore everyone could have the afternoon off.

At this, Jack said in a voice loud enough for all to hear, "Jenny, ask Mr. Levy if he'd like to play golf with me."

Ralph smiled and said, "Jenny, tell Mr. Benny that I haven't got my clubs here."

Jack said, "Tell Mr. Levy I will drive him to his house where he can pick up his clubs."

Ralph replied, "Tell Mr. Benny I accept."

Ralph recalls that they drove to his house and then to the Hillcrest Country Club in silence. Afterward, sharing a caddy and cart, they proceeded to play a dozen or so holes while carrying on all conversation through the medium of their confused caddy. When they finished, Jack drove Ralph home, once more in complete silence.

As Ralph got out of the car, he said, "Car, tell Mr. Benny that I appreciate this, and thank him for me."

Then, for the first time in several days, Jack addressed him directly. "You can thank me yourself," Jack said. "Now that the day is over, we can talk. You see, I'm not mad at Ralph Levy, my friend. I'm mad at Ralph Levy, my director."

When Levy told me of this display of temperament, he said that by the time they made up, he had forgotten what had caused the friction in the first place. Since Jack made no further mention of the squabble, Ralph, for fear of reviving a dead issue, never inquired as to the specific cause of the quarrel.

As the years passed, I continued to hear rumblings that while Jack was still among the best of bosses, he wasn't the perfect employer I so fondly remembered. However, because I had never experienced anything but the pleasantest personal relationship with him, I preferred to doubt these rumors.

Eventually the facts of these bickerings were confirmed to me via two of the persons most involved, Perrin and Balzer. When Jack stopped doing his weekly TV series, their agent submitted their names to me, in my role as Lucy's "Script Consultant," for writing assignments. Time has a habit of making the past seem more pleasant than the present, and we had forgotten our early differences. Even if I subconsciously harbored any resentment, they were excellent writers, and my job was to get the best scripts possible for Miss Ball, so I was happy to have them work for us.

It was during these periods of employment that they both confirmed the fact that with the passing years they were involved in increasing disagreements with Jack, blaming this situation on his mounting years and the grinding pressure of TV. However when I asked if both of these factors also couldn't have contributed to making them more difficult to work with, they reluctantly agreed.

I'll never know what actually caused the friction, but I do know—and I pointed this out to Sam and George—that in all the years since I had left the show, I had never had a harsh word with Jack. When they argued that I wasn't as constantly in his company as they were, since they had remained on his staff for ten years after my departure, for a total of twenty-two years, I suggested that it could very easily have been a case of the old adage, "Familiarity breeds contempt." Balzer replied: "Perhaps so. Maybe we were with him too much, and we were like family. You only saw him several times a year. He treated you like company."

I didn't argue the point then, and I won't dispute it at this time. I know that I feel far better now than I could possibly feel if I had ever had a serious argument with Jack that was the direct fault of either one of us.

I discussed this fact with Hugh Wedlock, Jr., who knew Jack longer than any of us. Hugh worked for him before any of us did and after any of us did, and his recollection coincided with mine.

Even in Jack's last year on earth he never said a sharp word to Wedlock or had anything remotely resembling an argument with him. But, then, maybe Jack treated Wedlock like company, too.

42

Thirty-Nine—And Ever Young

During my nearly four decades of association with Jack, friends, interviewers, and others asked me many questions about him. However, the most frequent ones were: (1) "What kind of man is he?" (2) "Is he actually stingy?" (3) "Can he play the violin well?" and (4) "What is his real age?"

Here are my answers: (1) He was a great man—perhaps the greatest man that show business, or any other business, ever produced. (2) Far from being stingy, he was the most generous person I ever met. (3) Jack played the violin well enough to earn his living as a soloist.

And now we come to the fourth question: "What is his real age?"

Age, as reckoned by the calendar, can be a misconception. I'm sure we have all known teenagers who acted as though they should buy rocking chairs and sit in senior citizen homes. And then there are those rare individuals who belie their birth certificates by remaining youthful no matter what their chronological ages are.

Jack was in the latter classification. He was the fountain of youth that Ponce de Leon failed to find. He was Peter Pan with a sense of humor. He was a perennial portrait of Dorian Gray without perversity or the penalty of deteriorating.

As he frequently reminded his public his birthday was February

14, and he gave a long-lasting Valentine's Day gift of laughter to the world. Unfortunately he didn't last long enough. He made his final exit almost exactly seven weeks short of his eighty-first birthday.

Almost all newspapers and the radio and television commentators said that Jack was past eighty years old. I agree on the number eighty, but when they append it to the word "old," I must object. In fact I take offense. Jack was not eighty, or seventy, or any other figure associated with the encroachment of years and approaching infirmity. He was ageless.

When I first met Jack, he was in his late forties. I joined him as a staff writer in the fall of 1943. Several months later, on February 14, 1944, newspapers printed the fact that Jack Benny was fifty years old, and this was the only occasion I ever recall him being down or depressed because he was allegedly aging. I remember that at one writing session his scripting staff, whom he occasionally referred to as his "Faithful Four," tried to cheer him up. We pointed out that times had changed, and that while, when he was a kid, a man of fifty was considered a patriarch, in these days fifty was no longer considered old. "In fact," one of us added, "fifty is merely middle-aged." Jack smiled sadly and said, "If fifty is only middle-aged, how come you don't see too many hundred-year-old men?" Later in life, when he was well into his seventies, inconsiderate interviewers would occasionally ask him, "How does it feel to be getting so old?" Jack frequently answered with the line credited to the late Maurice Chevalier (and Benny always gave the great French entertainer due credit for the observation), "It's great to grow old, especially when you consider the alternative."

Ask the average person fortunate enough to have heard (or seen) Jack what his age was, and the answer invariably is thirty-nine. However, Jack wasn't always thirty-nine. When we first fibbed about his age on the radio, his birth certificate indicated that he was in his fifties, but we made him thirty-six. The only reason for selecting this figure was because we could have him hammily say, "I'm thirty-six—a perfect thirty-six."

Jack remained thirty-six years old for three years, which is one year less than my wife did. He became thirty-seven with much flourish. Then on his next birthday we had a line, not on our radio program, but given to the press by Jack: "Thirty-seven is such a nice age I've decided to hold it over for another year." And he did. Thirty-eight lasted longer because we were fast approaching forty, a figure we were loath to reach. After trying on the age of thirty-eight for size and liking it, we stayed with it for another few years, and then we hit the final age, thirty-nine.

Jack never advanced past thirty-nine for many reasons. The writers, and Jack, had numerous discussions about it. Some thought we could have fun with the phrase "Life begins at forty." Others felt that if we had him hit forty, then we must progress through the forties. Like every other lasting facet of his radio character, this was not a quick decision. Each writer, and Jack, acted as the devil's advocate, listing his opinions of the assets and liabilities of adding an extra year to Jack's age. Eventually we decided to stop time at thirty-nine.

But no matter what radio, television, or calendars said, Jack wasn't thirty-nine. He was younger! He always retained the zest and enthusiasm he had for all things. Each new program he did was treated as though it were his very first. He tackled each line, routine, or bit of business like a tyro whose entire career depended on this particular program being the best ever.

Jack seemed to be a professional enthusiast. He thought and spoke in superlatives, and his friends and fellow comedians made a long-time running gag of his exuberance. Whenever he was a guest star on Lucille Ball's program—and I know these occasions were many because I wrote six shows starring Jack on Lucy's program—he would always be introduced to the studio audience prior to the filming, and Miss Ball's husband, Gary Morton, executive producer of the series, would make a production of his introduction of Benny to the waiting viewers. He changed his lines occasionally, but he always added the following remarks: "Jack Benny can get excited about anything. Last week Lucy and I went to dinner with Jack and Mary Benny at a new restaurant. We had just been seated at our table, and Jack took a sip of water and turned to his wife and said, 'Mary, I am sure this is a wonderful restaurant because this is the *greatest* glass of water I ever tasted.' Recently he played golf at the Hillcrest Country Club, and came rushing out of his shower to announce to everyone in the locker room, 'These are the *most fantastic* Turkish towels in the world.' One evening after an extremely important business meeting involving his program, and consequently millions of dollars, Jack arrived at his home in a state of great excitement. Mary asked him how the meeting went and he said, 'Oh, fine. But I made the *most amazing* discovery. If you drive along Wilshire Boulevard at exactly twenty-nine miles an hour you'll never get stopped by a red light.' " The studio audience would howl at Morton's lines, not realizing that they were all based on truth.

George Balzer, one of my co-writers on *The Jack Benny Show*, reminded me of a similar incident. We were at one of those parties usually given by the sponsor or network after the first program of the new season, and a group of epicures were discussing the best places to get the most delicious delicacies. One gourmet raved about the way one restaurant served poached fresh salmon encrusted in a thin bread-like covering. Another guest went into mouth-watering ecstasies describing another restaurant's broiled squab. Finally Jack, in all earnestness, said, "On the road between Palm Springs and Cathedral City there's a drive-in that serves the world's greatest chicken fried steak." Now the meat used in chicken fried steak was possibly the least expensive cut of steak, if indeed it could be called steak at all. It was sliced so thin that a wag once said it only had one side to it. Then it was dipped into a batter made out of some combination of flour, milk, and eggs, and fried, usually in oil that hadn't been changed in ten thousand meals. It was inexpensive, and while it was fairly tasty, personally I'd rather have Hamburger Helper. Yet there was a period when Jack Benny loved it and never hesitated plugging it as one of his favorite foods, while others were talking about Oysters Rockefeller and Beluga Caviar.

Jack's contagious enthusiasm covered every script, and especially applied to his work. When he had a script that pleased him more than most, he couldn't wait to do it, and if it contained a routine or joke that broke him up, it was hard for him to restrain himself.

I remember that once, a dozen or so years ago, I was writing a one-hour television special for Tennessee Ernie Ford on which Jack Benny was the guest star. I collaborated on the script with Hal Kanter who also served as producer and director. Mr. Kanter is one of the most multi-talented men in the industry, and not the least of his gifts is his ability to act as a master of ceremonies, a function he performs with never-failing quality at many industry dinners and charitable functions.

Normally when I work with a collaborator on a script, I function as the head writer. ("Head writer" is sometimes an empty title. In theory it means that he makes the final decision. However when two writers begin to collaborate they realize that they are entering into a relationship somewhat slightly more intimate than marriage. One of them can be boss, but the other reserves the right to tell him his idea or joke stinks, and he should shove it.) Hal is one of the writers I've willingly deferred to as head writer, and he has never resented my squabbling with him over the wording of a sentence or a punch line. He has kicked me several times, but he's never resented me.

However, when we began to write the routine for Jack Benny, we reversed positions because Hal realized that I was a more knowledgeable authority on Jack Benny's type of humor. The routine we wrote was simple and rather obvious. The program was slated to go on the air early in April, shortly before the deadline for paying income taxes. In our sketch we had Jack Benny earning a few extra dollars by opening an office as an income tax expert, with Tennessee Ernie as a customer coming in to have Jack help him fill and file his tax returns.

I only remember one joke in that routine. Perhaps the gag itself is not memorable, but what happened with it certainly is. In the course of the sketch Jack asked Ernie if he had any sources of income other than as an entertainer. Then the dialogue and action went as follows:

ERNIE

Yes, I own a farm. A cattle farm.

JACK

I see. And how many cattle do you have on this farm?

ERNIE

Five hundred cows.

JACK

Five hundred cows?

ERNIE

And one bull.

JACK

And one bull? (Picks up pen and begins writing feverishly on some notepaper on his desk)

ERNIE

What are you doing?

JACK

I'm taking depreciation on the bull.

The script was finally finished and rehearsals were scheduled. When Jack showed up at the first one, he was greeted by Ernie Ford who said, "Jack, I think we have a very good script here." In his usual enthusiastic fashion, Jack said, "Well, with writers like Hal Kanter and Milt Josefsberg, it should be better than good." Kanter caught his enthusiasm and tried to keep it going by saying, "It's a real goody, Jack. And Milt put in a joke that's sure to rank with the greatest you've ever done." Like a kid who had been promised a new toy, Jack wanted to hear it immediately, but we told him that it would lose a little zest and zing if he heard it out of context. However, we did tell him that it was in the scene where he played the part of the income tax expert.

We then sat around a table and read the script, with Jack obviously impatient for the income tax scene. When we reached it and he read the gag, it was greeted by a lovely roar of laughter from the cast and crew, with the loudest laugh coming from Jack himself, who was lying on the floor, doubled up with hysteria, with his head half under the table.

We rehearsed the script for several days, and each time he read the line about "taking depreciation on the bull," Jack reacted the same way. Not only that, but he would say that usually he hated to do jokes with sexual undertones, but that since this one concerned itself with cows and bulls instead of people, he felt that it would be permissible. He was visibly happy when we assured him that NBC's censor found nothing questionable about the routine.

Then came the night for filming the show. Most variety shows are filmed in front of live audiences so that the performers can benefit from the reaction of laughter and applause. This show was no exception, and the audience was most appreciative throughout the performance, up to, and including, the start of the income tax sketch.

And then we approached the joke that Jack had been waiting for all week. We reached the line where Ernie told Jack that he had five hundred cows and one bull, and Jack, in his usual style of comedy, repeated the lines as he had rehearsed them. Then, with the deadpan expression he was supposed to use in the scene, Jack started writing notes on a piece of paper. As per the script, Ernie asked, "What are you doing?" At this point Jack was supposed to say, "I'm taking depreciation on the bull." However he only said, "I'm taking depre—" and went into paroxysms of laughter. He slid off his chair and fell to the floor, helplessly guffawing at the gag he knew was coming.

There is a strange thing about filming shows in front of live audiences. When a performer fluffs a line or breaks up, the audience goes into hysterics. And the bigger the performer, the greater the hysterics. So when Jack lay on the floor laughing, the entire audience echoed his mirth—and since laughter is contagious, soon the cameramen, musicians, technicians, page boys, script girls, and everyone present had congealed into one screaming group.

It took several minutes to restore order, and then we started to refilm the scene from its start. Again it played very well until we hit the fateful phrase, "I'm taking depreciation on the bull." This time Jack didn't get as far as he did the first time. He barely said, "I'm taking . . ." when he was convulsed once more and again visited the floor. The audience didn't know the cause of his mirth, but the sight of him howling with laughter caused them to join him to such an extent that I'm quite sure that several of them went home with wet underwear that night.

Everybody was enjoying the unscheduled fun, but unfortunately we were wasting both time and money. Some economy-minded major domo suggested temporarily skipping the scene, and then filming it later on after the audience had gone, but Jack wouldn't hear of it, and Ernie Ford, who was footing the bills, sided with him. We tried the scene a third time. However this time, prior to the moment that the cameras started rolling, Jack stepped out to the front of the stage and made a short speech to the audience. In effect he said, "Ladies and gentlemen, please forgive me for being so unprofessional as to break up, but you see, I know what's coming, and it's so funny I can't control myself. However, if you have patience with me I'll get it right this time ... or the next ... or the next."

We started to shoot the scene again, and the performance went perfectly. Jack reached the line and delivered it with all his customary skill, "I'm taking depreciation on the bull." The audience, perhaps prepped by the two previous blowups, greeted the gag with a thunderous laugh, followed by long applause. Then, impishly (and he was always the oldest imp alive), Jack got up and started taking mock bows and ad-libbing to the audience about himself in the third person, "See, I told you to have faith in this kid. I knew the kid could do it." The laughter eventually subsided, and from the producer's booth, via the intercom public address system, Hal Kanter's voice boomed throughout the studio, "I'm sorry, Jack but we ran out of film. The cameras were empty, so you'll have to do it again." Benny's reaction was typical. He fell to the floor and was laughing so hard he shook like the Jell-O he sold for so many years.

P.S. Of course Kanter was kidding.

P.P.S. The critics reviewed the show more than just favorably, and several of them selected the "depreciation on the bull" line for special commendation.

43
The Final Years

According to the Old Testament the length of life that man is entitled to is three score and ten. If true, then God was good to Jack Benny by giving him nearly eleven additional years. God was also good to the rest of the world by letting us enjoy Jack for all that extra time.

In America some statistical and actuarial geniuses have figured that a man's usefulness ends when he reaches his sixty-fifth birthday. Sixty-five is the arbitrary retirement age that has been established, and continues to be maintained, by most big businesses in America. That's when Social Security begins. That's also when Jack got his "second wind." He speeded up instead of slowing down, continuing to work, and to work very hard, at his job of entertaining audiences for nearly sixteen years past the required retirement limits.

During those post-sixty-five years Jack was frequently asked if he was going to retire, and his usual response was a line first coined by George Burns: "Retire? To what?" Some time ago one of Jack's close friends, Frank Sinatra, announced that he was putting himself out to pasture, which, fortunately, did not turn out to be a permanent venture. During the period of Frank's temporary retirement, in December 1971, when he was nearly seventy-eight years

434

old, Jack was doing two shows nightly, playing a booking in Las Vegas at the Sahara Hotel's Congo Room. In his act he would joke about Frank. "Sure," he quipped to his audiences, "Sinatra can retire. He has hobbies. Women . . . girls . . . young girls. . . . What would I do if I retired?"

If the entertainment industry adhered to the usual rule that a person is no longer useful once he attains the age of sixty-five, Jack never would have been seen in a regular weekly television series. He was nearly sixty-seven years old when he ceased broadcasting on alternate weeks and began to appear every week on CBS.

Weekly television is nothing like the comparative cinch that radio was. It is a time-consuming chore for a performer, and in addition to all the hours Jack spent rehearsing, he still found time for many meetings with his writers—not as much as in the old days, but still much more than most comedians allot to their writing staffs.

Jack thrived on work, and in addition to his own TV series he was a frequent guest on the shows of other stars such as Lucille Ball and Bob Hope. These appearances were made primarily not for money, but for the good of his own program. Stars of the caliber of Benny, Ball, and Hope needed the extra money and extra work like, to quote Jack's favorite flop joke, "a moose needs a hatrack." However, they do need important guest stars to appear on their own programs to maintain their ratings. Therefore, they do exchanges, which are exactly what the name implies: "You appear on my show, I'll appear on yours."

Jack once got a sizable boff on a broadcast when he explained this to his audience. He said, in effect, "Bob Hope and I have an exchange agreement. You see, he appears on my program free, and I do his laundry."

In addition to his regular programs and guest appearances, Jack appeared several weeks each year—usually during the summer, or when his TV production schedule permitted—in the huge show rooms in Las Vegas and Lake Tahoe. Personal appearances were also made in regular theaters, theaters-in-the-round, tents, fairs, and other auditoriums. Add to this several annual appearances with financially troubled philharmonic orchestras, his informal appearances on late-night talk shows like Johnny Carson's, and the dozens and dozens of benefits at which he entertained, and you have some idea of the bone-wearying schedule that Jack maintained until he was past seventy.

Frequently Jack on a single evening would play not one but two benefits. For example, in December 1971, when he was nearly seventy-eight, he traveled to New York to speak at the Arthritis Foundation affair at the Plaza Hotel honoring Rosalind Russell, and he was the man who was selected to give Miss Russell her award.

Immediately after concluding these duties, he rushed outside to a waiting limousine and was whisked to the Waldorf-Astoria Hotel where, in the Grand Ballroom, he was toastmaster at the American Jewish Congress banquet honoring his dear friend and, as he put it, "rival," famed virtuoso Isaac Stern. Stern had recently completed the off-screen violin music that was so moving and important in the film version of the musical *Fiddler on the Roof.* In one of his jokes there that evening, Jack asserted that both he and Stern originally had been candidates for the heard but not seen title role in that picture: "Both Mr. Stern and I were offered this job. When I heard they were considering him as well as me, welllllll. I thought they called both of us because they were getting *estimates* on the job—until I found out what they really wanted. They wanted *him* to play —and *me* to sit on the roof."

It's easy to realize that for this banquet Jack had to have special material quite different from the earlier jokes he had told honoring Miss Russell. Whenever Jack played an affair of this type, he always insisted on several original lines appropriate for the guests in attendance on that occasion, in addition to his usual routines. Getting these gags written, plus the task of memorizing them, must have been a mental strain—not to mention the digestive strain it must have been on his stomach when he had to partake of two, or at least part of two, different dinners on a single night.

When Jack was in his early seventies, he gave up his weekly television show, but he still did one or two hour-long NBC specials each year, and because of this he still did guest appearances on the programs of other stars.

On March 20, 1968, Jack, now seventy-four, presented a one-hour special on NBC which I wrote with Al Gordon, Hal Goldman, and Hilliard Marks. Jack's featured full-time guest stars on this hour were Lucille Ball and Johnny Carson. I was then doing double duty as script consultant and head writer of the *Here's Lucy* series, which is probably one of the reasons I was hired for this program. Jack and Lucy figured that I knew their styles as well as any writer in the business. Furthermore, the fact that two other men I had worked for, Bob Hope and Danny Thomas, were doing "cameo" roles on the special may have been an influencing factor.

I am sure that no money changed hands for these deals, except for token fees to satisfy guilds and unions. Jack repaid Lucy by doing one of her programs, and of course he repaid Johnny Carson by dropping in frequently on his talk show. In fact, Jack did a routine about this, saying (and this is quoted from memory, so it may not be exact): "Anytime I appear here, on Johnny Carson's show, he introduces me by telling his audience how much he admires me and how I'm his idol. Then he very generously pays me three hundred and twenty dollars for my appearance. Recently I wanted him as a guest on my show. Do you know what this man who idolized me charged? I had to pay him fifteen thousand dollars to get him on my program."

When he was well into his seventies, without his regular series to keep him tied down, Jack increased his nightclub engagements in Las Vegas and Lake Tahoe to eight or ten weeks a year, and his personal appearances, both for free and for fee, increased. He now did many more benefits and concert appearances, and he maintained this schedule to the very end. He also began to do something he had never done before—he endorsed products. He did a series of memorable TV commercials for Texaco gasoline where he drove into their gas stations and always bought only one gallon of gasoline. (And that was before the price of gas took such a tremendous jump upward.) Later he appeared as a salesman pushing The American-Republic Life Insurance Company, and still later he appeared as a huckster for "The Wool Industry." However, he probably wanted the extra work more than the extra money, because he was bored with inactivity—very bored.

In addition to all of this, Jack took a weekly violin lesson, and he practiced two to four hours daily. One of the last times I was with him, in 1973 or 1974, I asked him why he didn't ease up a little on his work and practice a little less. He told me that, for him, playing the violin was not work but an enjoyable interlude, much as reading is for other people. "It's one of the things I enjoy most," he said. "Hell, at my age, it's practically the only thing I can enjoy." Then he added, "So spending three or four hours daily with the violin is relaxation and fun for me." Then he paused, obviously thinking of something, and he had a faraway look on his face. From what he soon said, I realized that he was thinking of his boyhood in Waukegan. He was recalling how his father had hounded him, ineffectually, to work on his music. It was several seconds before Jack spoke. Then he pointed toward heaven and said with a wistful smile, "I can just see my father watching me from up there and saying to himself, 'Now he practices.'"

Not only did Jack's energy show little sign of diminishing as he inexorably approached eighty, but Father Time was also kind to him in other ways. The only indication as to his age was the skin on his hands which was mottled with telltale liver spots. However, if I remember correctly he had them, although probably not as many, when I first met him, and at that time he was under fifty.

Jack's seeming agelessness gave birth to many rumors—that he had had his face lifted; that he had gone to Europe for a series of expensive injections, made of ground-up tissues of unborn animals, supposedly a fountain of youth to fellow comedian Charles Chaplin and others; that he had undergone plastic surgery. To my knowledge, all were untrue.

Jack said that nature had blessed him with the type of skin that doesn't show wrinkles. For personal appearances all he needed was a little make-up which he applied himself. When he went on television they used tiny pieces of invisible elastic, applied near the rear of his countenance, to pull the facial skin a trifle tighter, and a tiny hairpiece to hide the spot where his own hair was too thin. "And," added Jack when we discussed this once, "on TV shows I make sure that I have the best make-up man available. The camera can be very revealing and cruel, especially in close-ups."

To emphasize the last point, Jack told me the famous story about actress Marlene Dietrich. Long ago, after several years of absence from films, Miss Dietrich agreed to appear in a picture if she could have the same cameraman who had photographed her so beautifully in her last picture. They granted her this wish. However, when she viewed the first day's rushes she was unpleasantly surprised to see that, despite the judicious use of lights and silk screens, she didn't look as great as she had hoped she would. She began to berate the cameraman, asking in an annoyed tone, "How do you explain the fact that I don't look as well in these pictures as I did in the ones you took seven years ago?" And the cameraman, possibly the most tactful technician in the business, answered, "Well, you've got to understand that it's unavoidable. After all, the camera is seven years older."

How did Jack maintain his rigorous schedule as he passed his seventy-eighth birthday and was thirty-nine for the second time? He did nothing special, but just continued to lead the same type of life that he had always led. Never in his life did Jack dissipate. For all intents and purposes he gave up smoking at fifty, and even before that his only concession to the "filthy weed" was an occasional cigar. He may have carried them frequently, but he rarely lit them. They were like stage props, and they gave him confidence. As a hangover from his vaudeville days, he felt reassured when he held a violin or a cigar in his hands. Furthermore, Jack drank very little. If he had more than one drink he would frequently fall asleep in the midst of a noisy party.

Oddly enough, most of this also holds true for Bob Hope. Bob rarely drinks, and he doesn't smoke. In fact, in his early movies, when a scene called for him to smoke, Bob handled a cigarette as self-consciously as a kid taking his first secret puff. And Hope, like Benny, has a quality that I, an insomniac since my teens, envy. They both could fall asleep at any time, at any place, and under any conditions.

When I first went to work for Jack, I wasn't aware of his catnaping ability. One day he, the writers, and our secretary, Jane Tucker, were in his hotel suite at the Sherry-Netherland Hotel, and we were stuck for a line. The room became silent as all of the writers tried to think of something worthy of our new boss. Finally, one of us threw a fairly good gag, but there was no reaction from Jack. Then we nudged each other, for he was sitting in his chair sound asleep. We exchanged puzzled glances, but we kept silent for a couple of minutes.

Suddenly Jack was wide awake again, and fresher than before. The line was thrown once more, and he accepted it. When we left that afternoon I was understandably upset that our new boss had found us so boring that he had fallen asleep while we were offering him our funniest efforts. I mentioned this to our secretary, and Jane laughed and said, "Don't worry—he did that with the writers he had before you. In fact, he's been doing it all the years I've worked for him."

In his later years people would sometimes say to me, "Gee, Jack's really getting old. I was at a party with him, and suddenly I looked at him and he was sitting in a chair sound asleep." I heard this several times from friends who thought it was a sign of senility. I assured them that it wasn't, because Jack had been dropping off to sleep in noisy gatherings even when he was *really* thirty-nine.

Jack believed in the benefits of exercise, and he hardly cut down at all as the years built up. He was always an avid walker, and only a heavy rain would stop him from hiking from one to five miles daily. Weather permitting, he swam daily in the pools he had at his various houses. He also golfed a lot, but in the last few years he usually just played nine holes and not the full eighteen. Most people, when they play, have a caddy or a cart. Jack was a "C & C" man —he took *both* a caddy and cart. However, the cart was enjoyed mostly by the caddy who rode while Jack strode, not walked, around the course. The only golfing occasion on which Jack made any concessions to his age was when he played steep uphill holes. Then he used the cart.

In the final few years I saw Jack perform in person numerous times, in addition to all his television appearances. In the summer of 1972 he invited me and my wife Hilda to join him as his guests in Las Vegas where he was appearing at the Sahara Hotel. When we watched him at the dinner show there was no indication to me that he had changed vastly or even visibly in the over thirty years I had known him. Perhaps I could not be considered an impartial observer, but the loud laughs, and the audience applause that greeted his every routine, plus the standing ovation he received at the conclusion of his act, confirmed my opinion.

My wife Hilda and I stayed three days and two nights in the

gambling mecca, and we shared a couple of breakfasts and lunches with him, and spent much time basking around the pool, reminiscing and joking. Although I had many meetings with him subsequently, this was the last time we were able to enjoy so many hours of personal conversation.

Jack looked quite well—amazingly fit for a man his age. He was then halfway to his seventy-ninth birthday. He did complain that doing two shows each night was some small strain. As he pointed out, for each performance he had to be on his feet for from one hour to nearly an hour and a half. Furthermore, his dinner show usually started at about 9:15 P.M., and his late show began shortly after midnight. He said that several other stars shared his wish that their appearances in the lush Las Vegas hotels could be confined to once a night.

I told him in all honesty—although there was no doubt that I was also trying to reassure him—that the first night I had witnessed his performance at the dinner show, and that the second night I had stood in the back of the room and caught his midnight appearance, and that he hadn't shown the slightest indication of any tiring effects that his grueling work might have had on him.

He turned reflective. "I've been very lucky," he said. "From the start of my career as a comic I have had a slow delivery, with frequent pauses. This was one of my trademarks on all my programs, radio and TV. The critics always praised me for this as part of my timing. Now, the first sign that age is slowing down a performer is that he actually slows down. So I've been lucky because I always worked slowly. To the general public I still have the same timing. Maybe age *has* slowed me down, but audiences, familiar with the way I performed through the many years of broadcasting, don't notice that I'm working slow, because I always worked slow. I try to pause for shorter periods, and it comes out the same way as when I was a kid doing four and five shows a day in vaudeville houses. Once in a while if I take an unintentionally long pause in my delivery, or stall because the words have temporarily slipped my mind, the folks out front not only accept it, but laugh at it as master timing. Maybe, like rare wine, my delivery improves with age."

I said, "Maybe *you're* improving with age."

Jack answered, a bit bitterly, "Milt, after a certain point, nobody, nobody improves with age."

I tried to cheer him up by saying, "Maybe you haven't reached that point yet."

Jack laughed as he answered, "If you think I'm going to argue with *that*, you're a big *schmuck*."

Then he began reminiscing again: "Not only do I get this lucky break in my comedy performances, but the same holds true when I play the violin at all my concerts. I try to start by playing the violin the best I can, and that's pretty darn good. Later on, I get laughs from the audience for my blunders. I feel that for the audience to enjoy my musical mistakes, it's necessary that I first must prove I can play pretty good. But when I'm doing my best and some minor mishap occurs, like a hair breaking on my bow, I do what all the great violinists, Stern, Heifetz, Kreisler, Elman, Menuhin, do—I wait for a two-bar rest, and then I try to snap it off, or pull the loose hair off my bow. Every great soloist does this, and it's accepted. It's normal. When I do it, I get a scream from the audience, and dammit, I don't want them laughing then."

Jack once appeared performing a duet at a benefit performance with the great cellist Gregor Piatigorsky, and he complained about the above fact to him. Piatigorsky listened to Jack's lament, thought it over for a few seconds, and then said, "Jack, don't you realize that you are in a most enviable position? We do not dare make one mistake, but you, you can make hundreds of mistakes." Then the famed cellist smiled and added, "And you'd better go on making them."

Jack accepted this comment with a smile, but also with mixed emotions, for in his praiseworthy public life, he treasured two compliments. Jascha Heifetz once told him that his tone was excellent, and Isaac Stern, in a sincere tribute, told him that he had a brilliant technique.

Jack then told me of a conversation he had had with Stern when he said, "Isaac, if, through some miracle, God appeared before me right this minute and said, 'Jack, starting tomorrow I'm going to make you the world's greatest violinist, but you'll never tell jokes anymore or get another laugh,' I tell you, I'd make the deal immediately." Stern replied: "Sure, now you'd accept it, but ten or twenty years ago you wouldn't. And you'd be silly to do it, because right now you're appearing with the same symphony orchestras that would accompany you if you were the world's greatest violinist— only people are paying a hundred dollars to hear you instead of ten or twenty-five dollars—and you do play well for an amateur—and you're doing more for music than any person in history."

Shortly after the time that my wife Hilda and I were his guests at the Sahara Hotel, Jack was scheduled to appear at a hundred dollar-a-plate dinner given by ANTA in honor of Alfred Lunt and Lynn Fontanne. Jack asked me to write a few funny lines for him. Naturally I did, and I'm proud to report that my contributions played quite well.

However, Jack's biggest laugh at that dinner came when he took the above conversation with Isaac Stern and used it as the basis of a short routine, although with some slight changes. He said: "Folks, I'd rather be a great musician than anything. If, through some miracle, God appeared before me this very morning and said, 'Jack'—*he knows everybody*—'starting tomorrow I'm going to make you the world's greatest violinist,' etc., etc." The addition of those three words, "he knows everybody," an ad-lib, brought the house down. And I laughed harder than anyone, because it was only a short time ago that he had told me the story straight.

Afterward I congratulated Jack on his especially fine performance, and I mentioned how much I had enjoyed him and his ability to think of those three words at that time under the circumstances. He told me that he actually had used the line a couple of times before but would only throw it in when he thought the time propitious. I asked him why he hadn't used the line when he told me the story in Vegas. He smiled and said, "Milt, if you think I'm going to waste a great gag like that on just you, you're crazy."

Another affair at which Benny scintillated in an unusual way was the testimonial dinner honoring Milton Berle on Saturday, October 10, 1973. The banquet was given to Uncle Miltie to celebrate his sixtieth anniversary in show business and his sixty-fifty birthday, and never have I seen a dais so stacked with celebrities. In fact, it was a double dais, with one slightly raised table behind the other. The toastmaster was Frank Sinatra, and the speakers included Lucille Ball, Bob Hope (via film), Walter Matthau, Jan Murray, Buddy Hackett, Don Rickles, Jack Carter, Sammy Davis, Jr., Bishop Fulton J. Sheen, Robert Sarnoff of RCA, Carroll O'Connor, Pearl Bailey, Gary Morton, Redd Foxx, Jack Benny, and many others. The second dais was also loaded with various celebrities, but they merely took bows and didn't speak. Despite the fact that it was for a mixed audience and Bishop Sheen was present, some of the speakers, Redd Foxx in particular, told jokes more suitable for stag parties.

A week prior to this roast, I phoned Jack and asked if he needed some lines. Jack told me what he was going to do, a simple device that needed no assistance from any writer.

The evening was a long one—very long. Testimonials of this type usually run three hours—half the time for cocktails and dinner, and the remaining ninety minutes for entertainment. This night wore on and on and on, with the entertainment part taking slightly over three hours. And, as usual, Jack was called upon very late in the proceedings. They had bombarded Berle with insults ranging from rough to scatological.

When it was Jack's turn, he apologized for not having prepared any special material. He said, however, that he would like to tell them about the personal handwritten invitation that Sinatra, the

M.C., had sent to him. He took this note out of his pocket and then read it—slightly changed, I'm sure—to the largest laughs of the night.

"Dear Jack, on Saturday night, October 13th, at the Beverly Hilton Hotel, the Friars Club would like to pay tribute to one of the greatest comedians in showbusiness." Jack merely stared at Berle and the audience broke up. Jack continued: "When I read that my blood tingled and I got a lump in my throat—for a second I thought he meant me." Another laugh. Jack read a few more sentences from Sinatra's invitation, some with appropriate comments, some with mere inflections and the crowd roared. Jack got the biggest laughs of the night when he read "The evening promises to be a most memorable event." Jack's baby blues registered amazement and in conversational tones he explained to the audience: "Now my definition of a memorable event certainly differs from Sinatra's. When Henry Kissinger was sworn in as Secretary of State, that was a memorable event. . . . When Alexander Graham Bell said, 'Can you hear me, Jack?' . . . that was a memorable event. . . . I guarantee that somewhere upstairs in a room in this hotel is a grey-haired old man and a grey-haired old lady celebrating what they know is really a memorable event." Each of these three lines was loudly appreciated by the audience despite the fact that the affair was now nearly two hours longer than scheduled.

Jack continued reading and commenting. In his letter Sinatra had written that he himself would be honorary chairman for the affair. Jack dwelt on this and reminded the group that the previous year he was the honorary chairman at a dinner tendered to Sinatra. Then he added, "Let me tell you what an honorary chairman is. . . . An honorary chairman is like the fellow at a concert who turns the pages for Arthur Rubinstein. You have to be there, but really, nobody gives a damn."

Although the actual invitation consisted of a few short paragraphs Jack read it sentence by sentence stopping to stare at the audience, Sinatra, or Berle, and sometimes all three and the reactions on simple straight lines rewarded him with more laughs than most of the major comics received. Outside of his observations on the invitation's wording, Jack told no jokes, per se. But Jack was by far the hit of the evening and received a standing ovation from the audience, and the other famed roasters, who all scored well on the laugh meter that night. However their repartee ripped the guest of honor apart with caustic and clever insults mainly on the blue side. They assaulted Berle's ancestry, anatomy, sexual ability and inability and several other subjects usually read about in the writings of Sigmund Freud or Masters and Johnson. The evening's proceedings were taped for a television special and cutting that mass of material, nearly four hours, to the ninety minutes required for this television special was a Herculean task. Many of the biggest stars in the industry were excised completely because their routines were far too blue or not funny enough. Practically all who appeared had at least half of their material deleted because of taste or time limitations. Several were cut down to token bows. Jack's remarks remained almost intact. Some small deletions were made, not because of taste or lack of humor, but because they were considered dispensable since they were too inside, or show biz, for the general public.

Although he turned down my offer of assistance in preparing his routine for the Berle "roast," I wrote for Jack on several occasions during the latter part of 1973 and early 1974. Most of the time this consisted of giving him a few lines for a benefit appearance. Also, whenever he made a personal appearance anywhere, if anything topical happened and I thought of a suitable gag about it, I'd call and tell him.

The last time I worked for Jack for a fee was in September 1973. He was scheduled to open at the new Superstar Theater in Las Vegas. This showplace didn't intend to serve dinner and drinks, but just to feature the biggest name stars available, in the style of a Broadway theater, and do only one show nightly. Jack was to be the opening attraction, together with Pearl Bailey, and he wanted a few topical quips to augment his many routines.

I wrote a substantial amount of material, and one line he particularly liked for his opening monologue. He would say, "Frankly, I don't know whether I approve of them calling this 'The Superstar Theater.' It sounds so egotistical. . . . After all, how many superstars are there in show business? There's Frank Sinatra . . . Barbra Streisand . . . and Sammy Davis, Jr. . . . That makes four of us."

Jack called me and told me that while he liked much of the material I had given him, he would probably use very little of it because he felt too tired to try to memorize new routines. This was the first indication I had that Jack was waning. Then again, perhaps he wasn't. It might have been that he really didn't care for most of my submissions and was letting me down easy.

Early in 1974, Jack signed for a co-starring role in the movie version of Neil Simon's Broadway comedy hit, *The Sunshine Boys.* This play's plot told of two old-time comics who had starred in vaudeville as a team for years until they eventually had a falling out. Now both of them are retired, and they haven't seen or spoken to each other for many years. Then a television producer decides that he wants to use them on a TV special, and the play revolves around the reactions of these two former partners, who are now enemies, to the proposed reunion.

Jack Albertson (of television's *Chico and the Man*) and Sam Levene starred in the Broadway presentation. For the movie the original choices were Jack Benny and Red Skelton. Eventually Skelton stepped out and he was replaced by Walter Matthau. The producers hesitantly asked Benny if he would mind taking a screen test, and he had no objections. He made the test in September 1974.

In the picture Jack was to portray an eighty-year-old man. For the screen test he was supposed to perform a few small bits of business, do a few lines of dialogue, and then walk across a room. The test went well, except that the director assigned to film the test told Jack that his walk was much too youthful. "Remember," he added, "you're supposed to walk like you're eighty years old." Jack answered, "But that's the way I walk, and I *am* eighty years old."

They tried it again, with the director telling Jack to slow down a bit. Jack did so, but he still seemed too peppy. The director still wasn't satisfied and said, "Watch me, I'll show you." Jack watched the director; then he imitated him and everyone was satisfied. To pass his screen test, Jack had to have someone less than half his age show him how to walk like an eighty-year-old man.

Having passed his screen test, Jack now had some time to fill in prior to making the picture. He made many personal appearances, and one of them, in July, took him to Dallas. He never did this show because shortly before he went on, sitting in his dressing room, he felt a numbness in his arms, and at a doctor's suggestion he called off his performance and was hospitalized.

Television, radio, and newspapers told the world that Jack Benny had suffered a heart attack. He had not. He was flown back to Los Angeles, and after a few days of treatment for a digestive disorder in a local hospital, he was released.

Upon emerging from the hospital he had a laugh-filled interview with reporters from all the media. I talked to him by phone a few days later and he said, "I feel fine. At my age if I get a pain in my tummy, the newspapers make big headlines out of it." His only fear was that the adverse publicity on his health might imperil his appearing in *The Sunshine Boys.* He told me that he even momentarily contemplated suing some of the papers and TV newscasts that had really exaggerated the story, but he had never done this before, and besides it might give added publicity to the story, so he dropped it. He then disproved the "heart attack" story by making more personal appearances, notably a big outdoor benefit affair held at Universal Studio's huge amphitheater, starring Frank Sinatra.

During Jack's illness I sent him a humorous note, and after his recovery I phoned him and we chatted for a few minutes. We exchanged pleasantries and he inquired as to the health of my wife and sons. I told him that all was well, which was a white lie, but I saw no point in burdening him with my troubles.

In the spring of 1974, my older son, Alan Roy, was stricken with a mysterious malady. He was hospitalized for ten days, treated for viral pneumonia, and then released as cured. Two days later an ambulance rushed him to the USC Hospital's "Contagious Unit," where a dozen different doctors diagnosed a dozen different diseases, the least serious of which were encephalitis and a less virulent ailment optimistically described as "aseptic meningitis."

For three weeks he suffered from symptoms which were as unpleasant as they were mystifying. He was subjected to a battery of medical tests, none of which seemed to prove anything conclusively. Then he was discharged as cured.

During the second week in August, he had a relapse requiring a five-day stay at UCLA Medical Center. Eventually he recovered, but from what, we weren't sure. For obvious reasons, when I called Jack about his health, I made no mention of Alan's puzzling malady.

Late one autumn afternoon in 1974, my telephone rang. It was Jack Benny—a very upset Jack Benny. He had heard from a mutual friend that Alan had been terribly ill, and since he had known my son practically since his birth, and had attended his bar mitzvah, he was angry at me for not having even mentioned his illness.

I apologized to Jack, saying that it was an oversight, which it wasn't. I told him that Alan was currently healthy, and he made me reassure him that I was telling the truth. Then he said, "Gee, I'm so glad to hear some good news for a change. Lately all I seem to do is hear stories about friends in hospitals, and I usually attend two or three funerals a month. And after the funerals, the gang always goes to Hillcrest where they have a drink and reminisce about the deceased.

"What gets me, Milt," he said, "is they'll talk about the dear departed and someone will always say, 'Well, he lived a good long life. He was seventy-two. Never sick a day in his life.'" He paused and then, laughing, added, "I keep listening to them and I'm thinking, 'I'm eighty years old, and I've never really been sick.' Maybe I should limp a little to get sympathy."

I didn't know it at the moment, but that was the last time I was to talk to Jack Benny.

In late October, Jack made what was to be his last television appearance on a Dean Martin "roast" with Lucille Ball as the "roastee," or "Woman of the Hour." This program was not aired until February 7, 1975, after Jack was gone. Martin made an announcement at the start of the program eulogizing Jack and explaining that it was his last appearance.

446

I talked with two men who worked with Jack on the Dean Martin show, writer Harry Crane and one of the men on the production staff, Buddy Arnold. Both of these men had worked with Jack before. Both said that he seemed fine during the filming of the show and gave no indication that his performance on this program would be Jack's "Final Farewell Appearance."

In early December 1974, Jack began to work on his own annual one-hour TV special for NBC. This program was scheduled to be broadcast on January 23, 1975. It was never finished.

Hugh Wedlock, Jr., one of the writers on this special, occupied a special spot in Jack's affections. He had worked for him at various times since 1936, and Jack loved him as a talent and companion. Although Hughie wasn't on staff or salary for any extended period, Jack used his services any time an emergency arose. Wedlock worked with Jack more than any other writer during the final few weeks, and I am indebted to him for the following material.

"I don't keep a diary," said Wedlock, "so my dates may be off slightly, but the last time I did some writing on the script for the special with Jack was probably a week or ten days before he passed away. There seemed to be no definite indications that he was nearing the end. In retrospect, if I start adding little things together, they all may have been symptoms of something, but I had seen the same things happen numerous times over the years.

"He seemed vague, tired, and occasionally he had difficulty in remembering things. But he did not seem sick—no sicker than all those occasions we held script conferences in his bedroom when he had a cold or felt tired.

"The last day I worked with him Jack said, 'Hughie, you would have had a helluva laugh if you had walked into my bedroom early this morning. I woke up at about four A.M. because I had to go to the can. When I came back, just as I reached the bed, my legs wouldn't hold me and I dropped to my knees. My head came to rest on my mattress and I fell asleep and slept that way for three hours.'"

Wedlock thought it was a little frightening and asked, "What's so funny that I should laugh at that?"

Jack began to chuckle as he explained, "I must have looked like the oldest kid in the world saying his prayers."

Then they settled down to work, but Jack seemed tired. He couldn't concentrate. He would like an idea first, then cool off on it, then try it again. Finally he suggested that they temporarily quit working and that Wedlock should phone him daily, and when Jack felt like it they would get together and resume writing the special.

Wedlock said that the incident of collapsing in front of the bed should have been enough evidence that something was wrong, but

Jack treated the whole thing as funny, so Hugh didn't pay too much attention to it until afterward—with hindsight.

As per Jack's instructions, Hughie called him every day to set a date for the resumption of their work. His phone calls were not to the office, but to the Benny home, and were always answered by a maid. Each time Wedlock said that he wanted to talk to Jack, who had suggested he call him, and each time he was told to hold on. Then a minute or so later the maid would inform Wedlock that Jack was sleeping or resting and couldn't be disturbed.

Shortly before Christmas Wedlock received a letter containing a sizable check from Jack as a Christmas bonus. He immediately phoned to express his thanks, but was again informed that Jack was resting or sleeping. He called every day, including Christmas, but always with the same result.

Meanwhile there were constant rumors around town that Jack was ill, but no indications of exactly what ailed him. I had heard these rumors, and on Christmas Day I wrote him a short note inspired by a wonderful nostalgic newspaper article on him and George Burns written by Bob Thomas which appeared in the *Los Angeles Times* on Christmas Day. In my note I expressed the hope that the stories of his illness were greatly exaggerated, mentioned how much I enjoyed reading the article on him and George, and extended best wishes for the holidays and the coming new year. I mailed it on the morning of December 26. It probably arrived on the 27th or 28th, a day or two after he was gone.

Hugh Wedlock had to go to Beverly Hills for a meeting on another assignment on December 26. He finished this late in the afternoon, and as he started to drive to his home in the Valley, he decided he was so close to Jack's residence that he might as well drop in on him and thank him for the generous gift.

The Benny estate, in Holmby Hills, has a long driveway up an incline, leading to a large parking area at the rear of the house. As Hughie drove up, he could see that the place seemed jammed with cars. He thought that perhaps the Bennys were giving a post-Christmas party, but he figured that he knew them well enough to drop in, uninvited, for a friendly drink, and to personally express his best wishes and gratitude for the check. He rang the bell and was admitted by a maid who ushered him into the large, luxurious living room.

Wedlock said that he immediately sensed something was wrong because he saw a large gathering of top stars, and their expressions indicated no festive occasion. He remembered seeing Bob Hope, Frank Sinatra, Gregory Peck, Danny Kaye, Walter Matthau, Billy Wilder, Jack Lemmon, and several others, many of them with their wives.

Wedlock spotted Ned Miller, Jack's combination companion and personal helper. He approached Ned and asked what was happening. Tearfully Miller told him that the doctors had said that Jack wouldn't last a day—possibly not the night.

Stunned, Wedlock left. He never got to thank Jack for his Christmas gift. However, this was not the final check that Hughie got.

Jack had left instructions that all the writers who worked on the scheduled, but never broadcast, special be paid their full fees, and several days after Jack Benny was laid to rest, Wedlock received a check for his services.

I asked Hugh if he could remember the very last joke Jack had okayed for his never-finished program. Wedlock told me he not only remembered it, but he used it as the ending of an obituary he wrote for The Writers Guild Newsletter.

Jack had planned to say: "I'm going to make a movie, *The Sunshine Boys,* with Walter Matthau next month. This will be my first picture in twenty-eight years. If it is well received, I may do another one in twenty-eight years. That way the pressure won't be on me, and I'll be able to be around forever."

You will be, Jack.

44
Epilogue

At the conclusion of Jack Benny's funeral, Rabbi Magnin announced that there would be a *Mourners' Kaddish* said at the Wilshire Temple on the Friday night Sabbath services, January 3, 1975, and Saturday morning, January 4, in memory of Jack.

The *Mourners' Kaddish* is recited by the bereaved at the death of a loved one and on the anniversary of that death, yet it contains no reference to death. It is a reaffirmation of the faith of our fathers that God is just even though we do not comprehend His ways.

I went to Wilshire Temple that first sad Saturday of 1975 to pay my last respects to Benjamin Kubelsky, the man, and Jack Benny, the comedian. As I recited the Hebrew words of this ancient invocation I remembered my Orthodox upbringing, which was the same as Jack's. In the Orthodox branch of Judaism, it is customary for the *Kaddish* to be said for the dead by the direct male descendant—the sons for the parents.

I wasn't related to Jack by blood, but I will always be bound to him by a stronger bond—that of love. Because of this I will say the *Kaddish* and light the candle for him at each *Yahrtzeit,* the anniversary of his passing. Eventually my sons will say the *Kaddish* for my wife and me, just as I said it for my parents, and my father said it for his parents, and as our ancestors have been doing for the generations stretching back over the centuries. And from now on this all-embracing prayer will include Jack through myself, my sons, and their sons for generations yet to come.

In the Prologue to this book I said that I always felt Jack was immortal. The laughs he left behind will keep his physical memory alive by means of his frequently aired radio recordings, filmed television shows, and motion pictures. The *Kaddish* will bestow upon him the immortality that everyone receives if he is remembered. And Jack Benny will always be remembered.

*"Yis-gad-dal v'yis-kad-dash sh'may rab-bo."**

---

*"Magnified and sanctified be His great Name."

Eulogy of Jack Benny

by Bob Hope

It is said that a memorial service is for those who are left behind
... for those who mourn the loss of a loved one. If this is the case,
then this service is for the world, because last Thursday night the
world lost somebody it loved a lot.

When Benny Kubelsky was born, who in their wildest dreams
would imagine that eighty years later at the event of his passing
every television program, every radio show would stop ... and that
every magazine and newspaper would headline it on their front
pages? The millions of people who had never met him ... who had
only seen him or heard him ... would feel the pain of a very personal loss.

The void that is left with us at Jack's passing is quickly filled with
the happy memories that we have of him. That's the way Jack
would like it to be. He wants us to remember the happiness we
shared with him rather than the sadness of losing him. Any path
that Jack Benny crossed was left with more laughter, not less.

How do you say goodbye to a man who was not just a good friend,
but a national treasure? It's hard to say that no man is indispensable. But it's true just the same that some are *irreplaceable.* No one
has come along to replace Jolson, or Bogart, or Gable, or Will Rogers, or Chevalier. I think it's a safe bet that no one will ever replace

Jack Benny. Jack had that rare magic—that indefinable something called genius. Picasso had it. Gershwin had it. And Jack was blessed with it. He didn't just stand on a stage . . . he owned it.

For a man who was the undisputed master of comedy timing, you'd have to say that this was the only time when Jack Benny's timing was all wrong. He left us much too soon.

He was stingy to the end. He only gave us eighty years, and it wasn't enough.

And it's an amusing footnote that the pennypinching cheapskate we all knew and loved was portrayed by a man who gave so much of himself to all of us. Though the idol of millions, he remained modest. Though the homes of the great were open to him, he remained a simple man. Though blessed with a sharp wit, he never used it to injure or belittle.

Admired by presidents and royalty, he never lost the humble, down-to-earth quality of Benny Kubelsky from Waukegan. Kings and porters, they were all the same to Jack. He gave the same smile to everybody. He was getting ready to do a picture called *The Sunshine Boys*. But then Jack was always getting ready to do something, whether a concert, a television show, or a benefit, and besides he always was a Sunshine Boy. He brought more sunshine to this world than Easter morning.

Jack Benny long ago ceased to be merely a personality and became an institution. If there's a Mount Rushmore for humanitarians, *that* first stone face might easily resemble him. And if stone could talk it would say . . . "Well!"

Jack was one of the richest men I know. He was happy with who he was. He was happy with what he was. He was happy with where he was. Few are as rich as that.

Jack Benny, a gentle man, crossed all barriers, all boundaries, all countries, all races, all creeds. I'll never forget in 1958 when I made my first trip to Moscow and it was announced in the papers that America's leading comedian was visiting. That night I went to Ambassador Thompson's home and Mrs. Thompson met me at the door and said, "How wonderful that you could come. Did you bring your violin?"

His first love was the violin . . . which proves once again, as Jack used to say, you always hurt the one you love. And yet, with that violin, Jack raised more money and benefited more worthwhile causes and charities than a dozen violin virtuosos. His technique wasn't much, but God sure loved his tone.

It is a cliché to say that in times of darkness, Jack Benny brought light with his gift of laughter, making us forget our troubles. For Jack was more than an *escape* from life. He *was* life—a life that enriched his profession, his friends, his millions of fans, his family, his country.

Perhaps what made Jack Benny such a great laugh-maker was that he himself loved to *laugh.* He was the greatest audience a comedian could ever want ... and all of us would play jokes on him just to break him up and hear him laugh. I know it might sound corny, but there will be times from now on when the lightning will crackle with a special kind of sound, or thunder will peal with a special roar, and I'll think to myself that Cantor or Fields or Fred Allen must have just told Jack a joke.

Jack had *another* quality that's become as rare as nickel candy bars ... *taste.* When Jack was on the tube, you didn't have to chase the kids out of the room. And he was a perfectionist, a meticulous craftsman. His radio show was classic, a masterpiece of ensemble playing.

I think: How many generations grew up to the sound of Jack Benny? To the names of Mary Livingstone, Don Wilson, Dennis Day, Rochester, Phil Harris, Anaheim, Azusa, Cucamonga? For over forty years, first on radio, then on television, Jack was a pioneer, ever extending the frontiers of humor. He was one of the first, if not the first, to have great film stars on his show, playing themselves and getting big laughs. The Ronald Colmans, the Jimmy Stewarts, the Greg Pecks—they went on for Jack because they trusted him and his superb sense of what was exactly right.

Jack knew that the best laughs were the ones you worked the hardest for. He and Mary felt the same way about friends. They both cultivated lasting friendships because they were friends in return. This is the kind of love that surrounds Mary now, and will surround her as long as people remember Jack Benny and Mary Livingstone. That is the best definition of eternity that I know of.

When a man can leave as much of himself as Jack left us, then he can never be truly gone. He has to be immortal.

In his book *You Can't Go Home Again* Thomas Wolfe might have written these words about any of us:

If a man has talent and cannot use it
He has failed.
If a man has a talent and uses only half of it
He has partly failed.
If he has a talent and learns somehow to use the whole of it
He had gloriously succeeded
And won a satisfaction and a triumph
Few men ever know.

Jack had a great talent ... and he learned somehow to use the whole of it. In his beautiful, full lifetime, Jack succeeded . . . gloriously. Jack found a great joy in the joy he brought to others. I cannot say it better than these words:

His life was gentle
And the elements so mixed in him
That nature might stand up and say to all the world:
This was a man!

God keep him. Enjoy him. We did for eighty years.

Appendix A: Filmography

List of Movies in Which Jack Benny Appeared

TITLE	YEAR
Hollywood Review of 1929	1929
Medicine Man	1930
Chasing Rainbows	1930
Transatlantic Merry-Go-Round	1934
It's in the Air	1935
Broadway Melody of 1936	1935
College Holiday	1936
Big Broadcast of 1937	1936
Artists and Models	1937
Artists and Models Abroad	1938
Man About Town	1938
Buck Benny Rides Again	1940
Love Thy Neighbor	1940
Charley's Aunt	1940
To Be Or Not To Be	1942
George Washington Slept Here	1942
The Meanest Man in the World	1943
Hollywood Canteen	1944
The Horn Blows at Midnight	1945

It's in the Bag.. 1945
Guide for the Married Man 1967

Most of the early pictures were musicals where Jack appeared with numerous other stars. *Buck Benny Rides Again* was based on his radio show, and in addition to Jack it starred regular members of his radio cast. The last two pictures he made, *It's in the Bag* and *Guide for the Married Man,* had him featured in so-called "cameo" roles. (Jack also had a tiny walk-on part in Stanley Kramer's *It's a Mad, Mad, Mad, Mad World.*)

Of all the movies he made, Jack only liked a few: *Charley's Aunt, George Washington Slept Here,* and *The Meanest Man in the World.* He felt these were fair features. He was only proud of one movie, and justly so. That movie was *To Be Or Not To Be,* co-starring Carole Lombard in her last appearance, and directed by Ernst Lubitsch.

Hollywood Review of 1929

CAST

Jack Benny	Oliver Hardy
Conrad Nagel	Anita Page
John Gilbert	Nils Asther
Norma Shearer	Marion Davies
Joan Crawford	Buster Keaton
Bessie Love	Marie Dressler
Lionel Barrymore	Charles King
Cliff Edwards	Polly Moran
Stan Laurel	

Directed by Charles Reisner
Dances staged by Sammy Lee
Music and Lyrics by N. H. Brown, Arthur Freed, Gus Edwards
Cameramen: John Arnold, I. G. Ries, Maximilian Fabian
Edited by William Gray
An MGM Release

STORY: A variety "all talking" picture with Jack Benny acting as M.C. and introducing the roster of MGM stars, most of whom did specialties, dances, songs, or comedy routines.

Medicine Man

CAST

Jack Benny   Betty Bronson

Directed by Scott Pembroke, from the play by Elliot Lester. Adapted by Eva Unsell and Max Dupont and Art Reeves Photographers.

A Tiffany Production and Release (1930)
(All Dialogue)

STORY: Benny plays a traveling medicine man. As he goes from town to town he has a "love them and leave them" attitude toward women until he hits one town and falls in love with the downtrodden, father-beaten daughter of a tough grocery store proprietor. After a one-night courtship he falls for the sweet little daughter and marries her.

Chasing Rainbows

CAST

Bessie Love   Gwen Lee
Charles King   Nita Martan
Jack Benny   Eddie Phillips
George K. Arthur   Marie Dressler
Polly Moran

Directed by Charles F. Reisner
Cameraman: Ira Morgan
Author: Bess Meredyth
Scenarist: Wells Root
Dialogue: Charles F. Reisner, Robert Hopkins, Kenyon Nicholson
Editor: George Hively
Recording Engineer: Douglas Shearer
Distributor: MGM 1930

Transatlantic Merry-Go-Round

Directed by Benjamin Stoloff
Story by Leon Gordon
Additional Dialogue and Scenes by Joseph M. March
Comedy Dialogue by Harry W. Conn*
Cameraman: Ted Tetzlaff
Songs by Dick Whiting and Sidney Clare
Numbers staged by Sammy Lee and Larry Ceballos
Musical Direction by Al Newman
A United Artists Release of Reliance—Edward Small Productions (1934)

CAST

Gene Raymond   Sid Silvers
Jack Benny   Sidney Blackmer
Nancy Carroll   Ralph Morgan
Sydney Howard   Shirley Grey
Mitzi Green   Sam Hardy

*Conn was Jack Benny's first regular radio writer.

William Boyd
Robert Elliot
Frank Parker*
Carlyle Moore
Jean Sargent

Boswell Sisters
Rex Weber
Jimmy Grier Orchestra
and other specialty people

STORY: Jack Benny is the M.C. handling a transatlantic luxury liner's entertainment and acting as Nancy Carroll's "big brother" as he guides her and advises her on romances despite his unrequited love for her. As part of the shipboard show Jack presents a take-off on "Grand Hotel," titled "Grind Hotel," which he first presented on his radio broadcast.

It's in the Air

CAST

Jack Benny—Calvin
Ted Healy—Clip
Una Merkel—Alice

Nat Pendleton—Henry Potke
Mary Carlisle—Grace
Grant Mitchell—W. R. Gridley

An MGM Release (1935)

STORY: Jack Benny is a sure-thing gambler, so his wife leaves him until he goes straight.

Broadway Melody of 1936

CAST

Jack Benny—Bert Keeler
Robert Taylor—George Brown
Una Merkel—Kitty Corbett
Eleanor Powell—Iren-Mele Arlette

June Knight—Lillian
Vilma Ebsen—Sally
Buddy Ebsen—Buddy Burke
Sid Silvers— Snoop Blue

Also Frances Langford, Harry Stockwell, Nick Long, Jr., and Robert Wildhack

Directed by Roy Del Ruth
Story by Moss Hart
Produced by John W. Considine, Jr.
An MGM Release

STORY: Jack Benny and Sid Silvers portray a Broadway columnist and his stooge who incur Robert Taylor's wrath by printing gossip items about Taylor and his Broadway show.

---

 * Frank Parker was then the tenor on Benny's radio shows, preceding Kenny Baker and Dennis Day.

College Holiday

Jack Benny—J. Davis Brewster	Martha Raye—Daisy
George Burns—George Hyman	Marsha Hunt—Sylvia Smith
Gracie Allen—Calliope Dove	Leif Erikson—Dick Winters
Mary Boland—Carole Gaye	Eleanore Whitney—Eleanor Wayne

Director: Frank Tuttle
Producer: Harlan Thompson
Executive Producer: Frank Tuttle
First Assistant Director: Joseph Lefert
Based on Original Story by Harlan Thompson
Screen Play: P. McEvoy, Harlan Ware, Henry Meyers, and Jay Corvey
Story Treatment: Frederick Hazlitt Brennan, Walter McLeon, and Bobby Vernon
A Paramount Picture (1936)

STORY: Musical with college background

Big Broadcast of 1937

CAST

Jack Benny—Jack Carson (sic)
George Burns and Gracie Allen—Mr. and Mrs. Plott
Bob Burns—Bob Block
Martha Raye—Patsy
Shirley Ross—Gwen Holmes
Raymond Milland—Bob Miller
Frank Forest—Frank Rossman
Benny Fields—Benny Fields
Sam Hearn—Shlepperman
Stan Kavanaugh—Kavvy
Benny Goodman and his Orchestra
Specialties—Larry Adler
Leopold Stokowski and his Symphony Orchestra
Elinor Whitney

Director: Mitchell Leisen
Producer: Lewis E. Gensler
Executive Producer: William Le Baron
Photographed by Theodore Sparkuhl A.S.C.
1st Assistant Director: Edgar Anderson
Unpublished Story by Edwin Gelsey, Arthur Kober, and Barry Trivers
Screenplay by Walter DeLeon and Frances Martin
Additional Dialogue by Duke Atteberry, Sam Perrin, and Arthur Phillips

A Paramount Picture

STORY: Variety musical comedy about the radio industry.

Artists and Models

CAST

Jack Benny—Mac Brester   Ben Blue—Jupiter Pluvius
Ida Lupino—Paula   Judy Canova—Toots
Richard Arlen—Alan Townsend   "The Yacht Club Boys"
Gail Patrick—Cynthia   Hedda Hopper—Mrs. Townsend
Specialties—Martha Raye, Andre Kostelanetz and his Orchestra, Louis Armstrong

Directed by Raoul Walsh
Producer: Lewis E. Gensler
Executive Producer: William LeBaron
Unpublished Story by Sig Herzig and Gene Thackrey
Adaptation by Eve Greene and Harlan Ware
Screenplay by Walter DeLeon and Francis Marion
Additional Dialogue by Russell Crouse, Howard Lindsay, William Morrow and Ed Beloin
Photographed by Victor Milner, A.S.C
A Paramount Picture (1937)

STORY: Atop the dizzy heights of a New York skyscraper is the dizzier advertising agency presided over by Jack Benny, chairman of the committee staging the Artists and Models' Ball.

Artists and Models Abroad

CAST

Jack Benny—Buck Boswell   Charley Grapewin—James Harper
Joan Bennett—Patricia Harper   Joyce Compton—Chickie
Mary Boland—Mrs. Isabel Channing   Yacht Club Boys

Director: Mitchell Leisen
Producer: Arthur Hornblow, Jr.
Screenplay: Howard Lindsay, Russell Crouse, and Ken Englund
Original Story: Howard Lindsay and Russell Crouse
Based on an idea by J. P. McEvoy
Photographer: Ted Tetzlaff
Musical numbers staged by LeRoy Prinz
Music and lyrics by Ralph Rainger and Leo Robin
"You're Broke, You Dope" by the Yacht Club Boys

A Paramount Picture (1938)

STORY: Jack Benny and his troupe of entertainers are stranded in Paris but a wealthy American girl settles their problems.

Man About Town

CAST

Jack Benny	Monty Wooley
Dorothy Lamour	Isabel Jeans
Edward Arnold	Eddie (Rochester) Anderson
Binnie Barnes	Merriel Abbott Dancers
Matty Malneck's Orchestra and Pina Troupe	

Director: Mark Sandrich
Assistant: Holly Morse
Photography: Ted Tetzlaff
Producer: Arthur Hornblow, Jr.
Musical Director: Victor Young
Musical Advisor: Troy Sanders
Screenplay by Morrie Ryskind, based on a story by Morrie Ryskind, Allan Scott and Z. Myers
Musical numbers staged by LeRoy Prinz
Songs by Matty Malneck, Frank Loesser, and Frederick Hollander
Costumes: Edith Head
Art Direction: Hans Drier and Robert Usher
Edited by LeRoy Stone
A Paramount Picture (1939)

Buck Benny Rides Again

CAST

Jack Benny—Jack Benny	Phil—Phil Harris
Joan Cameron—Ellen Drew	Dennis—Dennis Day
Rochester—Eddie Anderson	Virginia—Virginia Dale
Andy—Andy Devine	and Lillian Corbett and Theresa Harris

Director: Mark Sandrich
Director of Photography: Charles Lang, A.S.C.
Screenplay by William Morrow and Ed Beloin, based on an adaptation by Z. Myers of a story by Arthur Stringer
Other Writers: Eddie Moran and Sam Hellman
Additional Dialogue: Everett Freeman and Sid Herzig
Songs and Lyrics by Frank Loesser

Music by Jimmy McHugh
Merriel Abbott Dancers
Songs:
"Say It"—Sung by Ellen Drew, Lillian Corbett, Virginia Dale
"My, My"—Sung by Rochester and Theresa Harris
"My Kind o' Country—Sung by Dennis Day
Recitation—Jack Benny
A Paramount Picture (1940)

STORY: "Buck Benny Rides Again" is a saga of a city boy who goes West to prove to his lady love that he is a virile, two-fisted, rootin'-tootin' son of the wide open spaces. He does it against real bad men, in as hectic a Western drama as ever Hollywood produced.

Press Preview at the Westwood Village Theatre, April 10, 1940

Love Thy Neighbor

CAST

Fred Allen

Jack Benny

Mary Martin

Verree Teasdale

Theresa Harris

Virginia Dale

Rochester

Merry Macs

Director: Mark Sandrich
Director of Photography: Ted Tetzlaff, A.S.C.
Original Screenplay by William Morrow, Ed Beloin, Ernest Pagano, and Zion Myers
Edited by LeRoy Stone
Song Lyrics by Johnny Burke
Music by Jimmy Van Heusen
Musical Director: Victor Young
Musical Advisor: Arthur Franklin
"My Heart Belongs to Daddy"
by Cole Porter
Dance Ensembles: Merriel Abbott Dancers
Edited by LeRoy Stone
Costumes: Edith Head
Songs:
"Dearest, Dearest I"—Sung by Rochester and Theresa Harris
"Isn't That Just Like Love?"—Sung by Mary Martin, Merry Macs, and Virginia Dale
"My Heart Belongs to Daddy"—Sung by Mary Martin
A Paramount Picture (1940)

STORY: Jack Benny is a retired Southern colonel who switches from this role to that of a Broadway producer.

464

Charley's Aunt

CAST

Jack Benny—Babbs Babberly
Kay Francis—Donna Lucia
Anne Baxter—Amy Spettegue
James Ellison—Jack Chesney
Edmund Gwenn—Stephen Spettegue
Reginald Owen—Mr. Redcliffe
Laird Cregar—Sir Francis Chesney
Arleen Whelan—Kitty Verdun
Richard Haydn and Ernest Cossard—Charley and James

Director: Archie Mayo
Executive Producer: Darryl F. Zanuck
Producer: William Perlberg
Assistant Producer: Aaron Rosenberg
Photography: Peverell Morley
Art Director: Nathan Juran
Edited by: Robert Bischoff
Based on a Play by Brandon Thomas
Screen Credits: George Seaton
Twentieth Century-Fox Picture (1941)

STORY: After ten years at Oxford, Babbs Babberly (Jack Benny) is still trying to pass the three-year course there. He has a chance but accidently angers the proctor and is in danger of being thrown out of the school. The only way he can remain at Oxford is to have Charley (Richard Haydn) and James (George Seaton) lie in his behalf. They are willing to do this if he will pose as Charley's aunt to help them out.

To Be Or Not To Be

CAST

Carole Lombard—Maria Tura
Jack Benny—Joseph Tura
Robert Stack—Lt. Stanislau Sokenski
Felix Bressart—Greenberg
Lionel Atwill—Rawitch

Directed and Produced by Ernst Lubitsch
Photographed by Rudolph Maté
Screenplay by Edwin Justus Mayer
Original Story by Ernst Lubitsch and Melchior Lengyel
Musical Score by Werner R. Heymann
Miss Lombard's costumes by Irene
A Twentieth Century-Fox Release (1942)

STORY: Jack Benny and Carole Lombard are Joseph and Maria Tura, the

Polish equivalent of Alfred Lunt and Lynn Fontanne, starring in the Polski Theater Group putting on Shakespearian plays in Warsaw. When the Nazis invade Poland the Turas are active in the Polish underground, foiling the enemy.

George Washington Slept Here

CAST

Jack Benny—Bill Fuller
Ann Sheridan—Connie Fuller
Charles Coburn—Uncle Stanley
Percy Kilbride— Mr. Kimber
Hattie McDaniel—Hester
William Tracy—Steve Eldridge
Joyce Reynolds—Madge

Lee Patrick—Rena Leslie
Charles Dingle—Mr. Prescott
John Emery—Clayton Evans
Douglas Croft—Raymond
Harvey Stevens—Jeff Douglas
Franklin Pangborn—Mr. Gibney

Executive in Charge: Jack L. Warner
Director: William Keighley
Producer: Jerry Wald
First Assistant Director: Frank Heath
Photographer: Ernie Haller
Music: Adolph Deutsch
Musical Direction: Leo F. Forbstein
Authors: Moss Hart and George S. Kaufman
Screen Play: Everett Freeman, from the stage play by Moss Hart and George S. Kaufman, produced by Sam H. Harris
Contributor to Dialogue: Wilkie Mahoney
Warner Brothers (Completed June 3, 1942)

STORY: The characteristic Jack Benny petulance gets a workout in this amusing farce of a soft-living, city-bred man tricked into the country and a remodeled ramshackle house by an antique-mad wife.

The Meanest Man in the World

CAST

Jack Benny—Richard Clark
Priscilla Lane—Janie
Rochester—Shufro
Edmund Gwenn—Mr. Leggitt
Margaret Seddon—Mrs. Leggitt
Anne Revere—Miss Crockett
Matt Briggs—Brown

Helene Reynolds—Wife
Don Douglas—Husband
Harry Hayden—Mr. Chambers
Arthur Loft—Mr. Bellings
Andrew Tombes—Judge
Paul Burns—Farmer
Lyle Talbot—Potts

Director: Sidney Lanfield
Producer: William Perlberg

Photography: Paverell Morley
Written by: Augustin MacHugh
Edited by: Robert Bischoff
A Twentieth Century-Fox Picture (1943)

STORY: Jack Benny is cast in the role of a struggling attorney who has been advised to stop being big-hearted and get downright mean in order to succeed. He is required to snatch a lollipop from a five-year-old youngster, who kicks him in the shins. He tosses a nickel into a man's tin cup and then decides he does not believe in charity.

Hollywood Canteen

This was a 1944 Warner Brothers revue loosely based on the Hollywood Canteen, an entertainment center for our men and women in uniform during World War II. It featured all of the stars under contract to Warner Brothers, including Jack Benny and Bette Davis. Jack Warner was extolled by the Hollywood trade papers for turning over forty percent of the gross to perpetuate the Hollywood Canteen.

The Horn Blows at Midnight

CAST

Athanael—Jack Benny   Elizabeth—Alexis Smith
Supporting Players: Dolores Moran, Allyn Joslyn, Reginald Gardiner, Guy Kibbee, John Alexander, Franklin Pangborn, Margaret Dumont, and Bobby Blake

Screenplay: Sam Hellman and James V. Kern, from an idea by Aubrey Wisberg
Producer: Mark Hellinger
Director: Raoul Walsh
Warner Brothers (1945)

STORY: Jack Benny plays a trumpet player in a radio orchestra who falls asleep and dreams he is an angel sent down to destroy the earth with a blast of his trumpet at midnight. Allyn Joslyn and John Alexander portray two "fallen angels" on earth who try to circumvent Jack. Alexis Smith is the angel Elizabeth with romantic leanings toward Jack.

It's in the Bag

CAST

Stars Fred Allen

With Jack Benny, Don Ameche, William Bendix, Victor Moore, and Rudy Valle as guest stars
Features Binnie Barnes, Robert Benchley, Jerry Colonna, John Carradine, Minerva Pious, and Sidney Toler

Director: Richard Wallace
First Assistant Director: Jack Sullivan
Producer: Jack H. Skirball
Associate Producer: Walter Batchelor
Screenplay: Jay Dratler and Alma Reville
Photography: Russell Metty
Musical Director: Charles Previn
Substantial Contributor: Morrie Ryskind
A United Artists Release (1945)

STORY: Fred Allen inherits five antique chairs, and after selling them he discovers that twelve million dollars is hidden in one of the chairs. The action concerns his trying to get back the chairs he sold.

Guide for the Married Man

CAST

Walter Matthau—Paul Manning
Inger Stevens—Ruth Manning
Sue Ann Langdon—Mrs. Johnson

Jackie Russell—Miss Harris
Robert Morse—Ed Stander

and

Wally Cox, Art Carney, Lucille Ball, Hal March, Carl Reiner, Sid Caesar, Phil Silvers, Louis Nye, Ben Blue, Polly Bergen, Terry-Thomas, Jayne Mansfield, Jack Benny, and Joey Bishop

Director: Gene Kelly
Producer: Frank McCarthy
First Assistant Director: Paul Helmick
Photography: Joe MacDonald
Art Direction: Jack Martin Smith and William Glasgow
Set Direction: Raphael Bretton
Music: Johnny Williams
Sound: Harry M. Lindgren
Film Editor: Dorothy Spencer
Associate Director: Paul Hemick
Panavision: De Luxe Color
Motion Picture Story by Frank Tarloff, from an unpublished novel and screenplay by Frank Tarloff
A Twentieth Century-Fox Picture (1967)

STORY: A sophisticated comedy, depicting a variety of ways for a man to cheat on his wife. Jack appeared in one of these cameo roles.

Appendix B:
Chronology of Jack Benny's Broadcasting Career

RADIO

1931

Jack made his first radio appearance as a guest on Ed Sullivan's radio show on May 2.

1932

Jack's first sponsor was Canada Dry, starting in May on CBS. With George Olsen's orchestra and Ethel Shutta as vocalist, the program ran through the summer.

In October Jack went on NBC for the first time. He was sponsored by General Motors (Chevrolet). During this period his orchestra leaders were Ted Weems, Frank Black, and Don Bestor. Jack's request for music from Bestor with the two words, "Play, Don," became a national catch phrase. His featured singer was Frank Parker. In those early days he also had Michael Bartlett and James Melton as his vocalists at various times. His early announcers include George Hicks, Paul Douglas, and Alois Havrilla.

1934

A girl appeared on Jack's program in the character of a fan from

Plainfield, New Jersey, and remained with Jack to become one of his most permanent stars. She was Mary Livingstone, his wife. Kenny Baker replaced Frank Parker as vocalist, and a *New York World-Telegram* poll picked Jack as radio's top comedian.

During this year Jack was dropped by General Motors because its president didn't think the Benny broadcasts were funny. The program was sponsored next by General Tires. This year also marked the beginning of Don Wilson's employment as the announcer.

1935

Jack remained with General Tires for just one season, and in the fall he signed with General Foods. His first three sponsors after Canada Dry were General Motors, General Tires, and General Foods. As Jack said, "Having three Generals in a row ain't bad for a guy who was in the Navy, not in the Army."

General Foods, which turned out many food products, decided that the Benny broadcasts would be sponsored by their gelatine dessert. Although it was a fairly successful product prior to this, Jell-O soon zoomed into phenomenal sales via Jack's opening lines, "Jell-O Again," and his constant kidding of the commercials with Don Wilson. Even pre-school-age children could rattle off Jell-O's "six delicious flavors."

This year saw Jack move his radio show to the West Coast. Don Wilson went with him, and, of course, so did Mary. Johnny Green became his orchestra leader for one year. Kenny Baker remained as the singer with the show, but about this time, through some contractual agreement that Kenny had made with Mervyn LeRoy (one of Jack's best friends), every program ended with a statement that "Kenny Baker appeared through the courtesy of Mervyn LeRoy."

Sam Hearn, who played the part of Shlepperman, and whose greeting, "Hello, Straynger," was used as a universal greeting by all who listened to radio, made his first appearance during this period. Also Jack's writer, Harry Conn, who was probably the first to really write a program instead of putting it together out of old jokes, had a spat with Benny and left. Benny at first felt he couldn't continue, but he replaced Conn with Bill Morrow, Ed Beloin, Hugh Wedlock, Jr., and Howard Snyder. Jack also used the writing team of Sam Perrin and Arthur Phillips briefly. Perrin eventually rejoined Benny.

1936

Johnny Green left the show and was replaced by Jack's best-

470

known orchestra leader, Phil Harris, whose comedic talents and personality were so sparkling that he eventually had his own successful radio series with his wife Alice Faye.

1937

The show added another regular when a black vaudeville performer, Eddie Anderson, played a one-shot role as a Pullman porter, and Rochester was born. That year also saw Andy Devine become a semi-regular on the series. It was during these early years that the Maxwell made its debut, as did "Carmichael," the polar bear. Mel Blanc made his first appearance on the Benny show as the "voice" of Carmichael. Later Mel became the voice of the parrot, the Mexican, the French violin teacher, and countless characters who only appeared on one or two programs.

Although the famed Fred Allen "feud" started on Fred's last program of 1936, when Allen had a ten-year-old violinist, Stuart Canin, play "The Flight of the Bumble Bee" and then made a disparaging remark about Benny, Jack and Fred didn't really start exchanging insults until this year.

1938

The Jack Benny Show was now firmly entrenched in first place in the national ratings. However, another comedian, who couldn't be called new because he had several different radio series canceled after short runs, began to make inroads. Bob Hope, who started his first successful series in September 1938 for Pepsodent, was soon to give Jack a fight for first place.

1939

Kenny Baker left Jack and wound up on, of all shows, Fred Allen's. Baker was replaced by another tenor, Eugene Patrick McNulty, better known as Dennis Day.

1940

Like Bob Hope, Jack began to do his shows at Army camps. However, his writers, by this time just the team of Bill Morrow and Ed Beloin, refused to alter the format of the show and aim their jokes at the uniformed audience as Hope was doing. Jack's broadcasts at Army camps were less than successful, and he couldn't talk his writers into tailoring the material for the soldiers. Because the program was suffering, and so was Jack, early in the 1940s he curtailed his broadcasts from Army bases. Despite the fact that he made numerous appearances in person to entertain our armed forces, some magazines and newspapers criticized him.

1941

Although Jack's popularity didn't decrease, Bob Hope's soared, and he was first in the radio ratings more often than Jack. In the early 1940s General Foods was selling all the Jell-O it could make and shifted Jack to another of its products, Grape Nuts.

1942

The Jack Benny Show slipped out of first place, not because Bob Hope was on the way up, but because Jack was on the way down. His slower-paced shows seemed somewhat dull compared to the speeded-up comedy of most programs, especially Hope's.

1943

The first program written by Jack's new staff of writers was aired on October 10, and it received fair reviews. For the first two weeks the new writers were Milt Josefsberg, George Balzer, John Tacka-berry, and Cy Howard. When the series, which did its initial broad-casts in New York, returned to Hollywood, Sam Perrin joined the staff. At the end of thirteen weeks, Cy Howard left. The remaining quartet began to streamline the program. They retained the basic format but speeded up the jokes. The ratings continued to skid.

1944

On January 16, 23, and 30, Jack's guest stars were actress Alexis Smith, director Raoul Walsh, and producer Mark Hellinger—all connected with a picture Jack was making, *The Horn Blows at Midnight.*

Jack's new scripting staff convinced him to start playing Army camps with programs aimed at the soldiers and sailors. Jack clicked and his slide in the ratings stopped. During this period he used such guest stars as Danny Kaye, Eddie Cantor, and Groucho Marx.

On October 1, Jack began broadcasting for a new sponsor, The American Tobacco Company. He was hired originally for Pall Mall but never broadcast for them. He became Lucky Strike's salesman. Despite wartime shortages and the extreme difficulty of getting any brand of cigarettes, Luckies kept Jack on the air through the war, and it paid off for them. Jack's ratings began to climb upward again. During this year Dennis Day went into the Navy and was replaced by Larry Stevens.

1945

On January 7 the show had one of the most memorable scripts in radio history, although it was not realized at the time. On this show the writers invented three devices and characters which were to remain among the most popular in broadcasting: "The Vault," "The Race Track Tout" and "Train Leaving on Track Five for Anaheim, Azusa, and Cuc————amonga."

In the early months of this year the show was on the road for seven and eight weeks at a time playing Navy bases, Army camps, hospitals, etc. The guest stars included Fred Allen, Amos 'n' Andy, and William Powell.

The April 29 show featured the first appearance of another very popular continuing character, Jack's French violin teacher, Professor LeBlanc, played by Mel Blanc. On May 20 the guest stars were Rita Hayworth and the then governor of California, soon to be Chief Justice of the Supreme Court, Earl Warren.

On September 30 Jack opened the show, the first of the fall season, by letting his two telephone operators, played by Bea Benaderet and Sara Berner, gossip about him. This was an innovation because the custom was for the comic to get on his opening show of the new season as soon as possible and do as many jokes as quickly as he could to prove to the audience that he was still funny.

On October 7 a device was used which became an annual affair— Jack trying to listen to the World Series on his radio but getting every station except the one he wants.

On October 21 the comedy gimmick was used of having a child actress play Phil Harris' daughter and phone him. She was a hit, as was the later addition of a second little actress to portray Phil's second daughter. The two little girls were so popular that they eventually became regulars on the series starring Phil Harris and Alice Faye.

October 28 marked the beginning of a contest called "I Can't Stand Jack Benny Because . . ." and the first prize was ten thousand dollars. The winners were announced on the broadcast of January 27, 1946—and the man who announced them was Fred Allen.

The December 9 program marked the first time that Mr. and Mrs. Ronald Colman were used. Their appearances, plus other innovations, helped boost the ratings, so that once again Jack was battling Bob Hope for first place.

1946

The new year started with a new character destined to be one of the most popular—Mr. Kitzle, played by Artie Auerbach. Jack first "met" Kitzle during the program based on his going to the Rose Bowl game where Kitzle was selling hot dogs with his "Peekle in the Meedle Mit the Mustard on Top" jingle.

The Colmans made repeated appearances on the show during this year, and it eventually led to their getting their own series, the

473

erudite *Halls of Ivy*. Dennis Day had returned to the program by this time.

On March 10, Ray Milland was the guest star and worked in a sketch based on his Academy Award-winning performance in *The Lost Weekend*.

The regular season came to an end in New York with two shows featuring Fred Allen on May 19 and May 26. On those same two shows Jack repaid a debt to the man on whose program he first appeared when he had the pre-TV Ed Sullivan as guest.

On the October 27 show of the fall season, Mary made one of her most famous fluffs when she ordered a "chiss sweese" sandwich. On this same program Jack's parrot was introduced for a one-shot appearance, but Mel Blanc got so many laughs as Polly's voice and squawk that it became another regular feature.

December 8 of this year saw the first of what was to become the annual Christmas shopping shows, with Jack always driving the same salesman crazy exchanging gifts moments after he bought them. The salesman, of course, was Mel Blanc.

1947

Numerous guest stars were used during this year, including many appearances by Ronald and Benita Colman. Occasionally an extra guest star would be added to appear with the Colmans, such as Leo Durocher and Isaac Stern.

A couple of years before, The Sportsmen Quartet had been added as a gimmick to spice up the integrated commercials. On the March 9 program Jack had supposedly fired The Sportsmen (Marty Spurzel, Bill Days, Thirl Ravenscroft, Max Smith, and John Rarig—yes, five of them—but one was always filling in), and the sponsor "insisted" that Jack rehire them or get a substitute quartet. On the March 16 program his quartet consisted of Bing Crosby, Andy Russell, and Dick Haymes—all famed baritones—plus Dennis Day. During one break in the song, Crosby musically ad-libbed to Dennis, a tenor, "Get your voice down here where the money is, Kid."

The March 30 broadcast was from San Francisco, where the guest star was Jane Wyman who won an Oscar and later divorced a presidential prospect, Ronald Reagan.

On April 6 the guest stars were famed producer Sam Goldwyn and songwriter Hoagy Carmichael whom, shortly before on an Academy Awards broadcast, Goldwyn had referred to as "Hugo" Carmichael.

On May 25 Jack's guest star was Fred Allen. Also appearing on the program was a new young comic Jack was using as his summer replacement—Jack Paar.

The November 23 script had Jack shopping for a Thanksgiving

turkey, and Kitzle was the salesman. They got so many laughs that they used up the allotted time before they finished the program and they were cut off the air. Rumors immediately spread that the network cut off the program because of a dirty joke.

On the very next show, November 30, the problem was not too many laughs, but not enough. It featured a sketch in which Jack dreamed he was on trial for murder because he had killed a Thanksgiving turkey, and the jury was made up of turkeys. The show itself was a turkey—one of the worst shows Jack ever did—yet the script looked good on paper.

Mary became ill the day before the December 28 show and Alice Faye read her part. Once before, Mary had been unable to make the show and Barbara Stanwyck filled in for her at the last minute. There was no time to exploit or advertise these substitutions of two of the biggest box-office attractions of that era.

1948

In 1948 Ralph Edwards' *Truth Or Consequences* program had mystery guests, and listeners would be given clues on each show as to the identity. Each week Edwards would make a phone call, and many prizes were waiting for the person he called who correctly guessed the identity of the mystery guest. One such mystery guest was "The Walking Man." With "The Walking Man" you only heard footsteps as the clues were read off. An early clue made Hilliard Marks and Milt Josefsberg guess that it was Jack by the second or third week. Jack went to Edwards and said, "Ralph, Marks and Josefsberg have guessed it's me—and I can't lie to them." Edwards insisted that Jack must keep up the deception, but by the fourth week newspaper columnists were printing Jack's name as the mystery man. Despite this, no one that Edwards called guessed correctly for several weeks until a Mrs. Florence Hubbard of Chicago named Jack and won a fortune in prizes. On March 14 *The Jack Benny Show* had Ralph Edwards and Mrs. Hubbard, an elderly widow, as guest stars. Jack asked Mrs. Hubbard if she contemplated remarrying, and she said that with all the prizes she had won she didn't feel she wanted to marry again. Jack asked, "But won't you be lonely?" Mrs. Hubbard answered, "Lonely, but loaded." The resulting audience reaction made it inevitable that those words would be used repeatedly in future shows, and "Lonely, but loaded" became a popular catch phrase.

The March 28 show featured the most quoted of all Jack Benny jokes, and perhaps the most quoted joke in broadcasting history, with Jack being held up by a crook, played by actor Eddie Marr, who threatened: "Your money or your life." There was a long pause as Jack stared at the studio audience, which roared at his dilemma.

Then the crook said, "Look, Bud, I said, 'Your money or your life.' "
And Jack answered, "I'm thinking it over." The gag was repeated over the years on both radio and TV.

The programs this year featured a running idea with Jack borrowing Roland Colman's Oscar—which the holdup man stole from Jack on the aforementioned program. The following week Jack borrowed Bing Crosby's Oscar to use as a replacement for Colman's missing one. The week after he borrowed Paul Lukas' Oscar, and when Frank Sinatra appeared as a guest, Jack borrowed the Oscar he had won for *From Here to Eternity*.

The May 16 program was a rarity, inasmuch as Jack took a week off. Robert Taylor filled in for Jack during his absence—and when Jack returned the following week, the program was highlighted by a phone call from his sponsor suggesting that Jack take another vacation.

By June, Jack had re-established his popularity to such an extent that he began making personal appearances in theaters in Cleveland, Detroit, and other major cities. In Cleveland a program featured famed baseball pitcher Bob Feller as a guest star, in addition to a man who calls Cleveland his hometown—Bob Hope. The season ended on June 27 with a broadcast from New York with Fred Allen as a guest.

The first shows of the new fall season were of the usual type, featuring guest stars like Barbara Stanwyck, the Ronald Colmans (several times), and opera singer Dorothy Kirsten who sang our comedy-integrated commercials; this resulted in several hundred letters of criticism being sent to the show.

On the November 21 show Jack used his four writers as actors for a gag, and he was taken completely by surprise when Don Ameche substituted for one of the writers to read the last line. Jack got so hysterical he couldn't even say "Good night" to the listeners.

On December 26 Jack did his last radio show on NBC. He sold his program and company to CBS, and started the new year, on January 2, with his first broadcast for CBS. As an ironic coincidence, Jack passed away on December 26, 1974—twenty-six years to the day that he did his last NBC radio show.

1949

After his initial show on CBS, Jack began to use guest stars because of a sliding scale of pay depending on his radio ratings on the new network as compared with those he had on NBC. Jack's first shows on CBS outrated his NBC ratings by about three points, proving that it was the star that had the pulling power and not the time slot. Jack used Jimmy Stewart, the Ronald Colmans (frequently), Claudette Colbert, Vincent Price, Jack Warner, Claude Rains, Van Johnson, Barbara Stanwyck, and others.

The opening show of the fall season, on September 11, amazed critics and listeners because Jack didn't appear until the final four minutes of the show. (Legends grow, and recently a story appeared saying that Jack only read one single line on the show. That wasn't true. He did a four-minute routine with Rochester.)

To finish out his first year at CBS impressively, Jack kept booking big name stars such as Tyrone Power, Frank Sinatra, Rosalind Russell, Gene Kelly, "Prince" Mike Romanoff, Fred Allen, Notre Dame football coach Frank Leahy, and the Ronald Colmans.

1950

On the January 8 show Don Wilson was supposed to say he had read something in Drew Pearson's column—but he said "Drear Pooson" instead. As the program was progressing the writers got Frank Nelson to change one of his lines. When Jack asked him if he was a doorman, he was supposed to say, "Well, who do you think I am in this red uniform, Nelson Eddy?" Instead he surprised Jack by saying, "Well, who do you think I am—Drear Pooson?" Jack collapsed in laughter, and it took many seconds before he could resume reading the script without giggling.

After a full year on CBS, Jack's ratings were as high as ever, and he and Bob Hope were usually fighting it out for first and second place in the national ratings. This rivalry, however, never prevented them from appearing as guests on each other's programs. In fact, Hope was the guest on the March 26 show Jack did from Palm Springs. Other guests during this year included Red Skelton, Fred Allen, and, of course, Ronald and Benita Colman, as well as Sarah Churchill, the daughter of Winston Churchill. We also used Frank Fontaine several times, as John L.C. Sivoney. Later Frank was a regular on Jackie Gleason's TV show working in the "Joe the Bartender" sketches.

The fall radio season was faced with the growing competition of television. Many radio shows were cancelled, but Jack kept going and maintained respectable ratings. However, he also did two live television shows during the first season (from September 1950 to June 1951).

Jack's second radio show of the new season, on September 17, was based on a "fade-back" to a trip he took to Venice. Later, this was successfully converted to a filmed TV show.

On October 22, the radio show story line was about Jack going to New York to do his first live television show. Despite the fact that big time radio was slowly sliding to oblivion, Jack still used such big name guests as the Ronald Colmans, Douglas Fairbanks, Jr., and Dinah Shore. (The show with Dinah had as its theme the command performance she and Jack actually had given for the Queen of England.) Other guest stars included Deborah Kerr, Amos 'n' Andy, and Frank Sinatra.

1951

On the March 11 show Jack was ill, and, to solve the problem, a tape of a previous show was used. The following week the program was based on the incident of Jack missing his show because of illness.

1952

Budget problems caused the show to cut down on guest stars and to rely on other gimmicks. One had Jack writing a song called "When You Say 'I Beg Your Pardon,' Then I'll Come Back to You." It was as lousy as its title, but Jack's attempts to get famed stars to plug or sing it led to guest appearances by several well-known personalities, including a quartet made up of Frank Sinatra, George Burns, Danny Kaye, and Groucho Marx on the March 2 show from Palm Springs.

On the March 16 show there was another appearance of the two income tax men from the previous year, this time trying to figure out how a man like Jack earned over half a million dollars, yet spent seventeen dollars on entertainment. Jack said he had receipts to prove he had spent the seventeen dollars.

On March 23 Jack tried to sing his song "When You Say 'I Beg Your Pardon'" at the Academy Awards.

The March 30 broadcast emanated from a Navy base. On April 20 he did another camp show, this time at the San Diego Naval Base. (Naturally, when doing shows for sailors, there was also always a reference or two about Jack's naval career in 1918. One joke had Jack bragging about how royally they had treated him as a sailor. Mary said, "Naturally! You owned the Navy." Jack snapped back, "Stop exaggerating! I only owned one little battleship, and you make a big thing out of it.")

Very few of the big-time radio shows were still on the air in 1952. Television was the new craze. Fred Allen said that people loved TV because now they could see *and* hear how lousy the shows were. Jack was transcribing his radio shows in advance now, sometimes two a week, so he could have time to devote to the several television shows he was doing each season. The radio show frequently served as a billboard advertising the television show. Phil Harris, who had been Jack's orchestra leader for sixteen years, left because of budgetary reasons and was replaced by Bob Crosby. However, Phil and Jack retained their affection and respect for each other, and Phil appeared as a guest star on many of Jack's TV shows. Guest star appearances were curtailed, but Jack still had them occasionally, including Bob Hope, Fred Allen, and the Ronald Colmans.

1953

September 13, 1953 to June 6, 1954 marked Jack's final season on radio. Fewer and fewer guest stars were used, and even those were inexpensive, although with a name value that could provide script ideas. They included Leo Durocher, Sam Goldwyn, and Jack Warner, the head of Warner Bros. The Jack Warner program on November 22 hinged on the fact that Jack was going to do a television version of the much-maligned movie, *The Horn Blows at Midnight.* Warner's appearance had him begging Jack not to revive this egregious epic. (Jack did the television version of *The Horn Blows at Midnight* on the *Omnibus* TV program, giving this series the highest rating it ever had. The narrator for the hour-long show was a then unheralded Professor Frank Baxter—and this single appearance helped catapult him into broadcasting history as TV's foremost Shakespearean lecturer.) Jack also used guest stars who would appear for a nominal fee because of friendship, and these included George Burns and George Jessel.

1954

The May 2 program was based on Jack's going to Santa Anita Race Track and losing $4.75. That night he dreamed of his loss, and every number mentioned was 475. Then, when he awakened, he found that the mailman had brought him a refund on his income tax amounting to $4.75. In real life, on the following day, countless thousands of people who played the numbers bet on 475 and its various combinations. The winning number was one of the combinations, resulting in the biggest losing day in the history of the policy game.

The June 6 show was the finale—the last radio broadcast. Jack used all his old standbys, and although most of the cast, writers, and crew knew they'd be working regularly on Jack's television series, there were many tears, some for personal reasons, and others because it was the end of an era. The radio series was off the air for about two years, and then a deal was made whereby electrical transcriptions of old programs were rebroadcast. These repeats had a remarkable history of good ratings, considering their age, lack of exploitation, and other hurdles, but they only continued for a couple of years. Today stations throughout the country play an occasional full program, and more frequently excerpts from shows, but as far as can be determined the shows are not being broadcast on any regular schedule.

TELEVISION

1949

In March, Jack participated in the dedication of the Hollywood-based TV station, KTTV (Channel 11).

1950–1951

Jack did his first two commercial TV shows in this period. The first was on a Saturday night, October 28, 1950, and ran from 8 to 8:45 P.M. On the program were Rochester, Don Wilson, The Sportsmen Quartet, Mel Blanc, and Mr. Kitzle. Special guest stars were Dinah Shore and Ken Murray. Hilliard Marks was the producer, and Dick Linkroum directed. The show, done live from New York City, received good reviews but not raves. The second show was on May 20, 1951. It was on this show that Mary Livingstone made her TV debut. The guests were Bob Crosby and Ben Hogan, the golfing great.

1951–1952

Jack did six shows this season. Ralph Levy became the director. Guests included the Ronald Colmans for the final show in June 1952, during which Jack did his famous sketch with George Burns where Benny is forced to dress in drag and appear as Gracie Allen because Gracie failed to appear for the show.

1953–1954

Thirteen shows were done this season. Jack's guest on his opening show was a starlet who was just becoming a star—Marilyn Monroe. That season he also had Johnny Ray, Danny Thomas, Humphrey Bogart, Irene Dunne, Gregory Ratoff, Vincent Price (in a sketch Jack had done several times on radio), and Liberace, as well as George Burns and Bing Crosby who, with Benny, played an old-time vaudeville trio called "Goldie, Fields, and Glide." Mary Livingstone and daughter Joan Benny also appeared in a revitalized radio sketch. Helen Hayes was also a guest, and the last show of the season saw Bob Hope appear with Jack in "The Road to Nairobi," with Dean Martin and Jerry Lewis coming in for a cameo for the blackout.

1954–1955 and 1955–1956

Jack was now appearing on twenty shows a season, alternating with Ann Sothern's series, *Private Secretary,* both for the same sponsor, Lucky Strikes. He continued this twenty-show-a-season routine for several years. His guests during this period included Fred MacMurray, Tony Martin, Dick Powell, Kirk Douglas, and

Dan Dailey, all of whom appeared on one program, forming an orchestra, with Benny the violinist and Fred MacMurray getting laughs on the program by pouting over his treatment and reminding Jack: "I'm a star." Guests on other shows included Jackie Gleason and the June Taylor Dancers, as well as Leo Durocher, Bob Lemon, and other baseball greats in a baseball-oriented takeoff on *The Caine Mutiny*.

1957–1958

Jack was now alternating with *Bachelor Father* on an every-other-week basis. Phil Harris made many appearances this season and was more of a regular than a guest star. Jack's guests included Gary Cooper, Bob Hope, Mitzi Gaynor, and the famed Marquis Chimps. Seymour Berns replaced Ralph Levy as director. Hilliard Marks was again producer. In addition to his regularly scheduled series, Jack did two one-hour specials with such guests stars as Phil Silvers and Julie Andrews. The producer and director of these shows was Bud Yorkin, who later teamed with Norman Lear to form Tandem Productions, the most successful operation in TV history. Their programs include *All in the Family, Maude,* and *Mary Hartman, Mary Hartman*.

1959–1960

After over a decade and a half with Lucky Strikes, Jack switched sponsors and broadcast for Lever Brothers. He now aired at 10 P.M. on Sundays, alternating weekly with George Gobel. The numerous guests include Jack Paar and ex-President Harry Truman.

1960–1961

Lever Brothers shared sponsorship with State Farm Insurance, and now Jack's program was on every week. His producer-director was Fred de Cordova. Guests included George Burns, Mike Wallace, Tony Curtis, and Robert Wagner. Jack also made several guest appearances, including one on a Red Skelton special.

1961–1962

Jack's ratings began to sag, and he tried to bolster them with guests like Alan King, Phil Silvers, Jack Paar, and Garry Moore.

1962–1963

In an effort to improve the ratings, CBS moved Jack's show (now weekly, and all filmed) to 9:30 P.M. Tuesday nights between two powerful programs, those of Red Skelton and Garry Moore. One of his guest stars was Sammy Davis, Jr.

This was Jack's last regularly scheduled CBS season. The ratings continued to drop, and as an attraction Jack even booked evangelist Billy Graham, but as Jack said, "Neither comedy nor prayer could help the program."

1964–1974

In the spring of 1964, CBS, which fifteen years earlier had paid Jack over two million dollars to entice him to their network, now canceled his series. Jack was picked up almost immediately by NBC, and he opened his new season on September 25, 1964. Guests included the noted news team of Huntley and Brinkley, but the ratings were not impressive.

After one season, the weekly series was canceled, but NBC hung on to Jack this time, giving him a deal where he could appear in a few special one-hour shows a year. In addition to this, Jack (though he felt he was prostituting himself) appeared on commercials for Texaco (where he would usually order just one gallon of gas), for The American-Republic Life Insurance Company, and for The Wool Industry. (The money was impressive, and Jack needn't have had qualms about these commercials because many big stars, including Fred MacMurray, Henry Fonda, and Bob Hope, made them. Nevertheless, Jack felt that it was degrading for him to do it.)

When Jack's ratings were really hurt at CBS by NBC's Western blockbuster, *Bonanza,* which was opposite him, Jack was philosophical about it. But when he returned to NBC for the 1964–65 series on Friday nights, his competition was an untried new series called *Gomer Pyle.* When it trounced him in the ratings, Jack said: "I didn't mind getting beat by *Bonanza*—but *Gomer Pyle!*" Then, after hastening to add that he thought that Jim Nabors, the star of that series, was very talented, he again disdainfully repeated *"Gomer Pyle!"*

Jack's NBC specials, at the rate of one or two a year, were star-studded events, and though he was well over seventy years old, most of them continued to draw satisfying numbers in the ratings game. His first special had Bob Hope, Elke Sommers, and The Beach Boys (a rock group, aimed at teenage viewers). On many of his later shows he featured currently hot rock 'n' roll groups such as Paul Revere and the Raiders.

Other specials had the Smothers Brothers, Phyllis Diller, and Trini Lopez. One, called *Carnival Nights,* had as regular guests Lucille Ball, Johnny Carson, Ben Blue, and Paul Revere and the Raiders, while cameo appearances were made by Bob Hope, Danny Thomas, Dodger pitcher Don Drysdale, George Burns, and several others. This show was one of the highest-rated specials on the air that season, and from that time on Jack's hour-long programs once or twice a year garnered satisfactory ratings.

Jack's subsequent specials included such guests as Eddie Fisher and Lou Rawls in a sketch based on *The Graduate,* and a Jack Benny birthday party with Lawrence Welk, Lucille Ball, Dennis Day, and Dan "Hoss" Blocker.

On his various shows Jack always got big stars to drop in for brief surprise appearances. These included Jack Lemmon, Rochester, Dan Rowan and Dick Martin, Walter Matthau, Jerry Lewis, Dean Martin, and Ann-Margret. He scored a coup when he got Gregory Peck to appear on one of his specials, and then added guests Nancy Sinatra, Rochester, and Gary Puckett and the Union Gap (another rock 'n' roll group).

Jack's next special marked his twentieth anniversary in television and included such guests as Bob Hope, Frank Sinatra, Dinah Shore, Mary Livingstone, Dennis Day, Don Wilson, and Rochester, while Lucille Ball and Red Skelton appeared as unscheduled guests. Film clips from many of Jack's previous TV shows, including the ones with President Harry Truman, Gary Cooper, Marilyn Monroe, and Humphrey Bogart, were used and received tremendous audience response.

Jack's next show was based on Dr. David Reuben's successful sex manual, and the title was *Everything You Always Wanted To Know About Jack Benny But Were Afraid To Ask.* Lucille Ball guested again, together with John Wayne, George Burns, and Dionne Warwick.

Next came *Jack Benny's First Farewell Appearance* with an impressive list of big name guests and a surprise ending to the show when California Governor Ronald Reagan came on for a few gags.

In January 1974, Jack did *Jack Benny's Second Farewell Special.* Unfortunately it turned out to be his final farewell special. It did very well, with guests Johnny Carson, Dinah Shore, George Burns, and Redd Foxx, plus a cameo appearance by Don Rickles.

Jack appeared as a guest on several big programs and numerous talk shows prior to his death. One of the specials was *The Dean Martin Roast of Lucille Ball* which aired several weeks after Jack passed away. Prior to that Jack himself was the "Roastee" on a Dean Martin show in February 1974. At the time of his death he was working on a one-hour special to be broadcast on NBC early in 1975. It was never done.

Jack appeared as a guest star on practically every big-time radio and TV variety show, and some of them, like Bob Hope's and Dinah Shore's, employed him many times. He was worked into the stories of many situation comedies. From 1963 to 1974 he was a guest star on four of Lucille Ball's programs—and he made at least that many cameo surprise appearances with Lucy. Other situation comedies also worked him in, and Jack rarely turned these appearances down if the script idea appealed to him.

Jack was also a favorite guest on talk shows. It is doubtful if Johnny Carson, Jack Paar, Merv Griffin, and the other talk show hosts could accurately give the number of Jack's appearances on their programs. He also was frequently seen with Joey Bishop, Mike Douglas, Irv Kupcinet, Dick Cavett, Dinah Shore, and others, both on network and local programs.

Index

491